Clashing Views in

Gender

FIFTH EDITION

Selected, Edited, and with Introductions by

Jacquelyn W. White
University of North Carolina at Greensboro

Mc
Graw
Hill

Connect
Learn
Succeed™

The McGraw·Hill Companies

Connect
Learn
Succeed™

TAKING SIDES: CLASHING VIEWS IN GENDER, FIFTH EDITION

1 2 3 4 5 6 7 8 9 0 DOC/DOC 1 0 9 8 7 6 5 4 3 2 1 0

MHID: 0-07-804994-6
ISBN: 978-0-07-804994-1
ISSN: 1526-4548

Managing Editor: *Larry Loeppke*
Director, Specialized Production: *Faye Schilling*
Senior Developmental Editor: *Jill Meloy*
Editorial Coordinator: *Mary Foust*
Production Service Assistant: *Rita Hingtgen*
Permissions Coordinator: *Lenny J. Behnke*
Editorial Assistant: *Cindy Hedley*
Senior Marketing Manager: *Julie Keck*
Senior Marketing Communications Specialist: *Mary Klein*
Marketing Coordinator: *Alice Link*
Project Manager: *Erin Melloy*
Design Specialist: *Brenda Rolwes*
Cover Graphics: *Rick D. Noel*

Compositor: MPS Limited, A Macmillan Company
Cover Image: Chad Baker/Getty Images

Library of Congress Cataloging-in-Publication Data

Main entry under title:
Taking sides: clashing views in gender/selected, edited, and with introductions by Jacquelyn W. White.—5th ed.
Includes bibliographical references.
1. Sex (Psychology). 2. Sex Differences. White, Jacquelyn W., *comp.*
                                                        306.7

Editors/Academic Advisory Board

Members of the Academic Advisory Board are instrumental in the final selection of articles for each edition of TAKING SIDES. Their review of articles for content, level, and appropriateness provides critical direction to the editors and staff. We think that you will find their careful consideration well reflected in this volume.

TAKING SIDES: Clashing Views in Gender
Fifth Edition

EDITOR

Jacquelyn W. White
University of North Carolina at Greensboro

ACADEMIC ADVISORY BOARD MEMBERS

Editors/Academic Advisory Board, continued

Preface

Issues having to do with females and males, "femaleness" and "maleness," are omnipresent in Western culture and around the world. Our lives revolve around presumed distinctions between females' and males' attitudes, characteristics, emotions, behaviors, preferences, abilities, and responsibilities. We have clear definitions of what females and males can and should do differently from one another. In some cultures, there are third and fourth gender categories, complete with their own expectations and proscriptions. What has triggered such a deep gender divide? Is it rooted in our biology? Is it a cultural creation that gets reproduced through socialization practices and interpersonal interaction? What is the future of gender? Controversy abounds.

Taking Sides: Clashing Views in Gender is a tool for stimulating critical thought about females and males, femaleness and maleness, and beyond. Consideration of the complexity of sex and gender necessitates a multidisciplinary perspective. Thus, you will learn about definitions and views of sex and gender from such fields as sociology, ethnic studies, women's studies, men's studies, gay and lesbian studies, queer studies, gender studies, transgender studies, education, language, political science, global studies, religion, history, medicine, law, psychology, and biology. The multidisciplinarity of inquiry on sex and gender has created a rich, exciting, and emotionally and politically charged body of theory, research, and practice. The study of sex and gender is so dynamic that it is one of the most fast-paced areas of inquiry, characterized by great fervor and rapid growth. It is also one of the most contentious areas of thought, distinguished by deep theoretical and philosophical differences. Such division also marks public discourse on sex and gender.

This book contains 20 issues, organized into 6 parts, that are being hotly debated in contemporary scholarly and public discourse on sex and gender. They are phrased as yes/no questions so that two distinct perspectives are delineated and contrasted. Each issue is prefaced by an *issue introduction* containing background material contextualizing the dual positions. Additional perspectives are presented in a *postscript* following each issue to enrich and enliven debate and discussion. No issue is truly binary, adequately represented by only two points of view. Considering other perspectives will broaden your understanding of the complexity of each issue, enabling you to develop an informed ideology. The *suggestions for further reading* that appear in each issue postscript should help you find resources to continue your study of the subject. At the back of the book is a listing of all the *contributors to this volume*, which will give you information on the various writers whose views are debated here. Also, on the *Internet References* page that accompanies each part opener, you will find Web sites that are relevant to the issues in that part. These Web sites should prove useful as starting points for further research.

You begin this quest with an existing personal gender ideology of which you may not even be aware. It serves as a filter through which you process information about females and males, femaleness and maleness. It draws your attention to some information and points of view and allows you to disregard other more dissonant perspectives. Your challenge is to probe your personal gender ideology (and intersecting ideologies such as ethnicity, sexual orientation, social class, gender identity) so that you can open your mind to other perspectives and information and develop a more informed ideology. To do so takes courage and active thought. As you work through this book, note your reactions to different points and perspectives. Exchange reactions and relevant experiences with your peers. "Try on" different perspectives by trying to represent a view with which you initially disagree. Explore *suggestions for further reading* and Web sites provided for each part or issue. Challenge yourself to explore all angles so that your own theories or views become more reasoned and representative.

No matter what field of study, career path, and/or other personal choices you pursue, issues of sex and gender will be pervasive. Great sociohistorical change in sex and gender marked the twentieth century, catalyzing even greater momentum for the twenty-first century. The goal of this book is to help you develop an ideological tool chest that will enable you to intelligently and responsibly navigate the changing gender landscape. Collectively, you will chart the course of the future of gender.

Changes to this edition   This edition contains 20 issues organized into six parts. The book outline has changed substantially, with the addition of 8 new issues and 20 new, more current selections added to reflect the YES and NO perspectives. Part openers, issue introductions, and issues postscripts have been revised accordingly. Each issue opener calls attention to the consideration of cross-cutting issues that enrich and complicate in meaningful ways the clashing views presented in each part. Students and instructors are encouraged to discuss each of these questions:

1. *The role of biology:* What does emerging research on brain differences tell us about gender-related patterns of behavior? How can one separate cause, consequence, and correlates in this growing body of knowledge?
2. *Intersecting identities:* How do race, ethnicity, class, and other status-defining attributes relate to gendered patterns of behavior? Does the consideration of how multiple identities intersect contribute to new understandings of gender?
3. *Media representations:* How do media portrayals of gender-related issues affect our understanding of the phenomenon? How and when do media portrayals, including images and language, reinforce or defy gender stereotypes?
4. *Cross-cultural and intra-cultural generalities:* To what extent is understanding of gender-related concepts shaped by culture? Can results of studies conducted in one country generalize to other countries? Do results of a study conducted in a particular country actually reflect the values of that entire country? That is, are there intra-cultural differences within a given country? For example, are students at a

university in a given country more similar to students at universities in other countries than similar to other social groups within their own country?

A word to the instructor   An *Instructor's Resource Guide with Test Questions* (multiple-choice and essay) is available through the publisher for the instructor using *Taking Sides* in the classroom. A general guidebook, *Using Taking Sides in the Classroom,* which discusses methods and techniques for integrating the pro-con approach into any classroom setting, is also available. An online version of *Using Taking Sides in the Classroom* and a correspondence service for *Taking Sides* adopters can be found at www.mhhe.com/cls.

    Taking Sides: Clashing Views in Gender is only one title in the Taking Sides series. If you are interested in seeing the table of contents for any of the other titles, please visit the Taking Sides Web site at www.mhhe.com/cls.

Acknowledgments   First and foremost, the contributions of Elizabeth Paul, editor of the first two editions, are acknowledged. The insights and knowledge she brought to this project have provided a solid platform from which to move forward into the following editions. Her understanding of the issues facing the study of gender and her ability to cogently frame the issues set a high standard. I also want to express great appreciation to my many undergraduates who helped me understand which issues resonate most with them. Many colleagues in the Women's and Gender Studies program at UNCG provided an articulate sounding board as I debated which issues to include and how to frame them. Also, the comments and feedback from my doctoral students Ashlyn Swartout and Kevin Swartout have been invaluable in developing the set of issues selected for this edition. I must also acknowledge Jill Meloy at McGraw-Hill/Contemporary Learning Series, who provided me with expertise, support, and encouragement at each step of the process. Lastly, my husband, and children Ian and Elaine were enormously supportive and patient, filling in for all those household tasks I simply ignored. I have learned much from them about what it means to have an equal partner and to attempt to raise children free of gender constraints in a society that really does not want that to happen.

Jacquelyn W. White
University of North Carolina at Greensboro

Contents In Brief

Contents

"nice guys," that is, those who were intelligent, stable, conscientious, better educated, with good social skills and political and religious compatibility.

Educator Qing Li found, in a survey of students, males reported more bullying and cyberbullying than female students, and female cyberbully victims were more likely to report the cyberbullying to adults than were males. Criminal justice expert Kirk Williams and psychologist Nancy Guerra found that boys were more likely to bully than girls, but there were no sex differences in cyberbullying.

The Human Rights Campaign (HRC), America's largest gay and lesbian organization, explains why same-sex couples should be afforded the same legal right to marry as heterosexual couples. John Cornyn, United States senator from Texas, says a constitutional amendment is needed to define marriage as permissible only between a man and a woman. Senator Cornyn contends that the traditional institution of marriage needs to be protected from activist courts that would seek to redefine it.

The American Psychological Association's Council of Representatives adopted this resolution that was drafted by a task force of expert psychologists. The resolution, based on a thorough review of the literature, opposes any discrimination based on sexual orientation and concludes that children reared by same-sex parents benefit from legal ties to each parent. Timothy J. Dailey, senior research fellow at the Center for Marriage and Family Studies, provides an overview of state laws pertaining to adoption by lesbian or gay parents. He points to studies showing that children do much better in family settings that include both a mother and a father, and that the sexual behaviors same-sex parents engage in make them, by definition, inappropriate role models for children.

Hilda Kahne, professor emerita at Wheaton College in Massachusetts, makes the argument that incomplete education and few training programs, rather than gender discrimination, makes it more difficult for low-wage single mothers to raise their earnings. In contrast, Hadas Mandel of the department of sociology and anthropology and Moshe Semyonov of the department of sociology and labor studies anthropology at Tel Aviv University review extensive data from 22 countries and conclude that social policies have the counterintuitive impact of decreasing women's opportunities for access to more desirable and powerful positions.

John Shackleton, a professor of economics and Dean of the Business School, University of East London, suggests that the gender gap is largely due to nondiscriminatory factors; most notable are those associated with compensation for the differential value of associated with women's choices due to lifestyle, preferences, attitudes, and expectations. Hilary Lips, a professor of psychology and the director of the Center for Gender Studies at Radford University, documents the continuing gender gap in wages and argues that a continuing undervaluing of women's work, whatever it happens to be, due to stereotypes and prejudice maintains the wage gap. She argues that the language of "choice" is deceptive.

Alice Eagly and Linda Carli contend that barriers exist for women at every stage of their career trajectories, resulting in, not a glass ceiling, but a labyrinth. Kingsley Browne asserts that the division of labor by sex is rooted in biologically based differences between women and men. Evolutionarily based natural selection has led to inclinations that make women and men better suited for different types of jobs.

Bridget Maher argues that far too much funding has gone into programs that teach young people about sexuality and contraception—programs that she concludes are ineffective. Debra Hauser, in an evaluation of numerous abstinence-only-until-marriage programs that received funding under the Title V Social Security Act, concludes that they show few short-term benefits and no lasting, positive effects; rather such programs may actually worsen sexual health outcomes.

Mercedes Allen, educator, trainer, and founder of Alberta Trans.org, recognizes the bias in the DSM's classification of Gender Identity Disorder as a mental disorder but argues that changes run the risk of leaving the trans community at risk of losing medical care and treatment. Kelley Winters, Ph.D., writer and founder of GID Reform Advocates, argues the inclusion of Gender Identity Disorder in the DSM adds to the stigma faced by transpersons and that reclassification is necessary to adequately address the population's health care needs.

Attorney and activist Lisa Mottet and program manager of the National Center for Transgender Equality Justin Tanis argue for recognizing diversity in all aspects of people's lives and reject efforts to categorize on the basis of rigid definitions. Jaimie Veale, a graduate student, along with university faculty compared the sexuality of male-to-female transsexuals to biological females and found a number of differences that distinguish the groups in terms of patterns of sexual attraction to males.

Correlation Guide

The *Taking Sides* series presents current issues in a debate-style format designed to stimulate student interest and develop critical thinking skills. Each issue is thoughtfully framed with an issue summary, an issue introduction, and a postscript. The pro and con essays—selected for their liveliness and substance—represent the arguments of leading scholars and commentators in their fields.

Taking Sides: Clashing Views in Gender, 5/e is an easy-to-use reader that presents issues on important topics such as *sexual orientation, gender and work, cultural boundaries,* and *gender in childhood.* For more information on *Taking Sides* and other *McGraw-Hill Contemporary Learning Series* titles, visit www.mhhe.com/cls.

This convenient guide matches the issues in **Taking Sides: Gender, 5/e** with the corresponding chapters in two of our best-selling McGraw-Hill Psychology textbooks by Yarber et al., and Hyde/DeLamater.

Taking Sides: Gender, 5/e	Human Sexuality: Diversity in Contemporary America, 7/e by Yarber et al.	Understanding Human Sexuality, 11/e by Hyde/ DeLamater
Issue 1: Is Anatomy Destiny?	**Chapter 5:** Gender and Gender Roles	**Chapter 4:** Sexual Anatomy
Issue 2: Is Sexual Orientation Innate?	**Chapter 7:** Sexuality in Adulthood	**Chapter 13:** Sexual Orientation: Gay, Straight, or Bi?
Issue 3: Do Sex Differences in Careers in Mathematics and Sciences Have a Biological Basis?	**Chapter 5:** Gender and Gender Roles	**Chapter 1:** Sexuality in Perspective
Issue 4: Are Women and Men More Similar Than Different?	**Chapter 5:** Gender and Gender Roles	**Chapter 1:** Sexuality in Perspective **Chapter 12:** Gender and Sexuality
Issue 5: Is Culture the Primary Source of Sex Differences in Communication Styles?	**Chapter 8:** Love and Communication in Intimate Relationships	**Chapter 1:** Sexuality in Perspective **Chapter 11:** Attraction, Love, and Communication **Chapter 12:** Gender and Sexuality
Issue 6. Do Nice Guys Finish Last?	**Chapter 9:** Sexual Expression	**Chapter 11:** Attraction, Love, and Communication
Issue 7: Gender Symmetry: Do Women and Men Commit Equal Levels of Violence Against Intimate Partners?	**Chapter 17:** Sexual Coercion: Harassment, Aggression, and Abuse	**Chapter 12:** Gender and Sexuality **Chapter 15:** Sexual Coercion

(Continued)

Taking Sides: Gender, 5/e	Human Sexuality: Diversity in Contemporary America, 7/e by Yarber et al.	Understanding Human Sexuality, 11/e by Hyde/DeLamater
Issue 8: Does Pornography Reduce the Incidence of Rape?	**Chapter 18:** Sexually Explicit Materials, Prostitution, and Sex Laws	**Chapter 16:** Sex for Sale **Chapter 17:** Sexual Disorders and Sex Therapy
Issue 9: Is Cyberbullying Related to Gender?	**Chapter 5:** Gender and Gender Roles	**Chapter 1:** Sexuality in Perspective
Issue 10: Should Same-Sex Marriage Be Legal?	**Chapter 1:** Perspectives on Human Sexuality **Chapter 17:** Sexual Coercion: Harassment, Aggression, and Abuse **Chapter 18:** Sexually Explicit Materials, Prostitution, and Sex Laws	**Chapter 1:** Sexuality in Perspective **Chapter 10:** Sexuality and the Life Cycle: Adulthood **Chapter 13:** Sexual Orientation: Gay, Straight, or Bi?
Issue 11: Can Lesbian and Gay Couples Be Appropriate Parents for Children?	**Chapter 12:** Conception, Pregnancy, and Childbirth	**Chapter 13:** Sexual Orientation: Gay, Straight, or Bi?
Issue 12: Are Fathers Necessary for Children's Well-Being?	**Chapter 7:** Sexuality in Adulthood	**Chapter 10:** Sexuality and the Life Cycle: Adulthood
Issue 13: Should Parents be Allowed to Choose the Sex of Their Children?	**Chapter 12:** Conception, Pregnancy, and Childbirth	**Chapter 19:** Ethics, Religion, and Sexuality
Issue 14: Does the "Mommy Track" (Part-time Work) Improve Women's Lives?	**Chapter 12:** Conception, Pregnancy, and Childbirth	**Chapter 1:** Sexuality in Perspective
Issue 15: Can Social Policies Improve Gender Inequalities in the Workplace?	**Chapter 5:** Gender and Gender Roles **Chapter 17:** Sexual Coercion: Harassment, Aggression, and Abuse	**Chapter 1:** Sexuality in Perspective **Chapter 15:** Sexual Coercion
Issue 16: Is Gender Wage Gap Justified?	**Chapter 5:** Gender and Gender Roles **Chapter 17:** Sexual Coercion: Harassment, Aggression, and Abuse	**Chapter 1:** Sexuality in Perspective **Chapter 15:** Sexual Coercion
Issue 17: Are Barriers to Women's Success as Leaders Due to Societal Obstacles?	**Chapter 5:** Gender and Gender Roles **Chapter 17:** Sexual Coercion: Harassment, Aggression, and Abuse	**Chapter 1:** Sexuality in Perspective **Chapter 15:** Sexual Coercion
Issue 18: Should "Abstinence-Until-Marriage" Be the Only Message to Teens?	**Chapter 6:** Sexuality in Childhood and Adolescence	**Epilogue:** Looking to the Future: Sexuality Education
Issue 19: Is "Gender Identity Disorder" an Appropriate Psychiatric Diagnosis?	**Chapter 5:** Gender and Gender Roles	**Chapter 17:** Sexual Disorders and Sex Therapy
Issue 20: Should Transgendered Women Be Considered "Real" Women?	**Chapter 7:** Sexuality in Adulthood	**Chapter 13:** Sexual Orientation: Gay, Straight, or Bi?

Introduction

Sex and Gender: Knowing Is Believing, but Is Believing Knowing?

As people go through their day-to-day lives, when is their sex or gender relevant, that is, in the foreground, and when is it in the background? Think about this question regarding your own life. Are you always aware of being a female or a male? Probably not. Does your femaleness or maleness cause you to behave the way you do all the time? Probably not. Thus, we arrive at the perplexing and complicated question: When do sex and gender matter? To begin to answer this question we need to consider what we mean by the terms *sex* and *gender*. We also need to identify and make explicit the fundamental assumptions that lead us to put so much importance on questions regarding sex and gender.

Within any species of living organisms, there is variation. In Western thought, a primary individual difference is sex. What do we "know" about the ways in which individuals differ by sex? Of course, an obvious response is that individuals are either female or male. We treat it as fact. What else do you *know* about human variation by sex? Are there other *facts* about human females and males? Perhaps you will state such facts as males' greater physical strength than females, males' taller stature than females, and females' unique capacity for childbearing. Make a list of what else you *know* about human variation by sex.

Most of us have a vast network of knowledge about human variation by sex. Many of the claims stem from knowledge of the differential biology of females and males and extend to variation in human emotion, thought, and behavior. In fact, some individuals maintain that females and males are so different that they are from different planets! For most of us, this is an interconnected network of "givens" about the far-reaching effects of femaleness and maleness. Given that we consider human sex variation to be an undeniable fact, we rarely question these claims. Instead we see them as essential truths or facts—unquestionable, unchangeable, and inevitable. The goal of this book is to guide your critical evaluation of this network of knowledge. What you may discover as you critically consider the controversial issues in this book is that many of the things we believe to be factually true and objectively provable about human sex variation are instead unsupported beliefs.

Knowledge and Beliefs in the Study of Sex and Gender

Cross-Cutting Issue: The Role of Biology

For decades, in public discourse and in numerous academic disciplines, there has been widespread debate and discussion of the extent of human variation by sex. In addition, there is extensive consideration of the cultural meaning and significance attached to femaleness and maleness. The terms *sex* and *gender* are used to refer to these various phenomena. Although sex and gender are commonly thought to be synonyms, many scholars attempted to assign different meanings to these terms. Sex was often used to refer to the biological distinction between females and males. Gender referred to the social and cultural meaning attached to notions of femaleness and maleness. Depending on one's theory of how sex and gender were related, there were varying degrees of overlap or interconnection between these two terms. Many scholars now question the usefulness of the distinction, suggesting that the notion of biological sex itself is socially constructed. This more contemporary view rests on two arguments. First, biological organisms cannot exist or be studied devoid of a social context, making the sex and gender dichotomy arbitrary. Second, as Myra Hird has suggested, there is a persistent yet unchallenged belief that biological sex is the "original sign through which gender is read." That is, what we know about a person's anatomy provides the basis for prescriptions and proscriptions regarding appropriate behaviors.

However, some recent feminist theorists, reflecting on transgenderism, suggest that gender identity, not anatomy, is core to a person's true self. Thus, if biological anatomy does not match identity, it is the anatomy that is "wrong," a medical condition worthy of fixing.

Biological features of sex have been assumed to include genetic factors of female and male chromosomes, hormones and the endocrine system, internal and external sexual and reproductive organs (appearance and functionality), and central nervous system sex differentiation. The assumption or the defined norm was that there is consistency among these different biological factors, differentiating individuals into females and males. However, research with transgendered people and intersexed individuals challenges the assumption that various biological features of organisms "naturally" co-occur. Research suggests that variations among these features occur naturally. Defining these variations as "normal" or "deviant" is a social construction.

Gender has been employed in theory and research in various ways and toward various goals. The study of gender has been used to assess the validity of claims of human sex differences. It has also been used to challenge assertions of biological roots of gendered behavior by testing alternate causal theories (e.g., environmental, learning, cognitive theories). Some studies of gender aim to analyze the social organization of female/male relations, elucidating gendered power dynamics and patterns of dominance and subordination. Gender studies have also been used to show how burdens and benefits are inequitably distributed among females and males in society. Other scholars have used conceptions of gender to explain the structure of the human psyche, individuals' sense of self, identity, and aspiration.

How are elements of gender produced? Biological essentialists believe that biological sex differences directly lead to behavioral, cognitive, and emotional differences (i.e., gender affects) between females and males. In other words, there are *essential* differences between females and males that stem from biology and pervade human psychology and sociality. Evolutionary theorists believe that ancestral responses to environmental challenges created physiological differences between females and males that underlie contemporary behavioral differences. In contrast, social constructionists believe gender to be a social or cultural creation. Infants and children are socialized and disciplined so as to develop sex-appropriate gender attributes and skills. As individuals mature, they develop a gender identity or a sense of self as female or male. They internalize the dominant cultural gender ideology, develop expectations for self and others, and assume sex-congruent gender roles, behaving in gender-appropriate ways. Symbolic interactionists point to the power of pervasive cultural gender symbolism in the production and reproduction of gender in cultures. They show how gender metaphors are assigned to cultural artifacts and how language structures gender meanings and dynamics, creating a dominant cultural meaning system. Standpoint theorists show us how our position in the social hierarchy impacts our perspective on and involvement in cultural gender dynamics. Throughout all the issues in this book, you will see these various perspectives being contrasted.

Recent technological advances are permitting greater opportunities to examine genetic constitution and expression, as well as neurological and hormonal functioning in humans. Sophisticated methods provide for careful evaluation of cardiovascular and immune functions as well. All of these have been applied to the study of sex differences. The big debate is whether this work is clarifying or confusing the study of sex and gender.

Cross-Cutting Issue: Intersecting Identities

Adding to the complexity is a growing appreciation that what it means to be female or male in a given culture is affected by one's race, ethnicity, social class, and sexual orientation, with some scholars arguing that these too are social constructs. Contemporary analyses suggest that the fundamental construct is *oppression*—that is, those in power have the authority to declare who is and is not "acceptable," with access to resources (such as education or political influence) based on criteria defined by the powerful. Thus, gender is seen as one system of power intersecting with other systems of power (such as race, ethnicity, heterosexuality, and social class).

The concept of intersecting identities suggests that some people may experience status incongruence as they forge a sense of identity. Identity is a dynamic ongoing process involving the negotiation of social relationships across time and contexts. The view that people's identities are dynamic and negotiated indicates that one's senses of self (e.g., psychological characteristics or traits, physical features, roles, abilities) are contextually dependent. The negotiation of power relationships can be informed by the dynamic process of identity development and maintenance and vice versa. Theories of identity bring social structural variables (e.g., ethnicity, gender, class) associated with varying degrees of status, to the individual and interpersonal levels. In any given situation, a person's perception of how social structural variables are incorporated into her/his identity may inform the perception of relative power. Different levels of social power may produce different behavioral, cognitive, and affective consequences, making the presentation of self, even at the biological level, fluid across time and context. It is likely that as we more consciously consider the notion of intersecting identities into discussions of sex and gender, much of what we think we know will need to be reevaluated. Such analyses provide opportunities to challenge the essentialist notion of the universal male and female.

Cross-Cutting Issue: Media Representations

Consider what constitutes "proof" for you. What are your standards of "truth"? How do we know that a piece of information is a fact rather than a belief? Do we base our classification on evidence? What kind of evidence do we require? What constitutes enough evidence to classify a claim as a fact rather than a belief? Starting with what we *know* to be the most basic fact about human variation by sex, that humans are either female or male, how do you know that? Did someone tell you (e.g., a parent, a teacher)? Did you read it somewhere, in a magazine or a scientific journal? Did you observe differences between yourself and others or among others? How did this information or observation get generalized from a few individuals to all humans? How have your observations played out in movies or television programs? Is this kind of generalization warrantable, based on human variation? Are there any exceptions (i.e., individuals that do not fit neatly into the categories of female or male)? Would such exceptions lead you to question the *fact* of sex as female or male? For something to be fact, must it be universally true of all individuals within a given species? Have you ever thought critically about this before? How have media portrayals challenged gender constructions? Think of *M. Butterfly* or *Brokeback Mountain*.

If gender is a culturally specific construct, then many time-honored assumptions about sex and gender are challenged. Scholars have asked that we pay close attention to differences between cross-cultural comparisons, studies of cultural processes, and intra-cultural differences. For example, some cultures, mainly Eastern cultures, are considered to be more collectivist in comparison to the more individualist orientation of Western cultures. Although this is an oversimplification of the rich diversity within any given culture, this general difference reveals that people from individualistic cultures have a tendency to self-enhance and brag in ways absent in Eastern cultures. North Americans tend to view individuals as free agents and ascribe autonomous and agentic dispositions to individuals, whereas East Asians view individuals as more constrained by the situation, less agentic, and more subject to collective level influence. Does this not sound quite similar to the ways in which masculinity and femininity are contrasted in Western culture? Thus, what does it mean when we observe that Asian men are more deferential and modest than American women? Similarly, cultural differences in values relate to aggression. We find that in more collectivist cultures people generally are less aggressive than people in more individualistic cultures, revealing that Westernized women may be more aggressive than Asian men. Similarly, there are cultural differences in the expectation that romantic love is a prerequisite for marriage, with more collectivistic cultures placing less emphasis on romantic love and more on the wishes of family and other group members. There are even cultural differences in views of gender identity and attitudes toward sex change surgeries. Consider, for example, that there are more of these surgeries in the Muslim countries of Thailand and Iran than in more Westernized countries. What are the teachings of the Quran that might make sex reassignment more acceptable than teachings of the Roman Catholic Church?

As intriguing as such cross-cultural comparisons are, critics of cross-cultural comparison research, similar to critics of sex differences research, warn of the dangers of looking at surface differences. These types of comparisons give no insight into the whys of the differences. Here, a deeper exploration of specific cultural practices is necessary. That is, causal processes may have less to do with being female or male or a member of one cultural group or another and more to do with some underlying dynamic, such as power, social systems, or socioeconomic level.

Furthermore, there are striking intra-cultural differences that are often ignored. Take, for example, research on the culture of honor among southern white males, which reveals that this particular group of men tends to be more aggressive than men in other regions of the United States. How does this observation challenge our assumptions about aggression as a universal, biologically based male attribute? As another example, consider a study of attitudes toward breast self-examinations in immigrant women from Mexico, Puerto Rico, Cuba, El Salvador, and South America now residing in the United States. The researchers identified various barriers, as well as facilitative factors, that affected the likelihood of breast self-exam. For this discussion, the findings revealed vast differences in various attitudes among these groups of Latina women. For women of Mexican and Puerto Rican descent, embarrassment about touching their breasts was a major barrier, whereas this was not the case for women from South America. So, can we make a sweeping generalization about Latina women's attitudes towards breast self-exam? No—intra-cultural diversity must be considered.

As you consider the various issues presented in this book, you are challenged to remain cognizant of whether results observed are generalizable across cultures as well as to various sub-cultures within any given culture.

Most people do not read scientific journals to get their facts. They rely on various media—magazines, television, and increasingly, the Internet.

Consider how current media reports of scientific findings may privilege an essentialist, causal role of biological forces in gender differences over social constructionist views. For example, an ABC News report proclaimed, "Scientists find sex differences in the brain" (Jan. 19, 2000). "The New Sex Scorecard" in *Psychology Today* (July/Aug. 2003) proclaimed that "men and women's minds really do work differently." What is the impact of such headlines from supposedly reputable sources on everyday people's understanding of the women and men?

A fundamental question is whether the media reflect reality or contribute to the creation of reality. Consider the marketers of Halloween costumes for children. Adie Nelson (*Psychology of Women Quarterly*, 2000) did a content analysis of 469 children's costumes and sewing patterns. She found that less that 10 percent was gender neutral. Costumes for both girls and boys were predominantly hero costumes. Costumes for girls tended to depict beauty queens, princesses, and other traditionally feminine images (including animals and foodstuffs). Costumes for boys often followed a warrior theme, featuring villains (agents or symbols of death). She concluded that "children's fantasy dress reproduces and reiterates more conventional messages about gender." The same conclusion can be said about many media messages. Exposure to sexist media has been shown to lead to less achievement in girls and more sexist attitudes in boys.

It is important to also consider what media messages say to members of various racial, ethnic, and cultural groups. How do these messages frame and reinforce the marginalized status of many groups? For example, to be beautiful is to be thin, blond, and heterosexual. One study found that the more mainstream TV young white women watch, the more negative their body image, but that the more black-oriented TV that young black women watch, the more positive their body image.

Finally, there is growing interest in how Internet use might change "doing gender." In the game world, gamers are known to take on many different personae, experimenting with different ways of interacting. We know that switching genders is common. In chat rooms, people may present themselves differently and express themselves in ways they might not in the real world. What implications does this have for gamers' and chat room participants' real world sense of themselves as females and males? Does experimenting in virtual reality matter? Research has only begun to scratch the surface of the myriad ways that Internet use can alter one's gender-related attitudes, cognitions, and behaviors.

Cross-Cutting Issue: Cross-Cultural and Intra-Cultural Generalizations

The concept of gender has been construed in many ways, spawning a highly complex field of inquiry. Some scholars perceive gender as an attribute of individuals or something we "have." Others see gender as something we "do" or perform; gender is seen as a product of interpersonal interaction. Gender has also been construed as a mode of social organization, structuring status and power dynamics in cultural institutions. Some see gender as universal; others believe gender to be historically—and culturally—specific. The latter perspective has yielded a proliferation of investigations into how, why, when, where, and for whom gender "works." Recently similar logic has been applied to biological sex. That is, the concept of biological sex itself is a social construction.

As you can see from this brief review of many of the ways in which gender has been construed and studied, there are differences and even contradictions among the various perspectives and approaches. Some individuals champion gender as stimulating complementarity and interdependence among humans; others see gender as a powerful source of segregation and exclusion. Some scholars emphasize differences between females and males; others allow for greater

individual variation that crosses sex and gender boundaries or they even emphasize similarity between females and males. Some people think of gender as invariant and fixed; others think of gender as malleable and flexible. Some scholars see
gender as politically irrelevant; others see gender as the root of all social and
political inequities. Some view "gender-inappropriate" behavior with disdain
and fear, labeling it problematic and pathological and in need of correction; others see gender variance as natural and cause for celebration. Some individuals
believe "traditional" differentiated sex roles should be preserved; others believe
that these conventional notions of gender should be redefined or even tran-
scended. Some individuals view gender processes and dynamics as personally relevant; others have little conception of the role of gender in their lived experience.
How do we deal with this controversy? How can we evaluate and weigh different
assertions and arguments?

Tools for Argument Analysis

What is the difference (if any) between facts and beliefs? Do we treat knowledge differently if we classify it as fact versus belief or opinion? Are facts more
important to us than beliefs? Do we question the veracity of facts as much as
that of beliefs? Why not? What are the ramifications of not submitting facts to
critical questioning? Rethink the facts you listed about human variation by
sex. How do you know these are facts? What is your evidence? Does your evidence indisputably support the claim as fact? Do you detect defensiveness
about or resistance to critically questioning facts? Why?

Each pair of selections in this volume presents opposing arguments about
sex and gender. How do you decide which argument is "right" or, at least,
which argument is better? Argument analysis is a field with many approaches
and standards. Here a few major components and criteria are briefly presented
to help you in making judgments about the quality of the arguments advanced
in the book.

To assess an argument's quality it is helpful to break it down into seven
components, including its *claim, definitions, statements of fact, statements of value,
language and reasoning, use of authority,* and *audience.* However, first we must touch
on the issue of *explicit versus implicit elements* within an argument. Real-world
arguments contain many implicit (unstated) elements. For example, they may
use unstated definitions of key terms or rely on value judgments that are not
made clear within the body of the argument itself. Occasionally these elements
are left out because the author wants to hide the weaknesses of her or his argument by omitting them. However, it is probably more often the case that they are
omitted because the author assumes the audience for their work knows about the
missing elements and already accepts them as true. The job of the argument analyst begins with identifying implicit elements in an argument and making them
explicit. Since we usually do not have direct access to the argument's author,
making implicit elements explicit requires a good deal of interpretation on our
part. However, few arguments would stand up to analysis for long if we did not
try our best to fill in the implicit content. Specific examples of making implicit
elements explicit are provided in what follows.

Claim

The first component one should look for in an argument is its claim. What, specifically, are the authors trying to convince us of? The notion of a claim in an argument is essentially the same as that of a thesis in a term paper. In almost all cases it is possible to identify a single overarching claim that the authors are trying to get their audience to accept. For example, in Issue 2 Diamond and Butterworth claim that fluidity in one's sexual orientation across time is evidence that it is not innate. Once the claim of an argument is identified, the analyst can begin to look for and evaluate supporting components. If no claim can be identified, then we do not have an argument that is well formed enough to evaluate fairly.

Definitions

At first thought, an argument's definitions might not seem a very interesting target for analysis. However, definitions are often highly controversial, implicit, and suspect in terms of their quality. This is especially the case in the study of sex and gender. How are the key terms in an argument's claim and supporting reasons defined, if at all? Does the author rely on dictionary definitions, stipulative definitions (offering an original definition of the term), definition by negation (saying what the term does not mean), or definition by example? Dictionary definitions are relatively uncontroversial but rare and of limited application. Stipulative definitions are conveniently explicit but often the subject of controversy. Other types of definitions can be both implicit and not widely accepted. Once you have identified definitions of the key terms in an argument's claim and supporting reasons, ask yourself if you find these definitions to be acceptable. Then ask if the argument's opponent is using these same definitions or is advocating a different set. Opposing arguments cannot be resolved on their merits until the two sides agree on key definitions. Indeed, many long-term debates in public policy never seem to get resolved because the two sides define the underlying problem in very different ways. For example, in Issue 6, Furnham defines male advantage in terms of number of sex partners.

Statements of Fact

Claims have two fundamentally different types of supporting reasons. The first type is statements of fact. A fact is a description of something that we can presumably verify to be true. Thus the first question to be answered about an argument's factual statements is how do we know they are true? For example, in Issue 16, we are given the fact that on average women earn 75 cents to each dollar earned by men. Authors may report original empirical research of their own. With an argument that is reporting on original research, the best means of checking the truth of their facts would be to repeat, or replicate, their research. This is almost never realistically possible, so we then must rely on an assessment of the methods they used, either our own assessment or that of an authority we trust. Authors may be relying on facts that they did not discover on their own, but instead obtained from some authoritative source.

Aside from the question of the truth of facts is the question of their sufficiency. Authors may offer a few facts to support their claim or many. They may offer individual cases or very broad factual generalizations. How many facts are enough? Since most arguments are evaluated in the context of their opponents, it is tempting to tally up the factual statements of both arguments and declare the one with the most facts the winner. This is seldom adequate, although an argument with a wealth of well-substantiated factual statements in support of its claim is certainly preferable to one with few statements of fact that are of questionable quality. In persuasive arguments it is very common to see many anecdotes and examples of individual cases. These are used to encourage the audience to identify with the subject of the cases. However, in analyzing these arguments we must always ask if an individual case really represents a systematic trend. In other words, do the facts offered generalize to the whole or are they just persuasive but isolated exceptions? On the other hand, it is also common to see the use of statistics to identify general characteristics of a population. The analyst should always ask if these statistics were collected in a scientific manner and without bias, if they really show significant distinct characteristics, and how much variation there is around the central characteristics identified. Debates about the gender pay gap are highly influenced by how the pay gap is measured (see Issues 15 and 16).

A final question about statements of fact concerns their relevancy. We sometimes discover factual statements in an argument that may be true, and even interesting reading, but that just don't have anything to do with the claim being advanced. Be sure that the forest is not missed for the trees in evaluating statements of fact—in other words, that verifying and tallying of factual statements does not preempt the question of how well an author supports the primary claim.

Statements of Value

The philosopher David Hume is famous for his observation that a series of factual statements (that something "is" the case) will never lead to the conclusion that something "ought" to be done. The missing component necessary to move from "is" to "ought," to move from statements of fact to accepting an argument's claim, are statements of value. Statements of value declare something to be right or wrong, good or bad, desirable or undesirable, beautiful or ugly. For example, "It is wrong for boys to play with dolls."

Although many people behave as if debates can be resolved by proving one side or the other's factual statements to be true, statements of value are just as critical to the quality of an argument as are statements of fact. Moreover, because value statements have their roots in moral and religious beliefs, we tend to shy away from analyzing them too deeply in public discourse. Instead, people tend to be *absolutist,* rejecting outright values that they do not share, or *relativist,* declaring that all values are equally valid. As a result, statements of value are not as widely studied in argument analysis and standards of evaluation are not as well developed for them as for factual statements.

At the very least, the argument analyst can expect the value statements of an argument to be part of what has been referred to as a "rational ideology." A rational ideology is one in which value statements are *cogent* and *coherent* parts of a *justifiable* system of beliefs. A cogent value statement is one that is relevant and clear. Coherent value statements fit together; they are consistent with one another and help support an argument's claim. A system of beliefs is justifiable if its advocate can provide supporting reasons (both facts and values) for holding beliefs. A morality that makes value judgments but refuses to offer reasons for these judgments would strike us as neither very rational nor very persuasive. Although we rarely have the opportunity to engage in a debate with authors to test their ability to justify their value statements, we can expect an argument's value statements to be explicit, cogent, coherent, and supported by additional statements of fact and value as justification. As in the case of definitions, it is also fruitful to compare the value statements of one argument with those of the opposing view to see how much the authors agree or disagree in the (usually) implicit ideology that lies behind their value statements.

Throughout the issues in this book you will see an implicit clash of values: The sexes *should* be different versus opportunity for variations should be encouraged.

Language and Reasoning

There are a vast number of specific issues in the use of language and reasoning within arguments. Any introductory book on rhetoric or argumentative logic will provide a discussion of these issues. Here just a sample of the most common ones will be touched on. The analyst gives less weight to arguments that use language that is overly emotional. Emotional language relies on connotation (word meanings aside from formal definition), bias or slanting in word choice, exaggeration, slogan, and cliché. Emotional language is sometimes appropriate when describing personal experience but it is not persuasive when used to support a general claim about what should be believed or done in society.

The analysis of reasoning has to do with the logical structure of an argument's components and usually focuses on the search for logical fallacies (errors in logic). A common fallacy has already been discussed under statements of fact: hasty generalization. In hasty generalizations claims are made without a sufficient amount of factual evidence to support them. When authors argue that one event followed another and this proves the first event caused the second, they are committing the *post hoc* fallacy (it may just be a coincidence that the events happened in that order). Two fallacies often spotted in arguments directed at opponents are *ad hominem* and straw man. The first involves attacking the person advocating the opposing view, which is generally irrelevant to the quality of their statements. The second is unfairly describing an opponent's argument in an overly simplified way that is easy to defeat. Fallacies directed at the argument's audience include false dilemma, slippery slope, and *ad populum*. Authors commit the fallacy of false dilemma when they argue that only two alternatives exist when, in fact, there are more than two. Slippery slope is an unsupportable prediction that if a small first step is taken it will inevitably lead to more change. An appeal to public opinion to support a claim is an *ad populum* argument if there is reason to believe that the public is prejudiced or plain wrong in its views, or if what the public believes is simply not relevant to the issue. In general, the argument analyst must not only look at the individual statements of an argument but must also ask how well they are put together in an argument that is logical and not overly emotional.

Use of Authority

The issue of authority is relevant in argument analysis concerning what is the authority of the argument's author. Analysts should use whatever information they can gather to assess the expertise and possible biases of authors. Are authors reporting on an issue that they have only recently begun to study, or have they studied the issue area in considerable depth? Do they occupy a professional position that indicates recognition by others as authorities in the field? Do you have reason to believe that their work is objective and not subject to systematic biases because of who pays for or publishes their work? Be careful not to commit *ad hominem* on this one yourself. The brief biographies of contributors to this volume give you a bit of information about the authors of the arguments that follow.

Audience

The final component of argument analysis is consideration of an argument's intended audience. Clues to the intended audience can be found in the type of publication or forum where the argument is presented, in the professional standing of its author, and in the type of language that the author uses in the argument itself. Knowledge of audience is critical in evaluating an argument fairly. Authors writing an argument for an audience that shares their core values and general knowledge of the subject tend to leave definitions and statements implicit and use language that is highly technical, dense, and symbolic. This applies equally well to scientists writing for a journal in their field and politicians addressing their supporters. Authors writing for an audience that is very different from them tend to make the various components of their arguments much more explicit. However, if an author believes the audience disagrees with them on, for example, an important value statement, they tend to make statements that are both explicit and yet are still very general or ambiguous (this is a skill that is highly developed in politicians). It is difficult to make a fair judgment across these two basic types of author-audience relationships, since the former requires much more interpretation by the evaluator than the latter.

Summary

Analyzing arguments by evaluating their quality in terms of the seven components listed above is by no means guaranteed to give you a clear answer as to which argument is better, for several reasons. The relevant criteria applicable to each component are neither completely articulated nor without controversy themselves. In the process of making implicit elements explicit, analysts introduce their own subjectivity into the process. It should also be clear by this point that argument analysis is a very open-ended process—checking the truth of statements of fact, the justifiability of statements of values, the qualifications of authorities—could go on indefinitely. Thus the logic of argument analysis is underdetermined—following each step exactly is still no guarantee of a correct conclusion. However, if you apply the analytical techniques outlined above to the essays in this volume you will quickly spot implicit definitions, hasty generalizations, unsupported value statements, and questionable authorities as well as examples of well-crafted, logical, and persuasive argumentation. You will be in a much stronger position to defend *your* views about the arguments you find in this book.

Issues in This Volume

The critical examination of sex and gender in this text is segmented into six units. In Unit 1, fundamental assumptions about sex and gender are considered, revealing that "simple" definitions of sex as female or male and gender as directly derivative from biology are shortsighted. Moreover, debate over these fundamental assumptions has yielded some of the most contentious controversy in this field. In Unit 2, the "difference model," the primary paradigm for conceptualizing and studying sex and gender, is critically analyzed. Sex and gender are usually construed as binary oppositions: female versus male, feminine versus masculine. Thus, a primary way in which sex and gender are studied is the comparison of groups of females and males (i.e., sex comparison or sex difference). In this section, you will grapple with underlying theoretical rationales for excavating such differences (including biological, evolutionary, and learning theories), and you will critically evaluate the difference model in terms of methodology, social meaning and significance, and political impact. Is the search for differences between females and males a useful approach to elucidating gender or is it meaningless and even politically dangerous?

Unit 3 focuses on violence in the daily lives of women and men. One of the most pervasive stereotypes is that of sex differences in aggression. It is often assumed that males have an inborn predisposition toward aggression and females do not. As a result, girls and women should give up authority to men in exchange for their protection. This section addresses the issue of the extent to which aggression is gender-based, whether girls and boys, women and men do or do not express aggression equally and in similar or dissimilar ways. In what ways does patriarchy (masculine/male) ways lead to dominance and control? Two issues related to gender and violence are gender symmetry and pornography. Gender symmetry, as used in the domestic violence domain, reflects the assertion that women and men are both aggressive toward intimate partners; hence, domestic violence is not about gender. Various perspectives on this issue influence research agendas, intervention programs, arrest policy (i.e., dual arrest), and services (should there be shelters for battered men?). Similarly affecting research agendas, intervention programs, public policy, and services is the debate over the causal role of pornography in rape. Does viewing pornography increase men's proclivity to rape or do men with a propensity to rape prefer to view pornographic material?

Unit 4 examines gender in a critical social domain—family. Gender is influential before conception, in making decisions to carry a fetus to term, and in the life expectancy of female and male children. Sex selection is a common practice in many cultures, including Western cultures. Why is higher value placed on male versus female offspring? From some theoretical perspectives, gender begins with early socialization and is affected by family composition. One of the most gendered social institutions is the family. Traditional Western family ideology is heterosexist (regarding the heterosexual union as the only acceptable family context) and sexist (prescribing different roles for husbands and wives). In Unit 4, these fundamental values and assumptions are examined. Gender ideology riddles the construction of parenthood. Does gender influence women's and men's capacities for and approaches to parenting? How are traditional family gender ideologies challenged by same-sex parents?

In Unit 5, the world of work is explored. It is a well-established fact that women on average earn 75 cents for each man's dollar. We want to know why. Is it career choice, and if so, what factors determine individuals' career choices? It is highly likely that advanced training in mathematics and the sciences opens more doors of opportunity and increases the likelihood of a larger paycheck. How do gendered factors, be they biological or societal, affect girls' and boys' career choices and opportunities for advancement? Do these factors justify the gender wage gap? It is well understood now that most families cannot achieve a comfortable lifestyle without two paychecks. What are the implications of this for single parents, especially poor women?

In Unit 6, issues of gender and sexuality are explored. In particular, this section is interested in exploring the double-standard and double-bind that women and men often find themselves in. When considering the circumstances of a transgendered person, the question of a triple-standard arises. What does it mean to be a sexual person and how can society go about teaching young people about responsible sexual behavior? Throughout history there has been greater acceptance of male than female sexuality. Societies traditionally have endorsed various explicit and implicit means of controlling sexual expression. For example, sex education programs in the schools are explicitly aimed to control adolescent sexuality.

Conclusion

Equipped with your new tools for analyzing arguments, begin your exploration of knowledge and belief in the study of sex and gender. Remain open to considering and reconsidering beliefs and knowledge in ways that you never imagined. Your "gender quest" begins now; where you will end up, no one knows!

Internet References . . .

The American Psychological Association's Help Center

The American Psychological Association's Help Center is an online resource for brochures, tips, and articles on the psychological issues that affect people's physical and emotional well-being, as well as information about referrals.

http://www.apahelpcenter.org/articles/article.php?id=31

Gender Talk

Gendertalk.com is a resource for trans persons and folks interested in learning about trans persons. Gendertalk.com provides comprehensive access to GenderTalk Radio, the leading radio program on transgender issues.

http://www.gendertalk.com/radio/about.shtml

PFLAG

PFLAG is an international organization with 490 chapters. Founded in 1981, its goal is to help families understand and accept gay, lesbian, bisexual, and transgendered family members. It offers help in strengthening families, support groups for families and friends, educational outreach, a newsletter, chapter development guidelines, grassroots advocacy, information, and referrals. Also has a Transgender Network (PFLAG TNET).

http://www.pflag.org

The New York Times

Read an article in the *New York Times* by Cornelia Dean that discusses the problems girls who are good at math encounter.

http://www.nytimes.com/2005/02/01/science/01math.html

Center for 21st Century Teaching Excellence, University of South Florida

The Center provides opportunities for scholarly dialogue on the art, science, and craft of university teaching. It sponsors publications, workshops, and research that critically examine and promote instructional excellence. The Gender, Race and Ethnicity Bibliography: Natural and Physical Science Web site provides a bibliography of research articles related to factors associated with relationships among sex, achievement, and science self-concept to the science career preferences of Black students.

http://www.cte.usf.edu/bibs/gre/science/bib_science.html

The National Gay and Lesbian Task Force

The National Gay and Lesbian Task Force was founded in 1973 to advocate and organize for the rights of gay, lesbian, bisexual, and transgendered people. Technical assistance for state and local organizers is provided, along with publications, materials, and a newsletter.

http://www.thetaskforce.org

Definitions and Cultural Boundaries: A Moving Target

*W*hat is sex? What is gender? What is gender identity? What is sexual orientation? Must there be congruence between biological aspects of sex (chromosomes, hormones, internal organs, and genitals) and social aspects of gender (assigned sex, gender identity, sexual orientations, and career aspirations)? These are controversial questions with a diversity of answers. In fact, the vast array of contradictory "answers" loosens the boundaries of these concepts to the point of losing any sense of certain definition. Definitions often reveal important theoretical standpoints underlying much of the controversy in the study of sex and gender. Moreover, they raise the question of cultural relativity of definitions. Can these concepts be objectively defined, or is the most objective and scientific definition still a product of culture? This section will explore the limits and limitlessness of definitions and boundaries of sex and gender within biology, psyche, and culture. As you read these selections, consider the role of biology. Is the newest scientific evidence convincing regarding the causal role of biological factors? Does correlation mean causation? Do issues of gender identity, sexual orientation, and career choice based on biological factors play out the same way across race, ethnicity, class, culture, and other status-defining categories? How do the media shape the public's understanding of these issues?

- Is Anatomy Destiny?

- Is Sexual Orientation Innate?

- Do Sex Differences in Careers in Mathematics and Sciences Have a Biological Basis?

1

ISSUE 1

Is Anatomy Destiny?

YES: John L. Rinn and Michael Snyder, from "Sexual Dimorphism in Mammalian Gene Expression," *Trends in Genetics* (2005)

NO: Mahin Hassibi, "Ending the Male Patina in Biology and Busting Bogus Biology and Beliefs from Our Genders, Our Rights," *On The Issues Magazine,* Summer–Winter 2009 (2008)

ISSUE SUMMARY

YES: Professor of pathology John Rinn and biologist Michael Snyder demonstrate that a number of molecular and genetic differences underlie behaviors and physiologies of mammalian sexes.

NO: Psychiatrist Mahin Hassibi suggests that environmental and social factors, combined with myths about biology, explain gendered behavior better than genetic and biological factors.

Do we really know what constitutes one's "sex" and "gender"? Typically people assume that being male or female is a clear and absolute distinction. Biologically based theories of sex differentiation support the argument that genetic make-up and resultant hormonal influences determine fundamental differences between women and men. Given the ethical constraints associated with doing research on humans, researchers have had to rely on animal experimentation to demonstrate that hormones contribute to sexual dimorphism (i.e., sexual differentiation) on neural systems, brains, temperament, and behavior. The assumption is that sex is an unquestionably natural dichotomy rooted in an organism's genetics.

In contrast, a large body of research with numerous species of animals, as well as with humans, suggests that environmental factors provide the major determinants of gender-related patterns of behavior. That is, gender is a socially constructed constellation of feelings, attitudes, and behaviors, thus, strongly influenced by cultural forces.

Critics have begun to question the immunity of biological constructs from cultural analysis, urging that we must recognize that the practice of science occurs within a sociopolitical context. Therefore, biological notions of sex are cultural, social, and political creations.

The dominant Western definition of sex delineates two "normal" categories: male and female. Notions of gender follow suit, typically contrasting masculine and feminine behavior patterns. Is this dichotomy universal? Anthropologists have uncovered compelling evidence that dichotomous definitions of sex are not universal, arguing instead that many cultures have multiple genders. They argue that when looking for binaries, we observe a dichotomous reality. But what remains unseen—gender diversity—is also an important reality.

Some revisionists have begun to "reinvent sex" by replacing dichotomous conceptions of sex with arrays reflecting the complexities of sexual variability in natural characteristics of humans. For example, concepts such as "gender-crossing" have been coined. The problem with such concepts is that they still rely on the fixed binary of male/female, and they problematize deviations. In contrast, construing diversity as multiple genders enables the transcendence of this binary and notions of deviance associated with nonmale and nonfemale genders.

In the following selections, two different perspectives on the basis of gendered patterns of behaviors are presented. On the one hand, Rinn and Snyder note that anatomical, hormonal, and chemical differences, as well as molecular differences between mammalian sexes, underlie and elucidate factors that regulate sex-biased gene expression. On the other hand, Hassibi suggests that assumptions about the genetic and biological basis of sex differences are biased and debunked, especially by recent advances in biotechnology and research on people with atypical chromosomal compositions. She concludes, "These converging developments will leave no solid basis in culture, society, or psychology for gender role differentiation."

YES

John L. Rinn and
Michael Snyder

Sexual Dimorphism in Mammalian Gene Expression

Overview

Males and females have obvious phenotypic differences; they also exhibit differences related to health, life span, cognitive abilities, and have different responses to diseases such as anemia, coronary heart disease, hypertension, and renal dysfunction. Although the anatomical, hormonal, and chemical differences between the sexes are well known, there are few molecular descriptors for gender-specific physiological traits and health risks. Recent studies using microarrays and other methods have made significant progress towards elucidating the molecular differences between mammalian sexes in a variety of tissues and towards identifying the transcription factors that regulate sex-biased gene expression. These findings are providing new insights into the molecular and genetic differences that dictate the different behaviors and physiologies of mammalian sexes.

Introduction

Nearly a century ago, Lillie demonstrated that mixing the placental blood supply of male and female calves produced a more-masculine female, suggesting that there was a chemical factor influencing sex. Jost later showed that sex hormones secreted by the gonads guide the developmental pathways of sex determination and that the different hormonal profiles of males and females last through adulthood. The 90 years since Lillie's first observation have yielded a rich understanding of how these hormonal differences ultimately produce large anatomical dimorphisms. Recent advancements in genome sequencing and microarray technology have provided new insights into the types of genes that are differentially expressed in each sex in a variety of tissues and the mechanisms of their transcriptional regulation.

Males and female mammals begin life phenotypically indistinguishable, despite an XX or XY genotype. At embryonic day 10.5 in the mouse, the male and female developmental pathways diverge. It is at this point that the sex-determining region on the Y-chromosome (SRY), a HMG box transcription factor, is expressed, which ultimately leads to the production of testosterone and the concomitant development of the bipotential gonad into the testis. The female developmental pathway is determined by the absence of SRY, resulting in estrogen production and ovary development. In addition, the presence of a nuclear hormone receptor . . . Dax1 in the XX bipotential gonad represses the male developmental pathways. Thus, gonadogenesis is guided by key transcription factors that produce different hormonal outputs. The plasma growth-hormone profiles are also different between the sexes. Both sex hormones and growth hormones produce different chemical environments in males and females that persist into adulthood.

The different hormonal stimuli between the sexes have well-documented developmental effects (e.g. reproductive tissue development). However, less is known about either the molecular mechanisms that prompt transcription after hormone exposure or the identity of resulting genes that are differentially expressed in each sex in adult tissues, particularly somatic tissues. This information will provide important insights into the different physiologies of mammalian sexes such as disease susceptibility and life span. In this article, we will discuss several recent studies that have made significant progress in identifying genes that are differentially expressed in each sex and the mechanisms of sexually dimporphic transcriptional regulation, a phenomenon that is shared among many phyla. This knowledge serves the dual purpose of indexing the molecular differences between the physiologies of mammalian sexes and potentially identifies markers for sex-specific health risks.

Gene Expression Differences in the Male and Female Reproductive Tissues

The reproductive tissues are the most sexually dimorphic tissues in the majority of mammals and demonstrate clearly the role of sex-hormone stimulation and development. For example, pubescent males experience spikes in testosterone levels that stimulate the development of seminiferous tubules. In contrast to the well-characterized anatomical and histological effects of hormone exposure, less is known about the global transcriptional response to sex-hormone exposure in the reproductive tissues. Interestingly, recent work by Sadate-Ngatchou and colleagues indicates that testosterone serves to suppress gene expression in the testis. . . .

The ovary and testis are derived from the same primordial tissue and later differentiate into different tissues. Unsurprisingly, a recent study found that hundreds of genes are differentially expressed in the ovary and testis. More than 500 genes were found to be enriched in the testis and >300 genes were enriched in the ovary (out of >30 000 genes examined . . .). These transcripts were at least three times as abundant in one gonad. Gene-ontology analysis of these genes revealed several interesting functional gene classifications that were differentially expressed in the reproductive tissues. The testis expresses few genes that encode proteins involved in the immune response (i.e., the genes needed to defend the tissue against foreign material). [There is] decreased expression level in 43 immune-response genes in the testis, but not in the ovary.

. . . These studies revealed interesting functional differences in the genes that are differentially expressed between the male and female reproductive tissues.

Sex-Biased Gene-Expression Differences in Somatic Tissues

Differences in gene expression between males and females were first reported >20 years ago in the rat liver. . . .

Males and females respond to disease differently. For example, kidney diseases progress faster in men than women, kidney transplants from women to men tend to fail more frequently and the effects of diabetes on the kidney differ between the sexes. In many diseases, sex hormones are thought to explain sex-dependent differences in the progression and extent of disease; in systemic lupus erythematosus, a primarily female autoimmune disease, estrogen has a major role in the progression and development of the disease. Perhaps sex hormones differentially affect gene expression in somatic tissues, which in turn results in sex-specific propensities to disease.

Although most studies of sex-related gene expression have focused on specific genes in the liver, the advancement of technologies such as DNA microarrays is making it possible to investigate several other tissues that have sex-related disease differences. A recent microarray study, surveying the levels of polyadenylated RNA, demonstrated that, in addition to the liver, there is extensive sex-specific gene expression in the kidney. A total of 27 genes were found to be differentially expressed in each sex in the mouse kidney. Similar to the liver, several of these were involved in drug metabolism. . . .

It will be important to investigate human tissues for sex-biased gene expression to determine if similar differences are found.

Limited Sex-Biased Gene Expression in the Adult Brain

The brain is perhaps the most sexually dimorphic somatic organ in the human body. Many physical characteristics differ between the male and female brain, including hemispheric asymmetry, grey-matter content, white-matter content, cerebral spinal-fluid volume, and the size of numerous anatomical regions. Moreover, males and females appear to have different propensities for cognitive motor skills, suggesting that there might be further variation in brain structure and organization.

Several studies show that many of these physical dimorphisms in the brain are directly caused by sex-hormone exposure at key developmental time-points; however, there is evidence for hormone-independent sex differences. . . . Studies provide compelling evidence for sex differences in the brain that are independent of hormone exposure.

In contrast to the prenatal brain, several studies have reported few gene expression differences between the male and female adult brain. The hypothalamus contains the sexually dimorphic nuclei of the pre-optic area (SDN-POA), one of the most dramatic sexual dimorphisms of the brain. The male rat SDN-POA is on average of five times larger than in the female. Despite these large anatomical dimorphisms, few genes are differentially expressed in both the adult mouse and human hypothalamus of each sex. In both mice and humans, the differentially expressed genes were either encoded on the Y-chromosome or involved in X-chromosome inactivation. Two other studies have found similar results in three different brain regions. . . . Studies of different regions of the brain found that sex-related expression differences are primarily limited to genes encoded on the sex chromosomes; interestingly, several of these genes encode proteins that are involved in translation. This suggests that sex differences can occur on the protein level. Another possibility is that the increased heterogeneity of cell types in the brain (unlike the more uniform cell distribution of the liver) masks potential gene expression differences between males and females. In summary, unlike in kidney and the prenatal brain, there are limited gene expression differences between the adult male and female brain.

Transcriptional Regulation of Genes Differentially Expressed in Each Sex

A large body of evidence demonstrates that dimorphic patterns of growth-hormone (GH) release regulates sex-specific gene expression in the liver. In both rat and human, males have a cyclical release of GH (high peaks of GH followed by low troughs); females in both species have smaller amplitudes with more frequent pulses, yielding a near continuous plasma level of GH. . . . The different growth-hormone profiles between adult sexes can affect the expression of numerous genes in an adult somatic tissue. It is also likely that these hormonal differences affect the transcriptome of other somatic tissues.

. . . STAT5b is activated by the oscillation of GH release exhibited in males and subsequently activates male-biased genes. Moreover, there is a partial loss of male-biased transcription in STAT5b-deficient mice. However, STAT5b is not sufficient to induce certain sex-specific gene expression patterns in the liver, suggesting that other transcription factors are involved.

Two recent studies in the mouse implicate HNF4α, RSL1 and RSL2 as the transcription factors responsible for regulating genes that are preferentially expressed in each sex. HNR4α is a member of the nuclear receptor superfamily and contains a zinc-finger DNA-binding domain. Wiwi *et al.* used reverse genetics to determine that HNF4α regulates sex-related transcription in the liver. This study determined that HNF4α-deficient mice lose sex-related expression of several Cyp450s. HNF4α upregulates *Cy4α12* and glutathione S-transferase (*GSTp*) in the male liver, and it downregulates the female-biased genes *Cyp2a4*, *Cyp2b9*, *Hnf3β*, and *Hnf6β*. Moreover, several female predominant (*Cyp2b10*, *2b13*, *3a41*, and *3a44*) and male predominant (*2d9* and *8b1*) Cyp450s are also regulated by HNF4α. Thus, it seems that HNF4α induces male-predominant expression in the liver in addition to suppressing the expression of two transcription factors that might have an active role in the female (i.e., HNF3β and HNF6β). . . .

A study recently identified other transcription factors in the liver that, unlike the other transcription factors mentioned previously, regulate sex-specific transcription in a hormone-independent fashion. The RSL region on chromosome 13 has long been implicated in the regulation of sexually dimorphic gene expression in the liver. Female mice with defective *Rsl* genes express male-biased genes, indicating that this region probably acts as a transcriptional repressor. . . . Genes differentially expressed in each sex are regulated in a hormone-dependant . . . and hormone-independent . . . manner in the rodent liver. These results indicate that a complex transcriptional circuitry is responsible for sex-specific gene expression in the rodent liver. . . .

Concluding Remarks

. . . A multifaceted transcriptional network produces genes that are differentially expressed in the rodent liver in each sex. It remains to be determined if these and/or other transcriptional mechanisms produce sex-biased gene expression in the kidney, reproductive, and other tissues.

. . . It is also plausible that sexually dimorphic gene expression in other tissues is regulated by growth or sex hormones using similar mechanisms as the liver. . . . There remains much to learn about the mechanisms of sex differences in transcriptional regulation in the liver and in several other tissues, but even less is known about the direct targets of these transcription factors. [Further research] . . . will lead to a more comprehensive understanding of the transcriptional network regulated by sex-biased transcription factors, potentially revealing new target genes and even other down-stream transcription factors that have a sexually dimorphic role in transcriptional regulation.

In humans, the lack of data on genes that are preferentially expressed in each sex is probably due to the difficulty in obtaining healthy adult-tissue samples and individual variation in gene expression. However, by using multiple human samples separated by sex in a variety of human tissues, a more complete understanding of this phenomenon can be obtained. Only a handful of tissues in rodent models have been examined for sex-specific gene expression. It is likely that other tissues contain genes that are differentially express in each sex, especially tissues that have myriad physiological differences and disease propensities between sexes (e.g., heart and colon). Finally, differences in protein levels and modifications between males and females are relatively unexplored; however, it is plausible that proteins and post-translational modifications are important to sex-specific physiology.

The studies discussed in this article have shed some light on the mechanisms and characteristics of sex-specific gene expression; however, many questions remain regarding the molecular contributions to the dimorphic physiologies of males and females.

Mahin Hassibi

→ **NO**

Ending the Male Patina in Biology and Busting Bogus Biology and Beliefs from Our Genders, Our Rights

For the past century and a half, every new discovery of biology has left intact, and even crystallized, the myth of women's inferiority. Now, galloping developments in biotechnology may alter this age-old script.

Still, the possibilities for manipulation of genes and genetic engineering are taking place with little or no public attention to the potential consequences in the male-female equation. The future they portend could be truly revolutionary.

Origin of Bias

The pattern of past biological bias emerges even from the groundbreaking work of Charles Darwin. While he delivered innovative analyses that shifted the understanding of plant and animal evolution, in his next stage, Darwin managed to reinforce entrenched cultural attitudes that females are subservient to males.

Initially, the publication of Darwin's *Origin of Species* in 1859 introduced the revolutionary concept of evolution by natural selection into the scientific stream of the western thought. Opposition was based largely on the glaring disagreement between Darwin's conclusions and the biblical story of creation. But for the younger generation of his day, Darwin's observations and methodology led logically to his results and, as such, were not refutable.

Darwin's next important work, published in 1871, took a sharp turn when it came to women. In *Descent of Man, and Selection in Relation to Sex,* Darwin concludes, "Males are more evolutionarily advanced than females." This determination not only reinforced the belief about the inferiority of women during the 19th century, but has remained the underpinning of attitudes about women today.

In the second work, Darwin does not consider cultural, social, economic or historical factors when discussing the real or imaginary distinctions between men and women, although in the theory of natural selection, environmental factors are of prime importance in determining which organism survives to reproduce. Darwin concludes, instead, that sexual selection favors weaker women with a smaller volume of brain, which, to his thinking, indicates lower

From *On the Issues,* Summer and Winter 2009. Copyright © 2009 by On the Issues Magazine. Reprinted by permission.

intelligence than men, while manly pursuits such as war and hunting have helped to weed out the weaker men and maintain those fittest to survive. Consequently, for women, the aim of evolution and natural selection was no longer "survival of the fit," but the survival of what best served men's interests.

Codified in the Myth of "Penis Envy"

Sigmund Freud, following in the decades after, hoped to construct his theories of psychology on the solid basis of biology and accepted the Darwinian ideas about women. Darwin held that "unchecked female militancy" posed a real danger to civilization and "the orderly process of evolution." Freud believed that "penis envy" explained much about female psychology and that the "castrating woman" threatened the social order.

One hundred years post-Darwin, the second revolution in biology resulted in the discovery of double helix of the DNA in 1953. Yet nothing had changed in the science and scientists' attitudes toward women.

Dr. Rosalind E. Franklin, an x-ray crystallographer, chemist, and molecular biologist, worked on the structure of the DNA. Her male contemporaries relied upon their observations of her meticulous 3D-photography of the DNA molecule and subsequently received the Nobel Prize for the discovery. They not only appropriated her work and failed to credit her, but denigrated her as a woman who was unsuccessful in "her feminine qualities," criticizing her dress, hair, makeup, and apparent lack of interest in appealing to men.

Sociobiology and evolutionary psychology are the more recent theoretical offspring of evolutionary theory. So far, these fields have managed to disclaim only the generalized statement of women's lower intellectual endowment, and little else. Much time and money is spent trying to map the attributes of the brain of "Man the Hunter" and address its various counter arguments, as opposed to what is considered to be the less challenging talents of "Woman the Gatherer." And substantial space is given discussing the possible biological causes of the smaller number of women in academic jobs monopolized by men or in the power positions denied women by the male network.

Laboratories Leap Ahead

In the meantime, the pace of biology is accelerating. In laboratories, scientists are rapidly mapping the genomes of many animals and plants, as well as humans. Research into DNA and all its many components has become so numerous, so mysterious and fascinating, that identifying all of the elements, functions and possible manipulation of their activities requires the collective effort of many academic centers. The Encode Project was established as a reservoir of the biological microcosm. The Encyclopedia of Life promises to document information about the 1.8 million species known on the planet. For the first time, it seems, biology may develop concrete information about the differences between male and female physiology. Science may determine the type and functions of specifically female genes, their pathogenesis, and differential treatments of their diseases. . . .

Busting Bogus Biology and Beliefs

The feminist movement began to raise questions about the cultural root of male supremacy. The simplified male-female concept of "gender" has never been simple. Unrelated to individual capabilities, "gender roles" throughout most of human history have subordinated the female to the male. In more recent years, reexaminations of "gender identity" along with developments in science and society have resulted in new understandings about what gender means to individuals. These developments, in turn, may reshape "gender roles."

The binary categorization of gender as male-female is based on observed external male and female sexual characteristics. But the binary categorization has very little to do with gender roles and the universal subordination of women to men. The subordination appears to derive from the difference in physical power of men and women. This was, of course, desirable for men, as well. Pregnancy made it difficult for even young and physically strong women to resist physical domination by men. Men also made and utilized various weapons for hunting animals, extending their ability to subjugate and exploit women. Since the timing of pregnancy was not controllable for each individual woman, no collective, coordinated resistance was possible. Cultural myths and religious beliefs reinforced and justified this division. For centuries, social constructs held that women owed allegiance and obedience to their husbands; children were the property of their fathers, who owned the children's mothers.

More complex cultures developed more complicated reasons for maintaining the systems by which men subjugated women. Women were not only viewed as morally, intellectually and even emotionally inferior to men, but they became the agent of men's "downfall." Pandora opened the box full of trouble; Eve was the author of the original sin.

The Enlightenment and the Age of Reason did not rethink or re-examine the prevalent ideas about women. Humanists did not question the inferior status of women. Even in Thomas More's Utopia, the women remained naturally inferior to men. Even though they were granted the ability to engage in constructive employment, that is, hard physical labor, the women were supposed to prostrate themselves before their husbands.

Studies of chromosomes in the second half of the 19th century and the discovery and synthesis of sex hormones in the early 20th century seemed to put sexual differentiation on a solid biological ground. Freud relied upon these ideas to develop his theories of psychology, in which the inferior status of women did not change.

Modern Times Shake Up Old Notions

The feminist movement in the early 20th century began to raise serious questions about the cultural root of male supremacy. Then, following the civil rights movement of the '60s and inspired by feminist militancy, gays and lesbians began to refuse to accept the way in which same-sex sexual attraction and desire had been pathologized and declared a sickness that required various forms of treatment.

The news from the biological field also became more confusing and complex during the decades of the '50s and '60s. Studies of sex chromosomes found "meta-females," that is, women who have one or more extra X chromosomes in each cell, making them triple X, or more rarely four or five Xs. Biologists also identified males with one extra X chromosome: they carried the genotype of XXY, or, more rarely, XXXY, XXXXY or XY/XXY mosaic. Furthermore, psychologists and psychiatrists knew that some individuals experience deep and persistent dissatisfaction with their biological sex and undergo years of pain and suffering, as well as extensive medical and surgical intervention, to change their sex. Starting with the Second World War when women replaced men in heavy industry and hazardous jobs, the rigid ideas of gender roles became untenable. The loosening of sex-based criteria for jobs, including in the armed forces, provided evidence that women's place was not divinely designated, but literally manmade.

Recently, the last remnant of gender-specific function, that is, reproductive specialization, has undergone significant changes. People with a desire for parenting are now able to procure eggs and sperm from unrelated, and even unknown, individuals. Individuals can rent-a-uterus to nourish the lab-fertilized eggs to delivery. Advances in cloning, however controversial, may dispense with some steps in this process, as well. It is also not inconceivable that the uterine environment can be replicated in vitro, in the not too distant future, and the whole of reproduction processes take place outside the human body.

These converging developments will leave no solid basis in culture, society, or psychology for gender role differentiation. Biologically, the majority of human beings will still be born with male or female sexual organs and sexual hormones, and it is likely that the hormonal differences will prove to have subtle influences on the brain and on psychological characteristics of the individuals, but the utility of maintaining the concepts of gender identity and gender roles will become untenable. New categories and divisions will have to be made. Interpersonal relations will have to be based on factors other than the age-old customs, a revision that may create the new men and women so desired by utopian visionaries.

POSTSCRIPT

Is Anatomy Destiny?

Nature versus nurture? Biology versus social determinism? Just as some scholars argue that we need to move beyond gender binaries to better understand human complexity, we must also move beyond neat either/or propositions about the causes of sex and gender. Traditional thought dictates that biology affects or determines behavior, that anatomy is destiny. But behavior can also alter physiology. Recent advances explore the complex interaction between biology (genes, hormones, brain structure) and environment. We have learned that it is impossible to determine how much of our behavior is biologically based and how much is environmental. Moreover, definitions of gendered behavior are temporally and culturally relative. Yet why do researchers continue to try to isolate biological from environmental factors?

Advancements in the study of biological bases of sex and critiques of applications of biological theory to human behavior, such as Hassibi discussed, challenge some of Rinn and Snyder's assertions. Many traditional biologists recognize species diversity in hormone-brain-behavior relationships, which makes the general application of theories based on animal physiology and behavior to humans problematic. Moreover, species diversity challenges male/female binaries. The validity of the presence/absence model of sex dimorphism has been challenged. In embryonic development, do females "just happen" by default in the absence of testosterone? No, all individuals actively develop through various genetic processes. Moreover, the sexes are similar in the presence and need of both androgens and estrogens; in fact, the chemical structures and derivation of estrogen and testosterone are interconnected.

Suggested Readings

Dina Anselmi, *Questions of Gender: Perspectives and Paradox* (New York: McGraw-Hill, 2006).

Jill B. Becker, *Sex Differences in the Brain: From Genes to Behavior* (New York: Oxford University Press, 2008).

Colin Hamilton, *Cognition and Sex Differences* (New York: Palgrave Macmillan, 2008).

Anne Fausto-Sterling, *Sexing the Body: Gender Politics and the Construction of Sexuality* (New York: Basic Books, 2000).

David C. Geary, *Male, Female: The Evolution of Human Sex Differences* (Washington, DC: American Psychological Association, 1998).

Michael S. Kimmel, *The Gendered Society* (New York: Oxford Press, 2000).

Steven Rhodes, *Taking Sex Differences Seriously* (San Francisco: Encounter Books, 2004).

ISSUE 2

Is Sexual Orientation Innate?

YES: Heino F. L. Meyer-Bahlburg, Curtis Dolezal, Susan W. Baker, and Maria I. New, from "Sexual Orientation in Women with Classical or Non-Classical Congenital Adrenal Hyperplasia as a Function of Degree of Prenatal Androgen Excess," *Archives of Sexual Behavior,* 2008

NO: Lisa M. Diamond and Molly Butterworth, from "Questioning Gender and Sexual Identity: Dynamic Links over Time," *Sex Roles,* 2008

ISSUE SUMMARY

YES: Clinical psychologist Heino F. L. Meyer-Bahlburg and his colleagues report that sexual orientation is related to specific molecular genotypes in women with classical congenital adrenal hyperplasia (CAH), supporting a sexual-differentiation perspective involving the effects of prenatal androgens on the development of sexual orientation.

NO: Psychologist Lisa M. Diamond and her student use a feminist theoretical framework of intersectionality to analyze data from the experiences of individuals who claim neither an unambiguously female nor male identity to demonstrate that sexual orientation, sexual identify, and gender identity are fluid and change over time.

P sychosexuality, or psychological behaviors and phenomena presumably associated with biological sex, has typically been defined as having three components: gender identity, gender role, and sexual orientation. A fundamental assumption is that these are congruent.

Gender identity is one's sense of self as belonging to one sex: male or female. Cognitive developmentalists such as Lawrence Kohlberg add the criterion of gender constancy. Gender constancy starts with the ability of a child to accurately discriminate females from males and to accurately identify her or his own status correctly, and develops into the knowledge that gender is invariant. The acquisition of gender identity is often affectively loaded and sometimes marked by negative emotion, otherwise known as gender dysphoria.

The term *gender role* refers to attitudes, behaviors, and personality characteristics that are designated by society (in particular sociohistorical contexts) as appropriately masculine or feminine (i.e., typical of the male or female role, respectively). Thus, assessments of gender role behavior in children have included toy preferences, interest in physical activities, fantasy role and dress-up play, and affiliative preference for same-sex versus opposite-sex peers.

Sexual orientation refers to the match between one's own sex and the sex of the person to whom the person is erotically attracted. Typically, sexual orientation has been considered categorically as heterosexual, homosexual, or bisexual.

Gender Identity Disorder (GID) is defined as a strong psychological identification with the opposite sex and is signaled by the display of opposite sex-typed behaviors and avoidance or rejection of sex-typed behaviors characteristic of one's own sex. It is not related to sexual orientation. Distress or discomfort about one's status as a boy or a girl frequently accompanies these behaviors. The age of onset is 2 to 4 years. Some children self-label as the opposite sex, some self-label correctly but wish to become a member of the opposite sex. Other children do not express cross-sex desires but exhibit cross-sex-typed behavior. Some children cross-dress, sometimes insistently. Less characteristic are cross-sex-typed mannerisms (e.g., body movements, voice, pitch). Cross-sex peer affiliation preferences, poor peer relations, and alienation are typical.

It has been reported that women with classical congenital adrenal hyperplasia (CAH), which is related to a deficiency of the enzyme 21-hydroxylase, show variable degrees of masculinization of the body, interests, and behavior due to excess adrenal androgen production. One result may be related to increased bisexuality and homosexuality.

There is considerable controversy concerning whether gender identity and sexual orientation are socially constructed or innate. Researchers studying the effects of prenatal hormones on brain structure, gender identity, and gendered behavior, including sexual orientation, have challenged the claim that gender identity is socially constructed.

A pivotal case was that of John/Joan, a boy (with a twin brother) who at eight months of age was injured in a botched circumcision and subsequently reared as a girl. This created the opportunity to study "naturalistically" whether or not gender identity could be socially constructed. But at the age of 14, upon learning the facts of his birth and sex reassignment, the child rejected his reassigned sex and began living as a man. In May 2004 he committed suicide.

The selections presented here argue from very different perspectives and rely on different research traditions. Meyer-Bahlburg and colleagues compared responses on self-report questionnaires, psychometric tests, and interviews of women with CAH for whom their molecular genetics had been determined with a group of non-CAH women (sisters and female cousins). In contrast to a "snapshot in time," Diamond and Butterworth considered interview data collected over a 10-year period in four young women who identified as non-heterosexual. The results are arguments that on the one hand consider sexual orientation as a result of prenatal androgens and on the other hand consider sexual orientation and gender identify as fluid and changing over time as a result of multiple factors.

YES

Heino F. L. Meyer-Bahlburg et al.

Sexual Orientation in Women with Classical or Non-Classical Congenital Adrenal Hyperplasia as a Function of Degree of Prenatal Androgen Excess

Introduction

Sexual orientation is a trait with very large differences between men and women . . . one of the largest for any gender-related behavior or trait. . . . The demonstration of familiality and heritability of homosexuality has led to numerous attempts to provide genetic explanations. Given the focus of evolutionary theory on reproduction and survival of the offspring, a sexual orientation of women to men and of men to women is eminently plausible. It is much more difficult to come up with a compelling evolutionary raison d'être for homosexuality and bisexuality. A number of non-endocrine explanatory hypotheses have been formulated. In the framework of evolutionary theory, overdominance kin altruism, and sexually antagonistic selection have been suggested as potential mechanisms explaining the gene polymorphism that is presumed to underlie homosexuality, and mathematical models have recently been formulated that should facilitate their empirical testing. However, the variability of homosexual behavior across vertebrate species has not led to a consensus on an explanation in terms of evolutionary theory, and the demonstration of learning mechanisms in the acquisition of sexual preferences in animal models has further complicated the issue. Identification of specific genes has not yet led to consistent success, but new findings on extreme skewing of X-inactivation by DNA-methylation in mothers of gay men have added additional genetic possibilities.

. . . New data from the AddHealth project . . . (indirectly) supports a social-influence hypothesis explaining same-sex attractions in adolescents. Other non-genetic explanations include the progressive immunization hypothesis, which is derived from the well-replicated association of homosexuality in males with the number of older brothers in the sibship and assumes that successive pregnancies with male fetuses leads in some mothers

From *Archives of Sexual Behavior*, Vol. 37, No. 1, 2008. Copyright © 2008 by Springer Journals (Kluwer Academic). Reprinted with kind permission of Springer Science + Business Media via Rightslink.

to the development of male-specific antigens. The developmental instability theory explains homosexuality as a perturbance of the complex processes of prenatal brain development by exogenous influences and was originally stimulated by findings of increased non-right handedness among homosexuals of both sexes, but attempts at finding an association of homosexuality with fluctuating asymmetry as a broader index of developmental instability have been unsuccessful.

The most commonly offered theory places sexual orientation in the context of the sexual differentiation of brain and behavior in general, with a focus on the role of pre- and perinatal sex hormones in this process. This approach was presumably prompted by the association of human homosexuality with gender-atypical (non-sexual) behavior and goes back to the mid-19th century, when scientific embryology began focusing on the development of the sex-dimorphic reproductive tract and its disorders. Such research yielded medical explanations of somatic hermaphroditism, and analogous medical concepts were applied to the explanation of homosexuality. In this context, homosexuality was often categorized as an inversion (of gender roles). With the rapidly advancing techniques of measurement and synthesis of sex hormones in the second half of the 20th century, behavioral-endocrinology research in non-primate mammals demonstrated the profound "organizational" influence of sex hormones during early developmental periods on later mating behavior and sexual orientation, with perinatal androgens and estrogens (derived by aromatization of androgens within brain cells) supporting the development of masculine behavior, and estrogens supporting the defeminization of behavior, followed by "activating" effects of sex-specific hormones from puberty on. The analogous processes in primates may be limited to androgen effects, but the determinants of sexual orientation in primates are not yet clear. Early attempts to identify sex hormone abnormalities in human homosexuality were unsuccessful in men and only partially successful in women. In the absence of systemic hormone abnormalities and of any signs of somatic intersexuality in human homosexuality, some investigators have suggested that causal endocrine abnormalities might be limited to the central nervous system (CNS-limited pseudohermaphroditism), which is compatible with the recently growing evidence of tissue specificity of hormone production and/or metabolism and of hormone receptors. During the last two decades, advances in genetics have broadened the focus of research on sexual differentiation to include the many genes involved in the sexual differentiation of the gonads and, possibly, of the brain. Although research on the specific genetic mechanisms involved in the brain is still in its early stages, the recent use of cellular-biology techniques to unravel the chain of mechanisms involved in the hormone-based sexual differentiation of specific sex-dimorphic nuclei of the limbic system and the amygdala in the neonatal and pubertal periods of development is likely to contribute in a major way to the identification of genes with specific functions in these processes.

Recent quite large-scale behavioral data on humans continue to support the "inversion" perspective regarding homosexuality, and the attempts to find a hormonal cause continue. Considerable efforts have been made to identify somatic markers of prenatal sex hormone effects, such as shifts in the second to fourth finger length ratio (2D:4D) in homosexuals of both sexes; the findings are suggestive, but far from uniform. Another such marker may be the reduction of spontaneous otoacoustic emissions in lesbians, which is awaiting replication by independent teams. Clearly, more direct evidence of prenatal sex hormone effects would be desirable.

However, experimental variations of the prenatal sex-hormone milieu solely for behavioral research purposes cannot be ethically justified. [A] team at Johns Hopkins introduced as an alternative the behavioral study of syndromes of intersexuality, which represent naturally occurring extreme variations of the sex-hormone milieu. Classical (prenatal-onset) congenital adrenal hyperplasia (CAH) in 46,XX individuals is the most prevalent of the classical intersex syndromes and by far the most thoroughly investigated in terms of endocrinology and psychology. About 90% of CAH patients suffer from the deficiency of the enzyme, 21-hydroxylase. As one of several endocrine consequences, 46,XX fetuses with CAH are exposed to unusually high levels of androgens during fetal development, which variably masculinize the genitalia and presumably also the brain and later behavior.

If sexual orientation is sexually differentiated in a similar fashion, 46,XX women with classical CAH should show an increase in bisexuality and homosexuality. . . .

Even if the majority of . . . findings . . . support an association of classical CAH with bisexual or homosexual orientation in women, a causative interpretation of these findings in terms of androgen effects on sexual orientation is not as compelling as would be findings from randomized control trials of androgen treatment. Human studies of this kind only use "quasi-experimental designs" with, in the best case, "patched-up controls." One could strengthen the case for the role of androgens by demonstrating a dose–response relationship between the degree of prenatal androgen exposure and the degree of later sexual orientation. Ideally, we would measure prenatal hormone levels repeatedly over the course of fetal development and derive from such measurements an index of the degree of prenatal androgen exposure. However, the health risks of even one-time cross-sectional determinations of androgen levels in the amniotic fluid, for instance, can be justified only if there are compelling medical indications for the procedures involved. A relatively crude alternative is the demonstration of dose–response relations on the group level using the clinical-endocrine or molecular-genetics classification of CAH subtypes that differ in severity, i.e., degree of 21-hydroxylase deficiency and, thereby, degree of androgen excess. Within classical CAH, commonly two major subtypes are distinguished, the more severe salt-wasting (SW) variant and the simple virilizing (SV) variant, and several studies have shown that bisexuality and homosexuality are increased more in the SW than the SV variant or in CAH women with higher Prader stages of genital masculinization at birth, which are also (moderately) correlated with CAH severity. . . .

Our current study had several goals: (1) To replicate the published findings on sexual orientation in a relatively large sample of adult women with classical CAH using a systematic assessment of multiple aspects of sexual orientation, and to establish at which age the women reach the respective romantic/erotic milestones; (2) to extend the dose–response approach to the mildest form of CAH, the non-classical (NC) variant, which becomes clinically symptomatic (in somatic terms) only after birth, in childhood or adolescence; (3) to examine to what extent sexual orientation and global measures of gender behavior other than sexual orientation are correlated; (4) to test whether the prediction of the behavioral phenotype from the endocrine phenotype can be enhanced by the molecular-genetics classification; (5) to answer the question how commonly CAH women see themselves as men in their romantic/erotic imagery; and (6) to perform a methodological study of the interrelationship of the sexual orientation variables.

Method

Participants

The current study is part of a comprehensive long-term follow-up project of women with CAH. . . . During an initial pilot phase of this project, a small number of women with CAH was recruited from two pediatric endocrine clinics in New York City. . . . Eligible were all adult women with CAH due to 21-hydroxylase deficiency for whom the molecular genetics of the 21-hydroxylase gene had been determined and who spoke English. Geographically, the participating women were spread over the entire United States and other continents. Transportation reimbursement was provided for women within the continental US.

The total analysis sample for CAH women in this report included 40 SW women, 21 SV women, and 82 NC women. Almost all CAH women were on glucocorticoid replacement treatment at the time of the study. A total of 24 non-CAH control women (labeled COS) consisted of sisters and female cousins of participating CAH women. Ages ranged from 18–61 years (subgroup means, 28.8–34.7 years). . . .

In addition to the control group of sisters and female cousins, we included for selected comparisons and illustrations two control groups (labeled COD) from our preceding project on the long-term behavioral after effects of prenatal diethylstilbestrol (DES) exposure. . . .

Study procedures were approved by the appropriate institutional review boards, and all participants gave written informed consent.

Measures and Procedure

All women underwent an 8–10 h protocol (often spread out over several days) of standard self-report questionnaires, psychometric tests, physical examinations, and systematic interviews. Sexual orientation was assessed as part of the Sexual Behavior Assessment Schedule, a comprehensive sexual-history interview schedule that covers psychosexual milestones, sexual orientation, sexual activity level, and sexual dysfunctions. Its administration takes approximately 1 h. The SEBAS-A was placed late in the overall protocol in order to facilitate rapport development between interviewer and interviewee and, thereby, increase disclosure of sensitive information, and the SEBAS-A instructions to the interviewee emphasized the importance of accuracy to enhance the participants' motivation. All SEBAS-A interviews (as well as most other study interviews) with women were conducted by female interviewers in order to facilitate self-disclosure. Interviewers were clinical psychologists who were specifically trained for sexual research interviewing. Procedures were introduced to keep the interviewers from identifying the group membership of the study participants along with instructions for the women against the disclosure of their medical histories to the interviewers. All interviews were audiotaped to permit monitoring of interviewer performance. Excellent interrater reliability of the SEBAS-A has been demonstrated.

SEBAS-A variables pertinent to sexual orientation covered masturbation fantasies, masturbation erotica, romantic/erotic fantasies during sexual relations with a partner, romantic/sexual daydreams, romantic/sexual nightdreams, sexual attractions, "Total Imagery," actual sex partners ("Actual Partners"), and overall sexual responsiveness ("Overall Kinsey"). The first six variables addressed "current" sexual orientation, with "current" defined as the 12 months prior to interview, and each was preceded by a question concerning its frequency (e.g., "How often did you have romantic or sexual nightdreams during the past 12 months?"). The remaining three aspects were rated separately for the past 12 months and for lifelong ("Lifetime") patterns (thus, yielding six variables), with lifelong defined as "since puberty" (for "Total Imagery" and overall sexual responsiveness), or as "since becoming sexually active, excluding prepubertal sexual activities" (for sexual relations); both definitions of lifelong included the past 12 months.

For each sexual-orientation variable, interviewers' ratings used the Kinsey Rating Scale with the following formulations: 0 = entirely heterosexual; 1 = largely heterosexual but incidentally homosexual; 2 = largely heterosexual but also distinctly homosexual; 3 = equally heterosexual and homosexual; 4 = largely homosexual but also distinctly heterosexual; 5 = largely homosexual but incidentally heterosexual; and 6 = entirely homosexual. Since the Kinsey team had not defined "distinct," "a distinct" homosexual history (Kinsey score 2 or "K2") was rated when the woman had experiences such as homosexual dreams or fantasies over a period of at least 1-year recurring with some regularity (not less than "about once a month"). Whenever a subscale was rated "K2," the corresponding global score could not be rated less than "K2."

The variables on actual sex partners were based on detailed structured interview sections concerning diverse romantic and sexual activities, separately for male and female partners. The definition of sexual relations as used here for actual sex partners required genital contact including but not limited to penile–vaginal intercourse; it did not require orgasm. Total Imagery was a global rating encompassing the preceding six variables on imagery and attractions and taking into consideration the frequencies of the respective experiences as reported by the interviewee. Overall sexual responsiveness was a global rating based on Total Imagery and Actual Partners. . . .

Results

Psychosexual Milestones

. . . Substantial minorities of women in all groups experienced same-sex crushes, while fewer women experienced same-sex love and same-sex genital sex. CAH women were increased above control women in all three categories, and SW women were highest. . . . The NC group was higher than the COS group on all 3 variables (significantly so for genital sex and marginally significantly for love). The ages at first occurrence of these states or events appeared to be relatively late. However, this does not indicate a general delay of psychosexual milestones (heterosexual and homosexual combined) in CAH. Rather, among those women with a history of both heterosexual and homosexual experiences, the first experience tended to be heterosexual. . . .

Sexual Orientation: Lifetime

. . . The data show a rather consistent progression of Kinsey score means . . . , except for the SV group on Actual Partners and Overall Kinsey, and of K-2-6% for all three variables with increasing degree of androgenization. . . .

The K2-6% for women with classical CAH (SV and SW combined) was 42% for Total Imagery, 15% for Actual Partners, and 37% for the Overall Kinsey rating. The NC group was significantly higher than the COS group on all three Kinsey scores. . . . The Kinsey scores for lifetime Total Imagery were higher than for lifetime Actual Partners. The number of women with any actual same-sex partner experience was relatively small, and the number of those with considerable experience in terms of same-sex partner numbers or same-sex occasions was even smaller. In interpreting these data, one has to take into consideration that women with classical CAH, and especially those with the SW variant, had significantly lower lifetime actual-partner numbers and lower total lifetime sex occasions (heterosexual and homosexual combined in both variables) than the other groups. . . .

Sexual Orientation: Current (Past 12 Months)

The current data on sexual orientation also show Kinsey scores for all three CAH subgroups in an apparent dose–response fashion. The gradual increase in Kinsey scores from non-CAH controls to the most severe SW variant applied to all variables, and was highly significant for all categories except for fantasies during partner sex. Again, the NC group had higher Kinsey scores than the COS group on all 9 variables . . . , the SW group was significantly higher than the two other CAH variants . . . , but the difference between SV and NC women reached conventional and marginal significance on only 1 variable each.

Sexual Orientation and Non-Sexual Gender-Related Behavior

The global lifetime and 12 months Kinsey scores were correlated with selected global variables of gender-related behavior (not including sexual orientation). The expected correlations were significant and in the predicted direction, but of modest size, and stronger for childhood measures than adulthood measures. . . .

Cross-Gender Imagery

At the end of the imagery section, the participant was asked about the frequency with which they saw themselves as "a person of the opposite sex" in their erotic imagery, separately for the past 12 months and lifetime (since puberty, excluding the past 12 months). All groups except SV included some women with such experience. The percent of women with such experience and the frequency of having that experience, especially for lifetime, was significantly increased in the SW subgroup above all other groups.

Predicting Sexual Orientation from Prenatal Androgenization and Gender Variables

. . . We tried to predict the Overall Kinsey Score for the past 12 months successively from the degree of prenatal androgenization in terms of the four CAH-severity groups, childhood gender-related behavior (the Gender scale of the RCGQ-R), adult gender-related behavior (the sum score of the Hobby Preferences Scale), and Seeing Self as Man during Romantic/Erotic Imagery, Frequency: Lifetime (Excluding the Past 12 Months). Prenatal androgenization and RCGQ-R Gender contributed significantly to the prediction . . . , but Hobby Preferences and Seeing Self as Man was not.

Role of the Molecular Genotype

Finally, we wanted to test whether the CAH subtypes as defined by endocrine criteria or their classification by molecular genotype is more closely associated with sexual orientation. . . . The two classifications did not differ in their association with the Kinsey score. In this particular sub-sample, the endocrine and genetic classifications correlated Pearson $r = .90$ with each other, i.e., there was little room for divergence between molecular genotype and endocrine phenotype. . . .

Discussion

Our data clearly showed increased sexual orientation towards females (i.e., bisexuality and homosexuality) in women with classical CAH (SV and SW combined) compared to non-CAH controls. . . . Thus, our study corroborates earlier findings on sexual orientation in CAH. We also clearly replicate earlier demonstrations of increased bisexual/homosexual orientation in SW women compared to SV women, and earlier reports indicating that these shifts are more strongly accentuated in romantic/erotic imagery than actual sex-partner experiences.

More surprising is the finding of increased bisexual/homosexual orientation in NC women above controls in the diverse variables evaluated here. This finding is in line with our earlier report on mild, but significant shifts of the same

NC women towards masculinized gender-related behavior other than sexual orientation. In the endocrine literature, NC is usually described as a syndrome characterized by onset of clinical (somatic, physiological) symptoms of androgen excess after birth, in childhood or later. Since there is consensus that the masculinization of gender-related behavior in classical CAH is due to the effect of prenatal androgens on the developing brain, these behavioral shifts in NC women were not expected. The finding raises the question whether the mild androgen excess that is likely to be present in NC fetuses from the first trimester on, but is insufficient to noticeably affect the sexual differentiation of the genitalia, is nevertheless sufficient to slightly affect the sexual differentiation of the brain. Alternatively, the data suggest an unexpected postnatal effect of mild but persistent androgen excess on brain and gender-related behaviors. Our study does not provide data that would help us to argue in favor of one or the other explanation.

In conjunction with the other CAH subgroups and the control women, our NC data further strengthen the notion of a dose–response relationships of androgens with sexual orientation, at least on the subgroup level, given that the other hormone abnormalities seen in the CAH syndrome (e.g., deficiency of cortisol and aldosterone, excess of ACTH and 17-hydroxyprogesterone) are not known to be associated with masculinization of gender-related behavior in animals or humans (although specific studies of this kind are yet to be conducted). As we had found analogous relationships with CAH severity for non-sexual gender-related behavior, we also could confirm significant, but modest-sized correlations of sexual orientation scores with non-sexual gender-related behaviors, which had been shown by others. Such findings are also in line with an understanding of sexual orientation in the context of sexual differentiation. Given the many differences in sexual orientation and associated variables between men and women, the question arises, whether the increased sexual orientation towards females associated with CAH severity in 46,XX individuals is a model of the role of androgens in sexual-orientation development in males rather than lesbian women. Early developmental research on non-sexual sex-dimorphic behavior in animals sought to explain sex differences in behavior, and experimental manipulations of pre- and perinatal androgen levels served to show to what extent one could create male-typical behavior in females so treated. Later, such findings were also used to explain interindividual variations of gender-related behavior among females, and there is some supportive evidence for this approach in humans. That this may apply also to sexual orientation in at least a subgroup of women is suggested by the fact that earlier research has repeatedly shown that about one third of homosexual women have (modestly) increased levels of androgens.

One of the major limitations of the interpretation of findings in classical CAH in relation to animal studies is the hormone treatment that females with classical CAH typically receive throughout postnatal life. The classical animal study of sexual differentiation of brain and behavior exposes the female fetus to androgen treatment during the known early hormone-sensitive period of sexual differentiation of the brain and then again around the time of puberty/young adulthood. That combination tends to maximize the development of cross-gender sexual behaviors, especially when ovariectomy after puberty preceded the treatment with testosterone propionate. By contrast, human 46,XX individuals with CAH are initially exposed to excess, endogenous androgens from their adrenals during the presumed hormone-sensitive prenatal period of sexual differentiation of the brain, and in the severe variants at even higher levels than normal males and more chronically so; however, from birth on, the excess androgen levels are suppressed by glucocorticoid replacement therapy (sometimes to levels even lower than is normal for healthy females), the ovaries are left in place, and female puberty is induced by an endogenous, largely normal female hormonal milieu. Unfortunately, there are no behavioral studies of non-human primates that mimic the androgen history of 46,XX humans with CAH, so that we cannot be sure if we should expect to see much more bisexuality and homosexuality in 46,XX individuals without postnatal androgen suppression. . . .

Another potentially confounding factor is the fact that insufficient glucocorticoid replacement or treatment interruptions lead to virilization, i.e., somatic symptoms of androgen excess, and, if occurring early enough during childhood development, also to stunting of growth, while overtreatment brings about variable degrees of obesity, all of which may reduce attractivity to men and romantic approaches by men, and to related body-image concerns of the CAH women. This raises the question whether associated inhibition of romantic practice in adolescence, perhaps also supported by less-stereotypic feminine leisure time activities and, at least for some CAH women, relative isolation in the peer group, might increase the chance of bisexual/homosexual development rather than exclusively a direct effect of androgens on brain circuits that regulate sexual behavior. If so, this might be an example of the interaction of social and biological factors in the development of bisexuality/homosexuality, for which Bearman and Brückner (2002) argued.

In our data set, the clinical-endocrine classification of CAH was highly correlated with the classification based on molecular genetics, and knowledge of one did not add to the predictive power of the other in terms of gender outcome. Thus, there is no suggestion that the molecular-genetic defect influences sexual-orientation outcome through any other physiological route than the hormonal abnormalities caused by the degree of enzyme deficiency.

It is noteworthy that our data suggest an influence of CAH severity on cross-gender identity in sexual situations. . . . Perhaps, gender-atypicality in non-sexual behavior along with later emerging atypical sexual orientation facilitate in some CAH women an identification with selected aspects of the male role, which may subsequently broaden and thereby lead to late overall gender identity change, as it has been documented to occur in some 46,XX individuals with CAH.

Our data show that current sexual orientation is not only predicted from the degree of prenatal androgen exposure as indicated by the CAH-severity classification, but in addition also from the degree of masculinization of gender-related behavior during childhood. The latter variable could reflect variable brain responsiveness to prenatal androgens as well as postnatal psychosocial influences, provided retrospective reporting bias can be ruled out. This study does not provide an opportunity to decide between these options. . . .

The current data set on sexual orientation suffers from the same overall limitations as the previous one on gender development, namely, small sample size, questionable representativeness, and cross-sectional design. However, our findings on a dose–response relationship of androgens and sexual orientation appear even stronger than for non-sexual gender-related behavior and make a persuasive case for the extension of this association to women with NC CAH. Overall, our findings support a sexual-differentiation perspective involving prenatal androgens on the development of sexual orientation.

Lisa M. Diamond and Molly Butterworth

➡ **NO**

Questioning Gender and Sexual Identity: Dynamic Links over Time

Introduction

Historically, research on both sexual identity development (generally understood as the process by which individuals come to acknowledge same-sex attractions and to gradually conceive of themselves as nonheterosexual) and gender identity development (understood as the process by which children come to think of themselves as unequivocally and permanently male or female) have adopted dichotomous and essentialist models of gender and sexuality, in which individuals possess and seek to publicly embrace one and only one true identity (male or female, heterosexual or gay-lesbian). Individuals whose experiences of gender and sexuality involve multiplicity and fluidity have been ill-described by such models. For example, sexual identity researchers have long critiqued traditional sexual identity models for failing to account for the experiences of men and women who experience attractions for both men and women, and who do not consider one form of desire to be a "truer" representation of their sexuality than another. Historically, such individuals' resistance to dichotomous models of sexual identity and orientation has been attributed to denial, internalized homophobia, or false consciousness.

These views are now changing. Research increasingly demonstrates that categories such as "gay," "lesbian," and "heterosexual" are not, in fact unproblematic natural "types." Furthermore, patterns of same-sex and other-sex desire show far more fluidity and complexity than previously thought. A similar adherence to fixed, categorical notions of identity has also historically characterized interpretations of transgender experience. Transgender is a broad category typically used to represent any individual whose gender-related identification or an external presentation either violates conventional conceptualizations of "male" or "female" or mixes different aspects of male and female role and identity. The word and concept "transgender" came into use specifically because many individuals with fluid experiences of gender felt that this phenomenon was not well-described by clinical discussions of transsexualism. The term "transsexual" is typically used to refer to individuals who feel that their true psychological gender is the opposite of their biological sex, and

From *Sex Roles: A Journal of Research,* Vol. 59, 2008. Copyright © 2008 by Springer Science and Business Media. Reprinted by permission via Rightslink.

who seek surgical or hormonal modifications in order to bring these two into alignment.

There has been increasing social scientific acknowledgment and investigation of transgender individuals, but much of this work presumes that the primary "dilemma" of all transgender experience is a conflict between one's psychological gender and one's biological sex that inhibits expression of the individual's "true" gender identity. Hence, just as the healthy endpoint of sexual identity development was once presumed to be a stable, integrated, unambiguous lesbian, gay, or heterosexual identity, the normative and healthy endpoint of transgender development is often thought to be adoption of a stable, integrated, unambiguous identification as 100% male or 100% female, often achieved via some form of physical transformation (for example, some combination of clothes, makeup, demeanor, hormones, or surgery) aimed at bringing one's psychological gender and one's physical gender presentation into direct alignment.

Yet just as research increasingly demonstrates the inadequacy of historical, dichotomous models of sexuality, there is increasing evidence that dichotomous models of gender fail to capture the complexity, diversity, and fluidity of transgender experience. . . . Theorists have argued against a "master narrative" of transgender experience in which all experiences of gender fluidity and multiplicity must be resolved in favor of a singular, unified gender identification/presentation. In resisting this universalized narrative, they challenge the presumed essential basis of sexual differentiation and the corresponding, sociopolitical (and fundamentally patriarchal) sex/gender hegemony. . . .

The Relevance of Intersectionality

In this article we maintain that the feminist theoretical framework of intersectionality provides a generative starting point for theorizing women's experiences of multiple, partial, and fluid gender identifications. Historically, intersectionality has been articulated as a framework for analyzing the way in which multiple social locations and identities mutually inform and constitute one another. A key tenet of theories of intersectionality is that the process of identifying with more than one social group produces altogether new forms of subjective experience that are unique, nonadditive, and not reducible to the original identities that went into them.

Although intersectionality is perhaps most widely used as a theoretical approach for analyzing relations among different forms of oppression, our focus is more intrapsychic in nature, and emphasizes intersectionality's challenge to the notion of primary sites of identity and selfhood. Contrary to interpretations of transgender experience, which emphasize conflicts between an individual's (true) psychological gender and (discordant) biological sex, the framework of intersectionality calls attention to experiences of multiplicity in gender identification, and how these experiences—embedded within specific social, cultural, and interpersonal contexts—create altogether new, emergent forms of experience and identity.

We also find intersectionality relevant to understanding how gender identity and sexual identity interact and co-create one another. Historically, gender and sexual identity have been viewed as orthogonal dimensions, and social scientists have taken pains to emphasize that variability in one dimension does not neatly map onto the other: Being gay/lesbian/bisexual obviously does not mean that one is transgendered (and being heterosexual does not mean that one is *not* transgendered), just as being transgendered does not mean that one is necessary gay/lesbian/bisexual. Rather, the linkage between sexual identity and gender identity takes a wide array of forms. But in emphasizing distinctions between gender and sexual identity, social scientists may have given short shrift to the complex processes through which individuals' experiences of gender and erotic desire mutually influence one another over time. We believe that such intersections and reciprocal influences deserve closer analysis if we are to create developmentally accurate models of gender and sexual identification over the life course. In other words, when examining women with "non-mainstream" gender and sexual identities, we must account for the fact that their attractions and identities are in dynamic interaction with one another, yielding diverse constellations of identity and erotic phenomenology over time. Theories of intersectionality call direct attention to these processes via their emphasis on the ways in which intersections between different identities and social locations give rise to altogether novel forms of subjective experience.

To elucidate how the framework of intersectionality helps to interpret complex, multiple, partial experiences of gender, in this article we discuss experiences of gender/sexual intersectionality as experienced by four women, each of which has been interviewed intensively over the past 10 years in the course of an ongoing longitudinal study of sexual identity development. These four women's journeys through nonheterosexual sexual identities eventually—and unexpectedly—prompted each of them to explore transgendered identifications. None of these women described feeling "trapped" in the "wrong" gender, and none sought to irrevocably replace her female body and identity with a male one. Rather, they all articulated experiences of multiplicity regarding their gender identities, and resisted selecting one form of identity as inherently "primary." These women's reflections about their own gender-sexual phenomenology resonate with the challenge that theorists of intersectionality have historically posed to dichotomous, essentialist models of identity and selfhood. . . .

Four Women's Unexpected Journeys

Cynthia/Mark was an avid tomboy growing up, and greatly enjoyed boys' company and games. She first began questioning her sexuality at the age of 12, when she developed a strong crush on a female friend and sent her a love poem. This unfortunately triggered a barrage of social stigma and school harassment. Yet Cynthia persevered, becoming an active and proud bisexual at the age of 14, and identifying as lesbian by the age of 15. By her mid-20s she had met the woman of her dreams and the two of them were planning a lesbian wedding. Several years later, however, she was working at a male-dominated profession and found that she was increasingly adopting a masculine "stance" when interacting with colleagues. She gradually began reflecting on her own subjective sense of gender, and increasingly felt that she would be more comfortable adopting a more masculine gender identity. Her lesbian partner urged her not to do so, and once Cynthia finally made the decision to change her name to Mark and began dressing and appearing as a man (although not consistently identifying as "male," as we will see below), her partner left her. Mark now identifies as queer; he continues to present himself as male on a day-to-day basis, but has no plans to pursue sex-reassignment surgery. At the time of the 10-year follow-up, Mark was 30 years old, and happily married to a bisexually-identified woman.

Lori was a proudly-identified bisexual woman when she first enrolled in the study at the age of 23. She had longstanding memories of experiencing attractions to both women and men, and enjoying satisfying friendships with both female and male peers, although her most substantive emotional ties were formed with women. As Lori's college years progressed, she started reading about transgender issues and meeting transsexual people, and began thinking more and more about her own sense of gender. By the time of our third interview, when she was 27 years old, she had started identifying as transgendered, and an important part of this identification was a rejection of the notion of "two and only two" genders. Although she has never adopted a male identity, she began taking testosterone, and by the time of the ten-year follow-up interview, at age 33, she described her physical appearance as decidedly masculine. Over the years she continued to experience attractions and relationships with both women and men, but had become seriously involved with a woman.

Ellen first remembers feeling attracted to women at the age of 12 or 13, and by age 14 she had admitted to herself that she was a lesbian. She regularly attended gay-lesbian support groups, and felt both certain and proud of her sexual identity when she first enrolled in the study at age 19. Questions of gender identity had always been lurking in the back of her mind, from a very early age. Sometimes she thought that it would just be easier to be a man, given that she knew she was attracted to women. Yet toward the end of adolescence, she realized that she actually enjoyed being a woman. As she progressed through her 20s, her lesbian identity remained rock-solid, while her gender identity continued to fluctuate. She eventually began an intensive process of spiritual questioning that led her to affirm her own complex, multidimensional experience of gender and sexuality. She still identifies as a lesbian, but remains deeply ambivalent about identifying as a "woman." By the 10-year point, at age 29, she was unsure whether she might someday pursue full-blown gender reassignment.

Karen identified as bisexual when she first participated in the study at age 17. She had long been aware of experiencing attractions to both women and men, and pursued relationships with both sexes. By the age of 18, she had also started to question her gender identity. She began taking testosterone and started describing herself as a female-to-male transsexual. Yet through this process, she became aware that "male" was not necessarily a more comfortable identity for her than "female," and that she was more comfortable living and identifying "somewhere in the middle." Around this time she also became increasingly aware that her attractions to other people, too, were not strongly oriented around gender, but instead revolved around personal attributes. She continued to pursue relationships with both women and men, but by the time of the 10-year follow-up, at age 27, she was happily involved with a man.

Multiplicity of Female and Male Identifications

A longstanding assumption about transgender individuals is that they uniformly and unequivocally desire permanent re-identification as the other gender. This can be seen in many first-person accounts collected from transsexuals, in which they recount having dressed or acted as the other gender from an early age. For individuals who seek complete re-identification as the other gender, this goal involves changes in self-concept and corresponding changes in the outward presentation of one's gender, including changes in name, in gender role behavior, and in physical gender presentation. The latter can be achieved through a variety of routes, pursued separately or concurrently, including alterations in hairstyle and clothing, hormonal modification of secondary sex characteristics, and most drastically, surgical modification of the genitals.

This developmental trajectory presumes that female and male identities are irreconcilable, and that one of these identities must occupy a psychologically primary status. Hence, the process of becoming more and more masculine— in one's appearance, demeanor, and physicality—gradually supplants one's previous femininity, and is desirable for this specific reason.

Yet none of the women profiled here were following such a trajectory. Rather, despite adopting observably masculine gender presentations, they expressed ambivalence about taking on a male identity. . . .

Two aspect's of Lori's experience stand out from the perspective of intersectionality. First, Lori is acutely aware—and wary—of the sociopolitical ramifications of taking on a conventional "male" identity in light of the other identity statuses that she would simultaneously occupy. Given her ethnicity and her sexual interest in women, she perceives that identifying as male would entail identifying as a heterosexual white male, suddenly placing her in a position of power and privilege that runs counter to her previous experience with, and political activism regarding, social marginality. Her ambivalence about "being a guy" reflects an implicit awareness—consistent with the framework of intersectionality—that she cannot simply subtract out the aspects of a male identity she finds troubling.

Second, and perhaps most notably, Lori's overall resistance to "picking a box" and designating either a female or male identity as her true identity resonates with intersectionality's challenge to the notion that any one particular identity status (i.e., ethnicity, social class, gender) must be personally and socially "primary," such that other identity statuses are analyzable chiefly with respect to how they add or subtract from forms of social marginality associated with the primary one.

This particular aspect of Lori's experience was echoed by other respondents. Mark, for example, also resisted adopting a wholly male identity, despite changing his name and presenting himself as male on a day-to-day basis. He had specifically elected not to pursue sex reassignment surgery or to pursue a formal legal change to his gender status, instead crafting his own, hybrid combination of maleness and femaleness. . . . Thus, for Mark a feeling of "otherness"—which, from the perspective of intersectionality, can be interpreted as the emergent product of Mark's social marginalization on the basis of both his gender and sexual identity—was not necessarily undesirable, and was not something to be obliterated and replaced with a more fixed, categorical sense of self. Rather, Mark had come to embrace dynamic, partial, and intersecting experiences of gender and sexuality.

The notion of dynamism and continued change and transformation is important, because although all of these individuals embraced gender-ambiguity to some degree, they did not turn it into its own fixed category (i.e., "androgynous"). Rather, their experience of gender identity involved continued movement between, around, and within gender polarities. Hence, for these women the experience of "transition" was not a unilateral movement from female to male, but an ongoing oscillation between more feminine and more masculine aspects of internal gender identity and outward physical presentation. This is perhaps the clearest challenge to conventional notions of transgender, because it posits change and transition as a potential outcome rather than just a temporary process. This, importantly, is consistent with feminist perspectives on intersectionality which emphasize the simultaneous occupation of multiple social and psychological identities, and how dynamic interactions among these identities, embedded within specific contextual, interpersonal, and developmental circumstances, create altogether new senses of selfhood. . . .

Written on the Body: Physical Transformation and Intersectionality

Many conventional understandings of transgender experience, particularly those drawn from the narratives and experiences of self-identified transsexuals, suggest that transgender women and men typically feel they were born with the "wrong body," and hence experience a persistent hatred of their bodies which can only be remedied through bodily transformation. Such transformations are supposedly aimed at replacing all signs and manifestations of one's given gender with one's desired (and ostensibly, psychologically primary) gender. Yet among the women profiled here, the aforementioned phenomenon of multiplicity in gender identification extended to the way in which they perceived and experienced their physical bodies, and their corresponding motives for different types of body modification. Although all of them pursued some form of physical transformation, these "body projects" did not involve the straightforward erasure of femininity and the taking on of an unambiguous male role. Rather, women pursued complex, contradictory forms of gender presentation that seemed to inscribe, in physical terms, the multiplicity and partiality that characterized their psychological sense of gender.

Lori, for example, was an avid bodybuilder with a long history of body modification, including tattoos, body piercing, and experimenting with different modes of dress and posture. When she eventually sought a breast reduction, it was not because of any sort of "female body hatred"—in fact she stated straight out that she loved her breasts—but was linked to a certain muscular aesthetic. . . .

Lori did, in fact, eventually have her breasts removed. Yet as with the breast reduction, her account reveals no persistent body hatred. . . . Lori also expressed no desire to change her genitals. Despite the fact that she had been taking testosterone and was passing as male on a day-to-day basis. . . . In fact, by the 10-year interview, she was considering going off of testosterone in order to get pregnant, and was clearly comfortable with the prospect of combining her masculine-appearing body with perhaps the ultimate symbol of femininity: A pregnant belly.

Karen, in fact, actually lived out this experience, having served as a surrogate mother for one of her relatives despite having transformed her body through years of testosterone. . . .

The framework of intersectionality is relevant to Karen's and Lori's approaches to their bodies because intersectionality directly counters essentialist assumptions about the primacy of biologically-based forms of identification over others. . . .

Of all the respondents, Ellen was the only one who gave voice to a distinct dissatisfaction with the gendered nature of her body. . . .

Ellen enacted her own questioning process by pursuing other forms of body modification, and at the time of the 10-year interview was engaged in a long-term tattoo project which would eventually cover 75% of her body. . . .

Ellen's tattoo had everything to do with her own personal experience of identity transformation and emergence, and replacing old scars (both psychological and physical, in her case) with powerful, healing images whose symbolic meaning was contextualized within her own personal history. . . .

Links Between Gender and Desire

Perhaps the most fascinating aspect of these women's experiences of multiplicity regarding gender identity is the effect that it has had on their erotic attractions. Of course, the notion that gender identity and sexual desire are fundamentally linked has a long history: In the 19th and early 20th century, it was widely believed that same-sex sexuality was caused by gender "inversion," as if the only way to be attracted to a woman was to be male, and the only way to be attracted to a man was to be female. In this formulation, all desire is fundamentally heterosexual desire. Accordingly, if you possess same-sex desires it is not because you are homosexual, but because your natural, heterosexual desires are trapped in the wrong gender identity.

Now, of course, the pendulum has shifted, and gender and sexual identity are considered to be orthogonal constructs. Yet the experiences of the women profiled here indicate that for many women who have undergone substantive processes of sexual questioning, it is impossible to completely disentangle one's own sense of femaleness and maleness from one's own understanding, experience, and interpretation of sexual desire for female and male partners.

Theories of intersectionality provide useful conceptual tools with which to make sense of this phenomenon. Whereas conventional understandings of gender identity and sexual identity presume that each has its own independent, essential basis, making it possible to analyze each separately from the other, intersectionality challenges this notion. According to the theoretical framework of intersectionality, no identity status is experienced—or can be meaningfully understood—in isolation. Hence, a sexual-minority woman's experiences of same-sex and other-sex desires are always embedded within the social and interpersonal context of her gender presentation and gendered experience, and changes in one domain necessarily shape the other. The relationship between gender and desire is dynamic and reciprocal, relating not only to a woman's own sense of gender, but her appraisal of how social others appraise and understand her.

It is not surprising, then, that women who began to explore multiplicity and fluidity with respect to their gender identity became progressively more aware of multiplicity and fluidity in their erotic attractions as well. This is perhaps most evident in the case of Mark, whose attractions were predominantly directed toward women prior to the point at which he began to question his gender identity. But as Mark delved deeper into the masculine sides of his personality, and took on an increasingly masculine role in self-presentation and interpersonal interaction, he found himself unexpectedly attracted to men. . . . Mark's own experience of desire for men was, to some degree, constituted by his appraisal of men's social location with respect to his own. Previously, men's position of power and privilege rendered their erotic reactions to Cynthia troublesome. Yet now that Cynthia identified as Mark, a man's desire was no longer experienced as threatening, and in fact represented a willingness to threaten conventional gender locations (because male desire for Mark was now same-sex desire). It is also notable that Cynthia/Mark experienced changes in the types of men she/he found attractive after taking on a masculine gender presentation, and these changes were directly related to issues of power and social location. Previously, Cynthia had found only "feminine" men attractive, but after identifying as Mark, he found a broader range of men—and masculinities—to be desirable. This suggests that the critical "trigger" for Cynthia/Mark's desire was never, in fact, some sort of stable, trait-like "degree" of femininity or masculinity, but instead a particular interpersonal dialectic regarding gender and—necessarily—social power. Mark noted that it was the traditional male-female heterosexual dynamic that he had always found distasteful, and which he had subverted—as Cynthia—by seeking "feminine" men. Now that he identified as Mark, all desires for men now fell outside the purview of the conventional male-female heterosexual dynamic, thereby opening up new erotic possibilities. . . .

Similar intersections among gender, desire, and power were voiced by the other three respondents, making it clear that our culture's complex interbraiding of gender and power fundamentally shapes individuals' experiences of erotic attractions. Thus, some of the new desires for men that women began experiencing as a function of their increasingly masculine gender presentations had to do with the distinct changes they began to experience in their relative power vis-à-vis men. . . . Although it is common to think about desire as located "within" individuals, and expressed outwardly through behaviors and expression, these women's experiences demonstrate that desire itself takes shape (and is reshaped) through direct engagement with different social partners across different social contexts. Just as no form of identity is inherently "primary," neither is any specific form of "desire." Changes in one domain necessarily change the terrain on which the other is experienced. Intersectionality provides a valuable framework for interpreting this phenomenon because of its emphasis on the nonadditive relations among different social categories, and the potential for intersections between these categories to create novel forms of experience. . . .

Giving Voice to Multiplicity

Each of the women profiled has made a certain amount of peace with her own experience of multiplicity in gender identity and sexual desire. Yet according to conventional norms regarding sexuality and gender, no such peace is truly possible. Rather, it is presumed that the most desirable, psychologically healthful state is to have a unitary, primary identity which provides not only a solid foundation for ego development, but a permanent social location that is understandable to the rest of the culture. The women profiled here have already experienced society's relentless pressure toward categorization in the domain of sexual orientation and identity. All of these women experienced attractions to both men and women (even if they did not all identify as bisexual), and all of them were well-aware of the cultural unintelligibility of such attractions. In order to avoid being misunderstood, some of them actively censored themselves with friends or family members to present a more categorical portrait of their desire/behavior than was actually the case. . . .

Our culture's difficulty in making sense of individuals with multiple identities, multiple subjectivities, and multiple social locations is manifested in the lack of language to describe such experiences. As noted earlier, the word "transgender" came into use because many individuals with fluid experiences of gender felt that this phenomenon was not well-described by discussions of transsexuality, which instead emphasize experiences of conflict between psychological gender and biological sex.

Similarly, each of the women profiled here expressed dissatisfaction with the term "bisexual," feeling that it failed to adequately convey the open, expansive way in which she experienced her sexual desires. Some found it ironic that although the phenomenon of bisexual attraction posed a challenge to categorical models of sexual orientation, slapping the "bisexual" label on this phenomenon seemed to be an attempt to revise and reinvigorate such categorical models. Why is it so difficult, some wondered, to get beyond these categories?

Some noted that their main problem with the word bisexual was that it placed so much emphasis on gender as a category of desire. . . .

This ambivalence about labeling was also reflected in the way that these women dealt with "the pronoun thing." In other words, did they think of themselves—and prefer to be called—"he," or "she?" None of the four respondents expressed a preference for a single pronoun usage across all contexts. Rather, each reported using both "he" and "she" in different contexts. . . .

The difficulty that society continues to experience in giving voice to complex, multiple, fluid experiences of gender is exemplified by the difficulty that we encountered in choosing and using pronouns for Mark. In deference to his own unwillingness to consistently use "she" or "he," we initially experimented with randomly alternating among "he," "she," "her," and "him." Yet it soon became apparent that to readers (and writers!) accustomed to consistency in linguistic gender-markers, this proved both confusing and distracting. We therefore settled on consistently male pronouns for Mark, despite our own ambivalence about the erasure of multiplicity that this necessarily entails.

Conclusion

The struggles recounted by the women profiled here in reaching awareness and acceptance of the multiplicity in their gender status demonstrate the importance of fostering an increased appreciation for intersectional gender and sexual identities. Continued longitudinal observation is obviously critical for understanding how the experiences of multiplicity that we have emphasized play out over time, and the degree to which theories of intersectionality can, in fact, make substantive contributions to their interpretation. It is also critical to examine how the dynamics described in this article manifest themselves with younger cohorts of transgendered individuals, who have greater awareness and appreciation for social constructionist perspectives on gender than do older generations. . . .

Clearly, much has changed, and continues to change. The last 20 years have witnessed incredible strides with respect to conceptualizations of sexual identity and orientation. Multiplicity and fluidity in patterns of sexual attraction—which were long considered "impossible," "invalid" or "transitional"—are now widely acknowledged and even celebrated by both activists and social scientists, and have become one of the most exciting and productive areas of social scientific inquiry into sexuality.

Multiplicity in gender identification deserves similar theoretical attention, and the framework of intersectionality provides a valuable starting point for such analyses via its dismantling of the historical emphasis on "primary," "core" loci of identity. This does not necessarily suggest that we are—or should be—headed toward a future in which there are *no* terms or concepts to represent gender and/or sexual identities. As Mark pointed out, identity labels play a potentially important role in helping individuals to "find others like yourself," to build alliances around salient or personally significant aspects of one's experience and identification. A greater appreciation of intersectionality, however, helps to guard against the fallacy that these identities—once claimed and named—function as stable and essential "types" of selfhood. From the perspective of intersectionality, adopting and proudly embracing an identity is fully compatible with a critical appreciation for the fact that these identities are always moving targets, reforming and reshaping themselves across diverse social and interpersonal contexts.

Along these lines, perhaps the greatest potential contribution of intersectionality to our understanding of transgender experience is the way in which it recasts and reconstitutes the phenomenon of *change*. Traditional perspectives on transgender experience examine change from the perspective of *transition:* men transitioning to a new (and purportedly permanent) female identity, or women transitioning to a new (and purportedly permanent) male identity. . . . Change, for these women, was an ever-present possibility rather than a temporary phase. Theories of intersectionality help to make sense of this experience by emphasizing how *all* subjective experiences of selfhood are continually transformed, reenacted, and renegotiated as a function of shifting landscapes of social context. From an intersectionality perspective, instead of representing a woman's journey to transgender identification as having a distinct beginning, middle, and end, we should treat each successive stage of her life course, each of her (fluid) social locations, and each of her intimate relationships as continually interacting with her experiences of gender and desire to produce multiple, dynamic senses of self over time. . . .

POSTSCRIPT

Is Sexual Orientation Innate?

The etiology (cause) of sexual orientation is still more unknown than known. The biological perspective explores the effects of prenatal androgens and maternal prenatal distress on gender atypicality. This research is primarily conducted on lower animals, intersexual humans, or persons with atypical hormonal exposure, such as CAH women (even though GID is not typical in intersexuals). Social scientists examine sex-related socialization practices, including parental attitudes, social reinforcement processes (consistently and without ambiguity rearing a child as a boy or a girl, including encouragement of same-gender behavior and discouragement of cross-gender behavior), and self-socialization. An interactionist perspective suggests that sexual biology makes some individuals more vulnerable to certain psychosocial rearing conditions.

Different ideologies about whether or not sexual orientation is a disorder seem to rest on this question: do we view sex, gender, and sexual orientation as distinct domains or as inextricably linked? Phyllis Burke notes in *Gender Shock: Exploding the Myths of Male and Female* (Anchor Books, 1996) that "when you look at what society pathologizes, you can get the clearest glimpse of what society demands of those who wish to be considered normal." It appears, then, that our society expects congruence among sex, gender, and sexual orientation and believes that to be the norm. But some critics caution that the biodiversity of nature is greater than our norms allow us to observe. Moreover, we have little understanding, beyond stereotype and presumption, of the association between this biodiversity and gender identity and sexual behavior. For example, how many of us have biological evidence (beyond visible external genitalia) that we are the sex that we believe ourselves to be? There have been cases where female athletes were surprised to find that they have a Y chromosome, yet by other biological measures they are clearly female. What, then, is this individual's "appropriate" gender identity? (See Issue 20.)

Currently, cross-cultural studies, such as Herdt's work in Papua, New Guinea, studies of transgenderism, and analyses of historical changes in lesbian/gay identities in the late nineteenth century have begun to challenge the biological, bipolar notion of sexual orientation. Furthermore, the definition of sexual orientation is becoming more "complicated" as scholars pay more attention to diversity in sexual, affectional, and erotic attraction; that is, they do not all fit together. Erotic and affectional feelings may or may not match fantasies and behaviors. Sexual identity, sexual behavior, and sexual desire appear to be fluid and changeable over time, context, and cultures. Thus, there are likely multiple pathways to sexual orientations.

Suggested Readings

Jennifer Finney Boylan, *She's Not There: A Life in Two Genders* (Random House, 2004).

Judith Butler, *Undoing Gender* (New York: Routlege, 2004).

Paula J. Caplan, *They Say You're Crazy: How the World's Most Powerful Psychiatrists Decide Who's Normal* (Perseus Books, 1995).

J. Colapinto, *As Nature Made Him: The Boy Who Was Raised as a Girl* (HarperCollins, 2000).

Lori Messinger and Deana F. Morrow, *Case Studies on Sexual Orientation and Gender Expression in Social Work Practice* (Columbia University Press, 2006).

Sharon E. Preves, *Intersex and Identity: The Contested Self* (Piscataway, NJ: Rutgers University Press, 2003).

Cheryl L. Weill, *Nature's Choice: What Science Reveals About the Biological Origins of Sexual Orientation* (Routledge/Taylor & Francis Group, 2009).

ISSUE 3

Do Sex Differences in Careers in Mathematics and Sciences Have a Biological Basis?

YES: **Steven Pinker**, from "The Science of Gender and Science: Pinker vs. Spelke," *The Edge* (May 16, 2005)

NO: **Elizabeth Spelke**, from "The Science of Gender and Science: Pinker vs. Spelke," *The Edge* (May 16, 2005)

ISSUE SUMMARY

YES: Steven Pinker reviews arguments supporting the claim that there is a biological basis for gender differences in math and science.

NO: Elizabeth Spelke argues that the underrepresentation of women in the sciences is due to environmental factors.

Cognition represents a complex system of skills that enable the processing of different types of information. Cognitive processes underlie our intellectual activities and many other daily tasks. For three decades, researchers have actively explored whether or not males and females differ in their cognitive abilities. The most common taxonomy of cognitive processes used in cognitive sex differences research is based on the type of information used in a cognitive task: verbal (words), quantitative (numbers), and visual-spatial (figural representations).

The study of cognitive sex differences became especially active after the publication of Eleanor Emmons Maccoby and Carol Nagy Jacklin's now famous book entitled *The Psychology of Sex Differences* (Stanford University Press, 1974). While concluding with a generally skeptical perspective on the existence of sex difference, the authors maintained that one area in which the sexes did appear to differ was intellectual ability and functioning. Specifically, the sexes appeared to differ in verbal, quantitative, and spatial abilities.

This compilation and synthesis of sex comparison findings spawned extensive research on sex differences in numerous areas of functioning but especially in the domain of cognitive abilities. Researchers began to use the quantitative technique of meta-analysis, which has been used to explore whether or not any sex differences change in magnitude over the life cycle or over time, whether or not there is cross-cultural consistency in any sex differences, and whether or not cognitive sex differences are found across various ethnic groups.

At an academic conference in January 2005, Harvard's president Lawrence Summers gave a talk in which he suggested that innate differences in the math ability of women and men help explain why so few women are found at the highest levels in careers in mathematics and sciences. His speech has generated a huge outcry from feminists and numerous scholars who dispute such claims.

Summers's comments have refueled the ongoing debate regarding the biological basis of math and science abilities. We know that in careers in mathematics and the sciences, women tend to earn 25 percent less than men. They are twice as likely to be out of a job. Consider as well that only 2.5 percent of Nobel Prize winners are female and only 3 percent of the members of the U.S. National Academy of Sciences are women.

There has been contradiction among findings. Some researchers document what they describe as important sex differences; others report negligible sex differences that have become smaller over time. When sex differences are described, males show better visual-spatial ability, especially the ability to mentally rotate three-dimensional figures. Males are also found to have greater mathematical ability. Females show better verbal fluency.

This is a politically charged area of research because the stakes are high for the more and less cognitively able. Cognitive abilities relate to valued and "marketable" occupational and societal skills, often putting males at an advantage for higher social status and advancement. This "cognitive ability hierarchy" is not determined by findings of sex differences but reflect differential societal valuation of different cognitive abilities. Critical questions are, What causes cognitive sex differences? Must cognitive ability differences between the sexes, and thus societal inequalities, continue?

A criticism of explanatory research (including both biological and sociocultural studies) is the lack of direct testing of causal links. For example, sex differences in brain structure may exist, as might sex differences in spatial test performance. But do sex differences in brain structure *cause* sex-differentiated performance on spatial tests? Evidence is lacking for such causal claims. Observers caution that we must discriminate between causal theory and scientific evidence when evaluating causal claims.

The debate falls into the classic concern that correlation does not mean causation. Consider a study that was done examining visual-spatial skills in children. Boys on average outperformed girls. However, the sex disparity was eliminated after girls had been given training in the requisite skills. In these selections, you will be reading a debate that was held at Harvard between two professors. Steven Pinker summarizes the mass of evidence supporting the claim that there is a biological basis for sex differences in math and science and believes that "social forces are over-rated as the causes of gender differences." Elizabeth Spelke could not disagree more. For her, social factors are by far the major forces causing the gap between the sexes in careers in math and science.

YES ⤶

Steven Pinker

The Science of Gender and Science: Pinker vs. Spelke, A Debate

(STEVEN PINKER:) . . . For those of you who just arrived from Mars, there has been a certain amount of discussion here at Harvard on a particular datum, namely the under-representation of women among tenure-track faculty in elite universities in physical science, math, and engineering. Here are some recent numbers:

As with many issues in psychology, there are three broad ways to explain this phenomenon. One can imagine an extreme "nature" position: that males but not females have the talents and temperaments necessary for science. Needless to say, only a madman could take that view. The extreme nature position has no serious proponents.

There is an extreme "nurture" position: that males and females are biologically indistinguishable, and all relevant sex differences are products of socialization and bias.

Then there are various intermediate positions: that the difference is explainable by some combination of biological differences in average temperaments and talents interacting with socialization and bias.

Liz [Elizabeth Spelke] has embraced the extreme nurture position. There is an irony here, because in most discussions in cognitive science she and I are put in the same camp, namely the "innatists," when it comes to explaining the mind. But in this case Liz has said that there is "not a shred of evidence" for the biological factor, that "the evidence against there being an advantage for males in intrinsic aptitude is so overwhelming that it is hard for me to see how one can make a case at this point on the other side," and that "it seems to me as conclusive as any finding I know of in science."

Well we certainly aren't seeing the stereotypical gender difference in *confidence* here! Now, I'm a controversial guy. I've taken many controversial positions over the years, and, as a member of *Homo sapiens*, I think I am right on all of them. But I don't think that in any of them I would say there is "not a shred of evidence" for the other side, even if I think that the evidence *favors* one side. I would not say that the other side "can't even make a case" for their position, even if I think that their case is not as *good as* the one I favor. And as for saying that a position is "as conclusive as any finding in science"—well, we're talking about social science here! . . .

These are extreme statements—especially in light of the fact that an enormous amount of research, summarized in these and many other literature reviews, in fact points to a very different conclusion. I'll quote from one of them, a book called *Sex Differences in Cognitive Ability* by Diane Halpern. She is a respected psychologist, recently elected as president of the American Psychological Association, and someone with no theoretical axe to grind. She does not subscribe to any particular theory, and has been a critic, for example, of evolutionary psychology. And here is what she wrote in the preface to her book:

> At the time I started writing this book it seemed clear to me that any between sex differences in thinking abilities were due to socialization practices, artifacts, and mistakes in the research. After reviewing a pile of journal articles that stood several feet high, and numerous books and book chapters that dwarfed the stack of journal articles, I changed my mind. The literature on sex differences in cognitive abilities is filled with inconsistent findings, contradictory theories, and emotional claims that are unsupported by the research. Yet despite all the noise in the data, clear and consistent messages could be heard. These are real and in some cases sizable sex differences with respect to some cognitive abilities. Socialization practices are undoubtedly important, but there is also good evidence that biological sex differences play a role in establishing and maintaining cognitive sex differences, a conclusion I wasn't prepared to make when I began reviewing the relevant literature.

This captures my assessment perfectly.

Again for the benefit of the Martians in this room: This isn't just any old issue in empirical psychology. There are obvious political colorings to it, and I want to begin with a confession of my own politics. I am a feminist. I believe that women have been oppressed, discriminated against, and harassed for thousands of years. I believe that the two waves of the feminist movement in the 20th century are among the proudest achievements of our species, and I am proud to have lived through one of them, including the effort to increase the representation of women in the sciences.

But it is crucial to distinguish the *moral* proposition that people should not be discriminated against on account of their sex—which I take to be the core of feminism—and the *empirical* claim that males and females are biologically indistinguishable. They are not the same thing. Indeed, distinguishing them is essential to protecting the core of feminism. Anyone who takes an honest interest in science has to be prepared for the facts on a given issue to come out either way. And that makes it essential that we not hold the ideals of feminism hostage to the latest findings from the lab or field. Otherwise, if the findings come out as showing a sex difference, one would either have to say, "I guess sex discrimination wasn't so bad after all," or else furiously suppress or distort the findings so as to preserve the ideal. The truth cannot be sexist. Whatever the facts turn out to be, they should not be taken to compromise the core of feminism.

Why study sex differences? Believe me, being the Bobby Riggs of cognitive science is not my idea of a good time. So should I care about them, especially since they are not the focus of my own research?

First, differences between the sexes are part of the human condition. We all have a mother and a father. Most of us are attracted to members of the opposite sex, and the rest of us notice the difference from those who do. And we can't help but notice the sex of our children, friends, and our colleagues, in every aspect of life.

Also, the topic of possible sex differences is of great scientific interest. Sex is a fundamental problem in biology, and sexual reproduction and sex differences go back a billion years. . . .

The nature and source of sex differences are also of practical importance. Most of us agree that there are aspects of the world, including gender disparities, that we want to change. But if we want to *change* the world we must first *understand* it, and that includes understanding the sources of sex differences.

Let's get back to the datum to be explained. In many ways this is an *exotic* phenomenon. It involves biologically unprepared talents and temperaments: evolution certainly did not shape any part of the mind to do the work of a professor of mechanical engineering at MIT, for example. The datum has nothing to do with basic cognitive processes, or with those we use in our everyday lives, in school, or even in most college courses, where indeed there are few sex differences.

Also, we are talking about extremes of achievement. Most women are not qualified to be math professors at Harvard because most *men* aren't qualified to be math professors at Harvard. These are extremes in the population.

And we're talking about a subset of fields. Women are not under-represented to nearly the same extent in all academic fields, and certainly not in all prestigious professions.

Finally, we are talking about a statistical effect. This is such a crucial point that I have to discuss it in some detail.

Women are nowhere near absent even from the field in which they are most under-represented. The explanations for sex differences must be statistical as well. And here is a touchstone for the entire discussion:

These are two Gaussian or normal distributions: two bell curves. The X axis stands for any ability you want to measure. The Y axis stands for the proportion of people having that ability. The overlapping curves are what you get whenever you compare the sexes on any measure in which they differ. In this example, if we say that this is the male curve and this is the female curve, the means may be different, but at any particular ability level there are always representatives of both genders.

So right away a number of public statements that have been made in the last couple of months can be seen as red herrings, and should never have been made by anyone who understands the nature of statistical distributions. This includes the accusation that President Summers implied that "50% of the brightest minds in America do not have the right aptitude for science," that "women just can't cut it," and so on. These statements are statistically illiterate, and have nothing to do with the phenomena we are discussing.

There are some important corollaries of having two overlapping normal distributions. . . . [E]ven when there is only a small difference in the means of two distributions, the more extreme a score, the greater the disparity there will be in the two kinds of individuals having such a score. That is, the ratios get more extreme as you go farther out along the tail. If we hold a magnifying glass to the tail of the distribution, we see that even though the distributions overlap in the bulk of the curves, when you get out to the extremes the difference between the two curves gets larger and larger. . . .

A second important corollary is that tail ratios are affected by differences in variance. And biologists since Darwin have noted that for many traits and many species, males are the more variable gender. So even in cases where the mean for women and the mean for men are the same, the fact that men are more variable implies that the proportion of men would be higher at one tail, and also higher at the other. As it's sometimes summarized: more prodigies, more idiots.

With these statistical points in mind, let me begin the substance of my presentation by connecting the political issue with the scientific one. Economists who study patterns of discrimination have long argued (generally to no avail) that there is a crucial conceptual difference between *difference* and *discrimination*. A departure from a 50-50 sex ratio in any profession does not, by itself, imply that we are seeing discrimination, unless the interests and aptitudes of the two groups are equated. Let me illustrate the point with an example, involving myself.

I work in a scientific field—the study of language acquisition in children—that is in fact dominated by women. Seventy-five percent of the members of the main professional association are female, as are a majority of the keynote speakers at our main conference. I'm here to tell you that it's not because men like me have been discriminated against. I decided to study language development, as opposed to, say, mechanical engineering, for many reasons. . . .

Now, all we need to do to explain sex differences without invoking the discrimination or invidious sexist comparisons is to suppose that whatever traits *I* have that predispose *me* to choose (say) child language over (say) mechanical engineering are not exactly equally distributed statistically among men and women. For those of you out there—of either gender—who also are not mechanical engineers, you should understand what I'm talking about.

Okay, so what *are* the similarities and differences between the sexes? There certainly are many similarities. Men and women show no differences in general intelligence or *g*—on average, they are exactly the same, right on the money. Also, when it comes to the basic categories of cognition—how we negotiate the world and live our lives; our concept of objects, of numbers, of people, of living things, and so on—there are no differences.

Indeed, in cases where there *are* differences, there are as many instances in which women do slightly better than men as ones in which men do slightly better than women. For example, men are better at throwing, but women are more dexterous. Men are better at mentally rotating shapes; women are better at visual memory. Men are better at mathematical problem-solving; women are better at mathematical calculation. And so on.

But there are at least six differences that are relevant to the datum we have been discussing. The literature on these differences is so enormous that I can only touch on a fraction of it. . . .

1. The first difference, long noted by economists studying employment practices, is that men and women differ in what they state are their priorities in life. To sum it up: men, on average, are more likely to chase status at the expense of their families; women give a more balanced weighting. Once again: Think statistics! The finding is not that women value family and don't value status. It is not that men value status and don't value family. Nor does the finding imply that every last woman has the asymmetry that women show on average or that every last man has the asymmetry that men show on average. But in large data sets, on average, an asymmetry is what you find. . . .

2. Second, interest in people versus things and abstract rule systems. There is a *staggering* amount of data on this trait, because there is an entire field that studies people's vocational interests. . . . [T]here are consistent differences in the kinds of activities that appeal to men and women in their ideal jobs. I'll just discuss one of them: the desire to work with people versus things. There is an enormous average difference between women and men in this dimension, about one standard deviation.

   And this difference in interests will tend to cause people to gravitate in slightly different directions in their choice of career. The occupation that fits best with the "people" end of the continuum is "director of a community services organization." The occupations that fit best with the "things" end are physicist, chemist, mathematician, computer programmer, and biologist. . . .

3. Third, risk. Men are by far the more reckless sex. In a large meta-analysis involving 150 studies and 100,000 participants, in 14 out of 16 categories of risk-taking, men were over-represented. The two sexes were equally represented in the other two categories, one of which was smoking, for obvious reasons. And two of the largest sex differences were in "intellectual risk taking" and "participation in a risky experiment." . . .

4. Fourth, three-dimensional mental transformations: the ability to determine whether the drawings in each of these pairs has the same 3-dimensional shape. Again I'll appeal to a meta-analysis, this one containing 286 data sets and 100,000 subjects. The authors conclude, "we have specified a number of tests that show highly significant sex differences that are stable across age, at least after puberty, and have not decreased in recent years." Now, as I mentioned, for some kinds of spatial ability, the advantage goes to women, but in "mental rotation, spatial perception," and "spatial visualization" the advantage goes to men.

   Now, does this have any relevance to scientific achievement? We don't know for sure, but there's some reason to think that it does. In psychometric studies, three-dimensional spatial visualization is correlated with mathematical problem-solving. And mental manipulation of objects in three dimensions figures prominently in the memoirs and introspections of most creative physicists and chemists, including Faraday, Maxwell, Tesla, Kéekulé, and Lawrence, all of whom claim to have hit upon their discoveries by dynamic visual imagery and only later set them down in equations. . . .

5. Fifth, mathematical reasoning. Girls and women get better school grades in mathematics and pretty much everything else these days. And women are better at mathematical calculation. But consistently, men score better on mathematical word problems and on tests of mathematical reasoning, at least statistically. Again, here is a meta-analysis, with 254 data sets and 3 million subjects. It shows no significant difference in childhood; this is a difference that emerges around puberty, like many secondary sexual characteristics. But there are sizable differences in adolescence and adulthood, especially in high-end samples. . . .

   Now why is there a discrepancy with grades? Do SATs and other tests of mathematical reasoning aptitude underpredict grades, or do grades overpredict high-end aptitude? At the Radical Forum Liz [Elizabeth Spelke] was completely explicit in which side she takes, saying that "the tests are no good," unquote. But if the tests are really so useless, why does every major graduate program in science still use them—including the very departments at Harvard and MIT in which Liz and I have selected our own graduate students?

   I think the reason is that school grades are affected by homework and by the ability to solve the kinds of problems that have already been presented in lecture and textbooks. Whereas the aptitude tests are designed to test the application of mathematical knowledge to unfamiliar problems. And this, of course, is closer to the way that math is used in actually *doing* math and science.

   Indeed, contrary to . . . the popular opinion of many intellectuals, the tests are *surprisingly* good. There is an enormous amount of data on the predictive power of the SAT. . . . [T]he tests predict earnings, occupational choice, doctoral degrees, the prestige of one's degree, the probability of having a tenure-track position, and the number of patents. Moreover this predictive power is the same for men and for women. . . .

6. Finally there's a sex difference in variability. It's crucial here to look at the right samples. Estimates of variance depend highly on the tails of the distribution, which by definition contain smaller numbers of people. Since people at the tails of the distribution in many surveys are likely to be weeded out for various reasons, it's important to have large representative samples from national populations. In this regard the gold standard is the *Science* paper by Novell and Hedges, which reported six large stratified probability samples. They found that in 35 out of 37 tests, including all of the tests in math, space, and science, the male variance was greater than the female variance. . . .

Now the fact that these six gender differences exist does not mean that they are innate. This of course is a much more difficult issue to resolve. A necessary preamble to this discussion is that nature and nurture are not alternatives; it is possible that the explanation for a given sex difference involves some of each. The only issue is whether the contribution of biology is greater than zero. I think that there are ten kinds of evidence that the contribution of biology *is* greater than zero, though of course it is nowhere near 100 percent.

1. First, there are many biological mechanisms by which a sex difference *could* occur. There are large differences between males and females in levels of sex hormones, especially prenatally, in the first six months of life, and in adolescence. There are receptors for hormones all over the brain, including the cerebral cortex. There are many small differences in men's and women's brains, including the overall size of the brain (even correcting for body size), the density of cortical neurons, the degree of cortical asymmetry, the size of hypothalamic nuclei, and several others.

2. Second, many of the major sex differences—certainly some of them, maybe all of them—are universal. The idea that there are cultures out there somewhere in which everything is the reverse of here turns out to be an academic legend. In his survey of the anthropological literature called *Human Universals,* the anthropologist Donald Brown points out that in all cultures men and women are seen as having different natures; that there is a greater involvement of women in direct child care; more competitiveness in various measures for men than for women; and a greater spatial range traveled by men compared to by women.

   In personality, we have a cross-national survey (if not a true cross-cultural one) in Feingold's meta-analysis, which noted that gender differences in personality are consistent across ages, years of data collection, educational levels, and nations. When it comes to spatial manipulation and mathematical reasoning, we have fewer relevant data, and we honestly don't have true cross-cultural surveys, but we do have cross-national surveys. David Geary and Catherine Desoto found the expected sex difference in mental rotation in ten European countries and in Ghana, Turkey, and China. Similarly, Diane Halpern, analyzing results from ten countries, said that "the majority of the findings show amazing cross-cultural consistency when comparing males and females on cognitive tests."

3. Third, stability over time. Surveys of life interests and personality have shown little or no change in the two generations that have come of age since the second wave of feminism. There is also, famously, *resistance* to change in communities that, for various ideological reasons, were dedicated to stamping out sex differences, and found they were unable to do so. These include the Israeli kibbutz, various American Utopian communes a century ago, and contemporary androgynous academic couples. . . .

4. Fourth, many sex differences can be seen in other mammals. It would be an amazing coincidence if these differences just happened to be replicated in the arbitrary choices made by human cultures at the dawn of time. There are large differences between males and females in many mammals in aggression, in investment in offspring, in play aggression versus play parenting, and in the range size, which predicts a species' sex differences in spatial ability (such as in solving mazes), at least in polygynous species, which is how the human species is classified. Many primate species even show a sex difference in their interest in physical objects versus conspecifics, a difference seen [in] their patterns of juvenile play. . . .

5. Fifth, many of these differences emerge in early childhood. It is said that there is a technical term for people who believe that little boys and little girls are born indistinguishable and are molded into their natures by parental socialization. The term is "childless."

   Some sex differences seem to emerge even in the first week of life. Girls respond more to sounds of distress, and girls make more eye contact than boys. And in [one] study . . . , newborn boys were shown to be more interested in looking at a physical object than a face, whereas newborn girls were shown to be more interested in looking at a face than a physical object.

   A bit later in development there are vast and robust differences between boys and girls, seen all over the world. Boys far more often than girls engage in rough-and-tumble play, which involves aggression, physical activity, and competition. Girls spend a lot time often in cooperative play. Girls engage much more often in play parenting. . . . There are sex differences in intuitive psychology, that is, how well children can read one another's minds. For instance, several large studies show that girls are better than boys in solving the "false belief task," and in interpreting the mental states of characters in stories.

6. Sixth, genetic boys brought up as girls. In a famous 1970s incident called the John/Joan case, one member of a pair of identical twin boys lost his penis in a botched circumcision. . . . Following advice from the leading gender expert of the time, the parents agreed to have the boy castrated, given female-specific hormones, and brought up as a girl. All this was hidden from him throughout his childhood.

   When I was an undergraduate the case was taught to me as proof of how gender roles are socially acquired. But it turned out that the facts had been suppressed. When "Joan" and her family were interviewed years later, it turned out that from the youngest ages he exhibited boy-typical patterns of aggression and rough-and-tumble play, rejected girl-typical activities, and showed a greater interest in things than in people. At age 14, suffering from depression, his father finally told him the truth. . . .

7. Seventh, a lack of differential treatment by parents and teachers. These conclusions come as a shock to many people. One comes from Lytton and Romney's meta-analysis of sex-specific socialization involving 172 studies and 28,000 children, in which they looked both at parents' reports and at direct observations of how parents treat their sons and daughters—and found few or no differences among contemporary Americans. In particular, there was no difference in the categories "Encouraging Achievement" and "Encouraging Achievement in Mathematics."

   There is a widespread myth that teachers (who of course are disproportionately female) are dupes who perpetuate gender inequities by failing to call on girls in class, and who otherwise have low expectations of girls' performance. In fact Jussim and Eccles, in a study of 100 teachers and 1,800 students, concluded that teachers seemed to be basing their perceptions of students on those students' actual performances and motivation.

8. Eighth, studies of prenatal sex hormones: the mechanism that makes boys boys and girls girls in the first place. There is evidence, admittedly squishy in parts, that differences in prenatal hormones make a difference in later thought and behavior even within a given sex. In the condition called congenital adrenal hyperplasia, girls in utero are subjected to an increased dose of androgens, which is neutralized postnatally. But when they grow up they have male-typical toy preferences—trucks and guns—compared to other girls, male-typical play patterns, more competitiveness, less cooperativeness, and male-typical occupational preferences. However, research on their spatial abilities is inconclusive, and I cannot honestly say that there are replicable demonstrations that CAH women have male-typical patterns of spatial cognition.

   Similarly, variations in fetal testosterone, studied in various ways, show that fetal testosterone has a nonmonotic relationship to reduced eye contact and face perception at 12 months, to reduced vocabulary at 18 months, to reduced social skills and greater narrowness of interest at 48 months, and to enhanced mental rotation abilities in the school-age years.

9. Ninth, circulating sex hormones. . . . Though it's possible that all claims of the effects of hormones on cognition will turn out to be bogus, I suspect something will be salvaged from this somewhat contradictory literature. There are, in any case, many studies showing that testosterone levels in the low-normal male range are associated with better abilities in spatial manipulation. And in a variety of studies in which estrogens are compared or manipulated, there is evidence, admittedly disputed, for statistical changes in the strengths and weaknesses in women's cognition during the menstrual cycle, possibly a counterpart to the changes in men's abilities during their daily and seasonal cycles of testosterone.

10. My last kind of evidence: imprinted X chromosomes. In the past fifteen years an entirely separate genetic system capable of implementing sex differences has been discovered. In the phenomenon called genetic imprinting, studied by David Haig and others, a chromosome such as the X chromosome can be altered depending on whether it was passed on from one's mother or from one's father. This makes a difference in the condition called Turner syndrome, in which a child has just one X chromosome, but can get it either from her mother or her father. When she inherits an X that is specific to girls, on average she has a better vocabulary and better social skills, and is better at reading emotions, at reading body language, and at reading faces.

   A remark on stereotypes. . . .

Are these stereotypes? Yes, many of them are (although, I must add, not all of them—for example, women's superiority in spatial memory and mathematical calculation). There seems to be a widespread assumption that if a sex difference conforms to a stereotype, the difference must have been *caused* by the stereotype, via differential expectations for boys and for girls. But of course the causal arrow could go in either direction: stereotypes might *reflect* differences rather than cause them. In fact there's an enormous literature in cognitive psychology which says that people can be good intuitive statisticians when forming categories and that their prototypes for conceptual categories track the statistics of the natural world pretty well. . . .

To sum up: I think there is more than "a shred of evidence" for sex differences that are relevant to statistical gender disparities in elite hard science departments. There are reliable average differences in life priorities, in an interest in people versus things, in risk-seeking, in spatial transformations, in mathematical reasoning, and in variability in these traits. And there are ten kinds of evidence that these differences are not *completely* explained by socialization and bias, although they surely are in part.

A concluding remark. None of this provides grounds for ignoring the biases and barriers that do keep women out of science, as long as we keep in mind the distinction between *fairness* on the one hand and *sameness* on the other. And I will give the final word to Gloria Steinem: "there are very few jobs that actually require a penis or a vagina, and all the other jobs should be open to both sexes."

The Science of Gender and Science: Pinker vs. Spelke Debate

(ELIZABETH SPELKE:) . . . I want to start by talking about the points of agreement between Steve [Pinker] and me, and as he suggested, there are many. If we got away from the topic of sex and science, we'd be hard pressed to find issues that we disagree on. Here are a few of the points of agreement that are particularly relevant to the discussions of the last few months.

First, we agree that both our society in general and our university in particular will be healthiest if all opinions can be put on the table and debated on their merits. We also agree that claims concerning sex differences are empirical, they should be evaluated by evidence, and we'll all be happier and live longer if we can undertake that evaluation as dispassionately and rationally as possible. We agree that the mind is not a blank slate; in fact one of the deepest things that Steve and I agree on is that there is such a thing as human nature, and it is a fascinating and exhilarating experience to study it. And finally, I think we agree that the role of scientists in society is rather modest. Scientists find things out. The much more difficult questions of how to use that information, live our lives, and structure our societies are not questions that science can answer. Those are questions that everybody must consider.

So where do we disagree?

We disagree on the answer to the question, why in the world are women scarce as hens' teeth on Harvard's mathematics faculty and other similar institutions? In the current debate, two classes of factors have been said to account for this difference. In one class are social forces, including overt and covert discrimination and social influences that lead men and women to develop different skills and different priorities. In the other class are genetic differences that predispose men and women to have different capacities and to want different things.

In his book, *The Blank Slate,* and again today, Steve [Pinker] argued that social forces are over-rated as causes of gender differences. Intrinsic differences in aptitude are a larger factor, and intrinsic differences in motives are the biggest factor of all. Most of the examples that Steve gave concerned what he takes to be biologically based differences in motives.

My own view is different. I think the big forces causing this gap are social factors. There are no differences in overall intrinsic aptitude for science and mathematics between women and men. Notice that I am not saying the genders are indistinguishable, that men and women are alike in every way, or even that men and women have identical cognitive profiles. I'm saying that when you add up all the things that men are good at, and all the things that women are good at, there is no overall advantage for men that would put them at the top of the fields of math and science.

On the issue of motives, I think we're not in a position to know whether the different things that men and women often say they want stem only from social forces, or in part from intrinsic sex differences. I don't think we can know that now.

I want to start with the issue that's clearly the biggest source of debate between Steve and me: the issue of differences in intrinsic aptitude. This is the only issue that my own work and professional knowledge bear on. Then I will turn to the social forces, as a lay person as it were, because I think they are exerting the biggest effects. . . .

Over the last months, we've heard three arguments that men have greater cognitive aptitude for science. The first argument is that from birth, boys are interested in objects and mechanics, and girls are interested in people and emotions. The predisposition to figure out the mechanics of the world sets boys on a path that makes them more likely to become scientists or mathematicians. The second argument assumes, as Galileo told us, that science is conducted in the language of mathematics. On the second claim, males are intrinsically better at mathematical reasoning, including spatial reasoning. The third argument is that men show greater variability than women, and as a result there are more men at the extreme upper end of the ability distribution from which scientists and mathematicians are drawn. Let me take these claims one by one.

The first claim . . . is gaining new currency from the work of Simon Baron-Cohen. It's an old idea, presented with some new language. Baron-Cohen says that males are innately predisposed to learn about objects and mechanical relationships, and this sets them on a path to becoming what he calls "systematizers." Females, on the other hand, are innately predisposed to learn about people and their emotions, and this puts them on a path to becoming "empathizers." Since systematizing is at the heart of math and science, boys are more apt to develop the knowledge and skills that lead to math and science.

To anyone as old as I am who has been following the literature on sex differences, this may seem like a surprising claim. The classic reference on the nature and development of sex differences is a book by Eleanor Maccoby and Carol Jacklin that came out in the 1970s. . . . At the top of their list of myths was the idea that males are primarily interested in objects and females are primarily interested in people. They reviewed an enormous literature, in which babies were presented with objects and people to see if they were more interested in one than the other. They concluded that there were no sex differences in these interests. . . .

Let me take you on a whirlwind tour of 30 years of research. . . . From birth, babies perceive objects. They know where one object ends and the next one begins. They can't see objects as well as we can, but as they grow their object perception becomes richer and more differentiated.

Babies also start with rudimentary abilities to represent that an object continues to exist when it's out of view, and they hold onto those representations longer, and over more complicated kinds of changes, as they grow. Babies make basic inferences about object motion: inferences like, the force with which an object is hit determines the speed with which it moves. These inferences undergo regular developmental changes over the infancy period.

In each of these cases, there is systematic developmental change, and there's variability. Because of this variability, we can compare the abilities of male infants to females. Do we see sex differences? The research gives a clear answer to this question: We don't.

Male and female infants are equally interested in objects. Male and female infants make the same inferences about object motion, at the same time in development. They learn the same things about object mechanics at the same time.

Across large numbers of studies, occasionally a study will favor one sex over the other. For example, girls learn that the force with which something is hit influences the distance it moves a month earlier than boys do. But these differences are small and scattered. For the most part, we see high convergence across the sexes. Common paths of learning continue through the preschool years, as kids start manipulating objects to see if they can get a rectangular block into a circular hole. If you look at the rates at which boys and girls figure these things out, you don't find any differences. We see equal developmental paths.

I think this research supports an important conclusion. In discussions of sex differences, we need to ask what's common across the two sexes. One thing that's common is infants don't divide up the labor of understanding the world, with males focusing on mechanics and females focusing on emotions. Male and female infants are both interested in objects and in people, and they learn about both. The conclusions that Maccoby and Jacklin drew in the early 1970s are well supported by research since that time.

Let me turn to the second claim. People may have equal abilities to develop intuitive understanding of the physical world, but formal math and science don't build on these intuitions. Scientists use mathematics to come up with new characterizations of the world and new principles to explain its functioning. Maybe males have an edge in scientific reasoning because of their greater talent for mathematics.

[F]ormal mathematics is not something we have evolved to do; it's a recent accomplishment. Animals don't do formal math or science, and neither did humans back in the Pleistocene. If there is a biological basis for our mathematical reasoning abilities, it must depend on systems that evolved for other purposes, but that we've been able to harness for the new purpose of representing and manipulating numbers and geometry.

Research from the intersecting fields of cognitive neuroscience, neuropsychology, cognitive psychology, and cognitive development provide evidence for five "core systems" at the foundations of mathematical reasoning. The first is a system for representing small exact numbers of objects—the difference between *one, two,* and *three.* This system emerges in human infants at about five months of age, and it continues to be present in adults. The second is a system for discriminating large, approximate numerical magnitudes—the difference between a set of about ten things and a set of about 20 things. That system also emerges early in infancy, at four or five months, and continues to be present and functional in adults.

The third system is probably the first uniquely human foundation for numerical abilities: the system of natural number concepts that we construct as children when we learn verbal counting. That construction takes place between about the ages of two and a half and four years. The last two systems are first seen in children when they navigate. One system represents the geometry of the surrounding layout. The other system represents landmark objects.

All five systems have been studied quite extensively in large numbers of male and female infants. We can ask, are there sex differences in the development of any of these systems at the foundations of mathematical thinking? Again, the answer is no. . . .

[Studies] support two important points. First, indeed there is a biological foundation to mathematical and scientific reasoning. We are endowed with core knowledge systems that emerge prior to any formal instruction and that serve as a basis for mathematical thinking. Second, these systems develop equally in males and females. Ten years ago, the evolutionary psychologist and sex difference researcher, David Geary, reviewed the literature that was available at that time. He concluded that there were no sex differences in "primary abilities" underlying mathematics. What we've learned in the last ten years continues to support that conclusion.

Sex differences do emerge at older ages. Because they emerge later in childhood, it's hard to tease apart their biological and social sources. But before we attempt that task, let's ask what the differences are.

I think the following is a fair statement, both of the cognitive differences that Steve described and of others. When people are presented with a complex task that can be solved through multiple different strategies, males and females sometimes differ in the strategy that they prefer.

For example, if a task can only be solved by representing the geometry of the layout, we do not see a difference between men and women. But if the task can be accomplished either by representing geometry or by representing individual landmarks, girls tend to rely on the landmarks, and boys on the geometry. . . .

Because of these differences, males and females sometimes show differing cognitive profiles on timed tests. When you have to solve problems fast, some strategies will be faster than others. Thus, females perform better at some verbal, mathematical and spatial tasks, and males perform better at other verbal, mathematical, and spatial tasks. This pattern of differing profiles is not well captured by the generalization, often bandied about in the popular press, that women are "verbal" and men are "spatial." There doesn't seem to be any more evidence for that than there was for the idea that women are people-oriented and men are object-oriented. Rather the differences are more subtle.

Does one of these two profiles foster better learning of math than the other? In particular, is the male profile better suited to high-level mathematical reasoning?

At this point, we face a question that's been much discussed in the literature on mathematics education and mathematical testing. The question is, by what yardstick can we decide whether men or women are better at math?

Some people suggest that we look at performance on the SAT-M, the quantitative portion of the Scholastic Assessment Test. But this suggestion raises a problem of circularity. The SAT test is composed of many different types of items. Some of those items are solved better by females. Some are solved better by males. The people who make the test have to decide, how many items of each type to include? Depending on how they answer that question, they can create a test that makes women look like better mathematicians, or a test that makes men look like better mathematicians. What's the right solution? . . .

A second strategy is to look at job outcomes. Maybe the people who are better at mathematics are those who pursue more mathematically intensive careers. But this strategy raises two problems. First, which mathematically intensive jobs should we choose? If we choose engineering, we will conclude that men are better at math because more men become engineers. If we choose accounting, we will think that women are better at math because more women become accountants: 57% of current accountants are women. So which job are we going to pick, to decide who has more mathematical talent?

These two examples suggest a deeper problem with job outcomes as a measure of mathematical talent. Surely you've got to be good at math to land a mathematically intensive job, but talent in mathematics is only one of the factors influencing career choice. It can't be our gold standard for mathematical ability.

So what can be? I suggest the following experiment. We should take a large number of male students and a large number of female students who have equal educational backgrounds, and present them with the kinds of tasks that real mathematicians face. We should give them new mathematical material that they have not yet mastered, and allow them to learn it over an extended period of time: the kind of time scale that real mathematicians work on. We should ask, how well do the students master this material? The good news is, this experiment is done all the time. It's called high school and college.

Here's the outcome. In high school, girls and boys now take equally many math classes, including the most advanced ones, and girls get better grades. In college, women earn almost half of the bachelor's degrees in mathematics, and men and women get equal grades. Here I respectfully disagree with one thing that Steve said: men and women get equal grades, even when you only compare people within a single institution and a single math class. Equating for classes, men and women get equal grades.

The outcome of this large-scale experiment gives us every reason to conclude that men and women have equal talent for mathematics. Here, I too would like to quote Diane Halpern. Halpern reviews much evidence for sex differences, but she concludes, "differences are not deficiencies." Men and women have equal aptitude for mathematics. Yes, there are sex differences, but they don't add up to an overall advantage for one sex over the other.

Let me turn to the third claim, that men show greater variability, either in general or in quantitative abilities in particular, and so there are more men at the upper end of the ability distribution. . . .

[However], males and females [have been found to take] equally demanding math classes and major in math in equal numbers. More girls major in biology and more boys in physics and engineering, but equal numbers of girls and boys major in math. And they get equal grades. The SAT-M not only under-predicts the performance of college women in general, it also under-predicts the college performance of women in the talented sample. These women and men have been shown to be equally talented by the most meaningful measure we have: their ability to assimilate new, challenging material in demanding mathematics classes at top-flight institutions. By that measure, the study does not find any difference between highly talented girls and boys.

So, what's causing the gender imbalance on faculties of math and science? Not differences in intrinsic aptitude. Let's turn to the social factors that I think are much more important. . . . I will talk about just one effect: how gender stereotypes influence the ways in which males and females are perceived.

Let me start with studies of parents' perceptions of their own children. Steve said that parents report that they treat their children equally. They treat their boys and girls alike, and they encourage them to equal extents, for they want both their sons and their daughters to succeed. This is no doubt true. But how are parents perceiving their kids?

Some studies have interviewed parents just after the birth of their child, at the point where the first question that 80% of parents ask—is it a boy or a girl?—has been answered. Parents of boys describe their babies as stronger, heartier, and bigger than parents of girls. The investigators also looked at the babies' medical records and asked whether there really were differences between the boys and girls in weight, strength, or coordination. The boys and girls were indistinguishable in these respects, but the parents' descriptions were different.

At 12 months of age, girls and boys show equal abilities to walk, crawl, or clamber. But before one study, Karen Adolph, an investigator of infants' loco-motor development, asked parents to predict how well their child would do on a set of crawling tasks: Would the child be able to crawl down a sloping ramp? Parents of sons were more confident that their child would make it down the ramp than parents of daughters. When Adolph tested the infants on the ramp, there was no difference whatsoever between the sons and daughters, but there was a difference in the parents' predictions.

My third example, moving up in age, comes from the studies of Jackie Eccles. She asked parents of boys and girls in sixth grade, how talented do you think your child is in mathematics? Parents of sons were more likely to judge that their sons had talent than parents of daughters. . . .

There's clearly a mismatch between what parents perceive in their kids and what objective measures reveal. But is it possible that the parents are seeing something that the objective measures are missing? Maybe the boy getting B's in his math class really is a mathematical genius, and his mom or dad has sensed that. To eliminate that possibility, we need to present observers with the very same baby, or child, or Ph.D. candidate, and manipulate their belief about the person's gender. Then we can ask whether their belief influences their perception.

It's hard to do these studies, but there are examples, and I will describe a few of them. A bunch of studies take the following form: you show a group of parents, or college undergraduates, video-clips of babies that they don't know personally. For half of them you give the baby a male name, and for the other half you give the baby a female name. (Male and female babies don't look very different.) The observers watch the baby and then are asked a series of questions: What is the baby doing? What is the baby feeling? How would you rate the baby on a dimension like strong-to-weak, or more intelligent to less intelligent? There are two important findings.

First, when babies do something unambiguous, reports are not affected by the baby's gender. If the baby clearly smiles, everybody says the baby is smiling or happy. Perception of children is not pure hallucination. Second, children often do things that are ambiguous, and parents face questions whose answers aren't easily readable off their child's overt behavior. In those cases, you see some interesting gender labeling effects. For example, in one study a child on a video-clip was playing with a jack-in-the-box. It suddenly popped up, and the child was startled and jumped backward. When people were asked, what's the child feeling, those who were given a female label said, "she's afraid." But the ones given a male label said, "he's angry." Same child, same reaction, different interpretation. . . .

I think these perceptions matter. You, as a parent, may be completely committed to treating your male and female children equally. But no sane parent would treat a fearful child the same way they treat an angry child. If knowledge of a child's gender affects adults' perception of that child, then male and female children are going to elicit different reactions from the world, different patterns of encouragement. These perceptions matter, even in parents who are committed to treating sons and daughters alike.

I will give you one last version of a gender-labeling study. This one hits particularly close to home. The subjects in the study were people like Steve and me: professors of psychology, who were sent some vitas to evaluate as applicants for a tenure track position. Two different vitas were used in the study. One was a vita of a walk-on-water candidate, best candidate you've ever seen, you would die to have this person on your faculty. The other vita was a middling, average vita among successful candidates. For half the professors, the name on the vita was male, for the other half the name was female. People were asked a series of questions: What do you think about this candidate's research productivity? What do you think about his or her teaching experience? And finally, Would you hire this candidate at your university?

For the walk-on-water candidate, there was no effect of gender labeling on these judgments. I think this finding supports Steve's view that we're dealing with little overt discrimination at universities. It's not as if professors see a female name on a vita and think, I don't want her. When the vita's great, everybody says great, let's hire.

What about the average successful vita, though: that is to say, the kind of vita that professors most often must evaluate? In that case, there were differences. The male was rated as having higher research productivity. These psychologists, Steve's and my colleagues, looked at the same number of publications and thought, "good productivity" when the name was male, and "less good productivity" when the name was female. Same thing for teaching experience. The very same list of courses was seen as good teaching experience when the name was male, and less good teaching experience when the name was female. In answer to the question would they hire the candidate, 70% said yes for the male, 45% for the female. If the decision were made by majority rule, the male would get hired and the female would not.

A couple other interesting things came out of this study. The effects were every bit as strong among the female respondents as among the male respondents. Men are not the culprits here. There were effects at the tenure level as well. At the tenure level, professors evaluated a very strong candidate, and almost everyone said this looked like a good case for tenure. But people were invited to express their reservations, and they came up with some very reasonable doubts. For example, "This person looks very strong, but before I agree to give her tenure I would need to know, was this her own work or the work of her adviser?" Now that's a perfectly reasonable question to ask. But what ought to give us pause is that those kinds of reservations were expressed *four times more often* when the name was female than when the name was male.

So there's a pervasive difference in perceptions, and I think the difference matters. Scientists' perception of the quality of a candidate will influence the likelihood that the candidate will get a fellowship, a job, resources, or a promotion. A pattern of biased evaluation therefore will occur even in people who are absolutely committed to gender equity. . . .

From the moment of birth to the moment of tenure, throughout this great developmental progression, there are unintentional but pervasive and important differences in the ways that males and females are perceived and evaluated.

I have to emphasize that perceptions are not everything. When cases are unambiguous, you don't see these effects. What's more, cognitive development is robust: boys and girls show equal capacities and achievements in educational settings, including in science and mathematics, despite the very different ways in which boys and girls are perceived and evaluated. I think it's really great news that males and females develop along common paths and gain common sets of abilities. The equal performance of males and females, despite their unequal treatment, strongly suggests that mathematical and scientific reasoning has a biological foundation, and this foundation is shared by males and females.

Finally, you do not create someone who feels like a girl or boy simply by perceiving them as male or female. That's the lesson that comes from the studies of people of one sex who are raised as the opposite sex. Biological sex differences are real and important. Sex is not a cultural construction that's imposed on people.

But the question on the table is not, Are there biological sex differences? The question is, Why are there fewer women mathematicians and scientists? The patterns of bias that I described provide four interconnected answers to that question. First, and most obviously, biased perceptions produce discrimination: When a group of equally qualified men and women are evaluated for jobs, more of the men will get those jobs if they are perceived to be more qualified. Second, if people are rational, more men than women will put themselves forward into the academic competition, because men will see that they've got a better chance for success. Academic jobs will be more attractive to men because they face better odds, will get more resources, and so forth.

Third, biased perceptions earlier in life may well deter some female students from even attempting a career in science or mathematics. If your parents feel that you don't have as much natural talent as someone else whose objective abilities are no better than yours, that may discourage you, as Eccles's work shows. Finally, there's likely to be a snowball effect. All of us have an easier time imagining ourselves in careers where there are other people like us. If the first three effects perpetuate a situation where there are few female scientists and mathematicians, young girls will be less likely to see math and science as a possible life.

. . . Let me end, though, by asking, could biological differences in motives—motivational patterns that evolved in the Pleistocene but that apply to us today—propel more men than women towards careers in mathematics and science?

My feeling is that where we stand now, we cannot evaluate this claim. It may be true, but as long as the forces of discrimination and biased perceptions affect people so pervasively, we'll never know. I think the only way we can find out is to do one more experiment. We should allow all of the evidence that men and women have equal cognitive capacity to permeate through society. We should allow people to evaluate children in relation to their actual capacities, rather than one's sense of what their capacities ought to be, given their gender. Then we can see, as those boys and girls grow up, whether different inner voices pull them in different directions. I don't know what the findings of that experiment will be. But I do hope that some future generation of children gets to find out.

POSTSCRIPT

Do Sex Differences in Careers in Mathematics and Sciences Have a Biological Basis?

From the 1940s to the 1960s boys tended to surpass girls in math and science, but those discrepancies have lessened more recently. Today girls and boys tend to be equal, especially in basic math skills, although in advanced math, high school girls tend to outperform boys in the classroom. Even at the college level, although males receive higher scores on standardized tests such as the SAT, females tend to earn higher grades in college math courses. It has been suggested that numerous factors affect females' math performance, such as differential treatment of girls and boys in the classroom and girls' lower expectation and lower confidence because of cultural messages that math is a male domain and that girls are not supposed to do well. There was briefly a Barbie doll on the market that said "math is tough." Additionally, even highly competent girls may suffer from the stereotype threat in standardized testing situations. That is, although they may know they are good at math, the testing context arouses anxiety because of the stereotype; ironically, this can impair their performance. Research has suggested that girls who resist the pressure to conform to gender role expectations are more likely to take more math and science courses, compete in sports, and be more creative and achievement-oriented. Interestingly, it helps to not have a brother, especially an older brother. Birth order as well as the sex composition of the siblings makes a difference. Girls without brothers tend to have higher self-esteem and find it easier to resist the pressure to conform to gendered expectations. Jacquelynne Eccles has proposed an Expectancy by Values Theory that helps explain girls' and boys' differential interest in math. She explains that one's expectations for success interact with the subjective value of various options. Women, as well as men, must believe they can do it and must enjoy doing it. Her research demonstrates that parental attributions are very important. Parents very strongly influence their children's beliefs about their skills, which in turn shapes their academic and ultimately, career choices. Very frequently men are socialized to value career over family and vice versa for women. This emphasis on the development of attitudes towards math and science and their impact on career choices is important because it gives us insight into why there is a gender wage gap and why so many single mothers find themselves on welfare. Recently organizations have launched campaigns to narrow the computer technology gap, which may contribute to the math and science gap for girls and boys. For example, in 2002 the American Association of University Women began the

Nebraska Girls and Technology Project in cooperation with the Girl Scouts. The project includes *Girls Click,* which is a computer-based hands-on learning experience.

What does it mean if we find that cognitive sex differences are more heavily accounted for by biology or by environmental reason? If individuals are differently predisposed for cognitive skill, should we and can we do something about it? If so, what? For example, evidence suggests that testosterone is implicated in spatial abilities. Should we give females more testosterone to boost their spatial abilities? Does this sound preposterous considering that thousands of athletes (predominantly males) inject themselves with steroids daily to boost their muscle mass?

Feminist scholars are fearful of biological causal evidence because it renders the environment irrelevant and implies that cognitive sex differences are unchangeable. Rather, they believe that sociocultural evidence provides more hope for social change. How much truth can be found in either claim? Psychosocially caused behavior has often been very difficult to reduce or eliminate (e.g., sex and racial bias). Furthermore, biological mechanisms (e.g., hormones and brain structure) change in response to environmental input. Recent evidence shows, for example, that just as brain structures and functions have been found to impact the way people select and respond to the environment, environmental input and experience alter brain structure and function throughout the life course. If so, then a radical move like injecting females with testosterone is not necessary. Simply engaging individuals in certain activities (even the performance of cognitive tasks) can boost testosterone levels naturally. Thus, many scholars have argued for an interactionist approach to studying cognition, examining the interaction of biology and environment.

Rather than think of sociocultural and biological arguments as necessarily in opposition and mutually exclusive, we must consider how they interact to explain cognitive sex differences. For example, individuals differ in their genetic potential or predisposition for good spatial skills. But genetically predisposed children might select environments that provide more spatial opportunity, augmenting brain structure and further fostering the development of spatial ability. The environment also intercedes in either developing or thwarting this potential. The biological makeup of individuals in the home may also influence the family environment (e.g., parents' and siblings' biological predisposition as impacted by past experiences and environmental inputs). Likewise, individuals might recognize and directly respond to the child's predisposition for spatial ability and provide spatial experiences. Macro-level cultural influences may also act on biological predisposition (e.g., cultural prohibition of certain experiences).

Scholars also urge that we need to go beyond descriptive and explanatory research to a consideration of what the differences *mean* for individuals and society, especially given differential societal valuation of the cognitive differences. Indeed, cognitive sex differences research has revealed the powerful effects of identification and reinforcement of sex role–appropriate behaviors, expectations, motivational variables, and explicit and implicit messages in cognitive sex differences. If individuals have poor mathematical or spatial skill, what does it mean to be excluded from opportunities because of these cognitive deficits (whether actual or presumed based on stereotypes)? Having cognitive deficits impacts identity and self-esteem: how we feel about our abilities, our role in society, and our potential for success. It also creates dependencies. (Think about how much more expensive life is for individuals who are not mechanically inclined.) Spending so much time in a devaluing environment provides constant reminders of the jeopardy incurred by cognitive sex differences to future income, status, and happiness. The restrictions to societal and occupational opportunities based on cognitive functioning have repercussions for individuals and also for society at large. How is society influenced by the fact that the majority of engineers, mathematicians, chemists, mechanics, and airplane pilots are male? Of course, critics point out that the sex differences in occupational representation are grossly disproportionate to the magnitude of cognitive sex differences. Thus, even if there is biological evidence for cognitive sex differences, there seem to be other social factors at work in creating this gulf.

Suggested Readings

Deborah Blum, *Sex on the Brain: The Biological Differences Between Men and Women* (New York: Penguin Books, 1998).

Simon Baron-Cohen, *The Essential Difference: The Truth about the Male and Female Brain* (New York: Basic Books, 2003).

Girl Scouts, *The Girls Difference: Short-Circuiting the Myth of the Technophobic Girl* (New York: Girl Scouts Research Institute, 2001).

Barbara A. Gutek, "Women and Paid Work," *Psychology of Women Quarterly*, 25 (2001): 379–393.

Diane F. Halpren, *Sex Differences in Cognitive Abilities*, 4th ed. (Mahwah, NJ: Lawrence Erlbaum, 2000).

Caryl Rivers and C. Barnett, *Same Difference: How Gender Myths Are Hurting Our Relationships, Our Children, and Our Jobs* (New York: Basic Books, 2005).

Janet Shibley Hyde and Kristen C. Kling, "Women, Motivation, and Achievement," *Psychology of Women Quarterly*, 25 (2001): 364–378.

E. S. Spelke, "Sex Differences in Intrinsic Aptitude for Mathematics and Science? A Critical Analysis," *American Psychologist*, 60 (2005): 950–958.

Internet References . . .

Men, Women, and Sex Differences: The Attitudes of Three Feminists—Gloria Steinem, Gloria Allred, and Bella Abzug

A paper by Russell Eisenman entitled "Men, Women, and Sex Differences: The Attitudes of Three Feminists—Gloria Steinmen, Gloria Allred, and Bella Abzug" is presented on this Web site. This paper is a case study of perspectives on sex differences of three prominent feminists.

http://www.theabsolute.net/misogyny/eisenman.html

Genderlect Styles of Deborah Tannen

This Web site on the genderlect styles of Deborah Tannen provides an overview of Deborah Tannen's popular work on gender and communication.

http://www.usm.maine.edu/com/genderlect/

Feminism and Women's Studies

This link is maintained by EServer, which is an e-publishing cooperative housed at Iowa State University. Hundreds of writers, editors, and scholars gather here to publish their work free of charge. This link provides access to articles, research papers, and reports that focus on gender, communication, and Internet issues.

http://feminism.eserver.org/gender/cyberspace/

Educational Communications Board

This Web site is a state agency focused on public radio and television programs throughout Wisconsin that reflect Guide to Healthy Dating, including a series of videos on intimacy, sex, breaking up, communication, the role of the media, dating violence, and date rape.

http://www.ecb.org/guides/dating.htm

Center for Young Women's Health

This Web site from the Children's Hospital of Boston provides information on different kinds of relationships, what makes them special, and how to communicate in a positive way. Stories and fun ways to work on many kinds of relationships are offered.

http://www.youngwomenshealth.org/healthy_relat.html

Different Strokes:
The Question of Difference

*W*hat is the most fruitful approach for better understanding sex and gender? For decades, the dominant approach in social scientific research on sex and gender is studying sex differences, termed a difference model. The goal is to examine whether or not sex differences exist and to describe the differing group tendencies. In this research, sex differences are identified from a comparison of the average tendency of a group of males to the average tendency of a group of females. The result is typically expressed in the form of generalizations of ways in which males and females differ, presuming within-sex homogeneity (i.e., all females are alike). Although most of the research is descriptive, assumptions and theories of what causes these sex differences abound. The aims of this section are to explore some ways in which the difference model has shaped our understanding of gender in various domains of human functioning, including communication and mating strategies.*

As you read these selections, consider the role of biology. Are new developments in neuron-imaging that show which areas of the brain are most active during various tasks clarifying or confusing our understanding of the role of biology in explanations of sex differences and similarities? How do issues of sex differences/similarities play out across race, ethnicity, class, culture, and other status-defining categories? Are women and men similarly alike or different across these various categories? Do media representations of women and men "fan the fires" of difference, especially when talking about gender and communication and mating strategies?

- Are Women and Men More Similar Than Different?
- Is Culture the Primary Source of Sex Differences in Communication Styles?
- Do Nice Guys Finish Last?

ISSUE 4

Are Women and Men More Similar Than Different?

YES: **Janet Shibley Hyde**, from "The Gender Similarities Hypothesis," *American Psychologist* (2005)

NO: **Kingsley R. Browne**, from *Biology at Work: Rethinking Sexual Equality* (Rutgers University Press, 2002)

ISSUE SUMMARY

YES: Psychology professor Janet Shibley Hyde of the University of Wisconsin at Madison argues that claims of gender differences are overinflated, resulting in serious consequences for women and men in the workplace and in relationships.

NO: Kingsley R. Browne, a professor at Wayne State University Law School, claims that the differences are real, rooted in biology.

Some feminist scholars warn of the overrepresentation of findings of sex differences in published scholarship. Many scholars argue that the comparison of males and females is as much a political as a scientific enterprise. Findings of similarities between groups is thought to be a "null" finding and thus not publishable in its own right. The popular press is eager to disseminate evidence of sex differences; indeed, findings of sex similarity are viewed as not newsworthy. Often, the description of a sex difference is accompanied by a presumption that the difference is innate and thus immutable.

An ongoing debate surrounds whether women and men are more similar than different and whether it is worthwhile to continue to study differences, especially if they are small. There appears to be a trade-off in the costs and benefits of each perspective. Noted feminist psychologist Rhoda Unger once said, "Consider a rainbow. Given the full spectrum of color, we perceive red and magenta as being similar. If, however, we eliminate all other hues, red and magenta are now perceived as being different. But the price of emphasizing this difference is the loss of the rest of the spectrum. Similarly, relationships relevant to both sexes have been obscured by the limitation of research to the difference between them."

Maccoby and Jacklin's work triggered other in-depth analyses of the existence or lack thereof of sex differences in numerous areas. In general, conclusions reflected skepticism about the presence of sex differences. In the 1980s, this area of research took another step forward by moving from an impressionistic normative reviewing process to a more formal, quantitative technique for synthesizing research: meta-analysis. Meta-analysis provides a common metric with which studies can be directly compared and the magnitude of sex differences can be represented. Moreover, meta-analysis looks at the consistency of findings across studies and tries to identify variables (such as measurement strategies, the historical moment when the study was conducted, and sample characteristics) that explain inconsistencies and even contradictions across studies.

Researcher and psychologist Jacquelyn James in "What Are the Social Issues Involved in Focusing on *Difference* in the Study of Gender?" *Journal of Social Issues* (Summer 1997), outlines five critical issues to consider when reviewing the status of the difference model:

1. *Very Small Differences Can Be Statistically Significant.* Because of the social weight of scientific evidence, even misrepresented and statistically weak differences get exaggerated by public accounts and therefore misused.
2. *False Universalism.* Interpretations of group differences often presume within-group similarity. In fact, other individual differences (e.g., social power) may explain differences better than sex.
3. *The "Tyranny of Averages."* Sex differences are usually based on group averages, interpreted as if they represent absolutes. Within-group variability or the overlap between distributions of males and females is not examined.
4. *The Revelations of Within-Group Differences.* Careful examination of within-group variation can be very effective in challenging gender stereotypes and examining the conditions under which differences do and do not occur. Furthermore, methodological practices may skew the meaning of sex differences (e.g., measurement bias).
5. *Some Differences Are Diminishing Over Time.* Weakening differences over time suggest that sociohistorical change is relevant to the "why" of difference.

Has the difference model outlived its purpose? In the following selections, Janet Hyde, using results of several meta-analyses, documents that women and men are quite similar in a number of psychological domains. Only for the domains of motor performance and physical aggression, behaviors that depend largely on muscle mass and bone size, and for sexuality (at least masturbation and attitudes accepting of casual sex) have moderate to large sex differences been found. She highlights the importance of considering social context when examining gender-related behaviors and concludes that the overinflation of sex differences is costly for girls and boys. In contrast, Kingsley Browne focuses on precisely the attributes for which Hyde claims women and men are the most similar. He claims that these domains have a biological basis and lead to inevitable differences between women and men. He argues that research on these differences can "assist us in an understanding of existing patterns as well as developing designs for change."

YES ⤶

Janet Shibley Hyde

The Gender Similarities Hypothesis

The mass media and the general public are captivated by findings of gender differences. John Gray's (1992) *Men Are From Mars, Women Are From Venus*, which argued for enormous psychological differences between women and men, has sold over 30 million copies and been translated into 40 languages. Deborah Tannen's *You Just Don't Understand: Women and Men in Conversation* argued for the *different cultures hypothesis*: that men's and women's patterns of speaking are so fundamentally different that men and women essentially belong to different linguistic communities or cultures. That book was on the *New York Times* bestseller list for nearly four years and has been translated into 24 languages. Both of these works, and dozens of others like them, have argued for the *differences hypothesis*: that males and females are, psychologically, vastly different. Here, I advance a very different view—the *gender similarities hypothesis*.

The Hypothesis

The gender similarities hypothesis holds that males and females are similar on most, but not all, psychological variables. That is, men and women, as well as boys and girls, are more alike than they are different. In terms of effect sizes, the gender similarities hypothesis states that most psychological gender differences are in the close-to-zero ($d \le 0.10$) or small ($0.11 < d < 0.35$) range, a few are in the moderate range ($0.36 < d < 0.65$), and very few are large ($d = 0.66$–1.00) or very large ($d > 1.00$).

Although the fascination with psychological gender differences has been present from the dawn of formalized psychology around 1879, a few early researchers highlighted gender similarities. Thorndike (1914), for example, believed that psychological gender differences were too small, compared with within-gender variation, to be important. Leta Stetter Hollingworth (1918) reviewed available research on gender differences in mental traits and found little evidence of gender differences. Another important reviewer of gender research in the early 1900s, Helen Thompson Woolley, lamented the gap between the data and scientists' views on the question:

> The general discussions of the psychology of sex, whether by psychologists or by sociologists show such a wide diversity of points of view

From *American Psychologist*, September 2005, pp. 581–582, 586–590. Copyright © 2005 by American Psychological Association. Reprinted by permission.

68

that one feels that the truest thing to be said at present is that scientific evidence plays very little part in producing convictions.

The Role of Meta-Analysis in Assessing Psychological Gender Differences

Reviews of research on psychological gender differences began with Woolley's (1914) and Hollingworth's and extended through Maccoby and Jacklin's watershed book *The Psychology of Sex Differences*, in which they reviewed more than 2,000 studies of gender differences in a wide variety of domains, including abilities, personality, social behavior, and memory. Maccoby and Jacklin dismissed as unfounded many popular beliefs in psychological gender differences, including beliefs that girls are more "social" than boys; that girls are more suggestible; that girls have lower self-esteem; that girls are better at rote learning and simple tasks, whereas boys are better at higher level cognitive processing; and that girls lack achievement motivation. Maccoby and Jacklin concluded that gender differences were well established in only four areas: verbal ability, visual-spatial ability, mathematical ability, and aggression. Overall, then, they found much evidence for gender similarities. Secondary reports of their findings in textbooks and other sources, however, focused almost exclusively on their conclusions about gender differences.

Shortly after this important work appeared, the statistical method of meta-analysis was developed. This method revolutionized the study of psychological gender differences. Meta-analyses quickly appeared on issues such as gender differences in influenceability, and aggression.

Meta-analysis is a statistical method for aggregating research findings across many studies of the same question (Hedges & Becker, 1986). It is ideal for synthesizing research on gender differences, an area in which often dozens or even hundreds of studies of a particular question have been conducted.

Crucial to meta-analysis is the concept of effect size, which measures the magnitude of an effect—in this case, the magnitude of gender difference. In gender meta-analyses, the measure of effect size typically is d (Cohen, 1988):

$$d = \frac{M_M - M_F}{S_W},$$

where M_M is the mean score for males, M_F is the mean score for females, and S_W is the average within-sex standard deviation. That is, d measures how far apart the male and female means are in standardized units. In gender meta-analysis, the effect sizes computed from all individual studies are averaged to obtain an overall effect size reflecting the magnitude of gender differences across all studies. In the present article, I follow the convention that negative values of d mean that females scored higher on a dimension, and positive values of d indicate that males scored higher.

Gender meta-analyses generally proceed in four steps: (a) The researcher locates all studies on the topic being reviewed, typically using databases such as

PsycINFO and carefully chosen search terms. (b) Statistics are extracted from each report, and an effect size is computed for each study. (c) A weighted average of the effect sizes is computed (weighting by sample size) to obtain an overall assessment of the direction and magnitude of the gender difference when all studies are combined. (d) Homogeneity analyses are conducted to determine whether the group of effect sizes is relatively homogeneous. If it is not, then the studies can be partitioned into theoretically meaningful groups to determine whether the effect size is larger for some types of studies and smaller for other types. The researcher could ask, for example, whether gender differences are larger for measures of physical aggression compared with measures of verbal aggression.

The Evidence

To evaluate the gender similarities hypothesis, I collected the major meta-analyses that have been conducted on psychological gender differences. They are . . . grouped roughly into six categories: those that assessed cognitive variables, such as abilities; those that assessed verbal or nonverbal communication; those that assessed social or personality variables, such as aggression or leadership; those that assessed measures of psychological well-being, such as self-esteem; those that assessed motor behaviors, such as throwing distance; and those that assessed miscellaneous constructs, such as moral reasoning. I began with meta-analyses reviewed previously. I updated these lists with more recent meta-analyses and, where possible, replaced older meta-analyses with more up-to-date meta-analyses that used larger samples and better statistical methods.

Inspection of the effect sizes . . . reveals strong evidence for the gender similarities hypothesis. . . . Of the 128 effect sizes, . . . 4 were unclassifiable because the meta-analysis provided such a wide range for the estimate. The remaining 124 effect sizes were classified into the categories noted earlier: close-to-zero ($d \leq 0.10$), small ($0.11 < d < 0.35$), moderate ($0.36 < d < 0.65$), large ($d = 0.66 - 1.00$), or very large (> 1.00). The striking result is that 30% of the effect sizes are in the close-to-zero range, and an additional 48% are in the small range. That is, 78% of gender differences are small or close to zero. This result is similar to [another analysis that] found that 60% of effect sizes for gender differences were in the small or close-to-zero range.

The small magnitude of these effects is even more striking given that most of the meta-analyses addressed the classic gender differences questions—that is, areas in which gender differences were reputed to be reliable, such as mathematics performance, verbal ability, and aggressive behavior. For example, . . . gender differences in most aspects of communication are small. [It] has [been] argued that males and females speak in a different moral "voice," yet meta-analyses show that gender differences in moral reasoning and moral orientation are small.

The Exceptions

As noted earlier, the gender similarities hypothesis does not assert that males and females are similar in absolutely every domain. The exceptions—areas in which gender differences are moderate or large in magnitude—should be recognized.

The largest gender differences . . . are in the domain of motor performance, particularly for measures such as throwing velocity ($d = 2.18$) and throwing distance ($d = 1.98$). These differences are particularly large after puberty, when the gender gap in muscle mass and bone size widens.

A second area in which large gender differences are found is some—but not all—measures of sexuality. Gender differences are strikingly large for incidences of masturbation and for attitudes about sex in a casual, uncommitted relationship. In contrast, the gender difference in reported sexual satisfaction is close to zero.

Across several meta-analyses, aggression has repeatedly shown gender differences that are moderate in magnitude. The gender difference in physical aggression is particularly reliable and is larger than the gender difference in verbal aggression. Much publicity has been given to gender differences in relational aggression, with girls scoring higher. According to [an earlier] meta-analysis, indirect or relational aggression showed an effect size for gender differences of -0.45 when measured by direct observation, but it was only -0.19 for peer ratings, -0.02 for self-reports, and -0.13 for teacher reports. Therefore, the evidence is ambiguous regarding the magnitude of the gender difference in relational aggression. . . .

Developmental Trends

Not all meta-analyses have examined developmental trends and, given the preponderance of psychological research on college students, developmental analysis is not always possible. However, meta-analysis can be powerful for identifying age trends in the magnitude of gender differences. Here, I consider a few key examples of meta-analyses that have taken this developmental approach.

At [one] time, . . . it was believed that gender differences in mathematics performance were small or nonexistent in childhood and that the male advantage appeared beginning around the time of puberty. It was also believed that males were better at high-level mathematical problems that required complex processing, whereas females were better at low-level mathematics that required only simple computation. Hyde and colleagues addressed both hypotheses in [an earlier] meta-analysis. They found a small gender difference favoring girls in computation in elementary school and middle school and no gender difference in computation in the high school years. There was no gender difference in complex problem solving in elementary school or middle school, but a small gender difference favoring males emerged in the high school years ($d = 0.29$). Age differences in the magnitude of the gender effect were significant for both computation and problem solving.

[In] a developmental approach in [a] meta-analysis of studies of gender differences in self-esteem, on the basis of the assertion of prominent authors such as Mary Pipher that girls' self-esteem takes a nosedive at the beginning of adolescence, [it was] found that the magnitude of the gender difference did grow larger from childhood to adolescence: In childhood (ages 7–10), $d = 0.16$; for early adolescence (ages 11–14), $d = 0.23$; and for the high school years (ages 15–18), $d = 0.33$. However, the gender difference did not suddenly become large in early adolescence, and even in high school, the difference was still not large. Moreover, the gender difference was smaller in older samples. . . .

[Another] analysis of age trends in computer self-efficacy is revealing. In grammar school samples, $d = 0.09$, whereas in high school samples, $d = 0.66$. This dramatic trend leads to questions about what forces are at work transforming girls from feeling as effective with computers as boys do to showing a large difference in self-efficacy by high school.

These examples illustrate the extent to which the magnitude of gender differences can fluctuate with age. Gender differences grow larger or smaller at different times in the life span, and meta-analysis is a powerful tool for detecting these trends. Moreover, the fluctuating magnitude of gender differences at different ages argues against the differences model and notions that gender differences are large and stable.

The Importance of Context

Gender researchers have emphasized the importance of context in creating, erasing, or even reversing psychological gender differences. Context may exert influence at numerous levels, including the written instructions given for an exam, dyadic interactions between participants or between a participant and an experimenter, or the sociocultural level.

[A]n important experiment, . . . demonstrated the importance of gender roles and social context in creating or erasing the purportedly robust gender difference in aggression. [The researchers] used the technique of deindividuation to produce a situation that removed the influence of gender roles. *Deindividuation* refers to a state in which the person has lost his or her individual identity; that is, the person has become anonymous. Under such conditions, people should feel no obligation to conform to social norms such as gender roles. Half of the participants, who were college students, were assigned to an individuated condition by having them sit close to the experimenter, identify themselves by name, wear large name tags, and answer personal questions. Participants in the deindividuation condition sat far from the experimenter, wore no name tags, and were simply told to wait. All participants were also told that the experiment required information from only half of the participants, whose behavior would be monitored, and that the other half would remain anonymous. Participants then played an interactive video game in which they first defended and then attacked by dropping bombs. The number of bombs dropped was the measure of aggressive behavior.

The results indicated that in the individuated condition, men dropped significantly more bombs than women did. In the deindividuated condition, however, there were no significant gender differences, and, in fact, women dropped somewhat more bombs than men. In short, the significant gender difference in aggression disappeared when gender norms were removed.

[W]ork on stereotype threat has produced similar evidence in the cognitive domain. Although the original experiments concerned African Americans and the stereotype that they are intellectually inferior, the theory was quickly applied to gender and stereotypes that girls and women are bad at math. In one experiment, male and female college students with equivalent math backgrounds were tested. In one condition, participants were told that the math test had shown gender difference in the past, and in the other condition, they were told that the test had been shown to be gender fair—that men and women had performed equally on it. In the condition in which participants had been told that the math test was gender fair, there were no gender differences in performance on the test. In the condition in which participants expected gender differences, women underperformed compared with men. This simple manipulation of context was capable of creating or erasing gender differences in math performance.

Meta-analysts have addressed the importance of context for gender differences. [O]ne of the earliest demonstrations of context effects meta-analyzed studies of gender differences in helping behavior, basing the analysis in social-role theory. [It was] argued that certain kinds of helping are part of the male role: helping that is heroic or chivalrous. Other kinds of helping are part of the female role: helping that is nurturant and caring, such as caring for children. Heroic helping involves danger to the self, and both heroic and chivalrous helping are facilitated when onlookers are present. Women's nurturant helping more often occurs in private, with no onlookers. Averaged over all studies, men helped more ($d = 0.34$). However, when studies were separated into those in which onlookers were present and participants were aware of it, $d = 0.74$. When no onlookers were present, $d = -0.02$. Moreover, the magnitude of the gender difference was highly correlated with the degree of danger in the helping situation; gender differences were largest favoring males in situations with the most danger. In short, the gender difference in helping behavior can be large, favoring males, or close to zero, depending on the social context in which the behavior is measured. Moreover, the pattern of gender differences is consistent with social-role theory.

[S]imilar context effects [were found in a] meta-analysis of gender differences in conversational interruption. At the time of their meta-analysis, it was widely believed that men interrupted women considerably more than the reverse. Averaged over all studies, however, [only] a small effect [was found]. The effect size for intrusive interruptions (excluding back-channel interruptions) was larger: 0.33. It is important to note that the magnitude of the gender difference varied greatly depending on the social context in which interruptions were studied. When dyads were observed, $d = 0.06$, but with larger groups of three or more, $d = 0.26$. When participants were strangers, $d = 0.17$, but when they were friends, $d = -0.14$. Here, again, it is clear that gender differences can be created, erased, or reversed, depending on the context.

[A] moderate gender difference in smiling ($d = -0.41$), with girls and women smiling more [has been reported]. Again, the magnitude of the gender difference was highly dependent on the context. If participants had a clear awareness that they were being observed, the gender difference was larger ($d = -0.46$) than it was if they were not aware of being observed ($d = -0.19$). The magnitude of the gender difference also depended on culture and age.

[Others have] also found marked context effects in their gender meta-analyses. The conclusion is clear: The magnitude and even the direction of gender differences depends on the context. These findings provide strong evidence against the differences model and its notions that psychological gender differences are large and stable.

Costs of Inflated Claims of Gender Differences

The question of the magnitude of psychological gender differences is more than just an academic concern. There are serious costs of overinflated claims of gender differences. These costs occur in many areas, including work, parenting, and relationships.

[The] argument that women speak in a different moral "voice" than men is a well-known example of the differences model. Women, according to Gilligan, speak in a moral voice of caring, whereas men speak in a voice of justice. Despite the fact that meta-analyses disconfirm her arguments for large gender differences, Gilligan's ideas have permeated American culture. One consequence of this overinflated claim of gender differences is that it reifies the stereotype of women as caring and nurturant and men as lacking in nurturance. One cost to men is that they may believe that they cannot be nurturant, even in their role as father. For women, the cost in the workplace can be enormous. Women who violate the stereotype of being nurturant and nice can be penalized in hiring and evaluations. [For example,] female job applicants who displayed agentic qualities received considerably lower hireability ratings than agentic male applicants ($d = 0.92$) for a managerial job that had been "feminized" to require not only technical skills and the ability to work under pressure but also the ability to be helpful and sensitive to the needs of others. The researchers concluded that women must present themselves as competent and agentic to be hired, but they may then be viewed as interpersonally deficient and uncaring and receive biased work evaluations because of their violation of the female nurturance stereotype.

A second example of the costs of unwarranted validation of the stereotype of women as caring nurturers comes from [a] meta-analysis of studies of gender and the evaluation of leaders. Overall, women leaders were evaluated as positively as men leaders ($d = 0.05$). However, women leaders portrayed as uncaring autocrats were at a more substantial disadvantage than were men leaders portrayed similarly ($d = 0.30$). Women who violated the caring stereotype paid for it in their evaluations. The persistence of the stereotype of women as nurturers leads to serious costs for women who violate this stereotype in the workplace.

The costs of overinflated claims of gender differences hit children as well. According to stereotypes, boys are better at math than girls are. This stereotype is proclaimed in mass media headlines. Meta-analyses, however, indicate a pattern of gender similarities for math performance. . . . One cost to children is that mathematically talented girls may be overlooked by parents and teachers because these adults do not expect to find mathematical talent among girls. Parents have lower expectations for their daughters' math success than for their sons' despite the fact that girls earn better grades in math than boys do. Research has shown repeatedly that parents' expectations for their children's mathematics success relate strongly to outcomes such as the child's mathematics self-confidence and performance, with support for a model in which parents' expectations influence children. In short, girls may find their confidence in their ability to succeed in challenging math courses or in a mathematically oriented career undermined by parents' and teachers' beliefs that girls are weak in math ability.

In the realm of intimate heterosexual relationships, women and men are told that they are as different as if they came from different planets and that they communicate in dramatically different ways. When relationship conflicts occur, good communication is essential to resolving the conflict. If, however, women and men believe what they have been told—that it is almost impossible for them to communicate with each other—they may simply give up on trying to resolve the conflict through better communication. Therapists will need to dispel erroneous beliefs in massive, unbridgeable gender differences.

Inflated claims about psychological gender differences can hurt boys as well. A large gender gap in self-esteem beginning in adolescence has been touted in popular sources. Girls' self-esteem is purported to take a nosedive at the beginning of adolescence, with the implication that boys' self-esteem does not. Yet meta-analytic estimates of the magnitude of the gender difference have all been small or close to zero. . . . In short, self-esteem is roughly as much a problem for adolescent boys as it is for adolescent girls. The popular media's focus on girls as the ones with self-esteem problems may carry a huge cost in leading parents, teachers, and other professionals to overlook boys' self-esteem problems, so that boys do not receive the interventions they need.

As several of these examples indicate, the gender similarities hypothesis carries strong implications for practitioners. The scientific evidence does not support the belief that men and women have inherent difficulties in communicating across gender. Neither does the evidence support the belief that adolescent girls are the only ones with self-esteem problems. Therapists who base their practice in the differences model should reconsider their approach on the basis of the best scientific evidence.

Conclusion

The gender similarities hypothesis stands in stark contrast to the differences model, which holds that men and women, and boys and girls, are vastly different psychologically. The gender similarities hypothesis states, instead, that males and females are alike on most—but not all—psychological variables. Extensive evidence from meta-analyses of research on gender differences supports the gender similarities hypothesis. A few notable exceptions are some motor behaviors (e.g., throwing distance) and some aspects of sexuality, which show large gender differences. Aggression shows a gender difference that is moderate in magnitude.

It is time to consider the costs of overinflated claims of gender differences. Arguably, they cause harm in numerous realms, including women's opportunities in the workplace, couple conflict and communication, and analyses of self-esteem problems among adolescents. Most important, these claims are not consistent with the scientific data.

 **NO**

Biology at Work: Rethinking Sexual Equality

To provide biological explanations is, some say, to confuse the *is* and the *ought*, apparently ignoring the fact that the primary function of science is to explain the natural world, not to justify or defend it. If it is a fallacy to argue that the biological roots of a phenomenon demonstrate its desirability—as it surely is—then it is equally fallacious to infer that an argument for the biological roots of a phenomenon is implicitly an argument that the phenomenon is good. Put another way, it is more commonly the opponents than proponents of biological explanations who draw inferences of value from assertions of fact.

The discovery that all manner of social ills, from rape to child abuse, derive in part from biological predispositions does not justify these behaviors, especially since our desire to prevent those ills probably stems from the same kind of predispositions. Nor does the biological argument imply that attempts to reduce the prevalence of such behaviors are necessarily doomed, for a central finding of evolutionary psychology is the flexibility (albeit along predictable lines) of human behavioral responses. Nonetheless, an understanding of the deep origins of the phenomena of interest may assist us in an understanding of existing patterns as well as in developing designs for change. . . .

Aggressiveness, Dominance Assertion, Competitiveness, Achievement Motivation, and Status Seeking

The sexes are consistently found to differ in a constellation of related traits: aggressiveness, dominance assertion, competitiveness, achievement motivation, and status seeking. Each of these terms has its own somewhat different definition, but the traits are highly correlated and often overlapping. Although "aggressiveness" may be defined narrowly to mean the infliction of harm on another, a broader definition of the term encompasses most of the traits listed above. Thus, when we speak of an "aggressive soccer player" or "aggressive businessman," we are not necessarily describing a person who wishes to inflict harm on another, although we may be describing a willingness to step on competitors—literally in the former case and figuratively in the latter—in pursuit of his goals. . . .

Competitiveness

Competition seems to come more easily to males than females and to be a more unalloyed positive experience for males. Competition significantly increases the intrinsic motivation of men, while it does not do so for women. A perception that an academic program is competitive may result in poorer performance by women but better performance by men. Women also report higher levels of stress attendant to competition.

Sex differences in competition appear in early childhood. Even preschool boys engage in more competitive activities than girls, activities that seem to elevate levels of adrenaline and noradrenaline. A study of second through twelfth graders found that girls reported more-positive attitudes toward cooperation in school and less-positive attitudes toward competition in all grades than did boys.

Sex differences in attitudes toward competition are reflected in children's play styles, as demonstrated in a well-known study of play by Janet Lever. Boys were much more likely to engage in "game" (competitive interactions with explicit goals), while girls engaged in more "play" (behaviors with no explicit goal and no winners). Even when both sexes played games, the games were of different types. Games like hopscotch and jump-rope are "turn-taking" games, in which any competition that exists is indirect. When boys competed, they were more likely to compete head-to-head in zero-sum competition. Because boys cared more about being declared the winner, their games were usually structured so that there would be a clear and definite outcome.

The boys in Lever's study seemed to display a more instrumental approach to competition. Exhibiting a difference that may have later workplace implications, boys were much better than girls at competing against friends and cooperating with teammates whom they did not like. Anecdotal accounts of childhood play suggest that when boys pick teams for games, they pick the people they believe to be the best players irrespective of whether they like them, while girls are more likely to choose their friends irrespective of skill. Although Lever observed that among boys there were repeated disputes over the rules, no games were terminated as a consequence of these disputes. In fact, she concluded, boys enjoyed the rule disputes as much as the game. In contrast, quarrels among girls over application of rules were likely to terminate the game, perhaps anticipating what primatologist Sarah Hrdy has referred to as "the well-documented problem that unrelated women have working together over a long period of time."

Competition is simply a greater part of male life, even among children. If one boy tells another boy that he can spit ten feet, the response is likely to be either "I bet you can't" or "I can spit farther"; if a girl tells another girl that she can spit ten feet, the response is likely to be either "So what?" or "That's gross." Psychologist Eleanor Maccoby observes that "even when with a good friend, boys take pleasure in competing to see who can do a task best or quickest, who can lift the heaviest weight, who can run faster or farther." A study of free-play activities in fourth and sixth graders found that boys were engaged in direct competition with other boys 50 percent of the time, while among girls direct competition occurred only 1 percent of the time.

This is not to say that girls do not compete, but they often employ different means and pursue different ends. Sarah Hrdy attributes the belief that females are less competitive than males to the failure of scientists to examine "women competing with one another in the spheres that really matter to them." . . .

Dominance Assertion

Dominance assertion is, in a sense, a form of competition. Dominance behaviors are those intended to achieve or maintain a position of high relative status—to obtain power, influence, prerogatives, or resources. When children get together, even in the preschool years, dominance hierarchies emerge spontaneously: some children are more influential and less subject to aggression by others. Boys engage in a significantly greater amount of dominance-related play than girls, such as playing with weapons and engaging in rough-and-tumble play. In mixed-sex groups in nursery schools, boys end up disproportionately at the top of the hierarchy within the classroom. Even among preschoolers, the expression by girls of their ideas seems to be significantly curtailed in the presence of boys.

Although boys generally assume the dominant positions in mixed-sex hierarchies, boys and girls mostly establish separate hierarchies, a division that occurs in large part because boys and girls spend most of their time with others of the same sex. One of the most robust sex effects of early childhood is the powerful tendency that young children exhibit toward sex segregation. Up until about age two, children show little preference regarding the sex of playmates, but during the third year, same-sex preference begin to emerge in girls, followed perhaps a year later by similar preference among boys. Although girls show an earlier same-sex preference, when the preference emerges in boys, it is stronger. After about age five, boys take a much more active role in policing the boundaries of sex-appropriate behavior. These findings have been replicated in a wide range of cultures.

After the preference for same-sex playmates develops, children continue to play with members of the opposite sex, especially if required to by adults or by the dearth of same-sex playmates. When children find themselves surrounded by large numbers of children of their own age, however, the impulse to self-segregation is strong. As children move into later stages of childhood, an increasingly large portion of their time is spent with same-sex others, despite pressures by teachers to require greater sexual integration. Eleanor Maccoby has suggested that part of the aversion that girls have to boys is that girls find it difficult to influence the boys. Jacklin and Maccoby found, for example, that among unfamiliar pairs for thirty-three-month-old children, boys were less likely to pay attention to instructions from girls than girls were to those from boys.

In their same-sex groups, both boys and girls establish hierarchies, but the hierarchies differ in strength and in the traits that lead to dominance. Boys' dominance hierarchies tend to be more stable and well defined than those of girls. That is, the boys largely agree about who is on top, and these rankings tend to persist over time. Among girls, on the other hand, hierarchies are more fluid and there is considerably less agreement concerning the relative rankings of individual girls. Hierarchies among boys tend to be established quickly, often during their first interaction. Among boys, the critical determinant is "toughness," both physical strength and unwillingness to back down. Among girls, however, status tends to be achieved through physical attractiveness and friendship with popular girls.

Important sex differences in dominance behaviors and aggressiveness are obscured by looking only at frequencies, since the sexes also differ in the types and causes of these behaviors. Psychologists Martin Daly and Margo Wilson, for example, have found a consistent worldwide pattern: homicides tend to be committed by and against unmarried young males. Many are what Daly and Wilson label "trivial altercations," either "escalated showing-off disputes" or "disputes arising from retaliation for previous verbal or physical abuse." Although to an outside observer the precipitating event may seem trivial, many of these disputes are "affairs of honor," in which the precipitating event "often takes the form of disparagement of the challenged party's 'manhood': his nerve, strength or savvy, or the virtue of his wife, girlfriend, or female relatives." Failure to respond to challenges to reputation or signs of disrespect leads to loss of face and of relative status.

The foregoing does not mean that women are not interested in achieving status. However, the route to female status, across history, has been quite different for men and women. Men have generally achieved status through dominance over other men; women have achieved status not primarily by achieving dominance over other women (or over men) but rather through their association with high-status men.

Achievement Motivation and Response to Failure

Although in many respects the sexes are similar in their motivation to achieve, some sex differences are consistently reported, many of which are associated with attitudes toward failure. For example, when given a choice of tasks to perform, males are more likely to select the more difficult task, and females the easier one. Females tend also to be more adversely affected by failure and more likely to give up than males, and they are somewhat more likely to attribute failure to lack of ability rather than lack of effort. Males, on the other hand, are more likely than females to improve in performance after failure.

Confidence is an important contributor to achievement motivation, and competition seems to exaggerate sex differences in confidence. Anticipation of competition results in lower confidence levels in females than males. Moreover, females' performance predictions tend to be relatively unstable and subject to change with single encounters, while males are less likely to allow one failure to diminish their performance expectations.

Females seem to have a greater need than males for feedback about performance in order to achieve or maintain high levels of self-confidence in their performance capabilities. Such feedback seems to be more central to women's self-esteem than is the case for men, who exhibit a weaker relationship between positive feedback and global self-esteem. [T]his need may contribute to the dissatisfaction that women who study science often feel in moving from high school to college, when they leave an environment in which they are lavished with attention and praise and enter an environment in which they join the relatively anonymous masses.

Competition and Dominance in Mixed-Sex Groups

Studies measuring only attributes of individuals often miss important dynamics of social interactions. Males and females sometimes exhibit different competitive and dominance behaviors in same-sex and mixed-sex groups. Within same-sex groups, for example, males engage in more dominance behaviors than females do. This tendency is moderated to some extent in mixed-sex groups, with male dominance behaviors tending to abate somewhat and female dominance behaviors to increase; still, males in mixed-sex groups continue to act more dominantly. Not surprisingly, in same-sex pairings, a high-dominance individual will assume a leadership role over a low-dominance individual. However, when a high-dominance woman is paired with a low-dominance man, the low-dominance man tends to assume the leadership role. It is not that he asserted dominance over the woman to become the leader, but rather that the dominant woman selected him to be the leader. Perhaps this represents the same phenomenon as the many examples of very able women pushing their somewhat less able husbands to be more successful than the husbands would have been on their own.

Mixed-sex competition seems to be a quite different experience for its participants from same-sex competition. A study comparing responses of competitors to male, female, and machine opponents in a video game found some interesting patterns. First, it appears that men do not like to compete against women. Men who were measured as being low in competitiveness demonstrated low physiological arousal when their competitor was a woman, apparently because they were less engaged in the competition than when their opponent was either a machine or a man. This result is consistent with suggestions that some men may reduce effort in situations in which they are concerned about being outperformed by women. High-competitive men, on the other hand, demonstrated the highest level of engagement and the highest level of negative affect at the conclusion of the competition when their opponent was a woman. Why should men feel discomfort when competing against a woman? One potential reason is that men may feel they will be criticized for playing to win against a woman. Another reason is that men may perceive these encounters as "no-win" situations for them because they do not get the same credit for winning if their opponent is "just a woman," but losing to a woman is worse than losing to a man.

The literature dealing with female performance in mixed-sex competition is not entirely consistent, but psychologist Carol Weisfeld summarizes the literature as revealing that "it is almost always the case that some females will depress their performance levels, resulting in victory for males." This female suppression of effort does not appear to be consciously motivated. Females who perform at their highest level against males tend to be those characterized by masculine or androgynous temperaments. For them, competition against males appears to be a positive experience, perhaps for precisely the opposite reason that competitive males do not like the same competition: if she wins, the credit for beating a male is high, but if she loses, there is no shame in losing to a male.

Head-to-head competition between the sexes for status in hierarchies is a relatively recent phenomenon. Humans, like other primates, may not be "wired" in such a way as to evoke competitive responses from members of the opposite sex. Thus, perhaps it should not be surprising that neither males nor females view competition with the opposite sex as equivalent to same-sex competition.

Risk Taking

As with the other traits, . . . the sexes differ in risk taking from childhood. One of the best measures of physical risk taking in children is the incidence of accidental death and injury. In most industrialized countries, including the United States, accidents are the leading cause of death for children older than one year. A World Health organization study of accidental-death rates in fifty countries found a substantially higher rate for boys in all countries, with a ratio of male to female deaths of 1.9:1 in Europe and 1.7:1 in non-European countries. Notwithstanding greater equality and socially sanctioned androgyny, the male/female accidental-death ratio actually increased in the United States from 1960 to 1979.

Greater risk taking among boys is a robust finding. Boys are exposed to greater risks not only because they are more likely to engage in risky behaviors but also because when engaging in the same activity as girls, they are more likely to perform it in a risky manner. Boys are substantially more likely to approach a hazardous item than girls, and they differ in how they approach them, with girls tending to look and point and boys tending to touch and retrieve them.

Several factors appear to account for the greater inclination of boys to engage in risky activity. Boys tend to have both a higher activity level and poorer impulse control, both traits that are associated with injury rates. Three factors are correlated with self-reported risk taking in both boys and girls: attribution of injuries to bad luck, a belief that one is less vulnerable to injury than one's peers, and downplaying the degree of risk. Boys score higher than girls on all three of these traits.

Boys are less likely than girls to abstain from a risky activity simply because they have seen a peer injured while engaging in the same activity. The best predictor of girls' willingness to take a particular risk is their belief about the likelihood of getting hurt, while for boys it is the perceived severity of the injury. That is, girls tend to avoid risks if they think they might get hurt, while boys seem to be willing to take risks if they do not think they will get *too* hurt. It is possible, however, that positive attitudes about risk may result in part from risk taking, rather than causing it.

In adolescence and adulthood, sex differences in risk taking increase. Men are disproportionately involved in risky recreational activities such as car racing, sky diving, and hang gliding. Indeed, sex is the variable most predictive of the extent of participation in high-risk recreation. The driving style of men also shows a greater propensity toward risk. Men are disproportionately represented in risky employment, as well. Over 90 percent of all workplace deaths in the United States are males. A list of dangerous occupations is a list of disproportionately male occupations: fisherman, logger, airplane pilot, structural metal worker, coal miner, oil and gas extraction occupations, water transportation occupations, construction laborer, taxicab driver, roofer, and truck driver.

Men's greater propensity to risk their lives is demonstrated by a study of the recipients of awards granted by the Carnegie Hero Fund Commission. Of the 676 acts of heroism recognized from 1989 through 1995, 92 percent were performed by males. Moreover, over one-half of those rescued by women were known to the rescuer, while over two-thirds of those rescued by men were strangers. Although this is not a random sample of heroes, since one must be nominated for the award, it is likely that, if anything, the sex difference is understated because acts of heroism by women would tend to attract more attention than those by men.

Risk taking is statistically correlated with a number of other stereotypically male traits. People who rate high on achievement and dominance, for example, tend to be high risk takers. Risk taking and competitiveness may be related, since competition-prone individuals tend to be willing to take greater risks in pursuit of their competitive objective. High risk takers also fight more frequently, are more socially aggressive, take more dares, and participate in more rough sports and physical activities such as hunting, mountain climbing, and auto racing. In contrast, risk taking is negatively associated with a number of stereotypically feminine traits: affiliation, nurturance, succorance, deference, and abasement.

Psychologist Elizabeth Arch has suggested that the sex differences in achievement-orientation previously discussed may be explained in part by sex differences in risk taking. From an early age, females are more averse not just to physical risk but also to social risk, and they "tend to behave in a manner that ensures continued social inclusion." This aversion to risk may be partially responsible for women's disproportionately low representation in positions involving "career risk," which may adversely affect their prospects for advancement. This pattern suggests that what is sometimes labeled women's "fear of success" is in fact the more prosaic and easier-to-understand "fear of failure."

One's willingness to take risks depends in large part upon the relative values that one places on success and failure. A person whose appetite for success exceeds his aversion to failure will be inclined toward action; a person whose aversion to failure exceeds his appetite for success will be inclined not to act. A strong motive to achieve or to avoid failure may also bias the actor's subjective probability of outcome. That is, an achievement-oriented person may have a higher expectation of success than is objectively warranted, while a person with a high motivation to avoid failure may consistently underestimate the chance of success.

Nurturance, Empathy, and Interest in Children

Females in all known societies exhibit more nurturing behavior than males both inside and outside the family. Everywhere it is women who are the primary caretakers of the young, the sick, and the old. Even among young children, girls tend to exhibit more nurturing behavior, and throughout the adolescent years, girls have a greater preference than boys for more caring, personal values. Girls' interest in infants increases substantially at menarche.

Just as the description of greater male aggressiveness, dominance assertion, and risk taking does not mean that women lack these traits altogether, to say that women seem to be higher in nurturance and empathy does not mean that men lack these traits or that they are not capable of caretaking behavior. Men are certainly as capable as women of learning many of the routine behaviors of parenthood, such as changing diapers and making dinner. The important question, however, is whether the connection to the infant and attunement to its state is the same for men as for women. There is some evidence to suggest that women's nurturant responses have a stronger physiological underpinning than men's.

Sex differences in parental care are universal across cultures. While the level of paternal involvement varies considerably among societies, there is no society in which the level of direct paternal care approaches that of mothers. Among the Aka pygmies of Central Africa, fathers provide more direct care to their children than in any other society known to anthropologists. Nonetheless, Barry Hewlett found that males, on average, hold their infants for a total of 57 minutes per day, compared to 490 minutes for mothers. The greater female contribution to child care in contemporary Western society is, of course, well known. The disparity between male and female care is exaggerated after divorce, with noncustodial mothers being far more likely to maintain close contact with their children than noncustodial fathers.

Psychological studies generally confirm that women are more empathic than men, in the sense that they experience a "vicarious affective response to another's feelings." As psychologist Martin Hoffman observed in 1977, the most striking feature of the empathy findings in a whole host of studies "is the fact that in every case, regardless of the age of the subjects or the measures used, the females obtained higher scores than did the males." While some subsequent studies have found no sex difference, they tend to be studies measuring the ability to identify other people's feelings rather than measuring the subject's emotional reaction to those feelings. Personality studies also show a substantial correlation between nurturance and empathy.

The more social orientation of females is reflected in a consistently found sex difference in "object versus person" orientation. Females of all ages tend to be "person oriented," while males tend to be more "object oriented." As early as the first year of life, girls pay more attention to people, and boys pay more attention to inanimate objects. In a study of college students, male and female subjects were shown a series of pictures of human figures and mechanical objects in a stereoscope so that a picture of a human figure and a picture of a mechanical object were falling on the same part of the subject's visual field. The theory behind the experimental design is that when two stimuli are competing, subjects will pay attention to the stimulus that is more interesting to them. Males had a greater tendency to report seeing the objects, while females tended to report seeing the human figure.

Differences in orientation affect the way people perceive themselves. Women's self-identity and self-esteem tend to be centered around sensitivity to and relations with others, while men's self-concepts tend to be centered around task performance, skills, independence, and being "better" than others. In one study, 50 percent of the women but only 15 percent of the men agreed with the statement, "I'm happiest when I can succeed at something that will also make other people happy." As psychologist Carol Gilligan has argued, "Women not only define themselves in a context of human relationship but also judge themselves in terms of their ability to care." . . .

e⁄⊚∕ɔ

This chapter has revealed that males and females differ, on average, in a number of temperamental traits. Men tend toward competition, women toward cooperation. Men seek to achieve dominance over others, while women seek to cement social relations. Men tend to be object oriented, while women tend to be person oriented. . . . These are just statistical generalizations, but they hold true not just in our society but also cross-culturally.

POSTSCRIPT

Are Women and Men More Similar Than Different?

The issue of similarity and difference is one of degree and perspective. Although many meta-analyses inform us that most differences between women and men are statistically quite small, there are differences. What do we make of small differences, especially when the differences within women and within men typically exceed the average difference between the groups?

Should we move beyond the difference model for studying sex and gender? Debate has focused on social costs and benefits incurred as a consequence of sex difference findings, the statistical and social meaning of sex difference findings, the overemphasis on difference and underrepresentation of findings of similarity, and the questionable efficacy of sex difference findings in elucidating the phenomena of sex and gender.

Whether or not scholars believe that the continuation of sex difference research would be beneficial or at least benign, there is widespread agreement that this research alone is insufficient to explore the complexities of sex and gender as social categories and processes. Difference research has been primarily descriptive in nature, even though assumptions abound about the "natural" causes of sex differences. But knowing what differences exist between males and females does not help us to understand why, how, when, and for whom they exist. Furthermore, descriptive research alone does not help us understand the social meaning or significance of such differences. Some assert that sex comparisons obscure an understanding of gender as social relations and do little to help us understand the processes that expand or delimit the significance of the difference. Others argue that focusing on categorical differences helps us to avoid the hard work we have to do to improve our society. At the very least, scholars urge that we move beyond the individual as the focus of difference research to examine the way gender is produced in interpersonal and institutional contexts.

In moving beyond the difference model, what other approaches can be used to better understand sex and gender? One suggestion calls for an approach to studying gender that transcends the difference model. The focus is on the *process* of gender. Research should explore and document "gender coding," or how society is gendered (e.g., unequal expectations, opportunities, power), and how individuals (particularly those who are disenfranchised) cope with or negotiate such inequality (ranging from acceptance to resistance). It is important to view individuals as having some agency to affect their environment but also as being constrained or shaped by social situations and structures.

Another suggested innovation reflects an effort to move beyond essentialist overgeneralizations about "generic" men and women as distinct groups.

What does a categorical variable like sex actually mean? Many argue that such variables are too simplistic and therefore meaningless for representing the complexity among individuals, identities, and experiences that make up the group. Some state that assertions about sex differences are usually based on comparisons of white middle-class men and women and therefore have limited generalizability. Thus, some scholars advocate exploring within-sex diversity and attending to a host of contextual and structural variables that are inseparable from sex.

This kind of approach has led some to ask, Can we move to a point where difference no longer makes so much of a difference? How do we get there? One view differentiates between approaches that "turn the volume up" versus "turn the volume down" on categories of difference. Should we eliminate sex and gender dichotomies from the definition of normal and natural (turn the volume down) or proliferate categories of sex and gender into as many categories as needed to capture human complexity? Or is the focus on categories obscuring more specific and critical concepts such as privilege, conflict of interest, oppression, subordination, and even cooperation?

Suggested Readings

R. Barnett and C. Rivers, *Same Difference: How Gender Myths Are Hurting Our Relationships, Our Children, and Our Jobs* (Basic Books, 2004).

J. B. James, ed., "The Significance of Gender: Theory and Research About Difference" (Special Issue), *Journal of Social Issues* (Summer 1997).

M. M. Kimball, "Gender Similarities and Differences as Feminist Constructions," in R. K. Unger, ed., *Handbook of the Psychology of Women and Gender* (John Wiley & Sons, 2000).

C. Kitzinger, ed., "Should Psychologists Study Sex Differences?" *Feminism & Psychology* (1994).

B. Lott, "The Personal and Social Correlates of a Gender Difference Ideology," *Journal of Social Issues* (1997).

ISSUE 5

Is Culture the Primary Source of Sex Differences in Communication Styles?

YES: Louann Brizendine, from *The Female Brain* (Morgan Road Books, 2006)

NO: Brenda J. Allen, from *Difference Matters: Communicating Social Identity* (Waveland Press, 2004)

ISSUE SUMMARY

YES: Louann Brizendine argues that women's brains are hard-wired to communicate differently from men, suggesting on the jacket of her book "men will develop a serious case of brain envy."

NO: In contrast, Brenda J. Allen argues that socialization leads to forms of communication that are based on power and privilege.

Feminists view the study of communication and gender as very important because language is a powerful agent in the creation and maintenance of the gender system. In 1978, a major review of the scientific literature on gender and language by Cheris Kramer, Barrie Thorne, and Nancy Henley entitled "Perspectives on Language and Communication" (*Signs: Journal of Women in Culture and Society,* vol. 3, 1978) was published. This review summarized the three central research questions: (1) Do men and women use language in different ways? (2) In what ways does language—in structure, content, and daily usage—reflect and help constitute sexual inequality? (3) How can sexist language be changed?

Twenty-five years later, these three questions continue to dominate the field, but they have been reframed in more contemporary work because of an interest in *specificity* and *complexity*. Rather than studying "generic" groups of males and females, we must study particular men and women in particular settings and examine the interactions of gender and other identity categories and power relations.

In an issue of *Ladies Home Journal* (June 2005), an article on "Why Communication Counts" declared "Over and over again, communication problems are targeted as the number-one cause of marital strife. In many cases, couples think they're communicating, but the messages aren't getting through. Communication problems stem from differences in conversational styles between men and women." The article then proceeded to give readers (presumably mostly women) tips on how to communicate more effectively with their partner. The popular press is quick to agree with assertions such as these. In fact, most of these claims are based on the widely cited work on gender and language by author Deborah Tannen. Following up on her classic *You Just Don't Understand: Women and Men in Conversation* (1991), she has examined women and men's "conversational rituals" in the workplace in *Talking from 9 to 5: Women and Men at Work* (2001). In her writings she argues that "men and women live in different worlds . . . made of different words," and that how women and men converse determines who gets heard and who gets ahead in the workplace, via a verbal power game.

Tannen parallels male-female difference to cultural difference and regards males and females as different but equal. She explores how this cultural difference manifests itself in male-female (mis)communication. Her aim in her popular publications is to reassure women and men that they are not alone in experiencing miscommunication and communication problems because of sex-differentiated communication styles. Moreover, she says that she does not value one style over the other. If anything, she praises women's communication styles. Tannen urges that males and females need to respect each other's differences so that they understand why they misunderstand each other.

Similarly, Louann Brizendine in the selection that follows suggests that gendered communication is a result of biological differences in the brain. She agrees with Tannen that women and men live in different worlds, and these worlds differ beginning at conception.

Critics claim that analyses such as Tannen's and Brizendine's universalize and generalize, thereby creating generic individuals. Questions of difference are misguided and counterproductive not only because they are invariably marked by a political agenda but also because sex comparisons locate gender in the individual rather than in social relations and processes. Responses to claims of sex difference in communication styles frequently involve blaming women for deficiencies or minimizing conflicts between men and women by reframing them as miscommunication for which we must develop tolerance. Sociocultural inequalities are not addressed.

What do we *know* about differences between males' and females' communication styles? In the following selections, Brizendine's analysis of brain differences leads to a conclusion supporting Tannen's claims. Regarding the question of sex differentiation in communication styles, she suggests, for example, that men use only 7,000 words a day compared to women's use of about 20,000. In contrast, Brenda Allen argues that gendered communication patterns are related to power and status differences.

YES ⤶   Louann Brizendine

The Female Brain

What Makes Us Women

More than 99 percent of male and female genetic coding is exactly the same. Out of the thirty thousand genes in the human genome, the less than one percent variation between the sexes is small. But that percentage difference influences every single cell in our bodies—from the nerves that register pleasure and pain to the neurons that transmit perception, thoughts, feelings, and emotions.

To the observing eye, the brains of females and males are not the same. Male brains are larger by about 9 percent, even after correcting for body size. In the nineteenth century, scientists took this to mean that women had less mental capacity than men. Women and men, however, have the same number of brain cells. The cells are just packed more densely in women—cinched corsetlike into a smaller skull.

For much of the twentieth century, most scientists assumed that women were essentially small men, neurologically and in every other sense except for their reproductive functions. That assumption has been at the heart of enduring misunderstandings about female psychology and physiology. When you look a little deeper into the brain differences, they reveal what makes women women and men men.

Until the 1990s, researchers paid little attention to female physiology, neuroanatomy, or psychology separate from that of men. . . .

The little research that was available, however, suggested that the brain differences, though subtle, were profound. . . .

What we've found is that the female brain is so deeply affected by hormones that their influence can be said to create a woman's reality. They can shape a woman's values and desires, and tell her, day to day, what's important. Their presence is felt at every stage of life, right from birth. Each hormone state—girlhood, the adolescent years, the dating years, motherhood, and menopause—acts as fertilizer for different neurological connections that are responsible for new thoughts, emotions, and interests. Because of the fluctuations that begin as early as three months old and last until after menopause, a woman's neurological reality is not as constant as a man's. His is like a mountain that is worn away imperceptibly over the millennia by glaciers, weather, and the deep tectonic movements of the earth. Here is more like the weather itself—constantly changing and hard to predict.

$\approx\textcircled{\otimes}\approx$

New brain science has rapidly transformed our view of basic neurological differences between men and women. . . .

As a result, scientists have documented an astonishing array of structural, chemical, genetic, hormonal, and functional brain differences between women and men. We've learned that men and women have different brain sensitivities to stress and conflict. They use different brain areas and circuits to solve problems, process language, [and] experience and store the same strong emotion. Women may remember the smallest details of their first dates, and their biggest fights, while their husbands barely remember that these things happened. Brain structure and chemistry have everything to do with why this is so.

The female and male brains process stimuli, hear, see, "sense," and gauge what others are feeling in different ways. Our distinct female and male brain operating systems are mostly compatible and adept, but they perform and accomplish the same goals and tasks using different circuits. . . .

Until eight weeks old, every fetal brain looks female—female is nature's default gender setting. . . . A huge testosterone surge beginning in the eighth week will turn this unisex brain male by killing off some cells in the communication centers and growing more cells in the sex and aggression centers. If the testosterone surge doesn't happen, the female brain continues to grow unperturbed. The fetal girl's brain cells sprout more connections in the communication centers and areas that process emotion. How does this fetal fork in the road affect us? For one thing, because of her larger communication center, this girl will grow up to be more talkative than her brother. Men use about seven thousand words per day. Women use about twenty thousand. For another, it defines our innate biological destiny, coloring the lens through which each of us views and engages the world. . . .

Baby girls are born interested in emotional expression. They take meaning about themselves from a look, a touch, every reaction from the people they come into contact with. From these cues they discover whether they are worthy, lovable, or annoying. But take away the sign-posts that an expressive face provides and you've taken away the female brain's main touchstone for reality. . . .

Don't Fight

So why is a girl born with such a highly tuned machine for reading faces, hearing emotional tones in voices, and responding to unspoken cues in others? Think about it. A machine like that is built for connection. That's the main job of the girl brain, and that's what it drives a female to do from birth. This is the result of millennia of genetic and evolutionary hardwiring that once had—and probably still has—real consequences for survival. If you can read faces and voices, you can tell what an infant needs. You can predict what a bigger, more aggressive male is going to do. And since you're smaller, you probably need to band with other females to fend off attacks from a ticked off caveman—or cavemen.

If you're a girl, you've been programmed to make sure you keep social harmony. This is a matter of life and death to the brain, even if it's not so important in the twenty-first century. . . .

Typical non-testosteronized, estrogen-ruled girls are very invested in preserving harmonious relationships. From their earliest days, they live most comfortably and happily in the realm of peaceful interpersonal connections. They prefer to avoid conflict because discord puts them at odds with their urge to stay connected, to gain approval and nurture. The twenty-four-month estrogen bath of girls' infantile puberty reinforces the impulse to make social bonds based on communication and compromise. . . .

It is the brain that sets up the speech differences—the genderlects—of small children, which Deborah Tannen has pointed out. She noted that in studies of the speech of two-to-five-year-olds, girls usually make collaborative proposals by starting their sentences with "let's"—as in "Let's play house." Girls, in fact, typically use language to get consensus, influencing others without telling them directly what to do. . . .

Boys know how to employ this affiliative speech style, too, but research shows they typically don't use it. Instead, they'll generally use language to command others, get things done, brag, threaten, ignore a partner's suggestion, and override each other's attempts to speak. . . .

The testosterone-formed boy brain simply doesn't look for social connection in the same way a girl brain does. In fact, disorders that inhibit people from picking up on social nuance—called autism spectrum disorders and Asperger's syndrome—are eight times more common in boys. Scientists now believe that the typical male brain, with only one dose of X chromosome (there are two X's in a girl), gets flooded with testosterone during development and somehow becomes more easily socially handicapped. Extra testosterone in people with these disorders may be killing off some of the brain's circuits for emotional and social sensitivity.

By age two and a half, infantile puberty ends, and a girl enters the calmer pastures of the juvenile pause. The estrogen stream coming from the ovaries has been temporarily stopped; how, we don't yet know. But we do know that the levels of estrogen and testosterone become very low during the childhood years in both boys and girls—although girls still have six to eight times more estrogen than boys. When women talk about "the girl they left behind," this is the stage they are usually referring to. This is the quiet period before the full-volume rock 'n' roll of puberty. It's the time when a girl is devoted to her best friend, when she doesn't usually enjoy playing with boys. Research shows that this is true for girls between the ages of two and six in every culture that's been studied. . . .

Many women find biological comfort in one another's company, and language is the glue that connects one female to another. No surprise, then, that some verbal areas of the brain are larger in women than in men and that women, on average, talk and listen a lot more than men. The numbers vary, but on average girls speak two to three times more words per day than boys. We know that young girls speak earlier and by the age of twenty months have double or triple the number of words in their vocabularies than do boys. Boys eventually catch up in their vocabulary but not in speed. Girls speak faster on average—250 words per minute versus 125 for typical males. Men haven't always appreciated that verbal edge. In Colonial America, women were put in the town stocks with wooden clips on their tongues or tortured by the "dunking stool," held underwater and almost drowned—punishments that were never imposed on men—for the crime of "talking too much." . . .

And why do girls go to the bathroom to talk? Why do they spend so much time on the phone with the door closed? They're trading secrets and gossiping to create connection and intimacy with their female peers. They're developing close-knit cliques with secret rules. In these new groups, talking, telling secrets, and gossiping, in fact, often become girls' favorite activities—their tools to navigate and ease the ups and downs and stresses of life. . . .

There is a biological reason for this behavior. Connecting through talking activates the pleasure centers in a girl's brain. Sharing secrets that have romantic and sexual implications activates those centers even more. We're not talking about a small amount of pleasure. This is huge. It's a major dopamine and oxytocin rush, which is the biggest, fattest neurological reward you can get outside of an orgasm. Dopamine is a neurochemical that stimulates the motivation and pleasure circuits in the brain. Estrogen at puberty increases dopamine and oxytocin production in girls. Oxytocin is a neurohormone that triggers and is triggered by intimacy. When estrogen is on the rise, a teen girl's brain is pushed to make even more oxytocin—and to get even more reinforcement for social bonding. At midcycle, during peak estrogen production, the girl's dopamine and oxytocin level is likely at its highest, too. Not only her verbal output is at its maximum but her urge for intimacy is also peaking. Intimacy releases more oxytocin, which reinforces the desire to connect, and connecting then brings a sense of pleasure and well-being. . . .

Why the Teen Girl Brain Freaks

Think about it. Your brain has been pretty stable. You've had a steady flow—or lack—of hormones for your entire life. One day you're having tea parties with Mommy, the next day you're calling her an asshole. And, as a teen girl, the last thing you want to do is create conflict. You used to feel like a nice girl, and now, out of nowhere, it's as though you can't rely on that personality anymore. Everything you thought you knew about yourself has suddenly come undone. It's a huge gash in a girl's self-esteem, but it's a pretty simple chemical reaction, even for an adult woman. It makes a difference if you know what's going on. . . .

Studies show that when a conflict or argument breaks out in a game, girls typically decide to stop playing to avoid any angry exchange, while boys generally continue to play intensely—jockeying for position, competing, and arguing hour after hour about who'll be the boss or who will get access to the coveted toy. If a woman is pushed over the edge by finding out that her husband is having an affair, or if her child is in danger, her anger will blast right through and she will go to the mat. Otherwise, she will avoid anger or confrontation the same way a man will avoid an emotion.

Girls and women may not always feel the initial intense blast of anger directly from the amygdale that men feel. . . . Women talk to others first when they are angry at a third person. But scientists speculate that though a woman is slower to act out of anger, once her faster verbal circuits get going, they can cause her to unleash a barrage of angry words that a man can't match. Typical men speak fewer words and have less verbal fluency than women, so they may be handicapped in angry exchanges with women. Men's brain circuits and bodies may readily revert to a physical expression of anger fueled by the frustration of not being able to match women's words.

Often when I see a couple who are not communicating well, the problem is that the man's brain circuits push him frequently and quickly to an angry, aggressive reaction, and the woman feels frightened and shuts down. Ancient wiring is telling her it's dangerous, but she anticipates that if she flees she'll be losing her provider and may have to fend for herself. If a couple remains locked in this Stone Age conflict, there is no chance for resolution. Helping my patients understand that the emotion circuits for anger and safety are differences in the male and female brains is often quite helpful.

Brenda J. Allen ➡ **NO**

Difference Matters: Communicating Social Identity

Communicating Social Identity

Our study of difference (and similarity!) centers on communication. I use the verb form, communicating, to represent the dynamic nature of processes that humans use to produce, interpret, and share meaning. Our study of communicating views these processes as constitutive of social reality. To see how communicating helps to create reality, we will explore various relationships between social identity and discourse. *Discourse* refers to "systems of texts and talk that range from public to private and from naturally occurring to mediated forms. . . ."

Scholars from disciplines such as sociology, psychology, communication, anthropology, and philosophy study identity as an individual and/or a collective aspect of being. As sociologists Judith Howard and Ramira Alamilla observe, identity is based not only on responses to the question "Who am I?" but also on responses to the question "Who am I in relation to others?" Our exploration of difference matters focuses on *social identity*, aspects of a person's self-image derived from the social categories to which an individual perceives herself/himself as belonging. Most human beings divide their social worlds into groups, and categorize themselves into some of those groups. In addition, we become aware of other social groups to which we do not belong, and we compare ourselves to them. We often define ourselves in opposition to others: "I know who I am because I am not you." Thus, social identity refers to "the ways in which individuals and collectivities are distinguished in their social relations with other individuals and collectivities."

Because social identity stems from perceptions of social group membership, social identity is somewhat distinct from personal identity, which encompasses the conception of the self in terms of variables such as personality traits. For instance, a person may be characterized as "shy" or "outgoing." However, "a person's self actually consists of a personal identity and multiple social identities, each of which is linked to different social groups."

An individual can "belong" to numerous social identity groups. I self-identify as: professor, black, woman, homeowner, U.S. citizen, baby boomer, middle-class, and volunteer. Although infinite possibilities exist for categories of social identity groups, I focus on six that are especially significant in contemporary society: gender, race, social class, ability, sexuality, and age. Nationality and religion also are important aspects of identity. . . .

Central are the interconnected ideas that all identity is relational, and that human beings develop their social identities primarily through communicating. This perspective represents the *social constructionist* school of thought, which contends that "self is socially constructed through various relational and linguistic processes." In other words, "our identity arises out of interactions with other people and is based on language." Let's look at how communication helps to construct social identity.

From the time we are born (and even prior to birth, due to tests that determine a baby's sex or congenital defects), socially constructed categories of identity influence how others interact with us (and vice versa), and how we perceive ourselves. When a child is born, what do people usually want to know? Generally, they ask if "it" is a boy or a girl. Why is the sex of the child so important? Sex matters because it cues people on how to treat the baby. If the newborn is a girl, relatives and friends may buy her pink, frilly clothes and toys designated for girls. Her parent(s) or guardian(s) may decorate her room (if she's fortunate enough to have her own room) or sleep area in "feminine" colors and artifacts, or she may share a room with other family members. These actions and others will help to "create a gendered world which the infant gradually encounters and takes for granted as her social consciousness dawns, and which structures the responses to her of others."

And that's just the beginning. As she develops, she will receive messages from multiple sources, including family members, teachers, peers, and the media about what girls are allowed and supposed to do (as contrasted with boys). This process is known as *socialization*. . . .

The same scenario applies for a male child. He too will receive numerous messages, blatant and subtle, that will mold his self-perception. Simultaneously, both female and male children will learn about additional identity categories like race, class, and ability. What they learn may vary depending on their identity composites. For instance, a white Jewish boy in a middle-class family probably will be socialized differently than a Latino Catholic in a working-class family, even as they each may receive similar messages about being male. Meanwhile, as both males receive comparable lessons about masculinity, a nondisabled Asian-American boy will probably receive different messages than a white boy labeled as "developmentally challenged." These individuals also will learn communication styles particular to their groups, such as vocabulary, gestures, eye contact, and use of personal space.

As these children become indoctrinated into social identity groups, they will receive information about other groups, including contrasts between groups, and "rules" for interacting (or not) with members of other groups. They will be exposed to stereotypes about groups, and they may accept these stereotypes as facts. They also will learn about hierarchies of identity. They may learn that being young is more desirable than being elderly, or that being heterosexual is preferable to being gay. These and other "lessons" about distinctions between and within groups will recur throughout their lives.

Due to socialization, children will accept social identity categories as real and natural designations. Yet, they are not. Historically, persons in power have constructed categories and developed hierarchies based on characteristics of groups. For example, in 1795 a German scientist named Johann Blumenbach constructed a system of racial classification that arranged people according to geographical location and physical features. He also ranked the groups in hierarchical order, placing Caucasians in the most superior position.

Although scientists have since concluded that race is not related to capability, many societies in the world still adhere to various racial classification systems because the idea of race has become essentialized. *Essentialism* refers to assumptions that social differences stem from intrinsic, innate, human variations unrelated to social forces. For example, so-called racial groups are viewed as if they have an "ultimate essence that transcends historical and cultural boundaries.

Thus, while we accept social identity groups as real and natural, we also perceive them as fixed (essentialized) and unchanging. However, not only are such categories artificial, but they also are subject to change. In different times and different places, categories we take for granted either did/do not exist or they were/are quite unlike the ones that we reference in the United States in the twenty-first century. Currently, the same person identified as black in the United States may be considered white in the Dominican Republic; in the nineteenth century, choices for racial designations in the United States included gradations of enslaved blacks (mulattos were one-half black, quadroons were one-quarter black, and octoroons were one-eighth black). . . .

The tendency to compartmentalize humans according to physical characteristics is logical because "labels can be helpful devices used to identify people." If we did not have labels to distinguish groups of items that are similar, we would have to create and remember a separate "name" for everything and everyone. What a pain that would be! Therefore, it makes sense that we use cues like skin color, facial features, body parts, and so forth to distinguish and group people.

However, problems can arise when people assign meaning to previously neutral descriptors. They may use categories not only to distinguish but also to discriminate and dominate. Categorizing can lead to in-group/out-group distinctions that may negatively affect intergroup interactions. For instance, *social identity theory* (SIT) describes humans' tendency to label self and others based on individual and group identity. This theory contends that members of social identity groups constantly compare their group with others, and they tend "to seek positive distinctiveness for one's own group." When an individual perceives someone else to be a member of an out-group, that person will tend to react more to perceived *group* characteristics than to the other person *as an individual*. Stereotypes and prejudice occur more frequently in this scenario. In contrast, stereotypes and prejudice are less likely when a communicator views another person as an individual, especially when both persons belong to the same social identity group(s).

[I]ndividuals often use identity markers like skin color to develop hierarchies. Moreover, many people accept and reinforce such hierarchies as natural and normal. Organizational communication scholars explain: "As people *internalize* the values and assumptions of their societies they also internalize its class, race, gender, and ethnicity-based hierarchical relationships." One consequence of these perceptions is the social construction of inequality, which results in favoritism and privilege for some groups and disadvantage for others. . . .

Privilege is a key concept in understanding how difference matters. *Privilege* refers to advantaged status based upon social identity. Sociologist Peggy McIntosh coined this term to refer to men's advantages in society, based upon her experiences teaching women's studies. McIntosh noticed that while men in her classes were willing to concede women's disadvantages, they were unaware of advantages they enjoyed simply because they were men. She later extended her analysis to encompass race, and she developed the concept of white privilege. . . .

Privilege tends to "make life easier; it is easier to get around, to get what one wants, and to be treated in an acceptable manner." On the Public Broadcasting System's video *People Like Us*, which explores social class in the United States, a white male plumber describes how sales clerks tend to treat men in suits better than they respond to him when he wears his work clothes. Similarly, a working-class college student reported that he would change out of his work clothes before going to campus because he felt that faculty and staff treated him less favorably when he wore them. . . .

Opposing standpoints of privileged and nonprivileged persons can negatively impact interactions. A person who is not privileged (or who does not feel privileged) may seem hypersensitive to an individual who is privileged. In contrast, the person who is privileged (or whom the other person perceives to be privileged) may seem totally insensitive. Privileged individuals sometimes diminish, dismiss, or discount experiences of others who are not advantaged. If a privileged person witnesses an incident in which a less privileged person is demeaned or humiliated, she or he may characterize it as exceptional rather than routine and may assess the less-privileged person's complaints about this type of treatment as an overreaction or misinterpretation of the situation. . . .

Most individuals simultaneously occupy privileged and nonprivileged social identity groups. Although I may experience discrimination based upon my race and/or gender, I also reap benefits associated with being heterosexual, nondisabled, and middle-class. We will consider the concept of privilege and its complexities as we study gender, race, class, ability, sexuality, and age.

In addition to constructing inequality, another consequence of internalizing dominant values and assumptions about social identity groups is that members of nondominant groups often help to perpetuate hierarchies because they believe that their group is inferior and that the dominant group is superior. Accepting these ideas and believing negative stereotypes about one's group is known as *internalized oppression*. . . .

To summarize, social identities are created in context; they emerge mainly from social interactions. We learn communication styles and rules based upon our membership in certain groups, and we communicate with other people based upon how we have been socialized about ourselves and about them. We learn who we are and who we might become through interaction with others, within a variety of social contexts, from a variety of sources. These sources also give us information about other groups. To every interaction, we bring preconceptions and expectations about social identities that can affect what, how, when, why, and whether or not we communicate. Most of these interactions occur "within prevailing normative and structural circumstances." . . .

Power Dynamics and Gender

Although scholars have studied gender and communication for over fifty years, academic and popular writing on the topic has surged in the past two decades. Two recurring topics that reveal power dynamics are sexist language and gender differences in styles of communicating.

Language

As communication scholars Diana Ivy and Phil Backlund observe, "English is a patriarchal language." However, as they also note, we did not invent this male-dominated language; we inherited it. Therefore, referring to English as patriarchal and sexist is not an indictment against those of us (men and women) who use it: "It's nobody's fault (nobody alive anyway) that we have a language that favors one sex over the other, but it's also not something that we 'just have to live with.'" As I share examples of the sexist nature of English, I hope you will reflect on how you might avoid them.

Language reflects patriarchy and sexism in numerous ways. Some of these are subtle; others are blatant. A prevalent example is the use of generic masculine pronouns. Although proponents of "he," "him," or "his" contend that these terms are neutral and inclusive of women and men, research indicates that exclusive masculine pronoun usage helps to maintain sex-biased perceptions and shape attitudes about appropriateness of careers for women or men. Such usage also helps to perpetuate a gender hierarchy. One compelling example is the volume of derogatory words in English for women with a smaller number of such terms for men. Among negative synonyms for women/girls and for men/boys, many have sexual denotations or connotations. Moreover, pejorative terms for men/boys often are feminine.

A gender hierarchy also is implied in gendered pairs of words such as "old maid" and "bachelor." Additional examples include gendered titles such as Mrs., Ms., Miss, and Mr., which differentiate women according to marital status, but not men. Man-linked terminology such as "mankind," "foreman," "man-hours" and feminine suffixes (-ette, -ess, -enne) are other examples. These uses of language help to inculcate the idea that men are more valuable than women.

Linguistic practices also reveal patriarchy. For instance, in everyday talk and writing, communicators usually place masculine words prior to feminine words. Consider the following phrases: "boys and girls," "he or she," "his and hers," "husband and wife," and "masculine and feminine." While writing this book, I found myself routinely enacting that norm. To resist this tendency, I conscientiously placed the feminine in the first position. Exceptions to this rule include "ladies and gentlemen," "bride and groom," and "mom and dad."

Why do you think these are exceptions? They may reflect patriarchal expectations about gender roles. For example, in writing or speaking contexts, placing "mom" before "dad" may emphasize the female's parental role. Although these and similar uses of language may seem trivial, they reflect deep structures of power that most people do not even realize exist.

Communication Styles

Another stream of research investigates differences in women's and men's communication styles. Rarely do such studies assess similarities between women's and men's communication. This body of research studies sex/gender differences in: (1) communication styles, and (2) perceptions about the function of communication.

A recurring depiction of women's speech as tentative encompasses several patterns. Women sometimes use tag questions such as "isn't that right?" or "don't you think?" Or, they employ question intonation in declarative contexts; that is, they say a statement as if it were a question and as if seeking approval. Other examples of speech styles frequently used by women include hesitation forms such as "um" or "like"; overuse of polite forms; and the frequent use of qualifiers and intensifiers like "sort of," "rather," "very," and "really." Some communicators overuse these ways of speaking to the extent that listeners may not take them seriously.

Rather than view these deferential differences in speech styles as gender-based, some scholars refer to them as "powerless" speech styles that anyone can employ. Although women tend to use powerless language more frequently than men, other users include poorly educated or lower status individuals. Thus, some linguists argue that this speech style is related more to women's relatively powerless position in society rather than to essentialist characteristics of females. Experimental courtroom research found that jurors and judges were less likely to view powerless speakers, regardless of gender, as credible.

Results of research on functions of communication tend to correspond with the femininity/masculinity clusters (nurturing-expressive/instrumental-active). For example, Ivy and Backlund offer a "relational/content" differentiation: "We believe that men approach conversation more with the intent of imparting information (the content aspect) than to convey cues about the relationship (the relational aspect)."

Sociolinguist Deborah Tannen offers similar perspectives on gender differences in her influential book entitled *You Just Don't Understand.* Tannen labels female communication style "rapport," meaning that women establish connections and negotiate relationships. In contrast, she terms the male style of communication "report," to indicate men's need to preserve independence and to impart information.

Communication differences between women and men may be due to socialization processes, including the proliferation of literature that asserts such differences. Men tend to be socialized to use language that is valued, while the opposite usually occurs for women. Several research conclusions support this claim: men tend to talk about their accomplishments using comparative and competitive terms, while women may understate their contributions and acknowledge others' assistance. Women often are more relational and dialogic; men tend to be more competitive and monologic. Women tend to provide support work in interaction. They offer verbal and nonverbal encouragement, such as nodding or smiling, ask questions returning to points made by earlier speakers, and attempt to bring others into the conversation.

Communication scholars Daniel Canary and Kimberley Hause criticize research on sex differences in communication for relying on and perpetuating sex stereotypes, using invalid measures of gender, a dearth of theory, and a tendency to polarize the sexes. In a meta-analysis of communication studies, they conclude, "given this research, we should *not* expect to find substantial sex differences in communication" (emphasis added). Indeed, they did not. Communication scholars Daena Goldsmith and Patricia Fulfs draw a similar conclusion in a refutation of Tannen's claims about gender differences. From their analysis of Tannen's evidence, they report that communication differences between women and men are typically minimal and are contingent upon situational factors. They conclude that differences tend to be nonverbal rather than verbal. Basically, they assert that women's and men's communication behaviors are more similar than different.

Some scholars critique researchers' propensity to denote females and males as a dualism with each embodying clear-cut, uniform characteristics. Rather than assuming a "two worlds" approach to gender interaction, they advocate research that explores different forms of femininity and masculinity. For instance, Deborah Cameron problematizes the tendency to homogenize women's and men's communication behaviors. She asserts a need in gender studies of language to consider contextual factors such as setting, purpose of communication, and relationship between communicators, as well as complex facets of communicators themselves.

Researchers have attended to both context and complexity of gendered communication. Some studies found that women and men behave differently according to context. These projects indicate differences among women or among men, instead of concentrating on differences between women and men. Men in all-male groups such as sports teams or in combat situations may exhibit caring characteristics that usually are attributed to women. Women in positions of authority often are more assertive than those who are in powerless jobs. Finally, the significance of context and complexity is evident in a volume of research projects about black women across a variety of contexts, including contemporary university students, nineteenth-century "club women" who worked for the social uplift of black people, and female hip-hop artists. The diverse perspectives shown in this collection underscore the need to consider intersections of social identity, rather than focusing only on one. . . .

Social Identities Are Social Constructions

Humans create schemes to classify groups of people based on characteristics such as skin color and perceived ability. These classifications designate social identity categories that we may assume to be natural and permanent. However, social identity categories are artificial and subject to change. Meanings and classifications of gender, race, class, ability, sexuality, and age have varied throughout history. Classifications of these groups always are products of their times, as humans engage in social processes to manufacture differences, conclude that some differences are more important than others, and assign particular meanings to those differences.

We do not have to accept traditional notions that social identity groups are natural and unchangeable. We can change our beliefs and behaviors regarding social identity groups. For example, we can imagine and enact alternative meanings of our own social identities. We can affirm our "humanity as free agents with a capacity to create, to construct, to wonder, and to venture. . . ."

It seems ironic that although the United States is defined as an individualist culture, people rarely seem to behave as individuals. Even though we are relatively free to choose how we enact identity, we usually are predictable. We tend to choose occupations, clothing, food, music, recreational activities, and so forth, based on the social identity groups to which we "belong." We often seem to make decisions based on group identity rather than considering our options.

I encourage you to make conscientious choices rather than be a puppet or a parrot. Snip the invisible strings that control your behaviors. Rewrite the scripts that tell you what to say in certain situations. Resist the pressure to conform to societal expectations about the social identity groups you belong to. Remember that your attitudes and actions help to create who you are.

Power Matters

Across history, humans have enacted power relations to construct social identity classifications. Authoritative sources such as those from science, politics, medicine, religion, the media, and so forth use dominant belief systems to create and disseminate hierarchies of human differences. Most people take for granted these hierarchies and the ideologies that undergird them. Persons in positions of privilege tend to reap the benefits of these hierarchies and their consequences, while people categorized in lower levels of classification systems are more likely to be disadvantaged.

However, throughout the history of the United States, some members of nondominant and dominant groups have challenged ideological systems that discriminate against certain groups and favor others. Advocates for change have initiated social movements, campaigned for laws, developed social and economic programs, and engaged in other actions to challenge the status quo. Countless individuals have endeavored to achieve freedom and equality for everyone in the United States.

Once you realize that dominant ideologies underlie beliefs and behaviors related to difference, that you and others have been socialized to believe many ideas about matters of difference, and recognize the power of socialization and the persistence of dominant ideologies, you can make a conscious decision to contest forces that compel humans to comply with unjust dominant belief systems.

Communication Rules!

Humans use communication to construct social identities. Communication comprises discourse and discursive practices that produce, interpret, and share meaning about social identity groups. Through communication, we develop and disseminate classifications and hierarchies of gender, race, class, sexuality, ability, and age. We create labels, ascribe meaning to them, and use them to refer to one another. And, we use communication to co-create and re-create our identities as we interact with one another. A significant proportion of these interactions occurs in the various organizations that pervade our lives.

Socialization practices, which are primarily communicative, teach us about in-groups and out-groups. We inherit meanings about social identity groups from our families, peers, the media, teachers, and other sources, and we accept those meanings as our own. We use communication to create and consume media reports about social identity groups and media portrayals (factual and fictitious) of social identity groups. Many, if not most, of these reports and portrayals reinforce dominant ideologies and stereotypes.

Even as communication can reinforce dominant meanings of difference, communication can facilitate social change. For instance, the media sometimes offer alternative narratives, depictions, and information that challenge mainstream conceptions of social identity groups. In addition, advocacy groups use communication to develop and distribute information, engage in marches and rallies, and construct symbols to represent and advance their causes. Groups that oppose social change also employ these communication processes. Thus, communication can impede or facilitate progress toward equal opportunity for life, liberty, and the pursuit of happiness for everyone in the United States. Therefore, communication is central to applying what you have learned.

To summarize how to apply what you learned: appreciate and value difference, contest and re-imagine conceptions of social identities, assume agency, and acknowledge the power of communication.

POSTSCRIPT

Is Culture the Primary Source of Sex Differences in Communication Styles?

It is important to situate discourse about sex differences in communication (indeed in any domain) in a sociopolitical context. Beliefs that the sexes differ, whether supported by empirical evidence or not, are deeply entrenched in our society. Indeed, while academic critics signal the lack of a scientific basis to Tannen's sweeping claims, her popular works have shot to the top of the bestseller list. We, the consumers, have to be very careful about scrutinizing how knowledge has been constructed and used. There is no such thing as a "simple" yes or no answer to a question of sex difference.

Scholarly and popular writing on sex differences is impacted greatly by what can be called the "hall of mirrors" effect. As described by Deborah Cameron in "Gender and Language: Gender, Language, and Discourse: A Review Essay" (*Signs: Journal of Women in Culture and Society*, 1998), "in the course of being cited, discussed, and popularized over time, originally modest claims have been progressively represented as more and more absolute, while hypotheses have been given the status of facts." Thus, for example, the originally modest claim made by researchers Don Zimmerman and Candace West in "Sex Roles, Interruptions and Silences in Conversation" (in Barrie Thorne and Nancy Henley, eds., *In Language and Sex: Differences and Dominance*, Newbury House, 1975), that men interrupt women more than the reverse may have been exaggerated by constant repetition and then critiqued for being overstated (much like the "telephone" game played by children).

As another example, it turns out that no study has actually counted the number of words used by women and men in natural conversations, that is, not until July 2007. In contradiction of Brizdendine's claim that women utter 200,000 words to men's 7,000 per day, Matthias Mehl and his colleagues found over of period of 17 working hours women average 16,214 words and men averaged 15,669, a highly statistically nonsignificant finding (*Science*, vol. 31).

Currently there is less interest in examining sex differences in language and more emphasis on how people use language in everyday life to create and maintain social realities. Mary Crawford points out that feminists have worked to create a more gender-balanced language through the coining of new words and putting old words to new uses. She notes that language is power.

Suggested Readings

Daniel J. Canary and Kathryn Dindia, eds., *Sex Differences and Similarities in Communication: Critical Essays and Empirical Investigations of Sex and Gender in Interaction* (2nd ed. New York: Lawrence Erlbaum, 2006).

Mary Crawford, "Gender and Language," in R. K. Unger, ed., *Psychology of Women and Gender* (pp. 228–244), (New York: John Wiley & Son, 2001).

K. M. Galvin and P. J. Cooper, *Making Connections: Readings in Relational Communication*, 4th ed. (Los Angeles: Roxbury Publishing Co., 2006).

Diana Ivy and Phil Backlund, *Gender Speak: Personal Effectiveness in Gender Communication* (New York: McGraw-Hill, 2003).

Charlotte Krolokke and Anne Scott Sorenson, *Gender Communication Theories and Analyses: From Silence to Performance* (Thousand Oaks, CA: Sage, 2005).

Deborah Tannen, *Talking from 9 to 5: Women and Men at Work* (San Francisco: HarperCollins, 2001).

J. Wood, *Gendered Lives: Communication, Gender, and Culture*, 4th ed. (Belmont, CA: Wadsworth Publishing, 2001).

ISSUE 6

Do Nice Guys Finish Last?

YES: **Peter K. Jonason, Norman P. Li, Gregory D. Webster, and David P. Schmitt,** from "The Dark Triad: Facilitating a Short-Term Mating Strategy in Men," *European Journal of Personality* (2009)

NO: **Adrian Furnham,** from "Sex Differences in Mate Selection Preferences," *Personality and Individual Differences* (2009)

ISSUE SUMMARY

YES: Psychologist Peter K. Jonason, taking an evolutionary perspective, demonstrates that the "Dark Triad" of attributes (narcissism, psychopathy, and Machiavellianism) promotes a reproductively adaptive strategy, especially for short-term mating behaviors.

NO: Psychologist Adrian Furnham found consistent sex differences that revealed women's preference for "nice guys," that is, those who were intelligent, stable, conscientious, better educated, with good social skills and political and religious compatibility.

$\mathbf{G}$oogle the phrase "What do women want?" and you will get over a 100 million hits. Similarly, if you Google "Do nice guys finish last?" you will get over 10 million hits. These are obviously questions that fascinate, provoke, and frustrate, and there is no shortage of Web sites claiming to have the answer. The stereotype is that the "bad boy" gets the girl. In this section, we want to examine what it is about men that women seem to want in a partner. All relationships begin with attraction. Research by relationship experts in psychology and sociology attempt to answer these questions using various scientific strategies such as surveys and experimental studies, and by posing theories to explain attraction and relationship development. Some research attempts to identify whether there are physical characteristics that make some people more appealing as a partner than others. In this research, women and men are presented with photos and asked to provide attractiveness ratings. Features of the individuals in the photos are then measured (size of chin, size of eyes, shape of eyes, distance between the eyes, etc.), and these measurements are then correlated with the attractiveness ratings. These studies find remarkable similarity across cultures. In general, large eyes, prominent cheekbones, and a big smile are found attractive in both women and men.

Other research focuses on status factors (education, income) or personality attributes, shared values, interests, and character. In these studies, researchers may ask people to rate the attributes they want in a partner and then present them with opportunities to interact with another person, giving them information about several people and letting them select which they would prefer to meet. Interestingly, these studies suggest that in spite of the fact that women say they value personality, values, and character over looks, physical attractiveness wins out over similarity, just as it does for men. One theory suggests that the physical-attractiveness stereotype is at work. Beautiful people are perceived to be more sociable, extraverted, and socially competent when compared to less attractive people. They are also seen as more sexual, happier, more fun loving, and successful. Thus, first impressions are likely to be based on looks because of the inferences we make about personality and status. However, in spite of this stereotype, we all know that all beautiful people do not have wonderful relationships and that many unattractive people do. So, what is going on? The answer lies in what we mean by terms such as "relationship" and "partner." When researchers are looking at what men and women want, are they looking at whom they want to hang out with, hook up with, or go on a first date, or are they looking at with whom they want a fifty-year marriage? Relationships have a life cycle. The first stage is the attraction stage, when emotions run high, and physical attractiveness plays a prominent role. The vast majority of attraction research has focused on the initial stage of a relationship. However, it turns out that excitement and good looks cannot sustain a relationship. As a relationship develops, its success becomes more dependent on factors such as trust and shared values and interests, with physical attractiveness becoming less important. Violations of trust, as well as the lack of shared values and interests, are often at the core of relationship dissolution. Research on long-term relationships finds that women and men in both heterosexual and same-sex relationships want remarkably similar things in their relationships, such as companionship and the ability to communicate.

In these selections, think about what stage of a relationship the authors are discussing. Peter Jonason and colleagues suggest that the dark triad of attributes contribute to a successful short-term mating strategy for men. This triad includes narcissism, psychopathy, and Machiavellianism. Typically, psychologists would consider these attributes to be abnormal and maladaptive. So why would women initially be attracted to men who are so clearly self-centered and manipulative? Jonason suggests that these attributes include a drive for power and extraversion that might have at least a short-term advantage in the dating game. Adrian Furnham's research seems clearly opposite in what he finds women desire in a mate. Women reported valuing intelligence, stability, conscientiousness, height, education, social skills, and political/religious compatibility as highly desirous in their ideal mates. Are they lying, or do they really not know what they want? Consider his research methods. Are his findings more reflective of attributes that would contribute to a successful long-term mating strategy?

YES ↵

Peter Jonason, et al.

The Dark Triad: Facilitating a Short-Term Mating Strategy in Men

Introduction

Machiavellianism, narcissism and psychopathy—collectively known as 'The Dark Triad'—are traits that are linked to negative personal and societal outcomes and are traditionally considered maladaptive. However, the persistence of these traits over time and across various societies, as well as linkages to positive traits, suggests that the Dark Triad can be advantageous in some ways. For instance, subclinical psychopathy is associated with a lack of neuroticism and anxiety, which may facilitate the pursuit of one's goals through adverse conditions. Similarly, narcissism is associated with self-aggrandisement, and Machiavellianism is associated with being socially manipulative, both of which may aid in reaping benefits for oneself at the expense of others, especially in initial periods of acquaintance. In the current study, we examine the links between the Dark Triad traits and a short-term mating orientation, and suggest that the Dark Triad traits represent one end of a continuum of individual differences that may facilitate a particular mating strategy.

The Dark Triad Traits: An Exploitative Social Strategy

The Dark Triad is composed of Machiavellianism, subclinical narcissism, and subclinical psychopathy. Machiavellian individuals tend to be manipulative, while demonstrating a "cool" or "cold" approach to others. Subclinical narcissists, sometimes called "normal narcissists," tend to have a sense of entitlement and seek admiration, attention, prestige, and status. Subclinical psychopaths are characterised by high impulsivity and thrill-seeking and tend to have low empathy. Associations among the three traits have been studied in both clinical and nonclinical settings. The three traits are moderately intercorrelated, and each contains a degree of self-aggrandisement, aggression and duplicity. We contend that the three traits may be best viewed as one particular social orientation towards conspecifics.

From *European Journal of Personality,* vol. 23, 2009. Copyright © 2009 by Wiley-Blackwell. Reprinted by permission.

Specifically, various lines of research suggest that the Dark Triad may facilitate a social style geared towards exploiting others in short-term social contexts. For instance, narcissists tend to be more agentic, with a desire for power and dominance, are less communally oriented, and have a lower tendency to feel guilt or shame. Those with high levels of Machiavellianism are described as charmers and as exploitative demonstrate less empathy, and are less willing to help others in need. Psychopaths have an exploitative nature, with high levels of egocentrism, impulsivity, and irresponsibility, and have low levels of empathy, shame, and guilt.

Clearly the three traits are associated with both high levels of self-interest and low levels of empathic qualities. As such, individuals who score high on the Dark Triad traits are not well suited for or interested in maintaining long-term relationships, where continued reciprocity is integral. Likewise, once their qualities are evident to others, excessively self-serving individuals should be viewed as undesirable, and thus, to be avoided by potential long-term partners. To the extent that this occurs, a self-serving, exploitative nature should be better suited to transacting with others in shorter-term durations (i.e., a "hit and run" strategy).

An Exploitative Short-Term Mating Strategy

In a mating context, those high on the Dark Triad traits may be especially well suited for an exploitative, short-term approach. For example, all three traits are correlated with low agreeableness, which is associated with conflict in long-term relationships and marital dissatisfaction. Machiavellianism is associated with promiscuous, as well as sexually coercive behaviour. Narcissists tend to have an unrestricted sociosexuality and higher levels of infidelity. Narcissists find it easy to start new relationships, but are less committed to and interested in staying in existing relationships, hence, they may pursue exploitative short-term matings to improve their own reproductive interests at the expense of their partners. We predicted that the three individual measures associated with the Dark Triad—narcissism, psychopathy, and Machiavellianism—would be positively associated with behavioural and attitudinal measures of short-term mating.

Pursuing an exploitative short-term mating strategy may be more advantageous for men than women. First, short-term mating may, on average, provide more reproductive benefits to men. That is, women—but not men—are physiologically required to undertake pregnancy and nursing. Because pregnancy was always a possible outcome of sexual intercourse in the ancestral past, casual sex resulted in higher potential costs for ancestral women than men. As such, women may have evolved to be less open than men towards casual sexual opportunities. Indeed, men tend to favour short-term sexual relationships much more than women do, and narcissistic men—but not women—have more illegitimate children. Second, men tend to score higher on the Dark Triad personality traits than women. Therefore, we would expect the facilitation of a short-term mating strategy from having high level of the Dark Triad traits to be more applicable to men than women. Thus, we predicted that the sex of the participant will moderate the positive correlations between scores on the Dark Triad, such that the correlation will be stronger in men than women.

This moderation prediction is informed by the pervasive fact that sex differences persist in mating behaviour. Men's greater interest in short-term sexual relationships compared to women is one of the most consistent and strongest sex differences in the field. However, personality traits like the Dark Triad may facilitate the pursuit of short-term mating in men. Thus, we conducted mediation analyses on the relationship between the sex of the participant and rates of short-term mating. Therefore, we predicted that when the Dark Triad is treated as a unit, it will partially mediate the relationship between the sex of the participant and rates of short-term mating behaviour.

However, only partial mediation is expected because numerous other individual differences, including extraversion, are likely to facilitate short-term mating. Extraversion may be related to extrapair mating in men and lower relationship commitment in women. Extraverts are generally more interested in short-term mating than introverts. Extraversion and the Dark Triad traits are positively correlated. In addition, variables such as age and sex of the participant are also associated with higher self-reports of sexual behaviour. Therefore, we also investigated the correlation between the Dark Triad and short-term mating when we control for the potential confounds of extraversion, age, and sex.

Method

Participants

Two hundred and twenty-four psychology undergraduate students at New Mexico State University (88 men, 136 women) aged 17–43 years (mean = 23.50, median = 21, SD = 6.40) received extra credit for participation. The majority of the sample (88%) was heterosexual, 5% was homosexual, and 6% was bisexual (1% nonresponsive).

Procedures

Participants received a packet that (a) informed them of the nature of the study, (b) asked demographic questions, and (c) asked them to respond to the self-report items described below. Participants completed the survey alone in a room with a closed door and a two-way mirror that allowed an experimenter to monitor the participant's progress. Upon completion, the participants were debriefed and thanked for their participation.

Measures of the Dark Triad

Narcissism was assessed with the 40-item Narcissistic Personality Inventory, a validated and widely used measure. For each item, participants chose one of two statements that they felt applied to them more. One of the two statements reflected a narcissistic attitude (e.g., "I have a natural talent for influencing people"), whereas the other statement did not (e.g., "I am not good at influencing people"). We summed the total number of narcissistic statements the participants endorsed to measure overall narcissism. . . .

The 31-item Self-Report Psychopathy Scale-III was used to assess subclinical psychopathy. This measure has good psychometric properties. Participants rated how much they agreed (1 = strongly disagree, 5 = strongly agree) with statements such as: "I enjoy driving at high speeds" and "I think I could beat a lie detector." The items were averaged to create an index of psychopathy. . . .

Machiavellianism was measured with the 20-item MACH-IV. This measure has good psychometric properties. Participants were asked how much they agreed (1 = strongly disagree, 5 = strongly agree) with statements such as: "It is hard to get ahead without cutting corners here and there" and "People suffering from incurable diseases should have the choice of being put painlessly to death." The items were averaged to create a Machiavellianism index. . . .

We also treated the three Dark Triad measures as a composite measure of an exploitive sexual strategy. We first standardised (z-scored) overall scores on each measure and then averaged all three together to create a composite Dark Triad score. Overall scores were used as opposed to using the complete set of items from all the scales because dichotomous data, like that in the NPI, is problematic in factor reduction procedures. We then conducted analyses on an overall Dark Triad score . . . in addition to the constituent parts. Such an estimate of internal consistency is reasonable for a three-item scale in basic research.

Measures of Short-Term Mating

Sociosexual orientation (SOI) was assessed, measuring both sociosexual attitudes (e.g., "I can imagine myself being comfortable and enjoying casual sex with different partners") and behaviours (e.g., "With how many different partners have you had sexual intercourse within the past year"). As in prior work, individual SOI items were standardised (z-scored) prior to computing an index of sociosexuality. . . .

Participants reported the degree to which they were seeking a short-term mate (1 = not strongly currently seeking, 7 = strongly currently seeking) using a single-item, face-valid question. Such a measure may provide a rough estimate of participants' sociosexual desires. Additionally, we assessed the degree to which participants were seeking a long-term mate as a means of briefly assessing a contrasting mating strategy. It was assessed just as the corresponding item for seeking a short-term partner.

Participants also reported their number of lifetime vaginal-sex partners. Because these numbers were positively skewed, we performed a log-transformation before analyses.

All the short-term mating measures were standardised (z-scored) and then averaged to create an index of attitudes, behaviours, and desires towards short-term mating. . . . The measures of short-term mating were moderately correlated with each other. . . . We did not include the item for degree of seeking a long-term partner in this composite.

Extraversion as a Covariate

Extraversion was measured with seven self-descriptive statements from the NEO-PI-R that are cross-culturally reliable and valid. Participants were asked how much a series of statements fit with their self-concept of how extraverted they were (1 = not at all; 5 = very much). Specifically they were asked: "I see myself as someone who. . ." (e.g., "Is talkative," "Generates a lot of enthusiasm"). The responses to these statements were averaged to create an index of extraversion (α = .75).

Results

Compared with women, men scored higher on Dark Triad traits, as well as short-term mating behaviours and attitudes. Men did not show a significantly . . . higher preference for seeking long-term mates . . . than women. . . .

To examine the possibility that the Dark Triad may reflect a single, underlying social strategy, we conducted three separate tests. First, we tested the intercorrelations among the three measures to determine how strongly correlated they were with one another. Narcissism was significantly correlated with Machiavellianism . . . and psychopathy . . . , and psychopathy was significantly correlated with Machiavellianism. . . . Next an exploratory factor analysis yielded a one factor solution when we considered all three measures of the Dark Triad. . . . Last, we conducted a confirmatory factor analysis to examine the possibility that the three measures reflected a single latent factor that we will call "an exploitive social style." . . . These . . . tests provide convergent evidence that the three measures of the Dark Triad can be treated as a composite. With this support in hand, subsequent analyses were conducted on the Dark Triad composite and its components.

To examine whether the Dark Triad was related to short-term mating, we assessed the intercorrelations between the Dark Triad measures and the short-term mating measures. People's standings on each of the three components of the Dark Triad were related to their history of, orientation towards, and interest in short-term mating, but not long-term mating.

To address the possibility that the Dark Triad is a suite of traits that facilitate short-term mating in men, we tested whether the sex of the participant moderated the relationship between a Dark Triad composite and a short-term mating composite. . . . The Dark Triad composite and short-term mating composite were correlated in men . . . and in women. . . . Second, . . . the Dark Triad was correlated with short-term mating in men . . . and women. . . . [Results] confirmed our prediction that the sex of the participant would moderate the relationship between the Dark Triad and short-term mating.

We hypothesised that the Dark Triad would partially mediate the sex difference in short-term mating. Mediation is present when the relationship between two variables is carried by a third variable that is related significantly to the first two variables. . . . We found significant partial mediation. . . .

To confirm that variables such as age, participant's sex, and extraversion were not driving the correlation between the Dark Triad and short-term mating, we built a hierarchical regression model. . . . The Dark Triad composite remained a significant predictor of short-term mating whereas extraversion did not. This analysis also demonstrated that the mediation was robust after controlling for other sources of variability that have been associated with short-term mating.

Discussion

Although most studies have focused on the negative aspects of the Dark Triad, our evidence suggests that there might be some up-sides to these anti-social personality traits. We found that the scores on the Dark Triad traits were positively related to having more sex partners, an unrestricted sociosexuality and a greater preference for short-term mates. We demonstrated that the association between the Dark Triad composite was correlated with short-term mating above and beyond effects of participant's age, sex and extraversion. We also provide evidence that the three measures of the Dark Triad can be compressed into a composite measure, most notably evidenced in the exploratory and the confirmatory factor analyses.

We confirmed sex differences in all three Dark Triad measures when using a college-student sample. We found a rather high sex difference in psychopathy which may reflect greater rates of secondary psychopathy in some college-aged American men than women. Because we had a smaller amount of men than women in our sample, a few men may have had an undue influence on this sex difference. We confirmed sex differences in short-term mating and a convergence in interest in long-term mating.

Results are consistent with the possibility that the Dark Triad traits may facilitate an exploitative, short-term mating style in men and with work on Machiavellianism, narcissism, and the complete Dark Triad. Our mediation tests showed that personality traits such as the Dark Triad partially mediate the relationships between the sex of the participant and short-term mating. However, this was merely a partial mediation, which we suspect is caused by (a) the reliance on a student sample which may mask some of the extremes of these traits in the population, (b) response biases endemic to self-reports of socially undesirable traits, and (c) the large array of possible individual differences that could also partially mediate the sex difference in short-term mating.

Adaptive Individual Differences?

Whereas personality psychology has been primarily concerned with documenting trait-level individual differences among people, evolutionary psychology has typically been concerned with identifying adaptive, species-typical traits and commonalities among peoples. In recent years, these two approaches have been integrated to yield powerful explanations of individual differences. It is via this adaptive individual difference perspective that we will interpret our results.

An evolutionary view of personality considers traits to have been naturally selected, allowing individuals to compete against conspecifics and deal with the environment. Although directional selection tends to decrease trait variation, localising it in species-typical traits, trait continuums can be maintained in a population if different levels of traits are reproductively useful. For instance, a trait may consist of a dimension whereby both poles of the trait can yield adaptive benefits or bear adaptive costs under certain conditions. That is, one end on a trait (e.g., dominance) might have associated costs and benefits (greater risk and rewards), and the other end of a trait (e.g., submissiveness) might have its own costs and benefits (e.g., lower risks and rewards). However, as long as net fitness gains are achieved by individuals at both ends, then individual differences on this trait may be maintained in the population via balancing selection.

Our study indicates a connection between the Dark Triad and more positive attitudes towards casual sex and more casual sex behaviours. To the extent that lifetime number of sexual partners is a modern-day marker of reproductive success, and given that the Dark Triad traits are heritable and exist in different cultures, we speculate that these traits may represent one end of a set of individual differences that reflects an evolutionarily stable solution to the adaptive problem of reproduction.

Limitations

Personality traits, such as those associated with the Dark Triad, are often considered to be global, continuous measures. We agree that global measures, such as SOI, may obscure the sophisticated or multidimensional nature of personality traits. Independently, the three Dark Triad measures may have distinct implications for psychological and interpersonal functioning. However, in the case of mating, it appears that all three may be measuring the same or a similar social strategy. Specifically, those who score high on the Dark Triad traits may be equipped to engage in exploitative (e.g., deceptive promises of commitment, behaviourally aggressive) short-term mating, which may be a viable reproductive strategy when the relative frequency of exploitable cooperators in a population is sufficiently high. Whereas such a strategy capitalises on quantity at the cost of receiving long-term benefits, individuals who are not high on the Dark Triad traits—the majority of populations—may be better equipped to form cooperative long-term relationships and, to a lesser degree, short-term relationships without deception. This long-term, nonexploitive strategy may represent a slower but more stable approach to reproduction. These two mating strategies have been described as the *Cad* and *Dad* strategies or in literature analyses, the "dark hero" and the "proper hero." Furthermore, because of the asymmetries in reproductive constraints between the sexes, a short-term mating strategy, and by extension, the Dark Triad traits, are more likely to benefit men's reproductive fitness than women's.

This study was based on self-report data offered by psychology undergraduate students from the southwestern United States, and thus, our results are limited in their generalisability. Future work should attempt to replicate our findings with a more diverse, cross-cultural sample. Additionally, we cannot exclude the possibility that the present results were partially caused by some individuals (i.e., high scorers on the Dark Triad measures) positively biasing their sexual success in the form of reported lifetime sex partners. We feel our utilisation of multiple measures of short-term mating should alleviate such concerns. Future research should examine whether scores on the Dark Triad traits mediate the sex difference in sexual success.

In our analyses, we used overall measures of narcissism, psychopathy, Machiavellianism, and sociosexuality. However, work suggests that these measures can be broken down into sub-dimensions. For instance, SOI can be divided into sociosexual attitudes and behaviours or into past behavioural experiences, attitudes towards uncommitted sex, and sociosexual desire; the NPI can be divided into four or seven components; psychopathy can be divided into primary and secondary psychopathy; and at least two different factor structures have been used with Machiavellianism. While we reported only the overall results, we did assess different scale dimensions during our analyses and did not find differences among them. For instance, both sociosexual behaviours and attitudes were moderately correlated with all three of the Dark Triad measures and with the composite variable of the Dark Triad.

All three Dark Triad traits are associated with an exploitative social style. However, actual exploitative behaviours in mating, and in general, are rarely addressed. Future work should examine the Dark Triad traits along with mating-related deception, mate-poaching, coercive mating, and other more general measures of this exploitative approach to conspecifics.

Conclusion

The personality traits that compose the Dark Triad have typically been considered abnormal, pathological, and inherently maladaptive. Although individuals with these traits inflict costs to others and themselves, the Dark Triad traits are also associated with some qualities, including a drive for power, low neuroticism, and extraversion, that may be beneficial. Together with low amounts of empathy and agreeableness, such traits may facilitate—especially for men—the pursuit of an exploitative short-term mating strategy. Although our study is limited, it suggests a potentially interesting new avenue of research to explore. More generally, the application of evolutionary reasoning to the study of personality traits may yield fruitful insights into the wide array of individual differences that exist on various dimensions.

Adrian Furnham

 **NO**

Sex Differences in Mate Selection Preferences

1. Introduction

There is an extensive literature on mate selection and preferences in evolutionary and social psychology. Studies in the area have been particularly concerned with two areas, namely sex differences and similarity preferences in mate attraction. The fact that women are particularly interested in "resources" and males in "attractiveness" has lead to various theoretical explanations.

The *sex-role socialisation* hypothesis suggests that females' "comparative structural powerlessness" leads them to hypergamy or marrying-upward in socio-economic status while men are more likely to accept the concept of "exchange object." Therefore physical attractiveness becomes the central mechanism or criterion for measuring relative value in exchange commodity. Traditional sex-role socialisation is assumed to be designed to support those structural differences. On the other hand, the evolutionary theory explanation is concerned with reproductive success: females focus on the social and material provisioning for offspring while males seek out fecundity. Whilst there appear to be different explanations for mate choice based on different theories, there is little evidence that they yield dramatically different hypotheses in terms of what they would predict. The aim of this study is primarily to look at sex, personality, and ideological predictors of mate choice.

There is also a *"birds of a feather"* and assortative mating literature which shows that people seek out those similar to themselves. It has been found that newlyweds showed substantial similarity on attitudes but not traits, yet a positive relationship between spouse similarity and marital quality for traits but not attitudes.

There is a literature on the influence of personality factors on their similarity, complementary and assortative mating concepts. My colleagues and I have proposed a "mating market model," which assumes that individuals examine competitors in the mate market and both negotiate and adjust their criteria based on their self and competitor ratings.

Various studies have specifically examined real, media-based personal or lonely-hearts advertisements.

There have been a number of studies using "lonely hearts," mate attraction published advertisements which have been surprisingly consistent. One analysed 800 lonely-heart advertisements of American men and women aged 20–59. They found women were more likely than men to offer attractiveness, seek financial security, express concerns about the potential partner's motives, and seek someone who was older. Men were more likely than women to seek attractiveness, offer financial security, profess an interest in marriage, and seek someone who was younger. Offers of, and demands for, financial security varied systematically with age, but concerns about appearance and character did not.

In an analysis of 98 advertisements it was found that males seek attractivity (health, sexiness) and offer resources, while females seek resources and offer attractivity. This is simple evidence of sexually dimorphic mating strategies. Yet another analysis of 1000 advertisements showed, as hypothesised, men sought women of reproductive value (young, attractive) while women looked for ability to acquire resources and provide resources (time, emotions, money, status) in the relationship. Men were more promiscuously indirect while women sought long-term monogamous relationships. . . .

Heterosexual women place emphasis on wealth and status as well as the man's willingness to invest time and effort in the relationship. Females also consistently specify physical attractiveness and social skills; males tend to emphasise physical attractiveness above all other features. The advertisements also indicate that males tend to advertise for females younger than themselves whereas females do the opposite. Further, both sexes know what the other wants. Women offer attractiveness and charm and seek commitment and resources. Men offer attractiveness, charm and resources but seek predominantly the first two.

Some studies have examined the desirability of traits in mate selection. For both males and females the top five most desirable traits are: sincerity, faithfulness, tenderness, reliability, and communicative. This suggests Conscientiousness and Agreeableness of the Big Five are the most desirable traits. In a study using experimentally designed advertisements matched to photographs, it was found that females prefer men of medium rather than high socio-economic status. The idea was that females would be worried that (very) high socio-economic status would be very desirable to all women some of whom might encourage the male to cheat or desert the partner.

In this study participants were asked to freely express what they would say about themselves and the people they are looking for. They were also asked to rate the importance of various characteristics. However, they were also asked to complete a Big Five personality measure and specific details like their height and weight, religious and political beliefs. Hence it was able to look at individual difference predictors of preferences. Whilst studies appear to support the socio-biological theories on mate choice, there appear to have been no individual difference correlates of these factors.

Based on the previous literature, it was hypothesised first, that females would place higher emphasis on education, social skills, emotional intelligence, and conscientiousness while males would place greater emphasis on attractiveness. Second, it was hypothesised that there would be a "birds of a feather"/assortative mating effect in that people would seek out those with personalities similar to themselves, specifically Extraverts would seek out Extraverts, Agreeable participants Agreeable partners, and Open participants, Imaginative partners. Third, it was hypothesised that there would be a strong ideological compatibility effect in that for those of stronger beliefs and commitments to religious and political causes this would be an overwhelmingly important factor in their preference. Specifically that those with strong ideological beliefs would emphasis the role of partner value compatibility.

2. Method

2.1. Participants

There were 250 participants of which 110 were all single male and 140 female. They ranged in age from 18 to 41 with a mean of 22.25 (SD = 5.03 yrs). They rated themselves 5.03 (SD = 1.16) on a 7-point attractiveness scale; 4.48 (SD = 2.03) on a 7-point religious scale (1 Very, 7 Not at All), and 3.98 (SD = 1.12) on a political scale (1 = right wing, 7 = left wing). Their mean weight was 62.38 kg (SD = 13.07) and height 169.80 cm (SD = 9.38). Around a third were Asian from Hong Kong, China, and Singapore, half European, mainly British, and the remainder from North America and Australasia. Around three quarters were students at a variety of higher education institutions, mainly universities.

2.2. Questionnaire

They completed either on-line (80%) or on paper (20%) a two page questionnaire. The first part required participants to write down five characteristics that they believed best describes themselves, then write down—in rank order—the five characteristics that they most want in a long-term romantic partner. They then rated the characteristics. These were rated on an 11-point scale where 0 = Not Desirable to 11 = Extremely Desirable.

Personality was assessed by a frequently used brief (15 item) measure of the Big Five questionnaire. It has adequate evidence of internal reliability as well as construct and predictive validity. They were also asked to indicate personal details like age, sex, height, weight, strength of religious beliefs, political leaning, marital status, etc.

2.3. Procedure

Ten research assistants contacted around 25 friends mainly by emailing, asking if they or their friends would complete a short and interesting questionnaire. This may mean this is a very unrepresentative sample. They were asked to ensure that they were roughly half male and half female, between the age of 18 and 35 yrs old, unmarried, and heterosexual. They reported on average a 96% response rate. Ethical approval was sought and obtained for the study.

3. Results

A content analysis of the free responses based on a frequency count of the qualities/traits mentioned by each participant was done. Some categories showed relatively big differences between the descriptions given by the male and female respondents. Females were more likely to describe themselves as outgoing/sociable/extraverted, cheerful/optimistic, and caring/loving compared to males who were more likely to describe themselves as intelligent/competent/capable and good looking/attractive.

The top three categories of adjective/descriptions listed by the males for what characteristics they wanted in a partner were looks/attractiveness, caring/loving, and intelligence. For females it was caring/loving, then funny/humorous, and third loyal/honest.

3.1. Rated Preference

. . . Females showed a significant higher preference compared to males for cognitive ability, emotional intelligence, conscientiousness, height, education, social skills, and political compatibility. It was only good looks where male ratings were significantly higher than females. This confirms the first hypothesis. Effect sizes were greatest for height, Conscientiousness, and social skills. . . .

The results showed Agreeableness, Emotional Intelligence and Emotional stability were rated highest (i.e., most desirable) while political and religious compatibility as well as height rated lowest (i.e., least desirable). Abilities and personality tended to be more highly rated than physical factors and looks.

Preferences were correlated with various individual difference factors, two demographic, one self-rating of attractiveness, and the final two of the "ideological" or belief variable. Age of participant showed few correlations. The importance of the physical attractiveness of the partner was confirmed by the ratings. The more religious the person the greater importance they attached to personality (stability, agreeableness, conscientiousness) and values, especially religious compatibility. Religious compatibility was more important to females than males, but the relationship was consistent for both sexes. Political beliefs of the participants had few significant relationships.

The participants' height, weight, and BMI were also correlated with the ratings. Heavier participants rated Conscientiousness . . . , height . . . , and education lower than lighter participants. Taller participants rated good looks more highly . . . but Conscientiousness lower . . . than shorter people. Participants' BMI was correlated negatively with the rated importance of partner conscientiousness . . . , height . . . education . . . and social skills. . . . Height of participant was correlated . . . with ratings of height in a partner. For males the correlation was .63, but for females it was $r = .23$.

Thereafter a set of regressions were performed to examine which, and to what extent, the participant individual difference variables predicted their separate ratings. . . .

> A. *Ability:* the only significant regression was for intelligence as criterion factor. Conscientious females rated this more highly. . . .

B. *Personality:* all except one regression was significant. The pattern showed that the participants' personality was the best predictor of personality trait preferences and that there was clear evidence of "like attracts like." Conscientious participants rated Conscientiousness in potential mates highly, as was the case with Openness which predicted ratings of Imaginativeness. Stable, Conscientious females rated Stability in a partner highly while open extraverts rated extraversion highly. However, Neurotic participants preferred stable partners and the participants' Agreeableness scores were unrelated to all ratings. This confirms the second hypothesis.

C. *Physical:* all four regressions were significant. Surprisingly neither sex, nor age, nor BMI were related to the overall ratings of physical characteristics. Agreeableness and Conscientiousness were the only predictors. Disagreeable Conscientious participants rated physical attractiveness highly. Age was related to looks; older, Disagreeable people rated looks less important than younger people. Sex was the only predictor of ratings of height (not BMI) and thus accounted for over 10% of the variance. Open, Disagreeable, Conscientious people rated health most highly.

D. *Social Factors:* again, all regressions were significant and results showed three participant characteristics were consistently significant predictors. Conscientious, low BMI, females rated the overall factor most highly. Slimmer, conscientious people rated education highly, while Conscientious females rated social skills highly. However, it is possible that slimness is a correlate of, and index of, higher socioeconomic status and education. This study did not measure socioeconomic status which would be desirable in future studies.

E. *Values:* all three regressions were significant. . . . Females with a conservative ideology (highly religious and right wing) placed high value on political compatibility. Low Openness participants with a conservative ideology placed considerable emphasis on religious compatibility. This confirms the third hypothesis.

4. Discussion

The results of this study provide broad support for the hypotheses, which are similar to other studies. Females did rate cognitive ability, social skills, height and conscientiousness more highly than males who in turn rated "good looks" more highly. This confirms nearly all the content analysis studies reviewed in the introduction. However, . . . differences in sex partner preferences are restricted to very specific areas. This study did not include wealth or profession but it could be argued that intelligent (cognitive ability), highly educated, Conscientious, and socially skilled males are most likely to have stable, well-paid, professional jobs. It is interesting to notice that height seemed of particular importance to females though overall it was the third lowest rated factor. Recent studies on height preferences showed that both men and women preferred relationships in which the woman was shorter than the man.

This study showed that there were individual differences, as well as simply sex differences in mate selection. For some factors there was general agreement that the rated factor cognitive ability, emotional intelligence, physical health, social skills—was desirable. However, personality factors did clearly play a part in preferences for personality traits, particularly extraversion and conscientiousness.

There was clear evidence of the "birds of a feather" personality-likeness factor. For each of the regressions, with the exception of Agreeableness, the trait score of the participants on each of the five factors was predictive of the desired trait in a mate. This was strongest for Extraversion and Conscientiousness and throws in dispute Jungian ideas of "opposites" attracting one another, which have not seen much empirical support.

Perhaps one of the most unique aspects of this study was to include political and religious beliefs as both a criterion and predictor variable. Overall religious and political compatibility was not rated as particularly important for these participants but religious compatibility more highly than political compatibility. Further the religious beliefs of participants were a more powerful predictor in their mate choice criteria than political beliefs. Other studies have documented the importance of religion in mate preferences. However, participant ideology did have predictively a very powerful impact on participants' preference for political and religious compatibility. Indeed, together with openness, participant ideology predicted 30% of the variance in the ratings of religious compatibility.

How would evolutionary psychologists explain this? Religion is a strong predictor of values and life style. Religions pre- and proscribe behaviour with respect to money, alcohol, child-rearing. People of similar beliefs are less likely to argue about important social issues and to have similar aims and goals. Most religions still seem conservative with respect to sex-roles and encourage both in-group marriages and having many children to support the youth. People who stay within the faith are likely to be protected and assisted by others while the opposite is true for those who marry out. In this sense there are probably evolutionary advantages to select out people of similar religious beliefs.

Like all others this study has its limitations. The participants were all young and it would have been better to have had a wider age range from a more representative population group. Further it would be most desirable to know about the nature and status of their current relationship and whether they had indeed ever used lonely hearts columns. There is also a problem with respect to questionnaire methodology. Various evolutionary psychology studies have shown that females respond to testosterone-related markers of male physical traits as well as cues to facial and body bilateral symmetry. This means that there may be a mismatch between what females say they may want in a partner and what they actually seek or respond to. This is an important theoretical and methodological issue.

Research using photographs and "live models" suggest that small visual cues have a powerful effect below consciousness on the ratings of attractiveness, . . . such as the symmetry, length and size of fingers, hands, feet and legs, skin-tone, facial hair as well as face structure and shape. These have predictable and consistent relationships with ratings of attractiveness, health, preferences and therefore mate selection. Yet few if any person-descriptions used in questionnaires contain such data preferring to mention more sociological markers like education or ability factors like intelligence or vocabulary. Thus, it may be that results in this area are very methodologically dependent because people actually respond more powerfully to physical cues they rarely mention and maybe are even unaware of. It may be possible to test the relative power of different factors experimentally by varying body-cues and verbal descriptions to see whether mate selection is based more on subtle physical markers of health, than sociological markers of status or wealth. It may also mean that ultimately the self-report methodology of questionnaires may lead to findings that are misleading in the sense that they do not represent how people behave when faced with visual cues.

POSTSCRIPT

Do Nice Guys Finish Last?

What do the more than 50 reality dating shows, from *The Bachelorette* to *Average Joe* to *Hell Date,* have in common? What assumptions do they reflect about what people are looking for in a relationship? What assumptions are they making about how relationships begin? What are the odds that the relationships formed on these shows will last? What can the lessons learned by relationship researchers tell us about these shows? Issues of women's and men's desired mating strategies abound and cover a range of relationships from one-night stands to short-term to long-term relationships. Two sets of explanations are advanced, one resting on evolutionary theory and one on sociocultural theories. Evolutionary theorists tell us that a combination of short-term and long-term mating strategies has the greatest reproductive advantage, especially for men. This approach is used to explain the greater tendency for infidelity among men than women and men's greater intolerance for sexual than emotional infidelity in their female partners. Sociocultural explanations, on the other hand, look at the historically lower status of women and dependence on men for care of themselves and their children. These explanations suggest that women have learned to be more pragmatic in their mate selection. Character traits, values, and status are better indicators of a man's willingness and ability to care for a family than his physical attractiveness. However, with greater opportunities for education and economic security, women may now have more choices than in earlier times for a variety of types of relationships. Yet, there are still questions about whether women can express their relationship desires free of societal constraints.

How do discussions of attraction and mate selection relate to issues of sexuality and sexual expression? Over the past three decades, women's sexuality has changed—by some accounts dramatically—in ways more commensurate with men's sexuality. In general, women are gaining greater sexual experience. They engage in intercourse at a younger age, they have more sex partners, they engage in sexual intercourse more frequently, and they are increasingly likely to engage in casual sex. Yet, despite this trend toward sex equality in behaviors, traditional gender socialization and the sexual double standard continue to act as an interpretive filter for sexual experience.

Competitiveness, assertiveness, and coercion often characterize males' sexual experience. Males' self- and peer-esteem are linked to sexual experience and performance. Many future-oriented sexologists caution that in striving for sexual equality, we must not limit ourselves to a preset "male" definition of sexual freedom.

Psychologist and sex researcher Leonore Tiefer argues that we need to encourage women's sexual experimentation and explore sexual possibilities.

Furthermore, new ideas need to be developed about desire and pleasure. To facilitate this, there needs to be freely available information, ideas, images, and open sexual talk. Tiefer asserts that if women develop sexual knowledge and self-knowledge, they can take more responsibility for their own pleasure.

Traditional sex education programming has overlooked the possibility of female desire and sexual pleasure, nor does it focus on relationship issues. Some argue that sex education programs can be used to help females not allow themselves to be treated as objects but think of themselves as sexual subjects. Women as sexual subjects would feel free to seek out sexual pleasure and know that they have a right to this pleasure. This argument supports the assertion that we also need to raise boys to avoid treating females as sexual objects. The challenge for sex education programming is to inform women about the possible risks of sexual relationships without supporting the double standard that limits, inhibits, and controls their sexuality.

Ideally, sex education programming would include education specifically about gender ideology, as it influences sexual perceptions, decisions, and experiences. Conformity to gender-based norms and ideals for sexual activity and relationships is the most important source of peer sexual pressure and risky sex among youth; youth "perform" gendered roles in sexual relations to secure gender affirmation.

Advocates of sex education reform also call for incorporating definitions of "good sex"—sex that is not coercive, exploitative, or harmful. Thus, greater attention to the meaning of healthy relationships is also necessary; young people could learn how to think about attributes to look for in an ideal partner and perhaps, in males in particular, can avoid the "dark triad" in potential mates. They caution not to impose rigid definitions of "sexual normality"; rather, identify some dimensions of healthy sexuality as examples upon which individuals can explore and develop their own unique sexual identity and style. It has been observed that a central practice in the social construction of gender inequality is *compulsory heterosexuality* or societal pressure to be heterosexual. Many sexual revolutionaries argue that an important condition of sexual freedom is freedom from pressures to be a particular "type" of sexual being or to be in a particular type of relationship.

Return to the questions asked at the beginning of this postscript about reality dating programs (RDP) and the impact of watching them in the context of this discussion about sex education programs. Unfortunately, watching RDPs has effects that run counter to good sex education programs. Research has shown that there is a correlation between the amount of RDP viewing and sexual attitudes and behaviors, such that greater consumption is associated with stronger endorsement of the sexual double standard, that dating is a game, the belief that appearance is important in dating, strong adversarial sexual beliefs, and that men are sex-driven. This finding is true for women and men, but men report using RDPs for learning more than women do. In discussing this research, Eileen Zurbriggen has said, "Thus, ironically, reality dating programs that purport to show 'real' people in dating situations may actually be an impediment to viewers who hope to create healthy intimacy in their own relationships and to make intelligent decisions about sexuality."

Suggested Readings

Joel D. Block, *Broken Promises, Mended Hearts: Maintaining Trust in Love Relationships* (McGraw-Hill, 2001).

Benjamin R. Karney et al., *Adolescent Romantic Relationships as Precursors of Healthy Adult Marriages: A Review of Theory, Research, and Programs* (RAND Corp., 2007).

George Weinberg, *Why Men Won't Commit: Getting What You Both Want Without Playing Games* (Simon & Schuster, 2004).

Leonore Tiefer, "Arriving at a 'New View' of Women's Sexual Problems: Background, Theory, and Activism," *Women and Therapy, 24* (2001): 63–98.

Deborah Tolman, *Dilemmas of Desire: Teenage Girls Talk about Sexuality* (Cambridge, MA: Harvard University Press, 2005).

Naomi Wolf, *The Beauty Myth: How Images of Beauty Are Used Against Women* (New York: HarperCollins, 2002).

Internet References . . .

Cyberbullying Research Center

This Web site is dedicated to providing up-to-date information about the nature, extent, causes, and consequences of cyberbullying among adolescents. It is a clearinghouse of information concerning the ways adolescents use and misuse technology. It is a resource for parents, educators, law enforcement officers, counselors, and others who work with youth. The site provides facts, figures, and detailed stories. It includes ways to help people prevent and respond to cyberbullying incidents.

http://www.cyberbullying.us/

MedlinePlus: Domestic Violence

This Web site is presented by the U.S. National Library of Medicine and the National Institutes of Health to provide accurate data on a variety of health issues. Information includes the basics, diagnoses, references, and resources.

http://www.nlm.nih.gov/medlineplus/domesticviolence.html

National Online Resource Center on Violence Against Women

This Web site is the online resource for advocates working to end domestic violence, sexual assault, and other violence in the lives of women and their children. It provides resources and research.

http://www.vawnet.org/

Men Against Violence

This group is a nonprofit corporation dedicated to reducing domestic violence. It is a group of committed men and women who actively provide early intervention to reduce domestic violence through the education and support of individuals who have been or may be at risk of offending.

http://www.menagainstviolence.org/

Same-Sex Dating Violence

This Web site is maintained by Student Services at Brown University to provide a wide range of information and resources regarding same-sex dating violence.

http://brown.edu/Student_Services/Health_Services/
Health_Education/sexual_assault_&_dating_violence/
dating_violence_in_LGBTQ_communities.php

Enough Is Enough

Enough.org is dedicated to protecting children and families from the Internet dangers of pornography and sexual predators. This Web site is the Internet safety site. It provides various resources, including information on the harms of pornography and tips for parents, such as how to report cybercrimes.

http://www.protectkids.com/effects/

UNIT 3

Violence in the Daily Lives of Women and Men

*V*iolence is an unfortunate part of many people's daily lives. It can range from exposure to violent images in the media, including television shows, movies, music videos, and electronic games, as well as pornography. Remarkably high percentages of children, adolescents, and adults report experiences with witnessing, experiencing, or engaging in name-calling, screaming, yelling, hitting, pushing, shoving, and slapping, with smaller numbers reporting violence that involves weapons. A major question regards the extent to which patterns of violence are gendered, for victims and for perpetrators. One of the most enduring stereotypes is that of aggressive men and passive women. But just how accurate is that stereotype? Research would suggest that the answer depends on how aggression is defined and whether one is looking at discrete behaviors or other forms of psychological control and abuse. Additionally, the meaning, motive, and outcome can alter how the gendered nature of violence is construed. Consistent with stereotypes, it has been assumed that level of testosterone plays a causal role in aggression, supporting the stereotype of male aggressiveness. However, recent research suggests that testosterone levels may be a result, not necessarily a cause. So, does aggression have a biological basis? Can studies of neurological and hormonal functioning better help us understand gendered patterns of experiences with violence? What insights does the study of race, ethnicity, and social class lend to our understanding of violence? How do media portrayals of aggressive women and men, as well as portrayals of male and female victims, fuel or challenge stereotypes?

- Gender Symmetry: Do Women and Men Commit Equal Levels of Violence Against Intimate Partners?
- Does Pornography Reduce the Incidence of Rape?
- Is Cyberbullying Related to Gender?

ISSUE 7

Gender Symmetry: Do Women and Men Commit Equal Levels of Violence Against Intimate Partners?

YES: **Murray A. Straus and Ignacio L. Ramirez**, from "Gender Symmetry in Prevalence, Severity, and Chronicity of Physical Aggression Against Dating Partners by University Students in Mexico and USA," *Aggressive Behavior* (2007)

NO: **Suzanne C. Swan and David L. Snow**, from "The Development of a Theory of Women's Use of Violence in Intimate Relationships," *Violence Against Women* (2006)

ISSUE SUMMARY

YES: Murray A. Straus and his colleague Ignacio L. Ramirez argue that women are just as likely to commit physical aggression against dating partners as are men, suggesting that gender symmetry exists in different cultural contexts.

NO: On the other hand, social psychologist Suzanne C. Swan and colleague David L. Snow argue that women's use of aggression does not equate to gender symmetry. Rather cultural context, motives, and history of trauma must be considered.

One of the most contentious and emotional issues in the intimate partner violence (IPV) literature surrounds the issue of "gender symmetry" in the use of aggression in relationships. For many years, the stereotype was of the male batterer and the female victim. Mental health, medical emergency room, and criminal justice data support this assumption. Many more women than men show up at shelters and emergency rooms suffering from the psychological and physical effects of abuse; many more women than men are likely to be murdered by an intimate partner. In contrast, most survey research that asks high school aged youth, college students, and community samples about their use of verbal and physical aggression in intimate relationships finds a very different pattern of results. In these studies, as many and sometimes more women as men report aggression against their partners, at least when the Conflict Tactics Scale (CTS) is the research instrument of choice. These data have led some researchers to conclude that such "gender symmetry" indicates that gender is not a central issue in intimate partner violence and that the study of IPV should move from the study of gender to other issues such as dominance. However, the same studies that use the CTS still find that women are more likely to be injured than men, suggesting to a different group of researchers that gender is still a central construct of interest. This perspective suggests that it is important to acknowledge and study women's aggression toward male partners, but to maintain a focus on gender. In fact, feminists have suggested that maintenance of the myth of the nonaggressive female contributes to continued discrimination against women. That is, if women are not aggressive, they must turn to men for protection (giving up their independence in exchange for the protection), they are not capable of leadership positions (based on the assumption that aggression is correlated with power, authority, and assertiveness), and if they are aggressive, they must be mentally ill (i.e., deviation from expected gender roles is an indicator of mental illness). Feminist research is challenging this myth in numerous ways, as reflected in several special issues of journals (*Violence Against Women, Psychology of Women Quarterly, Sex Roles*). In the selections that follow, Straus, the developer of the CTS, and his colleague demonstrate the typical pattern of gender symmetry found in survey research. In contrast, the selection by Swann and her colleagues examines the use of women's aggression toward intimate partners and presents a model for understanding female partner violence from a social contextual perspective that emphasizes one's own history of abuse along with the intersection of race, ethnicity, and class factors.

YES

Murray A. Straus and
Ignacio L. Ramirez

Gender Symmetry in Prevalence, Severity, and Chronicity of Physical Aggression Against Dating Partners by University Students in Mexico and USA

Introduction

A controversial issue in research on intimate partner violence (PV from here on) is whether this type of assault is primarily a crime perpetrated by men. A previous paper on this issue shows that when the statistics are based on data from the police or from surveys on crime victimization from 70 to 95% of PV perpetrators are men. On the other hand, the results of almost 200 studies using data from surveys of family problems and conflicts show that ". . . women are as physically aggressive, or more aggressive, than men in their relationships. . . . The aggregate sample size in the reviewed studies exceeds 58,000." The reason why police and crime survey data show PV to be a crime by males, whereas surveys of conflicts between partners in a couple relationship show that it is usually symmetrical or mutual were analyzed in a previous paper and will not be repeated here. Rather, this study is intended to move beyond tabulating the percent of men and women who had assaulted a partner during the time period covered by the study (typically the past year), by providing information on important additional aspects of PV such as the severity, chronicity of the assaults, and gender symmetry of assaults. Specifically, the purposes are:

- To determine the degree to which gender symmetry in PV is found in the diverse socio-cultural contexts in Mexico and the United States.
- To provide more detailed data on gender symmetry by
  - Providing data on the severity and chronicity of attacks by males and females.
  - Classifying couples into three groups: mutually violent, male partner only, and female partner only.
- To compare results based on data provided by male and female respondents.

From *Aggressive Behavior,* vol. 33, issue 4, 2007, pp. 281–289. Copyright © 2007 by John Wiley & Sons. Reprinted by permission.

Methods

Samples

The data [are] from the first four samples of the International Dating Violence *Study for which data became available. . . . The data were obtained by admin-*istering questionnaires to students in introductory sociology and psychology classes at the Universidad Autonoma de Ciudad Juarez, Mexico, University of Texas at El Paso, Texas Technological University, and the University of New Hampshire.

The data were gathered using procedures reviewed and approved by the boards for protection of human subjects at each of these universities. The purpose of the study and the students' right to not participate were explained orally as well as in printed form at the beginning of each session. Participants were told that the questionnaire asked about their attitudes, beliefs, and experiences they may have had, and that the questionnaire included questions on sensitive issues, including sexual relationships. They were assured of anonymity and confidentiality. A debriefing form was given to each participant as they left. The form explained the study in more detail and provided names and telephone numbers of area mental health services and community resources such as services for battered women. Although 1,554 students completed the questionnaire, as in other surveys, not everyone answered every question. Indeed, to respect the privacy and the voluntary nature of participation the instructions emphasized that respondents were free to omit any question they did not wish to answer. One hundred and eight students (6.9%) did not answer all the questions on violence against a partner. The number of cases analyzed was 1,446 for most of the analyses. However, some analyses are based on as few as 159 cases because they were restricted to the relatively small proportion of respondents who severely assaulted a partner. . . .

Measures

Physical Assault

The revised Conflict Tactics Scales or CTS2 was used to measure physical assault by the respondent. . . . The CTS has been used in many studies of both married and dating partners in the past 25 years and there is extensive evidence of reliability and validity. Respondents are asked to indicate how often they did each of the acts in the CTS and how often their partner did. This allows for analysis of symmetry, as well as patterns of the respondent's behavior. The CTS2 has scales to measure Physical Assault, Injury, Sexual Coercion, Psychological Aggression, and Negotiation. The analyses in this paper used data from the Physical Assault scale.

The CTS2 includes subscales for two levels of severity. The Minor Assault scale includes acts such as slapping or throwing something at the partner. The Severe Assault scale includes acts such as punching and choking. The difference between the minor and severe subscales is analogous to the US legal categories of simple assault and aggravated assault. The following scores were computed:

Prevalence.   Prevalence refers to whether respondents carried out one or more of the 12 acts of physical assault in the CTS in the previous 12 months. The analysis used two measures of prevalence, one for any versus no assault (referred to as "assault"), and one for severe assault versus both no assaults and minor assaults (referred to as "severe assault").

Severity level.   A problem with the Minor Assault scale is that some of the respondents who reported minor assaults probably also carried out more severe attacks on a partner. To have a variable in which the two are mutually exclusive, respondents were classified into one of three categories: 1 = none, 2 = minor only (i.e., one or more acts of minor violence but no instance of severe violence), and 3 = severe.

Chronicity.   The CTS asks respondents to indicate how many times in the previous year they have either perpetrated or been victim of each of the acts in the scale. Chronicity was calculated only for respondents who reported at least one instance of physical assault. Chronicity therefore indicates the number of times that subjects who were physically aggressive to a partner carried out acts of physical aggression. For a discussion of the rationale of the chronicity measure of the CTS2.

Symmetry types.   Three types were identified: *male-only* refers to couples in which violence in the relationship was perpetrated only by the male partner. *Female-only* violence refers to couples where the only violence in the relationship was perpetrated by the female partner. *Both* refers to couples in which both the male and female partner committed at least one of the acts of physical assault in the previous 12 months. Symmetry types were computed only if the respondent reported that they, and/or their partner had perpetrated an assault.

Social Desirability Response Bias

Criminological research that uses self-report data need to take into account defensiveness or minimization of socially undesirable behavior. The Limited Disclosure scale of the PRP [Straus and Mouradian, 1999; Straus et al., 1999] was used to control for the variation in individual respondents' tendencies to minimize socially undesirable behavior. This scale is a 13-item version of the widely used Crown–Marlow social desirability scale developed by Reynolds [1982]. The scale measures the degree to which respondents tend to avoid disclosing socially undesirable behavior.

Socioeconomic Status

Socioeconomic status was measured as a composite of the respondent's mother's and father's education, and family income. To control for differences in educational systems and for differences in incomes and purchasing power across countries and geographic regions, parent's education and family income were standardized (z-scored) separately for each sample, before being summed. For interpretability, the sum was then transformed to a z-score. Thus, in each sample, the score of a respondent indicates the number of standard deviations above or below the mean of respondents in that sample.

Results

Prevalence of Assaults on Dating Partners

Combined samples.   When all four samples are analyzed together, a third of the students (33.7%) reported they had physically assaulted a dating partner in the previous 12 months. This is consistent with many other studies of dating violence by university students.

Sample differences.   The percent of students reporting violence was high in all four samples, but also differed significantly between samples. . . . The lowest rate was in New Hampshire (29.7%), followed by Texas, Non-Mexican Whites (30.9%), Texas Mexican American (34.2%), and the highest rate of assault was in Juarez (46.1%).

Gender differences.   Although there were significant differences between samples, . . . the rates for males and females were similar. Thus, the four samples analyzed in this paper had similar rates of partner-assault by men and women. This finding is consistent with previous research on couple conflict discussed in the introduction.

Severe Assaults on Dating Partners

The similar rates of assaulting a partner by men and women could be misleading because the overall rate combines minor acts such as slapping and throwing things with more severe assaults involving punching, kicking, choking, etc. It is possible that the overall rate of assaults could be equal, but a larger proportion of the assaults by men could be in the form of attacks that are more likely to result in an injury. This possibility was investigated by examining the severity level of assaults.

Combined samples.   Overall, more than one out of ten students (11.4%) reported severely attacking a partner (acts such as punching, kicking, or choking).

Sample differences.   The samples differed significantly in the rate of severe violence. The differences were similar to the difference for the overall violence rate, i.e., the lowest rate was in New Hampshire (9.3%), followed by Mexican-Americans in Texas (12.4%), Non-Mexicans in Texas (14.2%) and highest in Juarez (15%).

Gender differences.   [T]he rates of severe assault are almost identical for men and women. Thus, the similarity between men and women in the overall rate of violence against a partner also applies to severe attacks.

When severity level scores were examined, controlling for age, SES, and score on the Social Desirability Response scale no significant differences in the scores of male and female students were found. The interaction of gender and sample was also non-significant indicating that the absence of a gender difference applied to all four samples.

Chronicity of Assaults

Combined samples.   The results from these four samples show that, among the couples where there was violence, it was not usually a one-time occurrence. Students who were physically aggressive to a partner carried out a mean of 14.7 acts of physical aggression in the previous 12 months. However, the mean overstates the typical pattern because of a relatively few cases in which violence occurred once a week or more, including a few where it was almost daily. Therefore, the median of four times in the previous year gives a better picture of the typical pattern of violence between dating couples.

A surprising finding was that average number of *severe* assaults (15.6) and the median number of severe assaults (4) was just about the same as mean and medians for the total assault scale. This indicates that when violence is severe, it also tends to be as chronic as minor assaults.

Sample differences.   The chronicity of overall assaults was similar across samples. The chronicity of severe assaults was also similar across samples. Thus, the mean chronicity of both overall and severe assaults is similar across the four samples.

Gender differences.   There was no significant difference between males and females in the chronicity of physical aggression overall. However, when severe assaults were considered separately, men hit their partner more than twice as frequently as women (mean of 21.9 times versus 9.3 times). The median for severe violence by men was four times in the previous year and for women three times. The large difference between the mean and the median indicates that for both men and women, but especially for men, the high mean score reflects a large influence of a relatively few extremely violent individuals. . . . [R]egardless of whether the mean or median is used, men who severely attacked their partner during the 12 month period covered by this study tended to do so more often than the women who engaged in severe assaults. Tests for a sample by gender interaction were non-significant for both overall and severe assaults. Thus, the analysis indicates that in all four samples, among individuals who assaulted their partners, men and women did so with similar frequency; in contrast, among individuals who were severely violent, men severely assaulted their partners more frequently than women.

Gender Symmetry in Assaults

Combined samples.   Among the 553 couples where one or both of the partners were violent, in almost three quarters of the cases (71.2%) gender symmetry was found, that is, both partners perpetrated one or more assault. When only one partner was violent, this was more than twice as likely to be the female partner (19.0%) as the male partner (9.8%). Among the 205 couples where there was an act of severe aggression, symmetry was less prevalent (56.6%), but when only one partner was violent, it was again twice as likely to be the female partner (29.8% female only versus 13.7% male partner only).

The finding that women are more likely to be the only violent partner differs from the results of studies of married and cohabiting couples in the general population. General population studies tend to show that, when there is violence by only one partner, it is as likely to be the male partner as the female partner. . . . [F]or [a] nationally representative sample of couples almost identical rates of partner assault by males and females, except for the youngest couples [has been found.] At ages 18–19, the rate for women is 47% greater than the rate for men. At ages 20–24 women exceed men by 18%, however, among respondents 25 and over, rates of partner assault are almost identical for men and women. A meta-analysis of 37 studies of college students and 27 studies of community samples found that in the community samples the rate of PV by women exceeded the male rate only very slightly. However, among the student samples, the female rate was greater than the rate of PV by males. Thus, the younger the individual, the more the female rate of assaulting a partner exceeds the rate for males. If that generalization is correct, the tendency in this sample of students for women to more often be the only violent partner probably reflects the youthfulness of the sample.

Sample differences. [G]ender symmetry in the overall assault rate across samples [was evident]. [T]he pattern of predominantly mutual violence described above was consistent when the four samples are examined individually. However, [there were] significant differences between samples for severe assaults. The most important difference is that students in the New Hampshire sample had by far the lowest percentage in both categories, and the highest percentage in the Female Only category.

The measure of gender symmetry was based on the questionnaire completed by one partner reporting on both their own behavior and the behavior of the partner. This procedure is open to the possibility that what seems to be symmetry could really be the result of men underreporting their violent behavior. To examine this possibility the Gender Symmetry measure was cross-tabulated by the sex of the respondent, [but] no significant difference in gender symmetry based on reports by male and female partners [emerged].

Discussion

The results of this study provide strong evidence of gender symmetry in respect to violence against a dating partner. First, the results were similar in four different samples with large differences in the socio-cultural setting. Second, the results showing gender symmetry and differences between samples remained after controlling for the age of the respondent, the severity and chronicity of violence, and controlling for socioeconomic status and for social desirability response bias. The results indicate that women and men have similar prevalence rates for both any and severe assaults, and for chronicity of minor assaults. Further, in the majority of couples where one partner is violent, both partners have committed one or more assaults. An important exception to the pattern of gender symmetry was that, among the subgroup of respondents who committed one or more acts of severe violence, men in all four samples did it more often than women. Finally, there is agreement between results based on data provided by males and females.

Methodological Implications

These results have important implications for the methodology of research on PV, and for primary prevention of PV. With respect to methodology, the results show that male or female respondents provide equivalent results. Thus, either partner can be the source of the data in research on PV in non-clinical populations. However, although it is not necessary to obtain data from both partners in a relationship, given that individuals of both sexes appear to underreport their own perpetration, and over-report assaults by partners, in any study of gender differences it is desirable to obtain data from both male and female respondents. Additionally, the parallel results in each of the four cultural settings suggests that the Conflict Tactics Scales is appropriate for use in cross-cultural research.

The robustness of the results cited, and the consistency of the results with many previous studies showing gender symmetry in PV, adds urgency to the need for steps to extend efforts at primary and secondary prevention of PV to women offenders. Also relevant are the studies showing that women initiate PV as often as men and the studies showing that women are injured more often and more seriously than men. Consequently, programs and policies aimed at primary prevention of PV *by women* are crucial for reducing the victimization of not only men but also women.

The High Proportion of Female Violence in New Hampshire

The high percentage in the Female Only and Both Violent category in New Hampshire could reflect the operation of two principles. One is the "convergence theory" of crime by women. This theory holds that as women become equal in other spheres of life, they will also tend to become more equal in respect to committing crime. The data for New Hampshire fit the convergence theory. First, New Hampshire had the highest degree of equality between women and men of the four samples. Second, although New Hampshire had the lowest overall rate of PV, among the couples where violence occurred, it had the largest proportion committed by women.

A second possibility is the cost-benefit theory formulated by Archer. He found that ". . . sex differences in partner aggression follow the perceived costs and benefits of physically aggressing in that social setting." In patriarchal social settings, violation of the male dominance principle in any form, and specifically by hitting a male partner, is likely to elicit severe physical retaliation. However, the social context in New Hampshire is almost the opposite. Women at the University of New Hampshire tend to come from high education and high-income families. Because of the small size of the state, many students live at home and even those living on campus are usually less than an hour from their home. They are thus in relatively protected positions. However, that also tends to be true of students in Ciudad Juarez and El Paso. Perhaps most important, women in New Hampshire have a relatively high degree of equality with men and physical violence against female partners is relatively low compared to other states of the USA. These characteristics may lower the costs women perceive of hitting a partner, and thus alter the cost-benefit ratio enough to produce a higher rate of violence by women than in the other samples.

These comments suggest some issues for future research. For example, why do women, who are on average weaker than men, engage in and initiate violence at least as often as men, whereas outside of family and dating relationships, women engage in a fraction of the violence perpetrated by men? Although Straus has outlined a theoretical model which might explain the discrepancy, it has yet to be tested. Another important avenue of research is twin studies which could provide information on genetic and environmental factors that predict PV. . . . Another needed type of research on gender symmetry in PV concerns the social context. One aspect of social context that has been investigated is the degree to which the society and the family system is male-dominant. However, the many other possible social context effects is illustrated by the Culture of Honor theory which states that violence in defense of honor will be more prevalent in ancestrally herding than in traditionally farming communities. The differences between samples in this study are consistent with that theory. . . .

Prevention Implications

Almost all primary and secondary prevention efforts are based on the assumption that PV is perpetrated primarily by men. There are several reasons for this false assumption. First, programs to end PV were initiated by and continue to be a major effort of the women's movement. Another reason is that women are much more likely to be physically, psychologically, and economically injured than men. Finally, about 90% of assaults and murders outside the family are perpetrated by men and it is easy to assume that this must also apply to PV.

PV by men, but not by women has been decreasing since the mid 1970s but PV by women on male partners have stayed about the same. The failure of prevention and treatment programs to address PV by women may partly explain why PV by men has decreased, but PV by women has remained constant. An ironic aspect is that although the number of male victims has remained high, there is no funding for services for male victims, and almost no research on male victims of PV.

Rather than ignoring assaults by female partners, primary prevention of PV requires strong efforts to end assaults by women. A fundamental reason is the intrinsic moral wrong of assaulting a spouse, as expressed in the fact that such assaults are criminal acts, even when no injury occurs. Second, males are the victims of about a third of injuries inflicted on partners, including about a third of homicides of partners. Third is the unintended validation by women of the traditional cultural norms tolerating a certain level of violence between spouses. A fourth reason for a strong effort to reduce PV by women is the danger of escalation when women engage in "harmless" minor violence. [I]f both partners were violent, it increases the probability that assaults are likely to persist or escalate in severity over [a] 2 year period; whereas if only one partner engages in physical attacks, the probability of a subsequent violence decreases. Finally, when a woman assaults her partner, it "models" violence for the children and therefore contributes to PV in the next generation. This modeling effect is as strong for assaults by women as is assaults by men.

Although it is essential that primary and secondary prevention of PV include a major focus on violence by women as well as men, the needed change must be made with extreme care for a number of reasons. First, it must be done in ways that simultaneously refute the idea that violence by women justifies or excuses violence by their partners. Second, although women may assault partners at approximately the same rate as men, assaults by men usually inflict greater physical, financial, and emotional injury. This means that male violence against women, on average, results in more severe victimization. Thus, a focus on protecting and assisting female victims must remain a priority, despite the fact that services for male victims (now essentially absent) need to be made available. Finally, in many societies women lack full economic, social, political, and human rights. In such cultural contexts, equality for women needs to be given priority as an even more fundamental aspect of primary prevention of PV. Otherwise focusing on PV by women can further exacerbate the oppression of women in those societies.

Suzanne C. Swan and
David L. Snow

NO

The Development of a Theory of Women's Use of Violence in Intimate Relationships

Several reports appeared in the popular press in the late 1990s concluding that women are just as violent as men. These reports often cite the many studies of self-reported physical aggression based on data from the Conflict Tactics Scale (CTS), a widely used measure of physical aggression between intimate partners. Indeed, a meta-analysis of gender differences in rates of physical abuse found that women were slightly more likely than men to use physical aggression against intimate partners. These findings have generated a great deal of controversy, in part because there has been no theoretical framework to explain women's violence.

The conclusion that "women are just as violent as men" is problematic. The studies on which these media reports are based typically examined only physical aggression, not other types of abuse; and they do not place the occurrence of women's violence within a broader social, cultural, or historical context. For example, [the] meta-analysis did not examine sexual assault, stalking, or coercive control; studies that include such behaviors tend to find higher rates of these types of violence committed by males, as do crime surveys. A theoretical framework to guide research on intimate partner violence (IPV) and, therefore, the popular discourse on women's violence, is sorely needed. A comprehensive theory of women's violence with intimate partners should include all types of abuse, not just physical aggression; the woman's abuse against the partner and the partner's abuse against the woman; the woman's relationship history, including experiences of childhood abuse or previous adult relationships that were abusive; her motivations for using abuse; the outcomes of her abuse, for herself, her partner, and her children; and the larger cultural context of gender, race and ethnicity, and social class. Without an understanding of women's violence in context, policy makers and others will draw erroneous conclusions from the data and will implement misguided "gender neutral" policies that penalize women and place them in increased danger.

In fact, "gender neutral" applications of domestic violence (DV) law already harm women. Although dual arrests and mutual restraining orders are necessary in some cases, the overreliance on these practices in some courts is

From *Violence Against Women*, vol. 12, no. 11, 2006, pp. 1026–1040. Copyright © 2006 by Sage Publications. Reprinted by permission.

misinformed at best, and at worst, it penalizes women who call on the criminal justice system because their lives are in danger. [O]ur cultural conception of a *battered woman* is that she deserves sympathy and protection by the law; however, a woman who fights back against her partner's violence violates our notion of acceptable feminine behavior. She thus shares the blame for her own victimization. However, it is likely that many battered women have used violence against their partners at some time, as a survival strategy and in retaliation for abuse and humiliation. For example, one study found that 33% of women residing in a DV shelter reported having used minor violence against their partners, and 24% reported using severe violence. [I]ntimate violence is gendered; that is, women's motivations for violence and the context in which the violence takes place are qualitatively different than those of men. A gendered, feminist theoretical approach, that is, one that "uses gender as a central organizing variable for understanding human behavior and social organization", is needed to understand women's violence.

The goal of this article is to provide an interpretive framework for women's violence by proposing a comprehensive, contextual model of women's violence in intimate relationships. A major emphasis is placed on the need for contextualism in the development of such a theory. Contextualism underscores that human behavior does not develop in a social vacuum but is situated within a sociohistorical and cultural context of meanings and relationships, like a message that makes sense only in terms of the total context in which it occurs. Without a focus on context in our development of theory, methods of inquiry, and interventions, there continues to be a strong tendency to locate problems in individuals. This increases the likelihood of "blaming the victim" and leaves us with limited understandings of complex social phenomena.

Based on these principles, the model of women's violence presented here includes: (a) women's violence in the context of their victimization by male partners; (b) factors that influence women's violence and victimization, namely, women's motivations for violent behavior and the coping strategies women utilize in response to relationship problems; (c) the historical context of women's experiences of childhood trauma; and (d) outcomes of depression, anxiety, posttraumatic stress disorder (PTSD), and substance use. This article briefly reviews the literature on each of these dimensions and presents a comprehensive model of women's violence and victimization, its antecedents, and its consequences. When developed, the model is examined within the context of *intersectionality*, that is, the intersection of important status variables, such as gender, race, and class that shape the experiences of women in violent relationships.

Women's Violence in the Context of Their Victimization

The evidence gathered to date strongly suggests that women are almost always violent in the context of violence against them by their male partners. Women's violence must be studied within this context. For example, in a study of 108 women who had recently used violence against an intimate male partner, women's self-reported rates of different types of violence were examined, including moderate and severe physical violence, sexual violence, emotional and/or verbal abuse, and coercive control behavior. Women reported the frequency of their male partners' commission of these behaviors as well. [This study] found that only six of the 108 participants experienced no physical victimization or injury from their male partners.

The types and prevalence of abusive behaviors committed by women also differ from those committed by men. [The study] found that women used equivalent levels of emotional and/or verbal abuse (e.g., yelling and screaming, name calling) as their partners used against them. Women also committed significantly more moderate physical violence (e.g., throwing something, pushing and/or shoving) than their partners used against them. However, women were more often victims of quite serious types of abuse, including sexual coercion, injury, and coercive control behaviors (e.g., restricting social contact, controlling the partner's activities and decisions).

These findings illustrate how the picture of women's violence changes with a more detailed examination of severity, frequency, and type of violence committed by both partners. [W]omen and men engaged in put-downs, insults, and yelling at equivalent rates. However, men much more frequently used coercive control tactics than women. This is not to say that women cannot be jealous or controlling; rather, it is much less common for a woman to have the ability to maintain significant control of a man's behavior because this type of control is maintained through fear. As a general rule, women simply do not inspire fear in men. Women were more frequently victims than perpetrators of the kinds of experiences that inspire terror, such as sexual violence and injury. Clearly, we cannot fully understand the nature, extent, and meaning of women's violence without considering the overall patterns of violence that occur in their intimate relationships. . . .

Women's Motivations for Violent Behavior

Self-defense.   Research suggests that the motivations for women's violent behavior in intimate relationships are often quite different from those for men. Several studies have found that women cite self-defense as a motivation for violence more frequently than men. For example, one study comparing the motivations for violence of college students found that 36% of women listed self-defense as a motivation compared to 18% of men. . . .

Fear.   Women also are more likely to report fear in DV situations. . . . This fear is well founded: In DV situations, women are much more likely than men to be injured, and injured severely. . . . Thus, some women's violence occurs in the context of fear of assault from their partners and the need to protect themselves from physical harm.

Defense of children.   It has been estimated that 30% to 60% of children whose mothers are battered are themselves victims of abuse. Children living with an abused mother have been found to be 12 to 14 times more likely to be sexually abused than children whose mothers were not abused. The effects of family violence on children, in terms of actual physical abuse of children and what children witness, affect how women behave in violent relationships. Some women behave violently toward their partners to protect their children and themselves.

Control.   Studies consistently show that men are more likely than women to use violence to regain control of the relationship or a partner who is challenging their authority. Findings from [a] study of men and women court ordered to a DV treatment program indicated that men were more likely to initiate and control the dynamics of violence, whereas women used violence but did not control those dynamics. However, this does not mean that control motives are completely absent from women's violence. [W]omen [have] stated that they had threatened to use violence at least sometimes to make their partner do the things they wanted him to do. . . .

Retribution.   Finally, several studies suggest that retribution for real or perceived wrongdoing is a common motivator of women's and men's violent behavior. . . . Women and men stated they used violence in retribution for their partners' attacks against them. However, men also reported using violence in retribution for their partners' unwanted behavior, such as infidelity or lying, while no women reported this motivation. In contrast, women stated they used violence in retribution for the partners' emotionally abusive behavior (e.g., "punishment for his insults"), while men did not. . . .

Women's Coping with Violent Relationships

The issue of how women cope with an abusive partner has received some attention in the DV literature; however, little research from a stress-and-coping framework has been conducted. In the general literature, coping is often grouped into three types: avoidant, problem solving, and support seeking. Studies relating coping to a variety of psychological and physical health outcomes typically find that avoidant strategies are related to poorer outcomes, and problem solving and support seeking are related to positive outcomes. Among victims of DV, avoidant coping strategies have been associated with the development of psychological problems such as depression. Problem-solving coping, on the other hand, has been related to well-being. Several studies document the variety of active coping strategies battered women use in response to abuse. Social support has also been found to be a protective factor for battered women; it has been found to be related to reduced symptoms of PTSD and depression.

. . . Problem-solving coping [has been found] negatively correlated with women's violence, indicating that the more problem-solving strategies women employed, the less violence they use. Avoidance coping was positively correlated with violence. . . .

Childhood Trauma

Evidence from several different studies indicates that rates of childhood trauma and abuse are very high among women who use violence. . . .

Several studies have found that experiences of childhood abuse are a risk factor for violent behavior and victimization as adults. A longitudinal study of 136 women who were treated at a hospital for sexual abuse as children examined the impact of childhood abuse on the women as adults. Childhood experiences of sexual abuse predicted women's use of violence against partners and their victimization from partners. Experiences of being hit or beaten by a parent also predicted women's violence against their partners. [D]ifferent types of childhood trauma correlated with women's violence and other related variables. Experiencing childhood sexual and physical abuse was positively correlated with women's use of violence and women's sexual victimization from their partners. Childhood emotional abuse experiences correlated with women's coercive control behavior and their use of avoidance coping strategies to deal with relationship violence. . . .

Outcomes

Four psychological outcomes have been associated with traumatic experiences in general, and DV victimization in particular: depression, anxiety, substance abuse, and PTSD. In a meta-analysis of IPV as a risk factor for mental disorders, the weighted mean prevalence of depression among battered women was approximately 50%. Battered women have a higher prevalence of anxiety disorders compared to the general female population. Battered women are also at risk for substance abuse. . . . Finally, the rate of diagnostic PTSD among women who experience IPV is around 40%. . . .

Sociocultural Context of Women's Violence

This section of the article examines women's violence within the context of the intersectionality of race, ethnicity, and culture. These contextual factors "color the meaning and nature of DV, how it is experienced by self and responded to by others, how personal and social consequences are represented, and how and whether escape and safety can be obtained". A focus on intersectionality in research on IPV enhances understanding of the phenomenon and increases the external validity of the study findings to different ethnic and cultural groups. . . .

African American Culture and Women's Violence with Intimate Partners

The literature on family violence within the African American culture reveals several protective and risk factors that may affect women's use of violence. One area that is relatively unique to African American culture, as compared to other American ethnic groups, is the expectation that African American women are "strong" and invulnerable. . . . [The] strong Black woman [has been defined] as self-sufficient, independent, and able to survive difficulties without assistance. The strong Black woman takes care of not only her own problems but also those of her family and community. However, without a balance between self-care and care for others, vulnerability to physical and mental health problems can result.

In the context of DV, a consequence of the "strong woman" expectation is that African American women may be expected to hold the family together and protect their men from the hostile mainstream culture, regardless of the cost to themselves. A woman striving to be strong and independent may be reluctant to ask for outside help and may be accused of disloyalty to the Black community if she "airs dirty laundry to White folks" by reporting the violence. Battered African American women may also be faced with the dilemma that if they report abuse, they are reinforcing negative stereotypes that intimate relationships between Black men and women are inherently dysfunctional, and that Black men are naturally violent.

As the "strong woman" construction of African American femininity implies, gender roles in African American culture differ from other ethnic groups. Some literature suggests that African American couples may be more egalitarian in some respects (e.g., acceptance of women's employment, more equitable distribution of child care). These egalitarian gender roles may in some cases reduce the risk of violence. On the other hand, when there is violence in the relationship, some African American women may hit back because their relationships are more egalitarian; that is, if the couple believes that the woman has the same rights as her male partner, then if he hits her, she has the same right to hit him. . . .

In addition, African American women may be reluctant to use legal interventions because of the history of mistreatment of African Americans by the criminal justice system. African American women who fight back may end up getting arrested themselves. Even if African American women have not fought back, they may still be perceived as "inauthentic victims" (Bell & Mattis, 2000). The "strong woman" socialization includes hiding one's vulnerability, especially in the presence of Whites. . . .

Other social services may also be less than helpful for African American women involved in violent relationships. One common problem is that service providers may not understand or be sensitive to the experiences of Black women. Thus, Black women may be less likely to use these services or, if they do, may not find them to be helpful. However, culturally appropriate social services (such as DV support groups), particularly those run by and for African American women, have been found to be very helpful.

Another problem African American women in abusive relationships may face is the lack of possibilities of alternative relationships. Many Black women, particularly middle-class women, have noted a shortage in eligible African American men of their status. Some women may remain in an abusive relationship because they do not believe they will be able to find another partner. Another risk factor may be the financial burdens faced by many African American women. Although poverty exists in all ethnic groups, it is disproportionately high among African Americans. Women with very limited finances, particularly those with children, may remain in abusive relationships for economic reasons.

A potential resilience factor for African American women is a positive racial identity. Racial socialization is the "responsibility of raising physically and emotionally healthy children who are Black in a society in which being Black has negative connotations". [R]acial socialization to take pride in Black heritage and culture, use spirituality and religion as coping mechanisms, draw on extended family for social support, and be aware of and cope with racism will all serve as protective factors for African Americans. This protection may extend to a decreased likelihood of involvement in DV as well.

A buffer against violence among some African American families may be a greater involvement with extended kin and community. . . . The extended family network may also exert social pressure to curb a male partner's violence against a woman. On the other hand, some African American women with strong family support may forgo that support because they want to protect their families from the risks of getting involved. Other buffers that may be particularly important in African American culture include religious supports, spirituality, and a strong sense of being embedded in one's community and neighborhood.

In sum, African American women may be trapped in violent relationships for a variety of reasons, including the "strong woman's" responsibility to keep the family together, lack of access to and help from legal or social services, and economic needs. From the perspective of women's violence, then, we propose that the more a woman is trapped as a result of these various factors in a violent relationship, the more likely she will be to use violence to protect herself. This may hold especially true for African American women because of cultural expectations regarding the strength of Black women and relatively egalitarian gender roles. Potential buffers include positive racial socialization and involvement with extended family and religious communities.

Latino Culture and Women's Violence with Intimate Partners

In an examination of family violence in Latino culture, it is important to consider not only the minority status of Latinos in the United States but also immigration, country of origin, and acculturation. According to the 2000 U.S. Census, 40% of Latinos living in the United States were born in other countries. Studies have found substantial differences in the prevalence of family violence based on country of origin. One large-scale survey found the highest rates of male-to-female violence in Puerto Rican families (20.4%), followed by Mexican Americans (14.2%), Anglos (9.9%), and Cubans (2.5%). These differences in prevalence are probably confounded in part by the socioeconomic status of people emigrating from those countries.

The role of acculturation in family violence appears to be critical for many Latinos who have immigrated to the United States. *Acculturation* has been defined as the process by which an immigrant's attitudes and behaviors change toward those of the predominant cultural group as a result of exposure to the new culture. Recent studies indicate that couples who are in the midst of undergoing the acculturation process—who are in between the gender roles of the country of origin and those of the mainstream United States—may be at the highest risk of partner violence. . . .

Why does acculturation appear to affect women's aggression toward partners more than men's behavior? Migration may change the rules of behavior more for women than for men. Aggression is much less acceptable for women in Latin America than in the United States. Some studies have explored the gender role conflict that can occur when Latino couples sort out the new roles they are exposed to through acculturation. . . . Mexican American women who were born in the United States had higher levels of education, and worked outside the home experienced more violence than women who were born in Mexico, had less education, and did not work. In addition, the more acculturated, educated, working women had different expectations about their role in the family than did their husbands, leading to conflict about men's and women's roles and abuse by their husbands. In contrast, when the women and their husbands agreed on gender roles, whether egalitarian or traditional, the incidence of violence was lower.

Traditional gender roles affect Latinas' perceptions of what constitutes abuse and how to respond to it. In one study, although Latina, African American, and Anglo women living in shelters reported similar severity of abuse, Latinas reported the longest duration of abuse and the fewest attempts to seek help. . . .

Barriers to seeking outside help may also increase Latina women's risk of abuse. Immigration status frequently prevents women from reporting DV to authorities. For example, Detroit police reported a large volume of calls from Latina women who had been victims of violence; however, many women did not want to prosecute the abusers because of fear of deportation. Language barriers also prevent many Latinas from seeking or receiving help. Among battered Mexican, Mexican American, and Puerto Rican women, Latinas who sought help had greater proficiency in English. Finally, the barriers to getting out of abusive relationships created by poverty cannot be overestimated. The issues related to poverty are manifold: unemployment, lack of affordable housing, inability to afford child care, lack of transportation—all of which can trap a woman in a violent relationship.

Protective factors for Latinas include strong family supports. Latinas will often seek help and advice from their families first before seeking help from outsiders. Latinas are more likely to live in larger households with extended family, and to marry and start families earlier than other ethnic groups. The family, then, provides a strong base of support; family members watch out for one another. In the case of battering, however, if the family is not able or willing to help the woman, she may be very reluctant to "betray" the family by going outside of it for help. In some cases, the extended family may contribute to the woman's oppression. For recent immigrants who left their extended families in their home countries, family supports may be absent. . . .

Spirituality can also be an important source of support for Latina women in DV situations. . . . However, the church can be nonsupportive of battered women as well, advising them to endure the abuse. Finally, as is the case for African Americans, positive ethnic identity has been proposed as an important protective factor for the well-being of Latinas.

Class and Socioeconomic Issues

Virtually every study of DV that examines socioeconomic status (SES) finds that poverty is consistently and robustly related to higher prevalence rates of IPV. In fact, in most studies that control for the effects of SES, differences in the prevalence rates of IPV between racial and/or ethnic groups disappear. However, very few studies have explored what it is about poverty that elevates the risk of IPV.

[A] study of the impact of race, SES, and neighborhood on the prevalence of DV . . . examined a number of objective indicators of social class, including neighborhood disadvantage (e.g., number of people below the poverty line, number of unemployed people), employment instability of the male partner, insufficiency of income to meet basic needs, and a subjective measure of financial strain. [It was] found that the relationship between male-to-female partner violence and SES was not linear; rather, those women living in the bottom 25% of the most disadvantaged neighborhoods experienced twice the prevalence of partner violence compared to those in the upper 75%. . . . After entering economic distress indicators into the model, the impact of race on rates of DV disappeared; [that is,] severe economic disadvantage in a neighborhood fosters anonymity and reduced social controls on IPV—neighbors are not looking out for one another, leaving DV unchecked. These neighborhood economic factors were found to increase the likelihood of women's and men's use of violence with their intimate partners.

Discussion

This article develops a theoretical framework for furthering our understanding of the phenomenon of women's violence. Particular emphasis is placed on the need to study women's violence within social, historical, and cultural contexts. The model proposes a number of risk and protective factors that appear to be related to women's use of violence with male partners, including the male partners' violence against women, experiences of childhood trauma, women's strategies for coping with problems in their relationships, women's motivations for using violence, and the outcomes of depression, anxiety, substance abuse, and PTSD. We argue for the importance of sociocultural contexts in developing theory regarding women's use of violence with intimate partners. Although only two ethnic groups were examined in detail in this article, future research should examine the effects of culture on women's violence with other ethnic groups.

Models of IPV, such as that proposed here, should also be examined longitudinally. Interrelationships among variables in the model are clearly dynamic; variables that are shown as mediators or outcomes in the various models may also operate as antecedents. For example, one possible alternative model is as follows: Women who have experienced childhood trauma are at risk of developing PTSD. PTSD increases the likelihood of developing maladaptive coping strategies, such as avoidance coping and poor problem solving, thereby increasing the likelihood that women with PTSD will get involved in, and remain in, violent relationships.

The model proposed here includes a number of critical dimensions that are relevant to women's violence; however, there are certainly other important factors that should be examined in future research. For example, the model does not include age, which has consistently been found to be related to DV, with younger individuals more likely to use violence against partners. It also does not focus on Axis II disorders, such as borderline personality disorder, and the extent to which such disorders may be involved in women's violence. The model only examines outcomes for women, not for their male partners or their children, and is presented in the context of heterosexual relationships. The relationships among variables proposed here may or may not apply to lesbians. The model proposed in this article, although serving as a framework for advancing a theory of women's violence, needs to be tested and refined. Through this process, the field will advance in developing a more comprehensive understanding of women's violence.

POSTSCRIPT

Gender Symmetry: Do Women and Men Commit Equal Levels of Violence Against Intimate Partners?

The debate about gender symmetry is fueled in part by a continued focus on the question of sex differences rather than on the factors and processes that contribute to intimate partner violence. A shift in focus would lead to questions of why some women and some men abuse their partners. Gender can be reintroduced into the discussion by focusing on how traditional constructions of masculinity and the power associated with it contribute to both women's and men's involvement in partner aggression as victim and/or perpetrator. For example, when women are aggressive, are they trying to gain power in a situation in which they feel powerless? Do men engage in aggression because they are attempting to counter threats to their masculinity? A shift in focus may also encourage researchers to more broadly define intimate partner violence so that it includes not only physical aggression, but also verbal and psychological aggression, as well as sexual assault. In doing so gender again enters the discussion in a way that asks whether there are different patterns of IPV. For example, men are much more likely to sexually coerce female partners than vice versa. Women may be more likely to persist in use of violence when they have partners who do not engage in aggression; this is known as the "rational choice" strategy. Maureen McHugh has suggested that a postmodern approach to conceptualizing women's use of aggression should include rejecting polarized stances in the debate on gender symmetry; that is, a sex difference approach is not useful. It ignores too much of the context and dynamic nature of intimate partner violence. Rather there should be a focus on human interactions, examining the meaning and consequences of the experience for all involved. There should be a recognition that patterns of intimate partner violence are multiple and varied, and that perpetrators can be victims and victims can be perpetrators. This latter point raises the possibility that intimate partner violence may be mutual, although it is not necessarily symmetric. Women and men may both commit acts of aggression but in the context of gendered constructions of power and status motives, meanings and consequences are highly unlikely to be symmetric.

Suggested Readings

Nicola Gavey, *Just Sex?: The Cultural Scaffolding of Rape* (Routledge, 2005).

Lisa Goodman and D. Epstein, *Listening to Battered Women: A Survivor-Centered Approach to Advocacy, Mental Health, and Justice* (Washington, DC: American Psychological Association, 2008).

Christopher Kilmartin and Julie Allison, *Men's Violence Against Women: Theory, Research and Activism* (Routledge, 2007).

Special issue: Female Violence Against Intimate Partners. *Psychology of Women Quarterly, 29*(3) (September 2005).

Special issue: Understanding Gender and Intimate Partner Abuse. *Sex Roles 52*(11/12) (June 2005).

Three-part special issue: Women's Use of Violence in Intimate Relationships. *Violence Against Women, 8*(11 & 12), *9*(1) (2006).

ISSUE 8

Does Pornography Reduce the Incidence of Rape?

YES: Anthony D'Amato, from "Porn Up, Rape Down," Northwestern University School of Law, Public Law and Legal Theory Research Paper Series (June 23, 2006)

NO: Judith Reisman, from "Pornography's Link to Rape," WorldnetDaily.com (July 29, 2006)

ISSUE SUMMARY

YES: Professor of law Anthony D'Amato highlights statistics from the most recent National Crime Victimization Survey that demonstrate a correlation between the increased consumption of pornography over the years with the decreased incidence of rape. Some people, he argues, watch pornography in order to push any desire to rape out of their minds, and thus have no further desire to go out and actually do it.

NO: Judith Reisman, president of the Institute for Media Education, asserts that sex criminals imitate what they see depicted in the media, providing examples of serial rapists and killers who had large stores of pornography in their possession, and research in which approximately 33 percent of rapists said that they had viewed pornography immediately prior to at least one of their rapes.

Since the creation of the Internet, the world has seen a huge increase in the amount and manner in which information is exchanged with others. This includes the adult entertainment industry, which has become an enormous, multi-billion dollar industry thanks in part to the anonymity and privacy that online pornography provides adults. One challenge, many argue, is that adults are far from the only ones who are able to access porn sites online. Children as young as middle school-age are accessing images online, some of which they search for and some of which is targeted to them through SPAM e-mails or pornographic Web sites that purchase the domain of a similarly sounding Web site, counting on minors to arrive at their sites by accident.

The debates about the effects of porn on its users are nearly endless: Does viewing porn encourage young people to become sexually active at earlier ages? Does viewing porn psychologically damage kids? Do adults who view porn develop unrealistic expectations of beauty and sexual expression in their own relationships? And so on.

This issue looks at the effects of visual pornography on the incidence of rape in the United States. Since pornography became available, there are many proponents who maintain that by depicting certain sexual acts, sexually explicit media encourages people to try these acts out. In particular, they say, porn that shows rape makes this type of behavior real and, in the rapists' mind, acceptable, thereby encouraging rape. Others maintain that there is no causality between viewing Internet porn and the incidence of rape, that people are exposed to a wide range of information, images, and behaviors every day and do not engage in all of the behaviors they see. These include, they say, sexual behaviors.

Still others, like one of the authors who appears in this issue, maintain that having pornography available actually *decreases* the incidence of rape. Depicting rape, which is a socially unacceptable (and criminal) behavior, this author argues, actually provides a potential rapist with an outlet for his unacceptable fantasies, thereby keeping him from acting upon them. In the following selections, Anthony D'Amato analyzes data that correlates a decrease in rapes in the United States with the increase of pornography availability. Judith Reisman counters with stories from actual rapists who discuss viewing porn immediately before raping a victim.

YES ↵

Anthony D'Amato

Porn Up, Rape Down

Today's headlines are shouting RAPE IN DECLINE![1] Official figures just released show a plunge in the number of rapes per capita in the United States since the 1970s. Even when measured in different ways, including police reports and survey interviews, the results are in agreement; there has been an 85% reduction in sexual violence in the past 25 years. The decline, steeper than the stock market crash that led to the Great Depression, is depicted in this chart prepared by the United States Department of Justice:

Rape rates
Adjusted victimization rate
per 1,000 persons age 12 and over

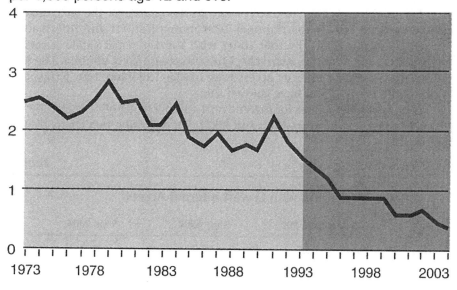

Source: The National Crime Victimization Survey. Includes both attempted and completed rapes.

As the chart shows, there were 2.7 rapes for every 1,000 people in 1980; by 2004, the same survey found the rate had decreased to 0.4 per 1,000 people, a decline of 85%.

D'Amato, Anthony, "Porn Up, Rape Down" (June 23, 2006). *Northwestern Public Law Research Paper* No. 913013 Available at SSRN: http://ssrn.com/abstract=913013. Reprinted by permission.

Official explanations for the unexpected decline include (1) less lawlessness associated with crack cocaine; (b) women have been taught to avoid unsafe situations; (c) more would-be rapists already in prison for other crimes; (d) sex education classes telling boys that "no means no." But these minor factors cannot begin to explain such a sharp decline in the incidence of rape.

There is, however, one social factor that correlates almost exactly with the rape statistics. The American public is probably not ready to believe it. My theory is that the sharp rise in access to pornography accounts for the decline in rape. The correlation is inverse: the more pornography, the less rape. It is like the inverse correlation: the more police officers on the street, the less crime.

The pornographic movie "Deep Throat" which started the flood of X-rated VHS and later DVD films, was released in 1972. Movie rental shops at first catered primarily to the adult film trade. Pornographic magazines also sharply increased in numbers in the 1970s and 1980s. Then came a seismic change: pornography became available on the new Internet. Today, purveyors of Internet porn earn a combined annual income exceeding the total of the major networks ABC, CBS, and NBC.

"Deep Throat" has moved from the adult theatre to a laptop near you.

National trends are one thing; what do the figures for the states show? From data compiled by the National Telecommunications and Information Administration in 2001, the four states with the *lowest* per capita access to the Internet were Arkansas, Kentucky, Minnesota, and West Virginia. The four states with the *highest* Internet access were Alaska, Colorado, New Jersey, and Washington. (I would not have guessed this.)

Next I took the figures for forcible rape compiled by police reports by the Disaster Center for the years 1980 and 2000. The following two charts display the results:

Table 1

States with Lowest Internet Access[2]

State	Internet 2001	Rape 1980	Rape 2000
Arkansas	36.9	26.7	31.7
Kentucky	40.2	19.2	27.4
Minnesota	36.1	23.2	45.5
W. Virginia	40.7	15.8	18.3

All figures are per capita.

While the nationwide incidence of rape was showing a drastic decline, the incidence of rape in the four states having the *least* access to the Internet showed an actual *increase* in rape over the same time period. This result was almost too clear and convincing, so to check it I compiled figures for the four

Table 2

States with Highest Internet Access[3]

Alaska	64.1	56.8	70.3
Colorado	58.5	52.5	41.2
New Jersey	61.6	30.7	16.1
Washington	60.4	52.7	46.4

All figures are per capita.

states having the *most* access to the Internet. Three out of four of these states showed declines (in New Jersey, an almost 50% decline). Alaska was an anomaly: it increased both in Internet access and incidence of rape. However, the population of Alaska is less than one-tenth that of the other three states in its category. To adjust for the disparity in population, I took the combined population of the four states in each table and calculated the percentage change in the rape statistics:

Table 3

Combined Per Capita Percentage Change in Incidence of Rape

	Aggregate per capita increase or decline in rape
Four states with lowest Internet access	Increase in rape of 53%
Four states with highest Internet access	Decrease in rape of 27%

I find these results to be statistically significant beyond the 95 confidence interval.

Yet proof of correlation is not the same thing as causation. If autumn regularly precedes winter, that doesn't mean that autumn causes winter. When six years ago my former Northwestern colleague John Donohue, together with Steven Levitt,[4] found that legalized abortion correlated with a reduction in crime, theirs would have only been an academically curious thesis if they had not identified a causal factor. But they did identify one: that prior to legalization there were many unwanted babies born due to the lack of a legal abortion alternative. Those unwanted children became the most likely group to turn to crime.

My own interest in the rape-pornography question began in 1970 when I served as a consultant to President Nixon's Commission on Obscenity and Pornography. The Commission concluded that there was no causal relationship between exposure to sexually explicit materials and delinquent or criminal behavior. The President was furious when he learned of the conclusion.

Later President Reagan tried the same thing, except unlike his predecessor he packed the Commission with persons who passed his ideological litmus test (small wonder that I was not asked to participate). This time, Reagan's

Commission on Pornography reached the approved result: that there does exist a causal relationship between pornography and violent sex crimes.

The drafter of the Commission's report was Frederich Schauer, a prominent law professor. In a separate statement, he assured readers that neither he nor the other Commissioners were at all influenced by their personal moral values.[5] . . .

Although the Reagan Commission had at its disposal all the evidence gathered by psychology and social-science departments throughout the world on the question whether a student's exposure to pornography increased his tendency to commit antisocial acts, I found that the Commission was unable to adduce a shred of evidence to support its affirmative conclusion. No scientist had ever found that pornography raised the probability of rape. However, the Commission was not seeking truth; rather, as I said in the title to my article, it sought political truth.

If pornography does not *produce* rape, I thought, then maybe it *reduces* rape. But no one apparently had any incentive to investigate the latter proposition. But the just-released rape statistics provide the necessary evidence.

Although neither Professor Schauer nor the other Commissioners ever responded to my William & Mary article, now they can forget it. For if they had been right that exposure to pornography leads to an increase in social violence, then the vast exposure to pornography furnished by the Internet would by now have resulted in scores of rapes per day on university campuses, hundreds of rapes daily in every town, and thousands of rapes per day in every city. Instead, the Commissioners were so incredibly wrong that the incidence of rape has actually declined by the astounding rate of 85%.

Correlations aside, could access to pornography actually reduce the incidence of rape as a matter of causation? In my article I mentioned one possibility: that some people watching pornography may "get it out of their system" and thus have no further desire to go out and actually try it. Another possibility might be labeled "Victorian effect": the more that people covered up their bodies with clothes in those days, the greater the mystery of what they looked like in the nude. The sight of a woman's ankle was considered shocking and erotic. But today, Internet porn has thoroughly de-mystified sex. . . .

I am sure there will be other explanations forthcoming as to why access to pornography is the most important causal factor in the decline of rape. Once one accepts the observation that there is a precise negative correlation between the two, the rest can safely be left to the imagination.

Notes

1. E.g., *Washington Post,* June 19, 2006; *Chicago Tribune,* June 21, 2006.
2. Statistics on Internet Access compiled from National Telecommunications and Information Administration. . . .
3. Statistics on forcible rape compiled from. . . .
4. Author of *Freakonimics* (2005).
5. U.S. Dept. of Justice, Final Report: Attorney General's Commission on Pornography 176–79 (1986) (personal statement of Commissioner Schauer).

Judith Reisman ➡ **NO**

Pornography's Link to Rape

Would you try to put out a fire with gasoline?

No? Then you might disagree with an MSNBC online article, "Porn: Good for America!" by Glenn Reynolds, a University of Tennessee law professor. Reynolds suggests that pornography *reduces* rape!

As proof, Reynolds quotes a U.S. Department of Justice claim that in 2004 rape of "people" *over age 12* radically decreased with an "85 percent decline in the per-capita rape rate since 1979" (DOJ's National Crime Victimization Survey of "thousands of respondents 12 and older").

But the FBI also estimates that "34 percent of female sex assault victims" are "under age 12" (National Incident-Based Reporting System, July 2000).

Since the DOJ data *excludes rape of children under age 12,* child rape may be *up 85 percent,* for all we know.

Although the FBI and local police departments are now swamped with teachers, police, professors, doctors, legislators, clergy, federal and state bureaucrats, dentists, judges, etc., arrested for child pornography and for abusing children *under age 12,* the Department of Justice excludes those small victims from its "rape" rates. Why?

Do DOJ, FBI Harbor Pedophiles?

You have to wonder: Are there pedophiles and other sexual predators in the governmental woodpiles?

When I worked for DOJ's Juvenile Justice and Delinquency Prevention in the 1980s, someone high up killed the order to collect crime-scene pornography as evidence in prosecutions. No Democrat or Republican administration has yet mandated such on-site pornography collections. Whom is DOJ protecting?

Reynolds writes less like an objective scholar than a pornography defender:

> *Since 1970 porn has exploded. But rape has gone down 85 percent. So much for the notion that pornography causes rape. [I]t would be hard to explain how rape rates could have declined so dramatically while porn expanded so explosively.*

He opines that pornography possibly prevents rape (the old discredited "safe-outlet" theory).

The DOJ's preposterous "85 percent" decrease in rape ignores the obvious. The U.S. FBI Index of Crime reported a *418 percent increase* in "forcible rape" from 1960 to 1999. That fear means we now keep our doors, windows, and cars locked. Women seldom walk alone at night. Parents rarely let children go anywhere unaccompanied. Many states let people carry guns for self-defense. Rape Crisis Centers do not report rapes to police. More women perform as sexually required. A conflicting DOJ 2002 report says "almost 25 percent of college women have been victims of rape or attempted rape since the age of 14."

Why Don't the Feds Call Child-Rape "Rape"?

In 1950, 18 states authorized the death penalty for rape; most others could impose a life sentence. Following Alfred Kinsey's "scientific" advice in 1948, many states redefined "rape" so the crime could be plea-bargained down to a misdemeanor like "sexual misconduct."

Missouri redefined rape to mean 11 different crimes for 11 different sentences, magically lowering "rape" rates. Like all states that have trivialized rape, Missouri relied on the Kinsey-based 1955 American Law Institute Model Penal Code.

"Rape" was eliminated from New Jersey's laws and replaced with a variety of terms during a 1978 penal law revision.

For example, Dr. Linda Jeffrey notes that the charge to which child-molesting teacher Pamela Diehl-Moore pleaded guilty was reduced to a second-tier crime, "sexual assault"—i.e., sexual contact with a victim under 13, or penetration where the "actor" uses physical force or coercion, but the victim doesn't suffer severe personal injury, or the victim is 16 or 17, with aggravating circumstances, or the victim is 13 to 15 and the "actor" is at least four years older. (Whew!)

Sex Criminals Copy What Porn Depicts

DOJ experts should read reports such as "Sex-Related Homicide and Death Investigation" (2003). Former Lt. Comdr. Vernon Geberth says today's "sex-related cases are more frequent, vicious and despicable" than anything he experienced in decades as a homicide cop.

In "Journey into Darkness" (1997), the FBI's premier serial-rape profiler, John Douglas wrote, "[Serial-rape murders are commonly found] with a large pornography collection, either store-bought or homemade. Our [FBI] research does show that certain types of sadomasochistic and bondage-oriented material can fuel the fantasies of those already leaning in that direction."

In "The Evil That Men Do" (1998), FBI serial-rape-murderer-mutilator profiler Roy Hazelwood quotes one sex killer who tied his victims in "a variety of positions" based on pictures he saw in sex magazines.

"Thrill Killers, a Study of America's Most Vicious Murders," by Charles Linedecker, reports that 81 percent of these killers rated pornography as their primary sexual interest. Dr. W.L. Marshall, in "Criminal Neglect, Why Sex

Offenders Go Free" (1990), says based on the evidence, pornography "feeds and legitimizes their deviant sexual tendencies."

In one study of rapists, Gene Abel of the New York Psychiatric Institute cited, "One-third reported that they had used pornography immediately prior to at least one of their crimes." In 1984, the U.S. Attorney General's Task Force on Family Violence reported, "Testimony indicates that an alarming number of rape and sexual assault offenders report that they were acting out behavior they had viewed in pornographic materials."

More pornography equals more rape of children and women. We need to ask whether Big Government is now selling out to Big Pornography as it did to Big Tobacco for half a century.

POSTSCRIPT

Does Pornography Reduce the Incidence of Rape?

Throughout history, people have looked for answers to why people perpetrate violent crimes on others. Mental health professionals, law enforcement officials, politicians, parents, and others have pointed fingers at many different potential causes without coming up with a clear answer. Is a person biologically determined to be a rapist? Is a rapist "created," and if so, by what or by whom?

One of the first sources people go to for these reasons is the media. One type of indictment against the media has been made since it has existed that it causes viewers to take actions that they would not otherwise take. Some argue, for example, that depictions of violence in the media leads to greater violence in real life. These arguments have even been brought to the legal system and used during trials. In a well-known court case at the time (*Huceg v. Hustler Magazine*, 1983), a family brought suit against *Hustler*, an adult pornographic magazine, in which a description appeared of autoerotic asphyxiation, a sexual practice in which a person restricts her or his breathing through partial hanging or other method, masturbates, and releases the air restriction at the moment of orgasm. The family's underage son tried this, did it incorrectly, and ended up hanging himself. The family sued *Hustler* magazine, arguing that if this had not been printed, their son would not have done it and died. The Court ruled for the magazine, saying that just reading a description of something does not necessarily encourage someone to do it—especially a young person for whom the material was not created.

To say, however, that the media has *no* effect on people's attitudes or behaviors would be inaccurate. Advertisers spend billions of dollars every year on television, print, Internet, and other ads to sell a wide variety of products. The ads are designed to influence people's behaviors—that if we see a particular commercial or hear a particular song, we will be more likely to purchase one product over another. If advertisers are successful at this—at actually influencing people enough to purchase something they may not have necessarily known they wanted—is it possible that the creators and producers of adult sexually explicit media could be doing the same?

For right now, the data are inconclusive—and there seem to be as many reports supporting each side of the debate. Be sure to consider a range of reasoning as you establish your own opinion on this topic. Is pornography always okay, as long as it's consumed only by adults? Is it never okay? Does it depend on what it depicts? And if there is some kind of causality shown, that pornography *does* indeed increase behavior, what role do you think the government should or should not play in regulating the industry?

Suggested Readings

M. Diamond, "Pornography, Rape and Sex Crimes in Japan," *International Journal of Law and Psychiatry,* 1999, 22(1): 1–22.

S. Ehrlich, *Representing Rape: Language and Sexual Consent* (New York: Routledge Press, 2001).

D. Linz, N. M., Malamuth, and K. Beckett, *Civil Liberties and Research on the Effects of Pornography.* American Psychological Association. . . .

D. J. Loftus, *Watching Sex: How Men Really Respond to Pornography* (New York: Thunder's Mouth Press, 2002).

P. Paul, *Pornified: How the Culture of Pornography Is Changing Our Lives, Our Relationships and Our Families* (New York: Times Books, 2005).

D. E. H. Russell, *Dangerous Relationships: Pornography, Misogyny and Rape* (Thousand Oaks, CA: Sage Publications, Inc., 1998).

A. Soble, *Pornography, Sex, and Feminism* (Amherst, NY: Prometheus Books, 2002).

G. A. Walp, *The Missing Link Between Pornography and Rape: Convicted Rapists Respond with Validated Truth* (Ann Arbor, MI: ProQuest/UMI, 2006).

ISSUE 9

Is Cyberbullying Related to Gender?

YES: Qing Li, from "Cyberbullying in Schools: A Research of Gender Differences," *School Psychology International* (May, 2006)

NO: Kirk R. Williams and Nancy G. Guerra, from "Prevalence and Predictors of Internet Bullying," *Journal of Adolescent Health* (2007)

ISSUE SUMMARY

YES: Educator Qing Li found, in a survey of students, males reported more bullying and cyberbullying than female students, and female cyberbully victims were more likely to report the cyberbullying to adults than were males.

NO: Criminal justice expert Kirk Williams and psychologist Nancy Guerra found that boys were more likely to bully than girls, but there were no sex differences in cyberbullying.

T here has been an explosion in the number of, and uses for, electronic technologies. As a result, virtually all aspects of our day-to-day lives are changing. We can shop online, take virtual tours of museums, take courses, play games, and listen to music, without ever needing to leave our homes. We can be connected to the Internet 24-7 if we wish. Some scientists are predicting that even the wiring of the brain will actually change as young people spend more time in cyberspace. Cyberspace may be also changing our notions about ourselves as males and females. There is evidence that in massively multiplayer online role-playing games, many people engage in gender swapping. Although most online gamers are male (80%), females are increasingly becoming involved. Also, in many online games, the player can choose the attributes of the characters they become, including the sex of the character. One study suggested that 60% of gamers have played a differently gendered character; another study suggested that about half the male and two-thirds of the female gamers had gender swapped. Reasons for gender swapping included the ability to experiment with aspects of one's self in a way that would be difficult in real life; that it's just fun and different; and using stereotypic attributes of one gender or the other allows one to be treated differently, i.e., a female character may be treated better and get free things—one gamer put it this way: "Nerd + Boob = Loot." One female gamer said she was tired of "creepy guys hitting on [her] female characters." Gender swappers can explore various styles of play and social interactions. Not surprisingly, if male and female gamers gender swap as a way of exploring, or exploiting, various dimensions of gender, it is not surprising that beyond the gaming environment, notions of relationships and human sexuality also are changing via the introduction of online dating, online forums, and chat rooms. Studies are beginning to examine how and why adolescents interact socially online. Cyberspace has become a common location for social interaction. Studies of social interactions online suggest that women and men may be more equal in the amount of disclosure of personal information than in face-to-face interactions, and one study found that males were more willing than females to respond online to others' sexual disclosures, especially under conditions of anonymity. What does all this mean for gendered patterns of behavior? Will online social interactions level the "playing field" for girls and boys, women and men? What are the implications of these changes in gendered behavior for the expression of aggression? Would females be more comfortable online than in the real world breaking away from cultural constraints on females' expressing aggression? Would males feel less pressure online to show they are "real men" and not behave aggressively when provoked? These are the types of questions researchers are beginning to explore as they enter cyberspace as a laboratory to explore issues of gender and aggression. In the present set of selections, we want to explore cyberbullying in particular, a topic that is just beginning to receive attention in the research literature. Two basic questions address whether there are gender differences in cyberbullying and why or why not.

According to the Cyberbullying Research Center, cyberbullying can be defined as "Willful and repeated harm inflicted through the use of computers, cell phones, and other electronic devices." It is also known as "cyber bullying," "electronic bullying," "e-bullying," "sms bullying," "mobile bullying," "online bullying," "digital bullying," or "Internet bullying." Some theorists suggest that cyberbullying is more akin to verbal aggression than physical aggression, and given that there are fewer sex differences in verbal than physical aggression, perhaps we might expect equivalent levels of cyberbullying in girls and boys. On the other hand, cyberbullying may be more akin to indirect than direct aggression and more akin to relational than direct aggression, in which case we might expect more girls than boys to engage in cyberbullying. The selections you will be reading provide some insight into these questions. Both rely on surveys of students regarding their experiences with cyberbullying. The Williams and Guerra study also assessed for experiences with verbal and physical bullying; likewise, Li also assessed for experiences with other forms of bullying. Thus, both studies provide a comparison of the prevalence of cyberbullying to traditional bullying. What do you think they found? Is cyberbullying or traditional bullying more common? Is the same pattern true for girls and boys?

YES ⤶

Qing Li

Cyberbullying in Schools:
A Research of Gender Differences

Introduction

School violence is a serious social problem and is particularly persistent and acute during the junior high/middle school period. Much of school violence involves students bullying their peers. . . . Bullying is related to more serious forms of aggression, and it is reported that in many school-shooting cases, bullying played a major role.

Although many teachers and administrators now recognize the problem of school bullying, few are aware that students are being harassed through electronic communication. Parallel to the fast development of technology and drastic increasing adoption of such technology, including the Internet and cell phones in society, many schools are enthusiastically embracing new technology. It has been found that the increasing access to new technology has the potential to increase students' social interaction and enhance collaborative learning experiences. Substantial research studies have shown that computers in classrooms can have positive effects on learning of all subjects. The introduction of electronic communication into classrooms, however, also brings problems that deserve our serious consideration. One such issue of concern is that cyberbullying has become a growing problem in schools, i.e., the use of electronic communication devices to bully others. The growing number and the level of severity of cyberbulling call for our educators, researchers, administrators, and authorities to take action.

But before we can tackle this problem, a better understanding of the issue is necessary. Because cyberbullying is a new territory, we know little about it. This study investigates the nature and the extent of adolescents' experience of cyberbullying, focusing on the effect of gender. A survey study of 264 junior high students in an urban city was conducted. In this article, "bullying" refers to bullying in the traditional sense, and "cyberbullying" refers to bullying via electronic communication tools.

Related Literature

Cyberbullying is a new phenomenon resulting from the advance of new communication technologies, including the Internet, cell phones, and Personal Digital Assistants. Cyberbullying can be briefly defined as "sending or posting

From *School Psychology International*, May 2006, pp. 157–170. Copyright © 2006 by Sage Publications. Reprinted by permission via Rightslink.

harmful or cruel text or images using the Internet or other digital communication devices." It can occur in various formats including flaming, harassment, cyberstalking, denigration (put-downs), masquerade, outing and trickery, and exclusion. Cyberbullying can involve stalking and death threats and can be very serious. Unlike face-to-face bullying, people often feel that cyberspace is impersonal and they can therefore say whatever they want. Further, it is reported that females prefer this type of bullying.

Many news stories have reported cyberbullying incidents all over the world. For example, in Australia, a nine-year-old grade 4 female student received very pornographic emails. Her parents assumed the sender of the emails was an adult. When the source was traced by local police, it was found that the sender was actually her classmate. A 15-year-old boy in Quebec, Canada became an unwilling

> celebrity when a film he made of himself emulating a Star War's fight scene was posted on the Internet by some classmates. Millions downloaded the two-minute clip . . . He was so humiliated he sought counseling [and dropped out of school], and his family has launched a lawsuit against his tormentors.

In Japan, cell phone pictures of an overweight boy, which were taken on the sly in the locker room, were distributed to many of his peers. Another incident happened in Calabasas High School in California. "It was a website—schoolscandals.com—on which vicious gossip and racist and threatening remarks grew so rampant that most of the school was affected."

Combating cyberbullying is more difficult for schools than people initially expected. Many bullies are anonymous. Further, under the free-speech rights, it is difficult to take down a website. In the case of the Calabasas High School, the principal did get involved after comments [on the website] caused many of his students to be depressed, angry, or simply unable to focus on school. . . .

Cyberbullying also takes various forms and electronic communication tools—from email, listserve, cell phone, to websites. In the US, a boy, using a photo-editing tool to paste a girl's face onto a pornographic photo, distributed the photo to his entire email list because he had a quarrel with the girl.

> Some used websites to circulate rumors, ask students to vote on the ugliest or fattest kid in school . . . When Will, a middle-schooler in Kansas, broke up with his girlfriend, she created a website devoted to smearing him. She outlined vivid threats, made up vicious rumors, and described what it would be like to see him torn apart.

Aside from the many reported news stories, several surveys have been conducted to explore cyberbullying issues. In a survey conducted in Britain in 2002, it was found that one in four youngsters aged 11 to 19 had been cyberbullied. An earlier survey conducted in New Hampshire in 2000 found that about 6 percent of youths had the experience of being harassed online. A survey conducted in Canada showed that one-quarter of young Canadian Internet users reported that they had experienced getting messages saying hateful things about others.

Further, a more severe form of bullying—harassment—has also been found in cyberspace. In a small sample of developmentally delayed adolescents, it was found that many adolescents experienced sexual harassment over the Internet. Other researchers reported that one-third of undergraduate students reported being stalked over the Internet. Text-based name calling, use of coarse language, profanity, and personal attacks have been discovered in computer-mediated communication environments.

In a survey to a females-only listserv, one-fifth of 500 subscribers reported that they had experienced online sexual harassment. This type of harassment or intimidation takes a variety of forms ranging from "'flaming' (overt attacks on a person) to highly sexual comments and visual pornography that dehumanize women" and "seduction under false pretences, electronic stalking, and virtual rape." For example, a textually enacted "rape" was conducted on MOO in which a male user controlled two female players' characters to force the performance of sexually degrading actions on themselves. Another incident occurred in a support MUD for sexual abuse survivors in which a male enacted graphic sexual abuse to all participants. Anonymity inherited in many electronic communication modes "not only fosters playful disinhibition but reduces social accountability, making it easier for users to engage in hostile, aggressive acts."

Two previous research studies in Canada have examined the extent and impact of cyberbullying. Cyberbullying not only occurs in schools, but increasingly becomes a significant problem. About one in four adolescents are cybervictims, and they experience various negative consequences, particularly anger and sadness. Over half of adolescents reported that they knew someone being cyberbullied. In addition, a close tie was identified amongst bullies, cyberbullies, and their victims. That is, bullies, compared to non-bullies, tended to be cyberbullies; while bully victims in the physical world were also likely to be bully victims in cyberspace. Further, cyberbullies were more likely to be victims in cyberspace than those who did not cyberbully.

Abundant research studies found that gender plays an important role in traditional forms of bullying. For example, males are more likely to be bullied than females. They also self-reported bullying others at significantly higher rates than their female counterparts. Males with atypical gender-related behaviours were at a much greater risk for peer assault than other young men. Also, females seen as less or more attractive than others were at the highest risk for harassment. Gender differences with respect to bullying were found in preschoolers as young as 3- to 5-years-old. Research indicates that males are significantly more physically victimized than females, while females were more relationally victimized. Both types of victims experienced bigger adjustment problems than did their counterparts. Males use their fists and physical threats to bully others, but females' weapons are words and behind-the-scenes school bully manipulation. These gendered patterns identified in traditional bullying lead to the question: when moved to cyberspace, does gender also affect cyberbullying related issues?

As studies and reports reviewed above suggested, cyberbullying indeed occurs, yet it is unclear whether gender plays a role in cyberbullying. This study, therefore, examines the nature and extent of students' experience of cyberbullying focusing on gender effect. Junior high students were chosen because adolescence is a time when physical aggression increases in frequency and intensity; for this reason it has been labelled a 'brutalizing' period. Correspondingly, and perhaps as an antecedent, this period also witnesses a series of abrupt changes in the social lives of youngsters.

The nature of new technology makes it possible for cyberbullying to occur more secretly, spread more rapidly, and be easily preserved (e.g., cutting and past[ing] messages). As this behaviour becomes recognized as a significant problem, researchers must provide information about its occurrence to inform and support educators and administrators. Considering that many Internet users are socially isolated and that some may even look for peer support on the Internet that incites them to act out in violence against their bullies, victims of cyberbullying may be at risk for experiencing poor psycho-social adjustment. Thus to support the appropriate use of technology in schools, teachers and administrators must be knowledgeable about cyberbullying, and as a result, develop appropriate preventive and intervention strategies to ensure the safety of all students.

Research Questions

This study was an exploration of the cyberbullying focusing on gender effects. The primary focus was on the examination of gender differences in students' cyberbullying experiences. A secondary focus was on the investigation of male and female students' perception of school climates. Particularly, the following research questions guide this exploration:

1. Do male and female students have different experiences in relation to cyberbullying?
2. Are there gender differences in student beliefs about adults' prevention of cyberbullying?
3. When cyberbullying occurs, do male and female students behave differently in terms of informing adults?

Methods

Subject and Instrument

The subjects for this study were randomly selected from three middle schools in a large city in Canada. A total of 264 grade 7–9 students (130 males and 134 females) completed the questionnaire. Among them, only 5.8 percent were ESL students. Further, 75.4 percent of the students were white, 6.4 percent Asian, and about 18 percent were Black, Hispanic, Aboriginal, or from other ethic groups. Over half of the students reported above average school grades, while close to 40 percent of them reported average grades. Only a couple of the students reported below average grades.

An anonymous survey adapted from previous research was used which includes two major areas: students' demographic data and their experience related to cyberbullying. A total of 26 questions including the frequency of using computers were analysed to answer the research questions of this study.

Analysis

Both descriptive and inferential statistics were used to examine gender differences in junior high students' experience of cyberbullying. . . . Descriptive statistics were employed to provide background information such as the extent and frequencies of cyberbullying. . . .

Results

We first examined the extent to which students experience cyberbullying in order to gain a basic understanding of the issue. In addition to cyberbullying, students' experience of bullying was also investigated considering that adolescents' experience of bullying can inform our understanding of cyberbullying. Overall, close to half of the students were bully victims and about one in four students had been cyberbullied. Over 34 percent of the students had bullied others in the traditional form, and almost 17 percent had bullied others using electronic communication tools. In addition, 53.6 percent of the students reported that they knew someone being cyberbullied.

When male and female students' experiences were considering separately, it was found that over 22 percent of males and close to 12 percent of females were cyberbullies. However, 25 percent of males and 25.6 percent of females reported that they were cyberbullied. . . .

Do Male and Female Adolescents Have Different Cyberbullying Experiences?

There was no significant difference between the proportion of male and female adolescents who reported being bullied. . . . However, males were more likely to bully . . . and cyberbully . . . others than were females.

How Often Did Cyberbullying Occur?

The answer to this question was grouped into two categories: one to three times and more than three times. Among the cybervictims, about 62 percent were cyberbullied one to three times and 37.8 percent were harassed more than three times. No significant gender difference was found in frequencies of cyberbullying victimization. . . . Further, close to 55 percent of cyberbullies harassed others between one to three times and over 45 percent did it more than three times using electronic means. No significant gender difference was found in frequencies of cyberbullying. . . .

What Were Student Beliefs about Adults' Prevention of Cyberbullying in Schools?

Only 64.1 percent of the students believed that adults in schools tried to stop cyberbullying when informed. No significant gender difference was found in student beliefs about this adult involvement in stopping cyberbullying. . . .

When cyberbullying occurred, who would tell adults, male or female students? The analysis showed that for the cybervictims, females were more likely to inform adults than males. . . . For the students who knew someone being cyberbullied, only 30.1 percent told adults but no gender difference was found. . . .

Discussion

This study explores a new and important issue related to cyberbullying. The preliminary analysis of survey data collected from junior high students in Canada sheds light on this evolving issue.

The first important issue concerns the large extent of young adolescents' experience of bullying and cyberbullying. In this study, about half of the students reported that they had been bullied during school. This supports the view that bullying is a significant problem in schools. The researcher is puzzled by this much higher percentage of bully victims as compared to previous research results. Initially, the researcher thought that the students' social economic background may have been a major factor. The fact that about half of the students were from the school where there are mainly middle class residences indicates that merely considering SES cannot explain this phenomenon. One possible explanation is the school climate—that is, perhaps no effective official policies toward bullying or anti-bullying programs are adopted and followed in the schools. Another explanation may be that bullying is becoming increasingly severe in terms of the scope and the extent in large cities. Further research studies are necessary to examine this issue.

A second issue that deserves our serious consideration is the scope of cyberbullying in schools. Over half of the students knew someone who had been cyberbullied. Further, over a quarter of the students in this study experienced being cyberbullied, and one in six students had cyberbullied others. This is consistent with previous studies, including a British survey conducted in 2002 which showed that 25 percent of children age 11–19 had been bullied or threatened via various electronic communication modes. An earlier survey conducted in 2000 in New Hampshire found that only about 6 percent of teenagers had experienced being cyberbullied or threatened. This suggests that cyberbullying may be on the rise and is becoming an increasingly critical issue of concern.

Third, when gender is considered, significant differences were identified in terms of bullying and cyberbullying. Although no gender difference was found in relation to victimization, males were more likely to be bullies and cyberbullies than their female counterparts. This is consistent with previous research that females are less likely to bully than are males. It also suggests that cyberbullying and bullying follow a similar pattern in terms of male and female involvement. This result, however, contradicts the theory that females prefer to use electronic communication mediums such as chatrooms and email to bully others.

Fourth, over a third of the cybervictims had been harassed more than three times, and close to half of the cyberbullies had bullied others more than three times using electronic means. This rate of cyberbullying is similar to the frequency of experiencing traditional bullying reported in several studies. One possible explanation is that bullies are also more likely to engage in cyberbully actions and there is a close relationship amongst bullying, cyberbullying and victimization, hence similar patterns are observed between bullying and cyberbullying.

Another issue worth noticing is the bystanders of cyberbullying. Previous research has demonstrated that up to 80 percent of regular bullying incidences are not reported to staff. This study shows that, just like in the real world, the vast majority of the students who were cyberbullied or knew someone being cyberbullied chose to stay quiet rather than to inform adults. One possible explanation may be that many students, over one-third of the students in this sample, do not think that adults in schools tried to stop cyberbullying when informed. Because of this belief that adults in schools would not help, many students, feeling either scared or powerless, chose not to report cyberbullying instances. This supports the literature that adolescents' perceptions of their school environments relate to their bullying related behaviours. It highlights the importance of building, and further strengthening, a trusty relationship between students and school staff (including teachers, administrators, and the like). Another explanation may be due to students' lack of appropriate strategies to deal with the problems.

As suggested by the data, most victims and bystanders do not report cyberbullying incidents. Female cybervictims, however, are more inclined to inform adults about the incidents than are male cybervictims. This is interesting and it may relate to the gender differences identified in conversational styles. In her work, Tannen indicates that "men are more likely to be aware that asking . . . for any kind of help, puts them in a one-down position." Therefore, males tend not to ask for help or inform others about their problems or troubles.

Conclusion

This study contributes to the extant literature on bullying in several conceptual areas. First, cyberbullying is a bullying problem occurring in a new territory. Few research studies have examined bullying issues in this new context. The astonishing high percent of adolescents who had experienced cyberbully tactics observed in this study suggests that cyberbullying is becoming an increasingly critical problem for schools and the whole society.

Second, in this article, bullying and cyberbullying are examined at a point where it had seldom been studied. Extant studies, for the most part, studied primary school children. The early adolescent period merits attention because it is a period, labelled a 'brutalizing period,' where disruptions in social networks afford opportunities for peer victimization and aggression to establish peer status. Consistent with this, the results of this study showed that a high percentage of the students were involved in bullying or cyberbullying.

Third, bullying, cyberbullying, and victimization are explored in this study considering the gender factor. This work examined for the first time the discrepancy between male and female adolescents' experience in relation to cyberbullying and victimization. It suggests that gender plays a significant role in cyberbullying. The gender difference identified in this study underscores the importance of differentiated approaches for the research and possible intervention programs related to cyberbully issues.

Fourth, the vast majority of adolescents choosing to be quiet bystanders further stresses the importance of systematic education of safety strategies from an early age. Just like dealing with traditional bullying issues, educating bystanders may provide some key strategies in dealing more effectively with cyberbullying. Focusing more attention on bystanders has the potential power to prevent a significant amount of cyberbullying. The gender difference identified in this study that male victims are less likely to inform adults underscores the importance of awareness. If students all understand cyberbullying related issues, aware of the strategies for combatting cyberbullying (e.g., informing adults), and know their own styles and limits, it would be much easier to fight cyberbullying.

The education dealing with cyberbullying related issues should be a joint endeavour of schools, families, communities, and the whole society. It supports the idea that our concern of the bully and cyberbully issue "must be at many levels, not only for the individuals themselves, and their families, but also society at large."

Like any research study, this study has limitations. For example, the data were collected from an urban city; we need to be cautious when generalizing the findings to other regions. In addition, although junior high is the time when bullying peaks, it is also important to examine cyberbullying in other age levels including elementary and senior high schools. The information obtained can be used to provide a fuller picture of the cyberbullying issue.

Kirk R. Williams and
Nancy G. Guerra

 **NO**

Prevalence and Predictors of Internet Bullying

Bullying is a form of aggression involving intentional and harmful behavior marked by repeated engagement and an asymmetric physical or psychological power relationship. The specific type of harmful behavior can vary considerably; previous studies of children's bullying have considered a range of diverse behaviors, including name calling, saying mean things, destruction or taking of property, demanding money, social exclusion, hitting, and kicking. What brands these behaviors as bullying rather than aggression is that they occur repeatedly, typically involving a weaker victim within the context of an ongoing social interaction. As such, research examining the prevalence, predictors, and prevention of bullying largely has examined this behavior as it unfolds within a specific social context. For children, schools have been the primary context for studying bullying behavior.

Over the last decade, interest in understanding and preventing bullying among school children in the U.S. and internationally has surged. Such interest coincides with a growing awareness of the detrimental consequences of being bullied on children's well-being as well as the recognition that bullying is a significant problem in schools. Still, prevalence rates vary as a function of how bullying is measured, what type of bullying (e.g., physical vs. verbal) is assessed, the age of respondents, and the country where the study takes place. Reported perpetration and victimization rates typically range from 10% of students reporting physical bullying or victimization to more than 50% reporting indirect bullying or victimization involving teasing, name calling, spreading rumors, or verbal aggression.

Because bullying has been framed as a schoolyard issue, the focus of research has largely been on bullying in schools—whether in the classroom, locker room, hallway, or bathroom—based on the assumption that personal contact is a prerequisite to bullying. Yet, in recent years, technology has transformed the landscape of children's social lives. With an estimated 45 million children between the ages of 10 and 17 in the U.S. alone using the Internet every day, social interactions have increasingly moved from personal contact in the school room to virtual contact in the chat room, and Internet bullying has emerged as a new and growing form of social cruelty. Such bullying

From *Journal of Adolescent Health*, vol. 41, no. 6, pp. S14–S21. Copyright © 2007 by Elsevier Health Sciences. Reprinted by permission.

is clearly not physical in nature and has more in common with verbal bullying. Intimidation is quickly being augmented by humiliation, destructive messages, gossip, slander, and other virtual taunts communicated through e-mail, instant messaging, chat rooms, and blogs. The Internet has become a new arena for social interactions, allowing children and youth to say and do things with a certain degree of anonymity and limited oversight by adult monitors. Internet bullying, as defined here, refers to the willful use of the Internet as a technological medium through which harm or discomfort is intentionally and repeatedly inflicted through indirect aggression that targets a specific person or group of persons.

The purpose of the present study is to contrast the prevalence of Internet bullying with physical and verbal bullying among 5th, 8th, and 11th grade boys and girls and to examine whether key predictors of physical and verbal bullying also predict Internet bullying. The focus is on youth involvement in such bullying as perpetrators, not victims. Perhaps because this type of bullying has unfolded on the fringes of the adult radar screen, it has only recently been considered in studies of bullying among children and youth. Relatively little is known about the prevalence of Internet bullying and how this compares with other types of bullying for boys and girls across different ages. Little is also known about whether Internet bullying is predicted (and potentially prevented) by the same types of factors that have been linked to physical and verbal bullying in schools. To date, information on the prevalence of Internet bullying comes primarily from anecdotal reports and a limited number of youth surveys. Findings suggest that Internet bullying and victimization rates are around 25%. This is higher than physical bullying rates but lower than indirect bullying rates from most school-based prevalence studies. Very few studies have examined age and gender differences for Internet bullying, although overall bullying appears to peak during early adolescence, with verbal bullying remaining high throughout the adolescent years. Furthermore boys are more likely to engage in physical bullying than girls.

Even fewer studies have examined the correlates and predictors of Internet bullying and whether these are similar or distinct from factors linked to bullying in schools. Overall, predictors of physical and verbal bullying are quite similar to predictors of aggression more generally. However studies of the etiology and prevention of bullying have emphasized a smaller set of predictors reflecting the social and normative context of bullying within peer networks and school settings. Two important predictors linked to bullying in both prediction and prevention studies are student perceptions of the acceptability (or moral approval) of bullying and student perceptions that school is an unsupportive context in which peers and adults cannot be trusted.

Bullying is behavior that is harmful to others and falls within the domain of behaviors with moral consequences: endorsement of the acceptability of bullying is akin to moral approval because harm to others is considered to be a key element of moral reasoning. A consistent finding in both the aggression and bullying literature is that children who endorse normative beliefs supporting such behavior are more likely to be perpetrators. A peer and school culture that supports bullying is more likely to have individuals who view this behavior as acceptable, further increasing normative support for bullying. Indeed a primary emphasis of many school-based bullying prevention programs is to change the normative climate so that bullying is seen as unacceptable.

Besides normative climate, several studies have examined the impact of various contextual characteristics of schools on bullying perpetration and victimization. For example, increases in student bullying over time are more likely in high-conflict, disorganized schools than in low-conflict, harmonious schools. Low levels of supervision within school settings have also been associated with higher rates of bullying. Disciplinary harshness, safety problems, and negative peer interactions have also been linked to behavior problems and bullying. The influence of peers is particularly noteworthy. Within the school setting, peers can escalate bullying through encouragement and validation. However, just as peers can enable bullying, they can also provide a supportive social context that encourages acceptance, belonging, and trust; many effective bullying prevention programs encourage students helping other students to form positive peer support systems.

If students believe that bullying is acceptable and if they feel disconnected and unsupported at school and by peers, they should be more likely to engage in all types of bullying behavior, including Internet bullying. However because both verbal and Internet bullying can occur behind the victim's back with a greater degree of anonymity than with physical bullying, both the prevalence and predictors of Internet bullying are expected to be more similar to verbal bullying than to physical bullying.

Methods

Data for the present research were collected as part of a larger study evaluating a statewide initiative in Colorado to strengthen the skills and willingness of youth and adults to intervene in bullying situations. The Bullying Prevention Initiative (BPI) is a 3-year, $8.6-million initiative funded by The Colorado Trust, a private grant-making foundation in Denver, Colorado. The grantees funded by this initiative represent school districts, individual schools, or community-based organizations, evenly split between rural and urban areas of the state and responsible for implementing bullying prevention programming in 78 schools across 40 of Colorado's 64 counties.

The larger BPI evaluation will provide an empirically based understanding of bullying and bystander behavior among youth, including an increased awareness of this behavior, social cognitive processes involved in the prevention of bullying, the social context surrounding bullying incidents, and the involvement of adults and youth in preventing such incidents. These issues are being addressed by collecting survey data from youth and adults in schools, collecting data from grantees concerning program implementation, and conducting a supplemental qualitative study seeking to acquire in-depth information from adults about challenges and successes in program implementation and from youth in terms of their awareness of the bullying prevention programs and their perceived effectiveness. A pre–post survey design collects data from youth in the fall and the spring of 3 academic years (2005–2006, 2006–2007, and 2007–2008) within the 78 schools. This design allows the assessment of single year changes in individual youth and contextual (school level) changes over the full 3 years of the BPI. All instruments developed to collect data from youth were piloted in the summer of 2005 before full implementation in the fall of that year, with all indices having acceptable reliabilities. . . .

Participants in the Present Study

The first year of the BPI was a start-up period for both the prevention programming as well as the evaluation study in refining its data collection instruments and procedures. During this year, 3,339 youth completed questionnaires in the 78 school sites during the fall of 2005, and another 2,293 youth in that original sample participated in a follow-up survey in 65 school sites in the spring of 2006. Data were collected in 5th, 8th, and 11th grades, representing transition years in elementary, middle, and high schools. All data collection was conducted in compliance with the protocol approved by the human subjects review board, including acquiring informed parental consent and youth ascent. To ensure the quality of data and that school samples are representative, a subsample of these first-year participants was selected for the present analysis based on two criteria: (1) schools must have successfully completed both fall and spring data collection, and (2) consent and completion rates at those schools must be 50% or greater. Applying these selection criteria yielded a subsample of 1,519 youth participating in both the fall and spring data collection, representing 46 school sites. The subsample has a greater percentage of rural participants, compared with the total first-year sample, and a greater percentage of 5th grade but a lower percentage of 11th grade participants, compared with the total first-year sample. The percentages for the remainder of the demographic characteristics are very similar between the subsample and the total first-year sample.

Procedures

Data were collected using two different electronic methods, with the choice of methods negotiated with schools in terms of what was deemed best for their students. However paper questionnaires were used by a small percentage of youth absent the day for which data collection was scheduled (4% of the total first-year sample and 1.6% of the subsample analyzed here). First, data collectors used a liquid crystal display projector to present questionnaire items in classrooms of approximately 30 students or less (used by 61.7% of the students in this subsample). After the data collectors read each question aloud, youth used a wireless response pad to enter their answers, which were automatically recorded in an electronic database and linked to the student identification code. The questionnaire was administered in English or Spanish as needed, using standard back-translation methods. Second, the questionnaire was adapted to a web-based format linked to the electronic database (36.7% of students in this subsample used this method). The youth web-based questionnaire was administered in school computer laboratories. Data collectors assisted youth in logging on to the password-protected question-naire and were available for assistance as youth answered questions at their own pace. No evidence was found that these different data collection proce-dures influenced responding.

Measures

Bullying perpetration. Items bearing on the perpetration (not victimization) of dif-ferent types of bullying were used. Youth were asked to respond to the following four items: "I pushed, shoved, tripped, or picked fights with students I know are weaker than me"; "I teased or said mean things to certain students"; "I spread rumors about some students"; and "I told lies about some students through e-mail or instant messaging." Numeric coding (in parentheses) and response options included (1) never, (2) one or two times, (3) several times, and (4) a lot. The first item was used to measure physical bullying perpetration, and the second and third items were combined to measure verbal bullying perpetration. Internet bullying perpetration was measured by the fourth item. . . .

As mentioned below, the appropriate temporal ordering between the predictors examined in this empirical analysis and these types of bullying per-petration requires using data collected in the fall of 2005 for the predictors and data gathered in the spring of 2006 for bullying perpetration. Therefore, the reference period for the four bullying items was "since the school year began." The distributions for these variables are highly skewed, with a high concentration of participants scoring one (i.e., never) and a precipitous decline in the distribution of participants across the higher scores. Hence these variables were dichotomized, with comparisons made between those participants who reported never engaging in these types of bullying (scoring 1) with those who reported doing so one or more times during the school year (scoring 2–4).

Moral approval of bullying. Moral beliefs about bullying perpetration and bystander involvement in bullying situations were assessed by asking partici-pants to evaluate six different items on a four point Likert-type scale ranging from "really wrong" to "perfectly ok." These items were taken from the Norma-tive Beliefs About Aggression Scale and were modified slightly to refer to bullying instead of aggression. The items included bullying perpetration as mentioned above (including Internet bullying), in addition to items pertaining to negative bystander involvement, such as encouraging others to fight smaller students or spread lies and rumors about them. These six items were summed to construct a summary additive index. . . . The distribution on the index was positively skewed, but it had a clustering of cases at the high end of the continuum of scores. The distribution of this measure was adjusted by sub-dividing it into six categories having approximately equal distributions. High scorers indicate par-ticipants who approve bullying perpetration and negative bystander behavior in general, not behavior-specific approval. Participants scoring low on this index disapprove of bullying and negative bystander behavior in general. This mea-sure is appropriate given the emphasis on capturing the normative orientation of students about bullying overall, not behavior-specific moral beliefs.

School climate. Student perceptions of school climate were assessed using the California School Climate Scale. This measure contains nine items about teachers, school staff and administrators, school policy, and a student's perceived personal connection to the school. For example, participants were asked whether they disagree or agree with statements like "My teachers respect me," "My teachers are fair," or "Teachers at my school are nice people." Other items addressed whether the principal in their school listens to the ideas of students, whether students who break school rules are treated fairly, and whether teachers and staff are doing the right things to prevent bullying in general, not specific forms of bullying in the school. The nine items were summed to form an additive index . . . with scores ranging from 9 to 36, given the response categories of the individual items. Respondents with high scores perceived a positive school climate, whereas those with low scores perceived a more negative school climate.

Perceived peer support. This four-item scale focused on positive and negative qualities of peers as a source of social support. It was adapted from the Generalized Perception of Peers Scale. Regardless of social context (e.g., schools), participants were asked to assess whether "students their age" care about what happens to them, will help them in time of need, can be trusted, and are sensitive to their feelings. Response options range from "no, not at all" to "yes, completely." The four items were summed to form an additive index, with scores ranging from a low of 4 to a high of 16, given the response categories for each of the individual items. High scores indicated higher perceptions of peers as supportive, whereas low scores indicated the opposite view. . . .

Results

The results presented below are arranged according to the two primary research objectives of this analysis: (1) to determine the prevalence of Internet compared with verbal and physical bullying perpetration in this sample of youth, and (2) to determine whether predictors of Internet bullying perpetration are similar to predictors of verbal and physical bullying perpetration. The first objective is addressed simply by tabulating the distributions of the three forms of bullying and examining whether these distributions vary by gender and grade level (5th, 8th, and 11th grades). The empirical examination by gender and grade was done by estimating their effects on each form of bullying perpetration through logistic regression, given the dichotomous bullying measures used.

The second objective is addressed by estimating the bivariate relations between each of the three predictors and the three forms of bullying perpetration. As noted above, these behavioral measures are dichotomized, differentiating between participants who report never perpetrating such behavior and those reporting they did so one or more times during the school year. . . .

Prevalence of Bullying

. . . Verbal bullying is clearly most prevalent for the total sample, followed by physical bullying and then bullying via e-mail or instant messaging. In short,

Internet bullying was a part of the behavioral repertoire of only a minority of youth in this sample during the last school year, but its prevalence is non-trivial. These three types of bullying perpetration are clearly interrelated, with ordinal associations (gamma coefficients) ranging from .66 for the relation between Internet and physical bullying to .87 for the relation between Internet and verbal bullying. However, distinctions remain, as suggested by 24.8% of the sample refraining from any type of bullying, 37.9% engaging in only one type, 30.7% perpetrating two types, and only 6.6% self-reporting involvement in all three types.

. . . No gender differences were found for Internet and verbal bullying, although such differences were pronounced for physical bullying, with males being more than twice as likely as females to report perpetrating such behavior. . . . Grade was significantly related to all forms of bullying perpetration, with the estimated effect being literally identical between Internet and verbal bullying . . . but substantially smaller for physical bullying. . . .

. . . About one third of 5th-graders reported engaging in verbal bullying in the past school year, with the prevalence rates then peaking in 8th grade and dropping off only slightly by 11th grade. A similar pattern holds for physical bullying as well, although the prevalence rates are lower than verbal bullying, especially among 5th and 11th-graders. A relatively small percentage of 5th-graders reported engaging in Internet bullying, with the distribution peaking in 8th grade and again declining slightly among 11th-graders. . . .

Predictors of Bullying

Moral approval of bullying. . . . The results show that this predictor is significantly and positively related to all three forms of bullying as expected; that is, beliefs endorsing bullying and negative bystander behavior are associated with self-reported involvement in verbal, physical, and Internet bullying. Specifically, an increase in one of the six ordinal categories of the moral beliefs measure (see description of measure above) is associated with a 43% increase in the odds of verbal bullying . . . , a 27% increase in the odds of physical bullying . . . and a 24% increase in the odds of Internet bullying. . . . However, the estimated effects for verbal bullying are significantly greater than those of both physical and Internet bullying . . . , but the difference between the estimated effects for physical and Internet bullying is not statistically significant. In short, although moral beliefs approving of bullying and negative bystander behavior are significantly and positively related to all three forms of bullying perpetration, the estimated effects for Internet bullying appear to be significantly lower than for verbal bullying.

Perceived school climate. . . . The more youth perceive themselves as connected to their schools, with the climate being trusting, fair, pleasant, etc. (i.e., a positive school climate), the lower is their self-reported involvement in verbal, physical, and Internet bullying perpetration. An increase of a single unit on the 9–36-point perceived school climate index (see description of measure above) is associated with a 7% decline in the odds of physical bullying . . . a

9% decline in the odds of Internet bullying . . . , and a 10% decline in the odds of verbal bullying. . . . Moreover, the difference between the estimated effects for Internet bullying and either physical bullying or verbal bullying is not statistically significant.

Perceived peer support. Youth perceptions that friends their age are trustworthy, caring, and helpful are significantly associated with lower self-reported participation in verbal, physical, and Internet bullying. Again, these empirical relations were anticipated. A single unit increase on the 4- to 16-point index of perceived peer support (see description of measure above) is associated with a 7% decline in the odds of physical bullying . . . , with the estimated effects being greatest for Internet . . . and verbal . . . bullying. Similar to the empirical relations between perceived school climate and these three forms of bullying perpetration, the estimated effects for Internet bullying are not significantly different from those of verbal or physical bullying.

Summary and Conclusion

The findings on the prevalence of bullying perpetration suggest that distributions vary by type, with verbal being most prevalent, followed by physical and then by Internet bullying. Physical and Internet bullying peaked in 8th grade and declined in 11th grade, whereas verbal bullying peaked in 8th grade and remained relatively high in the 11th grade. Males were more likely than females to report physical bullying perpetration. Consistent with the expectation that Internet bullying and verbal bullying would share common features, no gender differences were found for prevalence of Internet and verbal bullying.

Three predictors of bullying were empirically examined. One reflects an individual's normative orientation about the moral acceptability of bullying—that is, whether such behavior is right or wrong. However, the other two predictors capture perceptions of either the context in which youth regularly participate (i.e., schools) or the nature of peers with whom youth regularly interact (i.e., students their age). Regardless, Internet bullying was significantly related to all three predictors, and these empirical relations were similar to those of physical and verbal bullying, with the one exception of moral beliefs having a significantly greater positive estimated effect on verbal bullying than on Internet bullying. These findings suggest that the causal pathways to Internet bullying may not be unique; rather, it appears to share common causal pathways with other forms of bullying, particularly verbal bullying.

Technological advances (e.g., Internet e-mail, web sites, and blogs) merely provide yet another venue through which bullying among youth can occur. Indeed a limitation of the current study is that we did not consider a wider range of electronic bullying methods such as picture cell phones and text messages. However preliminary evidence from the second year of the larger study suggests that expanding the scope of the Internet question does not make a major difference. Specifically, the second-year student survey added cell phone text messaging and bullying on various websites. The result was an Internet bullying prevalence rate of 13.6% for the full pre-tested sample in year two, compared with 12.0% for the full pre-tested sample in year 1. These rates are comparable to more recent estimates of Internet bullying (13.1%) based on only 84 adolescents 13–18 years of age.

The present study highlighted common predictors of different types of bullying, including Internet bullying. The findings suggest that preventive interventions can impact these diverse types of bullying by changing normative beliefs about the acceptability of bullying while simultaneously considering how to increase trust and support among peers and within the school setting. For schools, this suggests a "whole school" approach to bullying prevention that facilitates changes in beliefs and behaviors toward greater support, trust, and cohesion. Furthermore, it is important to consider additional potential predictors uniquely linked to the anonymous nature of bullying via the Internet or other communication technologies (e.g., cell phone cameras, text messaging) that may further enhance an understanding of this behavior and thus preventive efforts in this domain. Once again, however, the findings reported here underscore a critical point of this paper: Common social forces influence the various ways in which bullying is expressed—through physical aggression, verbal aggression, or aggression perpetrated through new communication technologies.

POSTSCRIPT

Is Cyberbullying Related to Gender?

Because of the notion that aggression is a predominantly male attribute, researchers have disproportionately used male as opposed to female participants in their research studies. Even when female aggression has been the research focus, the conceptualization of aggression has stemmed from the "male" perspective on aggression. For example, much of the research on aggression has focused specifically on physical aggression using the teacher-learner paradigm. In this paradigm, the participant, acting as teacher, punishes the "learner" with electric shocks for incorrect responses. Research has shown, however, that women perceive electric shock more negatively and a less-effective deterrent than do men; thus, they are more reluctant than men to administer it. Research demonstrating gender differences in aggression might be reflecting gender differences in a willingness to behave physically aggressively rather than the potential for aggression.

A continued focus on types of aggression in which men consistently emerge as more aggressive than women fails to examine those situations in which women might aggress and the modes of aggression they might adopt. Cross-cultural analyses suggest that despite tremendous cross-cultural variation, men tend to be more physically aggressive, but women may use more indirect aggression. Men are more likely to use aggression that produces pain or physical harm, whereas women are more likely to use aggression that produces psychological or social harm. Because the majority of researchers have been male, they may have chosen questions and contexts regarding aggression of greatest personal relevance.

As the use of the Internet increases at exponential rates, questions about gender behavior in cyberspace abound. Research on how girls and boys, women and men, use the Internet as a tool for harm-doing is just beginning. Li's work, in a middle-school-aged sample, is perhaps the first to explicitly address gender differences, and she suggests that patterns of cyberbullying parallel patterns of traditional bullying, with boys more likely to be perpetrators than girls, and female victims more likely to report the bullying to adults than boys. Williams and Guerra, using a slightly older sample of students, find no differences in Internet or verbal bullying between girls and boys, although boys were more than twice as likely to engage in physical bullying. Reconciling the differences between these two studies remain a task for future research. However, results of these and future studies hold the potential to both challenge time-honored assumptions about gender and aggression and allow us to more fully explore how the expression of gender and aggression mutually define each other.

Thus, when asking questions about gender and aggression, aggression should be defined as any behavior directed toward another person or a person's property with the intent to do harm, even if the aggressor was unsuccessful. The behavior could be physical or verbal, active or passive, direct or indirect (i.e., aggressor may remain anonymous), occur in real space or cyberspace, and the consequence for the target could be physical or psychological. All forms of harm-doing behavior, including self-defense, should be considered because in some cases, such as domestic violence, it is difficult to distinguish retaliative from self-defense motives. Also, aggression, broadly defined, allows us to examine more fully the broad range of harm-doing behaviors available to human beings. Thus, rather than asking who is more aggressive, it might be more productive to ask what are the forms and functions of aggression for women and men, and to what degree is the expression of aggression shaped by cultural expectations regarding masculinity (power, dominance, strength) and femininity (nurturing, passive, weak).

Suggested Readings

American Association of University Women, *Tech Savvy: Educating Girls in the New Computer Age* (Washington, DC: AAUW Educational Research Foundation, 2001).

A. J. Baker, *Double-Click: Romance and Commitment among Online Couples* (Cresskill, NJ: Hampton Press, 2005).

Sameer Hinduja and Justin W. Patchin, *Bullying Beyond the School Yard: Preventing and Responding to Cyberbullying* (Thousand Oaks, CA: Corwin Press, 2009).

Robin M. Kowalski and S. E. Limber, *Cyber Bullying: Bullying in the Digital Age* (Malden, MA: Wiley/Blackwell, 2007).

N. E. Willard, *Cyberbullying and Cyberhearts* (Champaign, IL: Research Press, 2007).

Also see the journal *CyberPsychology & Behavior*.

Internet References . . .

Tufts University's Child and Family Web Guide

This Web site provides links to the best sites on same-sex parents.

http://www.cfw.tufts.edu/topic/2/189.htm

Parade

This Web site provides the full text of President Barack Obama's June 21, 2009, father's day speech.

http://www.parade.com/news/2009/06/barack-obama-we-need-fathers-to-step-up.html

National Organization of Single Mothers, Inc.

The National Organization of Single Mothers, Inc. is an organization dedicated to "helping single moms by choice or chance face the daily challenges of life with wisdom, wit, dignity, confidence, and courage."

http://singlemothers.org/cms/index.php

Work and Family: National Partnership for Women and Families

This public education and advocacy site aims "to promote fairness in the workplace, quality health care, and policies that help women and men meet the dual demands of work and family." This site includes a wealth of information about relevant public policy issues, including the Family Medical Leave Act.

http://www.nationalpartnership.org

The Family Economic Strategies

The Family Economic Self-Sufficiency Project describes six strategies that families, especially women, can follow as they move from welfare to self-sufficiency. See the "Setting the Standard for American Working Families" report.

http://www.sixstrategies.org/

The Future of Children

This Web site is sponsored by the Woodrow Wilson School of Public and International Affairs at Princeton University and the Brookings Institution. Its goal is to promote effective policies and programs for children by providing policymakers, service providers, and the media with timely, objective information based on the best available research.

http://www.futureofchildren.org/

The Children's Defense Fund

This nonprofit organization, begun in 1973, advocates for preventive programs to help children stay healthy and out of trouble.

http://www.childrensdefense.org

From *Ozzie and Harriet* to *My Two Dads:* Gender in Childhood

*I*n contemporary America, the "ideal" family continues to be defined as one in which mother and father are married, father is the breadwinner, and mother maintains the home and cares for the children. This ideal is no longer matched by actual family structure, with more and more alternative family structures, including families with same-sex parents and single-parent families being developed to meet personal desires and needs and to cope with societal pressures and changes. Nonetheless, traditional family ideology remains dominant in America. Traditional family ideology institutionalizes conventional gender roles, so much so that many gender scholars view the family as a "gender factory." The institutionalization of gender roles also extends to parental desires regarding the sex of one's children.

In this section, we examine issues surrounding what constitutes a "normal" family, from the perspective of couples themselves. In evaluating the readings in this section, consider what role biology plays in the construction of parenthood. One argument supporting traditional families rests on the assumption that women and men have biologically based attributes that renders each uniquely suited for particular parenting roles, and that having sons and daughters creates a more balanced family. Do data support such an assumption? Is there a maternal instinct? How do race, ethnicity, class, culture, and other status-defining attributes contribute to definitions of family? How might variations in family arrangements across these dimensions challenge essentialist notions of mother and father? Traditional media representations of the family supported a 1950s Ozzie and Harriet view of a stay-at-home-mother and a working father. What views are presented in contemporary media? Consider movies such as Three Men and a Baby and Transamerica. How do media portrayals of parenting affect our understanding of healthy relationships? How and when do media portrayals, including images and language, reinforce or defy gender stereotypes?

- Should Same-Sex Marriage Be Legal?

- Can Lesbian and Gay Couples Be Appropriate Parents for Children?

- Are Fathers Necessary for Children's Well-Being?

- Should Parents Be Allowed to Choose the Sex of Their Children?

ISSUE 10

Should Same-Sex Marriage Be Legal?

YES: **Human Rights Campaign,** from *Answers to Questions about Marriage Equality* (Human Rights Campaign, 2009)

NO: **John Cornyn,** from "In Defense of Marriage," *National Review* (July 2009)

ISSUE SUMMARY

YES: The Human Rights Campaign (HRC), America's largest gay and lesbian organization, explains why same-sex couples should be afforded the same legal right to marry as heterosexual couples.

NO: John Cornyn, United States senator from Texas, says a constitutional amendment is needed to define marriage as permissible only between a man and a woman. Senator Cornyn contends that the traditional institution of marriage needs to be protected from activist courts that would seek to redefine it.

Many people believe that a person should have the same rights as anyone else, regardless of their race, age, gender—or sexual orientation. When this discussion moves into the arena of same-sex marriage, however, those beliefs start to waver a bit. The past few years have seen the topic of same-sex marriage rush into the forefront of the news and other media.

Vermont became the first state to make civil unions legal between two people of the same sex. Although a same-sex couple cannot have a marriage license or refer to their union as a marriage, the benefits are the same as they would be for a heterosexual marriage. These unions are not, however, recognized in any other state. This is due in great part to the Defense of Marriage Act, which was signed into law in 1996 by President Bill Clinton. This Act says that no state is required to recognize a same-sex union, and defines marriage as being between a man and a woman only. Therefore, same-sex unions that are legal in one state do not have to be recognized as legal in another. In anticipation of efforts to have state recognition of civil unions, over 30 states have passed legislation saying they would not recognize a same-sex union that took place in another state.

In the 2004 national election, few issues were more hotly debated than same-sex marriage. In that election, 11 states passed constitutional amendments that effectively banned same-sex marriage. President Bush was quoted as saying "The union of a man and a woman is the most enduring human institution, honored and encouraged in all cultures and by every religious faith." Political conservatives claimed that the election results indicated that the country generally rejects same-sex marriage. President Obama also opposes same-sex marriage but does not believe a constitutional ban is necessary. However, beneath the political rhetoric are questions about what is really wrong with gays and lesbians being granted the same legal rights of heterosexual couples.

Those who oppose same-sex marriage believe that marriage is, and always has been, between a man and a woman. They believe that a key part of marriage for many heterosexual couples is reproduction or another type of parenting arrangement, such as adoption. In those cases, they believe that any child should have two parents, one male and one female (see Issue 11). Many do not oppose granting domestic partner benefits to same-sex partners, or even, in some cases, civil unions. They do, however, believe that if lesbian and gay couples were allowed to marry and to receive the legal and social benefits thereof, it would serve only to further erode the institution of marriage as it is currently defined, which, in the United States, boasts one divorce for every two marriages.

Supporters of same-sex marriage believe that if lesbian and gay couples wish to make a lifetime commitment, they should be afforded the same rights, privileges, and vocabulary as heterosexual couples. While some would be as happy with the term "civil union," accompanied by equal rights, others believe that making marriage available to all is the only way to go.

An argument that is raised in this debate is that granting same-sex couples the right to marry would open the door for adult pedophiles to petition to marry the children with whom they engage in their sexual relationships. Most lesbian and gay individuals and their supporters find this offensive, as well as an invalid comparison. What do you think?

As you read, consider what is at the base of each argument. Consider the assertions pertaining to the effects of same-sex couples or their unions on different-sex couples. Do you agree? What effect do you think the relationship status, choices, and behaviors of heterosexual couples have on lesbian and gay individuals and couples?

In the following sections, information from the Human Rights Campaign provides facts about same sex marriages and addresses commonly raised concerns opponents, such as Senator John Cornyn, raise, such as why do we need a federal constitutional amendment, when we already have the Defense of Marriage Act? He argues that the traditional institution of marriage is the "gold standard" for raising children.

Answers to Questions about Marriage Equality

10 Facts

1. Same-sex couples live in 99.3 percent of all counties nationwide.
2. There are an estimated 3.1 million people living together in same-sex relationships in the United States.
3. Fifteen percent of these same-sex couples live in rural settings.
4. One out of three lesbian couples is raising children. One out of five gay male couples is raising children.
5. Between 1 million and 9 million children are being raised by gay, lesbian and bisexual parents in the United States today.
6. At least one same-sex couple is raising children in 96 percent of all counties nationwide.
7. The highest percentages of same-sex couples raising children live in the South.
8. Nearly one in four same-sex couples includes a partner 55 years old or older, and nearly one in five same-sex couples is composed of two people 55 or older.
9. More than one in 10 same-sex couples include a partner 65 years old or older, and nearly one in 10 same-sex couples is composed of two people 65 or older.
10. The states with the highest numbers of same-sex senior couples are also the most popular for heterosexual senior couples: California, New York, and Florida.

Why Same-Sex Couples Want to Marry

Many same-sex couples want the right to legally marry because they are in love—either they just met the love of their lives, or more likely, they have spent the last 10, 20, or 50 years with that person—and they want to honor their relationship in the greatest way our society has to offer, by making a

---

These facts are based on analyses of the 2000 Census conducted by the Urban Institute and the Human Rights Campaign. The estimated number of people in same-sex relationships has been adjusted by 62 percent to compensate for the widely-reported undercount in the Census. . . .

public commitment to stand together in good times and bad, through all the joys and challenges family life brings.

Many parents want the right to marry because they know it offers children a vital safety net and guarantees protections that unmarried parents cannot provide.

And still other people—both gay and straight—are fighting for the right of same-sex couples to marry because they recognize that it is simply not fair to deny some families the protections all other families are eligible to enjoy.

Currently in the United States, same-sex couples in long-term, committed relationships pay higher taxes and are denied basic protections and rights granted to married heterosexual couples. Among them:

- **Hospital visitation.** Married couples have the automatic right to visit each other in the hospital and make medical decisions. Same-sex couples can be denied the right to visit a sick or injured loved one in the hospital.
- **Social Security benefits.** Married people receive Social Security payments upon the death of a spouse. Despite paying payroll taxes, gay and lesbian partners receive no Social Security survivor benefits— resulting in an average annual income loss of $5,528 upon the death of a partner.
- **Immigration.** Americans in binational relationships are not permitted to petition for their same-sex partners to immigrate. As a result, they are often forced to separate or move to another country.
- **Health insurance.** Many public and private employers provide medical coverage to the spouses of their employees, but most employers do not provide coverage to the life partners of gay and lesbian employees. Gay employees who do receive health coverage for their partners must pay federal income taxes on the value of the insurance.
- **Estate taxes.** A married person automatically inherits all the property of his or her deceased spouse without paying estate taxes. A gay or lesbian taxpayer is forced to pay estate taxes on property inherited from a deceased partner.
- **Retirement savings.** While a married person can roll a deceased spouse's 401(k) funds into an IRA without paying taxes, a gay or lesbian American who inherits a 401(k) can end up paying up to 70 percent of it in taxes and penalties.
- **Family leave.** Married workers are legally entitled to unpaid leave from their jobs to care for an ill spouse. Gay and lesbian workers are not entitled to family leave to care for their partners.
- **Nursing homes.** Married couples have a legal right to live together in nursing homes. Because they are not legal spouses, elderly gay or lesbian couples do not have the right to spend their last days living together in nursing homes.
- **Home protection.** Laws protect married seniors from being forced to sell their homes to pay high nursing home bills; gay and lesbian seniors have no such protection.
- **Pensions.** After the death of a worker, most pension plans pay survivor benefits only to a legal spouse of the participant. Gay and lesbian partners are excluded from such pension benefits.

Why Civil Unions Aren't Enough

Comparing marriage to civil unions is a bit like comparing diamonds to rhinestones. One is, quite simply, the real deal; the other is not. Consider:

- Couples eligible to marry may have their marriage performed in any state and have it recognized in every other state in the nation and every country in the world.
- Couples who are joined in a civil union in Vermont (the only state that offers civil unions) have no guarantee that its protections will even travel with them to neighboring New York or New Hampshire—let alone California or any other state.

Moreover, even couples who have a civil union and remain in Vermont receive only second-class protections in comparison to their married friends and neighbors. While they receive state-level protections, they do not receive any of the *more than 1,100 federal benefits and protections of marriage.*

In short, civil unions are not separate but equal—they are separate and unequal. And our society has tried separate before. It just doesn't work.

Marriage:	Civil unions:
• State grants marriage licenses to couples.	• State would grant civil union licenses to couples.
• Couples receive legal protections and rights under state and federal law.	• Couples receive legal protections and rights under state law only.
• Couples are recognized as being married by the federal government and all state governments.	• Civil unions are not recognized by other states or the federal government.
• Religious institutions are not required to perform marriage ceremonies.	• Religious institutions are not required to perform civil union ceremonies.

"I Believe God Meant Marriage for Men and Women. How Can I Support Marriage for Same-Sex Couples?"

Many people who believe in God—and fairness and justice for all—ask this question. They feel a tension between religious beliefs and democratic values that has been experienced in many different ways throughout our nation's history. That is why the framers of our Constitution established the principle of separation of church and state. That principle applies no less to the marriage issue than it does to any other.

Indeed, the answer to the apparent dilemma between religious beliefs and support for equal protections for all families lies in recognizing that marriage has a significant religious meaning for many people, but that it is also a legal contract. And it is strictly the legal—not the religious—dimension of marriage that is being debated now.

Granting marriage rights to same-sex couples would *not* require Christianity, Judaism, Islam, or any other religion to perform these marriages. It would not require religious institutions to permit these ceremonies to be held on their grounds. It would not even require that religious communities discuss the issue. People of faith would remain free to make their own judgments about what makes a marriage in the eyes of God—just as they are today.

Consider, for example, the difference in how the Catholic Church and the U.S. government view couples who have divorced and remarried. Because church tenets do not sanction divorce, the second marriage is not valid in the church's view. The government, however, recognizes the marriage by extending to the remarried couple the same rights and protections as those granted to every other married couple in America. In this situation—as would be the case in marriage for same-sex couples—the church remains free to establish its own teachings on the religious dimension of marriage while the government upholds equality under law.

It should also be noted that there are a growing number of religious communities that have decided to bless same-sex unions. Among them are Reform Judaism, the Unitarian Universalist Association, and the Metropolitan Community Church. The Presbyterian Church (USA) also allows ceremonies to be performed, although they are not considered the same as marriage. The Episcopal Church and United Church of Christ allow individual churches to set their own policies on same-sex unions.

"This Is Different from Interracial Marriage. Sexual Orientation Is a Choice."

"We cannot keep turning our backs on gay and lesbian Americans. I have fought too hard and too long against discrimination based on race and color not to stand up against discrimination based on sexual orientation. I've heard the reasons for opposing civil marriage for same-sex couples. Cut through the distractions, and they stink of the same fear, hatred, and intolerance I have known in racism and in bigotry."

— Rep. John Lewis, D-Ga., a leader of the black civil rights movement, writing in *The Boston Globe*, Nov. 25, 2003

Decades of research all point to the fact that sexual orientation is not a choice, and that a person's sexual orientation cannot be changed. Who one is drawn to is a fundamental aspect of who we are.

In this way, the struggle for marriage equality for same-sex couples is just as basic as the fight for interracial marriage was. It recognizes that Americans should not be coerced into false and unhappy marriages but should be free to marry the person they love—thereby building marriage on a true and stable foundation.

"Won't This Create a Free-for-All and Make the Whole Idea of Marriage Meaningless?"

Many people share this concern because opponents of gay and lesbian people have used this argument as a scare tactic. But it is not true. Granting same-sex couples the right to marry would in no way change the number of people who could enter into a marriage (or eliminate restrictions on the age or familial relationships of those who may marry). Marriage would continue to recognize the highest possible commitment that can be made between two adults, plain and simple.

Organizations That Support Same-Sex Parenting

American Academy of Pediatrics

American Academy of Family Physicians

Child Welfare League of America

National Association of Social Workers

North American Council on Adoptable Children

American Bar Association

American Psychological Association

American Psychiatric Association

American Psychoanalytic Association

"I Strongly Believe Children Need a Mother and a Father."

Many of us grew up believing that everyone needs a mother and father, regardless of whether we ourselves happened to have two parents, or two *good* parents.

But as families have grown more diverse in recent decades, and researchers have studied how these different family relationships affect children, it has become clear that the *quality* of a family's relationship is more important than the particular *structure* of families that exist today. In other words, the qualities that help children grow into good and responsible adults—learning how to learn, to have compassion for others, to contribute to society and be respectful of others and their differences—do not depend on the sexual orientation of their parents but on their parents' ability to provide a loving, stable and happy home, something no class of Americans has an exclusive hold on.

That is why research studies have consistently shown that children raised by gay and lesbian parents do just as well on all conventional measures of child development, such as academic achievement, psychological well-being, and social abilities, as children raised by heterosexual parents.

That is also why the nation's leading child welfare organizations, including the American Academy of Pediatrics, the American Academy of Family Physicians and others, have issued statements that dismiss assertions that only heterosexual couples can be good parents—and declare that the focus should now be on providing greater protections for the 1 million to 9 million children being raised by gay and lesbian parents in the United States today.

"What Would Be Wrong with a Constitutional Amendment to Define Marriage as a Union of a Man and Woman?"

In more than 200 years of American history, the U.S. Constitution has been amended only 17 times since the Bill of Rights—and in each instance (except for Prohibition, which was repealed), it was to extend rights and liberties to the American people, not restrict them. For example, our Constitution was amended to end our nation's tragic history of slavery. It was also amended to guarantee people of color, young people, and women the right to vote.

The amendment currently under consideration (called the Federal Marriage Amendment) would be the only one that would single out one class of Americans for discrimination by ensuring that same-sex couples would not be granted the equal protections that marriage brings to American families.

Moreover, the amendment could go even further by stripping same-sex couples of some of the more limited protections they now have, such as access to health insurance for domestic partners and their children.

Neither enshrining discrimination in our Constitution nor stripping millions of families of basic protections would serve our nation's best interest. The Constitution is supposed to protect and ensure equal treatment for *all* people. It should not be used to single out a group of people for different treatment.

TEXT OF PROPOSED FEDERAL MARRIAGE AMENDMENT

"Marriage in the United States shall consist only of the union of a man and a woman.

Neither this [C]onstitution [n]or the constitution of any state, nor state or federal law, shall be construed to require that marital status or the legal incidents thereof be conferred upon unmarried couples or groups."

— H.J. Resolution 56, introduced by Rep. Marilyn Musgrave, R-Colo., in May 2003. It has more than 100 co-sponsors. A similar bill was introduced in the U.S. Senate in November 2003. In February 2004, President Bush said that he would support a constitutional amendment to define marriage as between only a man and a woman.

"How Could Marriage for Same-Sex Couples Possibly Be Good for the American Family—or Our Country?"

"We shouldn't just allow gay marriage. We should insist on gay marriage. We should regard it as scandalous that two people could claim to love each other and not want to sanctify their love with marriage and fidelity."

— Conservative Columnist David Brooks, writing in
The New York Times, Nov. 22, 2003.

The prospect of a significant change in our laws and customs has often caused people to worry more about dire consequences that could result than about the potential positive outcomes. In fact, precisely the same anxiety arose when some people fought to overturn the laws prohibiting marriage between people of different races in the 1950s and 1960s. (One Virginia judge even declared that "God intended to separate the races.")

But in reality, opening marriage to couples who are so willing to fight for it could only strengthen the institution for all. It would open the doors to more supporters, not opponents. And it would help keep the age-old institution alive.

As history has repeatedly proven, institutions that fail to take account of the changing needs of the population are those that grow weak; those that recognize and accommodate changing needs grow strong. For example, the U.S. military, like American colleges and universities, grew stronger after permitting African Americans and women to join its ranks.

Similarly, granting same-sex couples the right to marry would strengthen the institution of marriage by allowing it to better meet the needs of the true diversity of family structures in America today.

"Can't Same-Sex Couples Go to a Lawyer to Secure All the Rights They Need?"

Not by a long shot. When a gay or lesbian person gets seriously ill, there is no legal document that can make their partner eligible to take leave from work under the federal Family and Medical Leave Act to provide care—because that law applies only to married couples.

When gay or lesbian people grow old and in need of nursing home care, there is no legal document that can give them the right to Medicaid coverage without potentially causing their partner to be forced from their home—because the federal Medicaid law only permits married spouses to keep their home without becoming ineligible for benefits.

And when a gay or lesbian person dies, there is no legal document that can extend Social Security survivor benefits or the right to inherit a retirement plan without severe tax burdens that stem from being "unmarried" in the eyes of the law.

These are only a few examples of the critical protections that are granted through more than 1,100 federal laws that protect only married couples. In the absence of the right to marry, same-sex couples can only put in place a handful of the most basic arrangements, such as naming each other in a will or a power of attorney. And even these documents remain vulnerable to challenges in court by disgruntled family members.

"Won't This Cost Taxpayers Too Much Money?"

No, it wouldn't necessarily cost much at all. In fact, treating same-sex couples as families under law could even save taxpayers money because marriage would require them to assume legal responsibility for their joint living expenses and reduce their dependence on public assistance programs, such as Medicaid, Temporary Assistance to Needy Families, Supplemental Security Income disability payments, and food stamps.

Put another way, the money it would cost to extend benefits to same-sex couples could be outweighed by the money that would be saved as these families rely more fully on each other instead of state or federal government assistance.

For example, two studies conducted in 2003 by professors at the University of Massachusetts, Amherst, and the University of California, Los Angeles, found that extending domestic partner benefits to same-sex couples in California and New Jersey would save taxpayers millions of dollars a year.

Specifically, the studies projected that the California state budget would save an estimated $8.1 million to $10.6 million each year by enacting the most comprehensive domestic partner law in the nation. In New Jersey, which passed a new domestic partner law in 2004, the savings were projected to be even higher—more than $61 million each year.

(Sources: "Equal Rights, Fiscal Responsibility: The Impact of A.B. 205 on California's Budget," by M. V. Lee Badgett, Ph.D., IGLSS, Department of Economics, University of Massachusetts, and R. Bradley Sears, J.D., Williams Project, UCLA School of Law, University of California, Los Angeles, May 2003, and "Supporting Families, Saving Funds: A Fiscal Analysis of New Jersey's Domestic Partnership Act," by Badgett and Sears with Suzanne Goldberg, J.D., Rutgers School of Law-Newark, December 2003.)

"Where Can Same-Sex Couples Marry Today?"

In 2001, the Netherlands became the first country to extend marriage rights to same-sex couples. Belgium passed a similar law two years later. The laws in both of these countries, however, have strict citizenship or residency requirements that do not permit American couples to take advantage of the protections provided.

In June 2003, Ontario became the first Canadian province to grant marriage to same-sex couples, and in July 2003, British Columbia followed suit—becoming the first places that American same-sex couples could go to get married.

In November 2003, the Massachusetts Supreme Judicial Court recognized the right of same-sex couples to marry—giving the state six months to begin issuing marriage licenses to same-sex couples. It began issuing licenses May 17, 2004.

In February 2004, the city of San Francisco began issuing marriage licenses to same-sex couples after the mayor declared that the state constitution forbade him to discriminate. The issue is being addressed by California courts, and a number of other cities have either taken or are considering taking steps in the same direction.

Follow the latest developments in California, Oregon, New Jersey, New Mexico, New York and in other communities across the country on the HRC Marriage Center. . . .

Other nations have also taken steps toward extending equal protections to all couples, though the protections they provide are more limited than marriage. Canada, Denmark, Finland, France, Germany, Iceland, Norway, Portugal, and Sweden all have nationwide laws that grant same-sex partners a range of important rights, protections, and obligations.

For example, in France, registered same-sex (and opposite-sex) couples can be joined in a civil "solidarity pact" that grants them the right to file joint tax returns, extend social security coverage to each other and receive the same health, employment and welfare benefits as legal spouses. It also commits the couple to assume responsibility for household debts.

Other countries, including Switzerland, Scotland, and the Czech Republic, also have considered legislation that would legally recognize same-sex unions.

"What Protections Other Than Marriage Are Available to Same-Sex Couples?"

At the federal level, there are no protections at all available to same-sex couples. In fact, a federal law called the "Defense of Marriage Act" says that the federal government will discriminate against same-sex couples who marry by refusing to recognize their marriages or providing them with the federal protections of marriage. Some members of Congress are trying to go even further by attempting to pass a Federal Marriage Amendment that would write discrimination against same-sex couples into the U.S. Constitution.

At the state level, only Vermont offers civil unions, which provide important state benefits but no federal protections, such as Social Security survivor benefits. There is also no guarantee that civil unions will be recognized outside Vermont. Thirty-nine states also have "defense of marriage" laws explicitly prohibiting the recognition of marriages between same-sex partners.

Domestic partner laws have been enacted in California, Connecticut, New Jersey, Hawaii, and the District of Columbia. The benefits conferred by these laws vary; some offer access to family health insurance, others confer co-parenting rights. These benefits are limited to residents of the state. A family that moves out of these states immediately loses the protections.

10 Things You Can Do

Every Family Deserves Equal Protections.
How Can I Help?

1. Urge your members of Congress to oppose the Federal Marriage Amendment, or any constitutional amendment to ban marriage for same-sex couples. Make a personal visit if you can. HRC's field team can help you. Or fax a message through HRC's Action Network. . . .
2. Sign the Million for Marriage petition . . . and ask 10 friends and family to do the same.

3. Talk to your friends and family members about the importance of marriage for same-sex couples and their children. Recent polls of the GLBT community show that many people have not yet talked to parents, siblings, or other family members about the discrimination they face. Nothing moves the hearts and minds of potential straight allies more than hearing the stories of someone they know who is gay, lesbian, bisexual, or transgender. For more information, download "Talking about Marriage Equality" from HRC's Online Action Center.

4. Write a letter to the editor of your local newspaper saying why you support marriage for same-sex couples and why a constitutional amendment against it is a bad idea.

5. Next time you hear someone say marriage is only meant for heterosexual couples, speak up. If you hear this on a radio program, call in. If you hear it on television, call or send an e-mail. If it comes up in conversation, set the record straight.

6. Host a house party to educate your friends and family about marriage equality. Invite a diverse group and inspire them to write letters to Congress and your state government at your house party. . . .

7. Meet with clergy and other opinion leaders in your community and ask them to join you in speaking out in support of marriage equality and against the Federal Marriage Amendment. Let HRC know the results. . . .

8. Share your story about why marriage equality matters to you and send it to HRC's family project. . . . Personal stories are what move hearts and minds.

9. Become a member of HRC and support our work on behalf of marriage equality. . . .

10. Register to vote and support fair-minded candidates. . . .

Additional National Resources

Human Rights Campaign . . .

HRC is the nation's largest national organization working to advance equality based on sexual orientation and gender expression and identity to ensure that gay, lesbian, bisexual, and transgender Americans can be open, honest, and safe at home, at work, and in their communities. Of particular interest to people following the marriage issue:

The Human Rights Campaign Foundation's FamilyNet

Project . . . offers the most comprehensive resources about GLBT families, covering marriage, parenting, aging, and more. HRC's Action Center . . . offers important updates about what's happening in legislatures nationwide and the latest online grassroots advocacy tools.

Other important resources include:

American Civil Liberties Union . . .

ACLU works in courts, legislatures, and communities throughout the country to defend and preserve the individual rights and liberties guaranteed by the Constitution and laws of the United States.

Freedom to Marry Collaborative . . .

A gay and non-gay partnership working to win marriage equality.

Children of Lesbians and Gays Everywhere (COLAGE) . . .

Fosters the growth of daughters and sons of GLBT parents by providing education, support, and community, advocating for their rights and rights of their families.

Dignity USA . . .

Works for respect and justice for all GLBT persons in the Catholic Church and the world through education, advocacy, and support.

Family Pride Coalition . . .

A national education and civil rights organization that advances the well-being of GLBT parents and their families through mutual support, community collaboration, and public understanding.

Federation of Statewide LGBT Advocacy Organizations . . .

The GLBT advocacy network of state/territory organizations committed to working with each other and with national and local groups to strengthen statewide advocacy organizing and secure full civil rights in every U.S. state and territory.

Gay & Lesbian Advocates & Defenders . . .

The GLBT legal organization that successfully brought the case that led to the civil union law in Vermont and the recognition of marriage equality in Massachusetts.

Gay & Lesbian Victory Fund . . .

Committed to increasing the number of openly gay and lesbian public officials at federal, state, and local levels of government.

Lambda Legal . . .

A national legal group committed to achieving full recognition of the civil rights of, and combating the discrimination against, the GLBT community and people with HIV/AIDS through impact litigation, education, and public policy work.

Log Cabin Republicans . . .

Operates within the Republican Party for the equal rights of all Americans, including gay men and women, according to the principles of limited government, individual liberty, individual responsibility, free markets, and a strong national defense.

Marriage Equality USA . . .

Works to secure the freedom and the right of same-sex couples to engage in civil marriage through a program of education, media campaigns, and community partnerships.

National Center for Lesbian Rights . . .

A national legal resource center devoted to advancing the rights and safety of lesbians and their families through a program of litigation, public policy advocacy, free legal advice and counseling and public education.

National Black Justice Coalition . . .

An ad hoc coalition of black GLBT leaders who have come together to fight against discrimination in our communities, to build black support for marriage equality, and to educate the community on the dangers of the proposal to amend the U.S. Constitution to discriminate against GLBT people.

National Gay & Lesbian Task Force . . .

Dedicated to building a national civil rights movement of GLBT people through the empowerment and training of state and local leaders, and research and development of national policy.

National Latina/o Lesbian, Gay, Bisexual & Transgender Organization (LLEGÓ) . . .

Develops solutions to social, health, and political disparities that exist due to discrimination based on ethnicity, sexual orientation, and gender identity affecting the lives and well-being of Latina/o GLBT people and their families.

Parents, Families & Friends of Lesbians & Gays (PFLAG) . . .

Promotes the health and well-being of GLBT people, their families and friends, through support, education, and advocacy with the intention of ending discrimination and securing equal civil rights.

Soulforce . . .

An interfaith movement committed to ending spiritual violence perpetuated by religious policies and teachings against GLBT people through the application of the principles of non-violence.

Universal Fellowship of Metropolitan Community Churches . . .

A worldwide fellowship of Christian churches with a special outreach to the world's GLBT communities.

John Cornyn ➡ **NO**

In Defense of Marriage:
The Amendment That Will
Protect a Fundamental Institution

In 1996, three fourths of the House and Senate joined President Bill Clinton in a strong bipartisan effort to defend the traditional institution of marriage, by enacting the federal Defense of Marriage Act (DOMA). That act defined, as a matter of federal law, the institution of marriage as the union of one man and one woman—reflecting the views of the vast majority of Americans across the country. Today, as it debates a constitutional amendment to defend marriage, the Senate will revisit precisely the same question: Should the institution of marriage continue to be defined as the union of one man and one woman—as it has been defined for thousands of years?

Since the 1996 vote, two things have changed. First, activist courts have so dramatically altered the meaning of the Constitution, that traditional marriage laws are now under serious threat of being invalidated by judicial fiat nationwide—indeed, the process has already begun in numerous states across the country. Second, the broad bipartisan consensus behind marriage that was exhibited in 1996 has begun to fracture. Some who supported DOMA just a few years ago are, for partisan reasons, unwilling to defend marriage today. Although the defense of marriage should continue to be a bipartisan endeavor—and kept out of the hands of activist lawyers and judges—there is no question that both the legal and the political landscapes have changed dramatically in recent years.

Commitment to Marriage

One thing has never changed, however: Throughout our nation's history, across diverse cultures, communities, and political affiliations, Americans of all stripes have remained committed to the traditional institution of marriage. Most Americans strongly and instinctively support the following two fundamental propositions: Every human being is worthy of respect, and the traditional institution of marriage is worthy of protection. In communities across America, adults form caring relationships of all kinds, while children are raised through the heroic efforts of parents of all kinds—including single parents,

From *The National Review,* July 2004. Copyright © 2004 by Senator John Cornyn. Reprinted by permission of the author.

foster parents, and adoptive parents. We admire, honor, and respect those relationships and those efforts.

At the same time, most Americans believe that children are best raised by their mother and father. Mankind has known no stronger human bond than that between a child and the two adults who have brought that child into the world together. For that reason, family and marriage experts have referred to the traditional institution of marriage as the "gold standard" for raising children. Social science simply confirms common sense. Social science also confirms that, when society stops privileging the traditional institution of marriage (as we have witnessed in a few European nations in recent years), the gold standard is diluted, and the ideal for raising children is threatened.

There are a number of important issues facing our nation—and the raising and nurturing of our next generation is one of them. Nearly 120 years ago, in the case of *Murphy v. Ramsey,* the U.S. Supreme Court unanimously concluded that "no legislation can be supposed more wholesome and necessary in the founding of a free, self-governing commonwealth" than "the idea of the family, as consisting in and springing from *the union for life of one man and one woman in the holy estate of matrimony*" (emphasis added). That union is "the sure foundation of all that is stable and noble in our civilization; the best guaranty of that reverent morality which is the source of all beneficent progress in social and political improvement." Moreover, that same Court unanimously praised efforts to shield the traditional institution of marriage from the winds of political change, by upholding a law "which endeavors to withdraw all political influence from those who are practically hostile to its attainment."

False Arguments

Today, however, the consensus behind marriage appears to be unraveling. Of course, those who no longer support traditional marriage laws do not say so outright. Instead, they resort to legalistic and procedural arguments for opposing a marriage amendment. They hope to confuse the issue in the minds of well-meaning Americans and to distract them from the importance of defending marriage, by unleashing a barrage of false arguments.

For example:

- *Why do we need a federal constitutional amendment, when we already have DOMA?*

The need for a federal constitutional amendment is simple: The traditional institution of marriage is under constitutional attack. It is now a national problem that requires a national solution. Legal experts and constitutional scholars across the political spectrum recognize and predict that the *only way* to preserve the status quo—the *only way* to preserve the traditional institution of marriage—is a constitutional amendment.

Immediately after the U.S. Supreme Court announced its decision in *Lawrence v. Texas* in June 2003, legal experts and commentators predicted that, under *Lawrence,* courts would begin to strike down traditional marriage laws around the country.

In *Lawrence,* the Court explicitly and unequivocally listed "marriage" as one of the "constitutional" rights that, absent a constitutional amendment, must be granted to same-sex couples and opposite-sex couples alike. Specifically, the Court stated that "our laws and tradition afford constitutional protection to personal decisions relating to *marriage,* procreation, contraception, family relationships, child rearing, and education. . . . Persons in a homosexual relationship may seek autonomy for these purposes, just as heterosexual persons do" (emphasis added). The *Lawrence* majority thus adopted the view endorsed decades ago by one of its members—Justice Ruth Bader Ginsburg. While serving as general counsel of the American Civil Liberties Union, she wrote that traditional marriage laws, such as anti-bigamy laws, are unconstitutional and must be struck down by courts.

It does not take a Supreme Court expert to understand the meaning of these words. And Supreme Court experts agree in any event. Legal scholars are a notoriously argumentative bunch. So it is particularly remarkable that the nation's most recognized constitutional experts—including several liberal legal scholars, like Laurence Tribe, Cass Sunstein, Erwin Chemerinsky, and William Eskridge—are in remarkable harmony on this issue. They predict that, like it or not, DOMA or other traditional marriage laws across the country will be struck down as unconstitutional by courts across the country.

Indeed, the process of invalidating and eradicating traditional marriage laws nationwide has already begun. Most notably, four justices of the Massachusetts Supreme Judicial Court invalidated that state's marriage law in its *Goodridge* decision issued last November, which it reaffirmed in February.

Those decisions were breathtaking, not just in their ultimate conclusion, but in their rhetoric as well. The court concluded that the "deep-seated religious, moral, and ethical convictions" that underlie traditional marriage are "no rational reason" for the institution's continued existence. It argued that traditional marriage is a "stain" on our laws that must be "eradicated." It contended that traditional marriage is "rooted in persistent prejudices" and "invidious discrimination," rather than in the best interest of children. Amazingly, it even suggested abolishing the institution of marriage outright, stating that "if the Legislature were to jettison the term 'marriage' altogether, it might well be rational and permissible." And for good measure, the court went out of its way to characterize DOMA itself as unconstitutionally discriminatory.

Without a federal constitutional amendment, activist courts, and judges will only continue striking down traditional marriage laws across the country—including DOMA itself. Lawsuits challenging traditional marriage laws are now pending in courtrooms across America—including four lawsuits in federal court.

In 2000, Nebraska voters ratified a state constitutional amendment protecting marriage in that state. Yet that state constitutional amendment has been challenged in federal district court as violating federal constitutional law. As Nebraska's attorney general, Jon Bruning, testified last March, the state expects the federal district judge to strike down its constitutional amendment. A federal lawsuit has also been filed in Florida to strike down DOMA as unconstitutional under *Lawrence*. Lawyers are similarly claiming that DOMA is unconstitutional in a pending federal bankruptcy case in Washington state. And in Utah, lawyers have filed suit arguing that traditional marriage laws, such as that state's anti-polygamy law, must be struck down under *Lawrence*. And that just covers lawsuits in federal court—in addition, dozens of suits have been filed in state courts around the country.

A representative of the Lambda Legal organization—a champion of the ongoing nationwide litigation campaign to abolish traditional marriage laws across the country—recently stated: "We won't stop until we have [same-sex] marriage nationwide." This nationwide litigation campaign also enjoys the tacit, if not explicit, support of leading Democrats—including Sens. John Kerry and Ted Kennedy, Rep. Jerrold Nadler, and former presidential candidates Howard Dean and Carol Moseley Braun. All of them have attacked DOMA as unconstitutional, and thus presumably *want* DOMA to be invalidated by the courts—and without a constitutional amendment, their wishes may very well come true. The only way to stop the lawsuits, and to ensure the protection of marriage, is a constitutional amendment.

- *Why do we need an amendment now?*

Last September, the Senate subcommittee on the Constitution, Civil Rights and Property Rights examined the threat posed to the traditional institution of marriage by the *Lawrence* decision.

Detractors of the hearing scoffed that the threat was a pure fabrication, motivated by partisan politics. But then, just two months later, the Massachusetts *Goodridge* decision, relying specifically on *Lawrence,* struck down that state's traditional marriage law—precisely as predicted at the hearing.

Detractors then scoffed that the *Goodridge* decision would not stick. They argued that the state's own constitutional amendment process would be sufficient to control their courts. But then, the Massachusetts court reaffirmed its decision in February. The court even refused to bend after the Massachusetts legislature formally approved a state constitutional amendment—an amendment that can only take effect, if ever, no earlier than 2006.

Detractors then scoffed that DOMA had not been challenged, so there was no reason to take constitutional action at the federal level. But then, lawyers began to challenge DOMA. Cases are now pending in federal courts in Florida and Washington. Additional challenges are, of course, inevitable.

The truth is that, for these detractors, there will never be a good time to protect the traditional institution of marriage—because they don't want to protect the traditional institution of marriage. The constitutional amendment to protect marriage is not a "preemptive strike" on the Constitution, as detractors allege—it's a precautionary solution. Parents take responsible precautions to protect their children. Spouses take responsible precautions to protect their marriage. Likewise, government has the responsibility to take precautions to protect the institution of marriage.

- *Why can't the states handle this? After all, isn't marriage traditionally a state issue?*

This argument borders on the fraudulent. There is nothing that a state can do to fully protect itself against federal courts hostile to its laws except a federal constitutional amendment. Nebraska has already done everything it can, on its own, to defend marriage—up to and including a state constitutional amendment. Yet its amendment has already been challenged in federal court, where it is expected to be struck down. As state and local officials across the country have repeatedly urged, when it comes to defending marriage, the real threat to states' rights is judicial activism—not Congress, and certainly not the democratic process.

Moreover, the Constitution cannot be amended without the consent of three-fourths of the state legislatures. States can protect marriage against judicial activism—but only if Congress provides them the opportunity to consider a federal constitutional amendment protecting marriage.

- *Isn't our Constitution too sacred for such a political issue as defending marriage?*

No one is suggesting that the Constitution should be amended lightly. But the defense of marriage should not be ridiculed as a political issue. Nor should we disparage the most democratic process established under our Constitution by our Founding Fathers.

Our Founding Fathers specifically insisted on including an amendment process in the Constitution because they humbly believed that no man-made document could ever be perfect. The constitutional amendment process was deliberatively considered and wisely crafted, and we have no reason to fear it.

We have amended the Constitution no fewer than 27 times—most recently in 1992 to regulate Congressional pay increases. The sky will not fall if Americans exercise their democratic rights to amend it again. Surely, the protection of marriage is at least as important to our nation as the regulation of Congressional pay, the specific manner in which we coin our money, or the countless other matters that can be found in our nation's charter.

Moreover, there is a robust tradition of constitutional amendments to reverse constitutional decisions by the courts with which the American people disagree—including the 11th, 14th, 16th, 19th, 24th, and 26th Amendments.

Opponents of the marriage amendment apparently have no objection to the courts amending the Constitution. Yet the power to amend the Constitution belongs to the American people, through the democratic process—not the courts. The courts alter the Constitution—under the guise of interpretation—far more often than the people have. Because of *Lawrence,* it is inevitable that the Constitution will be amended on the issue of marriage—the only question is how, and by whom. Legal scholars across the political spectrum agree that a constitutional amendment by the people is the only way to fully protect marriage against the courts.

- *Why would we ever want to write discrimination into the Constitution? Why would we ever want to roll back the Bill of Rights?*

This argument is offensive, pernicious—and revealing.

Marriage is not about discrimination—it is about children. It is offensive to characterize the vast majorities of Americans who support traditional marriage—individuals like Reverend Ray Hammond of the Bethel African Methodist Episcopal Church in Boston, Reverend Richard Richardson of the St. Paul African Methodist Episcopal Church in Boston, and Pastor Daniel de Leon, Sr., of Alianza de Ministerios Evangélicos Nacionales (AMEN) and Templo Calvario in Santa Ana, California—as bigots. It is offensive to characterize the laws, precedents, and customs of all fifty states as discriminatory. And it is offensive to slander the 85 senators who voted for DOMA as hateful.

Moreover, it is *precisely because* some activists believe that traditional marriage is about discrimination, and not about children, that they believe that all traditional marriage laws are unconstitutional and therefore must be abolished by the courts. These activists leave the American people with no middle ground. They accuse others of writing discrimination into the Constitution— yet they are the ones writing the American people out of our constitutional democracy.

Just last week, representatives of Sens. John Kerry and John Edwards said that the marriage amendment would "roll back rights." If you believe that traditional marriage is only about discrimination and about violating the rights of adults—as Sens. Kerry and Edwards apparently believe—then you have no choice but to oppose all traditional marriage laws. Any other position is incoherent at best—and deceptive at worst.

Marriage Protection

So the issue has been joined—precisely as it was in 1996. Despite typical Washington Beltway tricks to overcomplicate and confuse matters, the question remains a simple one: Should marriage, defined as the union of one man and one woman, be protected against judicial activism and the will of legal and political elites? If you believe that the answer is yes—as vast majorities of Americans do—then you have no legal option but to support a federal constitutional amendment protecting marriage.

The American people believe that every human being deserves respect, and the traditional institution of marriage deserves protection. As members of Congress continue to debate this issue, we should also remember what else the American people deserve: honesty. . . .

POSTSCRIPT

Should Same-Sex Marriage Be Legal?

Part of this discussion is that marriage is a civil right, not an inherent or moral one. Those supporting marriage rights for lesbian and gay couples cite the struggles of the civil rights movement of the 1960s in their current quest for equality for all couples. Among the points they make is that up until 1967, it was still illegal in some states for people of different races to marry. Many opponents find the idea of comparing same-sex marriage to the civil rights struggles of the 1960s and earlier offensive, that it is like comparing apples and oranges. Many of these individuals believe that sexual orientation is chosen, rather than an inherent part of who one is—unlike race, which is predetermined. Most sexuality experts, however, agree that while we do not know for sure what "causes" a person to be heterosexual, bisexual, or homosexual, it is clear that it is determined very early in life, perhaps even before we are born. Regardless, is marriage a civil right? A legal right? An inherent right?

It has also been argued that if sexual orientation is not "normal," then same-sex couples would not have "healthy" relationships. However, there is no evidence that would support such a claim. In fact, some studies would suggest that some aspects of same-sex relationships are in fact healthier than heterosexual relationships. At least two factors may contribute to this. First, neither person in a same-sex couple is constrained by gender role expectations; that is, each person has more latitude to be himself or herself rather than the "bread-winner" or "homemaker." Second, because there are few role models for same-sex couples, they may actually spend more time negotiating aspects of their relationships in ways that heterosexual couples do not. Currently no heterosexual has to pass a "mental health test" in order to marry. Additionally, heterosexual couples do not have to demonstrate a "healthy" relationship in order to either marry or remain married. Is it possible that heterosexual couples could learn something from same-sex couples?

Suggested Readings

George Chauncey, *Why Marriage? The History Shaping Today's Debate over Gay Equality* (Basic Books, 2004).

Linda Hollingdale, *Creating Civil Union: Opening Hearts and Minds* (Common Humanity Press, 2002).

Jonathan Rauch, *Gay Marriage: Why It Is Good for Gays, Good for Straights, and Good for America* (Owl Books, 2004).

A. Sullivan and J. Landau, *Same-Sex Marriage: Pro and Con* (Vintage Books, 1997).

ISSUE 11

Can Lesbian and Gay Couples Be Appropriate Parents for Children?

YES: American Psychological Association, from *APA Policy Statement on Sexual Orientation, Parents, and Children* (Adopted July 2004)

NO: Timothy J. Dailey, from "State of the States: Update on Homosexual Adoption in the U.S." *Family Research Council* (2004)

ISSUE SUMMARY

YES: The American Psychological Association's Council of Representatives adopted this resolution that was drafted by a task force of expert psychologists. The resolution, based on a thorough review of the literature, opposes any discrimination based on sexual orientation and concludes that children reared by same-sex parents benefit from legal ties to each parent.

NO: Timothy J. Dailey, senior research fellow at the Center for Marriage and Family Studies, provides an overview of state laws pertaining to adoption by lesbian or gay parents. He points to studies showing that children do much better in family settings that include both a mother and a father, and that the sexual behaviors same-sex parents engage in make them, by definition, inappropriate role models for children.

Currently, there are thousands of children awaiting adoption. In many cases, there are strict requirements as to who can and cannot adopt. In one country, for example, a heterosexual couple must be married for at least four years—and if they already have one child, they can only adopt a child of a different sex. Most countries do not allow same-sex couples or openly lesbian or gay individuals to adopt children.

In the United States, same-sex couples can adopt in a number of ways. Some will adopt as single parents, even though they are in a long-term, committed relationship with another person, because the state or agency does not permit same-sex couples to adopt together. Others will do what is called "second parent" adoption—where one partner is the biological parent of the child, and the other can become the other legal parent by going through the court system.

In other cases, the biological parent must terminate her or his own rights so that there can be a "joint adoption." Both parents jointly adopt the child and become equal, legal parents. This applies to unmarried different-sex couples, too.

There are a range of feelings about who should or should not parent children. Some individuals feel that children should be raised by a man and a woman who are married, not by a gay or lesbian individual or couple. Starting with the premise that homosexuality is wrong, they feel that such a relationship is an inappropriate context in which to raise children. For some of these opponents of lesbian and gay parenting, homosexuality is defined by behaviors. Opponents believe that children would be harmed if they grew up in gay or lesbian families, in part because they would grow up without a mother figure if raised by gay men or without a father figure if raised by lesbians. Additionally, because they fear that sexual orientation and behaviors can be learned, they also fear that children raised by a lesbian or gay couple will be more likely to come out as lesbian or gay.

Other people do not believe that a person's sexual orientation determines the ability to parent. Whether a person is raised by one parent, two men, two women, or a man and a woman is less important than any individual's or couple's ability to love, support, and care for a child. They oppose the concept that a heterosexual couple in which there is abuse or where there are inappropriate sexual boundaries would be considered preferable to a lesbian or gay couple in a long-term, committed relationship who care for each other and their children. They point to the fact that most lesbian, gay, and bisexual adults were raised by heterosexual parents. Therefore, they believe, being raised by a lesbian or gay couple will not create lesbian, gay, or bisexual children, any more than being raised by a heterosexual, married couple would guarantee heterosexuality.

Some state laws support same-sex couples' right to adopt children, and some do not. In New Jersey, California, Connecticut, and Massachusetts, for example, joint or second parent adoption is currently available. In Utah, married heterosexual couples are given priority for foster or adoptive children, and in Mississippi, there is a law that outright bans a same-sex couple from being able to adopt children.

As you read this issue, think about what you think the characteristics of a good parent are. Can these characteristics be found only in heterosexual relationships, or can they be fulfilled by a same-sex relationship? Does the gender of a same-sex relationship affect your feelings on the subject? For example, do you find two women raising a child more or less threatening than two men?

In the following selections, the American Psychological Association's resolution concludes that there is no empirical evidence to support the claim that children raised by same-sex parents are harmed psychologically and that all children benefit from legal ties to both parents. Timothy Dailey asserts that gay men are sexually promiscuous, and are therefore poor role models and parents for children. Lesbians, he believes, are ineffective parents because they are raising a child without the presence and influence of a father figure, which theorists, he maintains, argue is vital to the psychosocial development of children, male and female.

YES ↵

APA Policy Statement on Sexual Orientation, Parents, and Children

Research Summary

Lesbian and Gay Parents

Many lesbians and gay men are parents. In the 2000 U.S. Census, 33% of female same-sex couple households and 22% of male same-sex couple households reported at least one child under the age of 18 living in the home. Despite the significant presence of at least 163,879 households headed by lesbian or gay parents in U.S. society, three major concerns about lesbian and gay parents are commonly voiced (Falk, 1994; Patterson, Fulcher & Wainright, 2002). These include concerns that lesbians and gay men are mentally ill, that lesbians are less maternal than heterosexual women, and that lesbians' and gay men's relationships with their sexual partners leave little time for their relationships with their children. In general, research has failed to provide a basis for any of these concerns (Patterson, 2002, 2004a; Perrin, 2002; Tasker, 1999; Tasker & Golombok, 1997). First, homosexuality is not a psychological disorder (Conger, 1975). Although exposure to prejudice and discrimination based on sexual orientation may cause acute distress (Mays & Cochran, 2001; Meyer, 2003), there is no reliable evidence that homosexual orientation per se impairs psychological functioning. Second, beliefs that lesbian and gay adults are not fit parents have no empirical foundation (Patterson, 2000, 2004a; Perrin, 2002). Lesbian and heterosexual women have not been found to differ markedly in their approaches to child rearing (Patterson, 2002; Tasker, 1999). Members of gay and lesbian couples with children have been found to divide the work involved in childcare evenly, and to be satisfied with their relationships with their partners (Patterson, 2000, 2004a). The results of some studies suggest that lesbian mothers' and gay fathers' parenting skills may be superior to those of matched heterosexual parents. There is no scientific basis for concluding that lesbian mothers or gay fathers are unfit parents on the basis of their sexual orientation (Armesto, 2002; Patterson, 2000; Tasker & Golombok, 1997). On the contrary, results of research suggest that lesbian and gay parents are as likely as heterosexual parents to provide supportive and healthy environments for their children.

Paige, R. U. (2005). Proceedings of the American Psychological Association, Incorporated, for the legislative year 2004. Minutes of the meeting of the Council of Representatives July 28 & 30, 2004, Honolulu, HI. Retrieved November 18, 2004, from the World Wide Web http://www.apa .org/governance/.

Children of Lesbian and Gay Parents

As the social visibility and legal status of lesbian and gay parents has increased, three major concerns about the influence of lesbian and gay parents on children have been often voiced (Falk; 1994; Patterson, Fulcher & Wainright, 2002). One is that the children of lesbian and gay parents will experience more difficulties in the area of sexual identity than children of heterosexual parents. For instance, one such concern is that children brought up by lesbian mothers or gay fathers will show disturbances in gender identity and/or in gender role behavior. A second category of concerns involves aspects of children's personal development other than sexual identity. For example, some observers have expressed fears that children in the custody of gay or lesbian parents would be more vulnerable to mental breakdown, would exhibit more adjustment difficulties and behavior problems, or would be less psychologically healthy than other children. A third category of concerns is that children of lesbian and gay parents will experience difficulty in social relationships. For example, some observers have expressed concern that children living with lesbian mothers or gay fathers will be stigmatized, teased, or otherwise victimized by peers. Another common fear is that children living with gay or lesbian parents will be more likely to be sexually abused by the parent or by the parent's friends or acquaintances.

Results of social science research have failed to confirm any of these concerns about children of lesbian and gay parents (Patterson, 2000, 2004a; Perrin, 2002; Tasker, 1999). Research suggests that sexual identities (including gender identity, gender-role behavior, and sexual orientation) develop in much the same ways among children of lesbian mothers as they do among children of heterosexual parents (Patterson, 2004a). Studies of other aspects of personal development (including personality, self-concept, and conduct) similarly reveal few differences between children of lesbian mothers and children of heterosexual parents (Perrin, 2002; Stacey & Biblarz, 2001; Tasker, 1999). However, few data regarding these concerns are available for children of gay fathers (Patterson, 2004b). Evidence also suggests that children of lesbian and gay parents have normal social relationships with peers and adults (Patterson, 2000, 2004a; Perrin, 2002; Stacey & Biblarz, 2001; Tasker, 1999; Tasker & Golombok, 1997). The picture that emerges from research is one of general engagement in social life with peers, parents, family members, and friends. Fears about children of lesbian or gay parents being sexually abused by adults, ostracized by peers, or isolated in single-sex lesbian or gay communities have received no scientific support. Overall, results of research suggest that the development, adjustment, and well-being of children with lesbian and gay parents do not differ markedly from that of children with heterosexual parents.

Resolution

> WHEREAS APA supports policy and legislation that promote safe, secure, and nurturing environments for all children (DeLeon, 1993, 1995; Fox, 1991; Levant, 2000);

WHEREAS APA has a long-established policy to deplore "all public and private discrimination against gay men and lesbians" and urges "the repeal of all discriminatory legislation against lesbians and gay men" (Conger, 1975);

WHEREAS the APA adopted the Resolution on Child Custody and Placement in 1976 (Conger, 1977, p. 432);

WHEREAS Discrimination against lesbian and gay parents deprives their children of benefits, rights, and privileges enjoyed by children of heterosexual married couples;

WHEREAS some jurisdictions prohibit gay and lesbian individuals and same-sex couples from adopting children, notwithstanding the great need for adoptive parents (*Lofton v. Secretary,* 2004);

WHEREAS There is no scientific evidence that parenting effectiveness is related to parental sexual orientation: lesbian and gay parents are as likely as heterosexual parents to provide supportive and healthy environments for their children (Patterson, 2000, 2004; Perrin, 2002; Tasker, 1999);

WHEREAS Research has shown that the adjustment, development, and psychological well-being of children is unrelated to parental sexual orientation and that the children of lesbian and gay parents are as likely as those of heterosexual parents to flourish (Patterson, 2004; Perrin, 2002; Stacey & Biblarz, 2001);

THEREFORE BE IT RESOLVED That the APA opposes any discrimination based on sexual orientation in matters of adoption, child custody and visitation, foster care, and reproductive health services;

THEREFORE BE IT FURTHER RESOLVED That the APA believes that children reared by a same-sex couple benefit from legal ties to each parent;

THEREFORE BE IT FURTHER RESOLVED That the APA supports the protection of parent-child relationships through the legalization of joint adoptions and second parent adoptions of children being reared by same-sex couples;

THEREFORE BE IT FURTHER RESOLVED That APA shall take a leadership role in opposing all discrimination based on sexual orientation in matters of adoption, child custody and visitation, foster care, and reproductive health services;

THEREFORE BE IT FURTHER RESOLVED That APA encourages psychologists to act to eliminate all discrimination based on sexual orientation in matters of adoption, child custody and visitation, foster care, and reproductive health services in their practice, research, education and training ("Ethical Principles," 2002, p. 1063);

THEREFORE BE IT FURTHER RESOLVED That the APA shall provide scientific and educational resources that inform public discussion and public policy development regarding discrimination based on sexual orientation in matters of adoption, child custody and visitation, foster care, and reproductive health services and that assist its members, divisions, and affiliated state, provincial, and territorial psychological associations.

References

Armesto, J. C. (2002). Developmental and contextual factors that influence gay fathers' parental competence: A review of the literature. *Psychology of Men and Masculinity, 3,* 67–78.

Conger, J. J. (1975). Proceedings of the American Psychological Association, Incorporated, for the year 1974: Minutes of the Annual meeting of the Council of Representatives. *American Psychologist, 30,* 620–651.

Conger, J. J. (1977). Proceedings of the American Psychological Association, Incorporated, for the legislative year 1976: Minutes of the Annual Meeting of the Council of Representatives. *American Psychologist, 32,* 408–438.

DeLeon, P. H. (1993). Proceedings of the American Psychological Association, Incorporated, for the year 1992: Minutes of the annual meeting of the Council of Representatives August 13 and 16, 1992, and February 26–28, 1993, Washington, DC. *American Psychologist, 48,* 782.

DeLeon, P. H. (1995). Proceedings of the American Psychological Association, Incorporated, for the year 1994: Minutes of the annual meeting of the Council of Representatives August 11 and 14, 1994, Los Angeles, CA, and February 17–19, 1995, Washington, DC. *American Psychologist, 49,* 627–628.

Ethical Principles of Psychologists and Code of Conduct. (2002). *American Psychologist, 57,* 1060–1073.

Fox, R. E. (1991). Proceedings of the American Psychological Association, Incorporated, for the year 1990: Minutes of the annual meeting of the Council of Representatives August 9 and 12, 1990, Boston, MA, and February 8–9, 1991, Washington, DC. *American Psychologist, 45,* 845.

Levant, R. F. (2000). Proceedings of the American Psychological Association, Incorporated, for the Legislative Year 1999: Minutes of the Annual Meeting of the Council of Representatives February 19–21, 1999, Washington, DC, and August 19 and 22, 1999, Boston, MA, and Minutes of the February, June, August, and December 1999 Meetings of the Board of Directors. *American Psychologist, 55,* 832–890.

Lofton v. Secretary of Department of Children & Family Services, 358 F.3d 804 (11th Cir. 2004).

Mays, V. M. & Cochran, S. D. (2001). Mental health correlates of perceived discrimination among lesbian, gay, and bisexual adults in the United States. *American Journal of Public Health, 91,* 1869–1876.

Meyer, I. H. (2003). Prejudice, social stress, and mental health in lesbian, gay, and bisexual populations: Conceptual issues and research evidence. *Psychological Bulletin, 129,* 674–697.

Patterson, C. J. (2000). Family relationships of lesbians and gay men. *Journal of Marriage and Family, 62,* 1052–1069.

Patterson, C. J. (2004a). Lesbian and gay parents and their children: Summary of research findings. In *Lesbian and gay parenting: A resource for psychologists.* Washington, DC: American Psychological Association.

Patterson, C. J. (2004b). Gay fathers. In M. E. Lamb (Ed.), *The role of the father in child development* (4th Ed.). New York: John Wiley.

Patterson, C. J., Fulcher, M., & Wainright, J. (2002). Children of lesbian and gay parents: Research, law, and policy. In B. L. Bottoms, M. B. Kovera, and

B. D. McAuliff (Eds.), *Children, social science and the law* (pp. 176–199). New York: Cambridge University Press.

Perrin, E. C., and the Committee on Psychosocial Aspects of Child and Family Health (2002). Technical Report: Coparent or second-parent adoption by same-sex parents. *Pediatrics, 109,* 341–344.

Stacey, J. & Biblarz, T. J. (2001). (How) Does sexual orientation of parents matter? *American Sociological Review, 65,* 159–183.

Tasker, F. (1999). Children in lesbian-led families—A review. *Clinical Child Psychology and Psychiatry, 4,* 153–166.

Tasker, F., & Golombok, S. (1997). *Growing up in a lesbian family.* New York: Guilford Press.

Timothy J. Dailey

→ **NO**

State of the States: Update on Homosexual Adoption in the U.S.

The legal status of homosexual adoption varies from state to state, and is constantly changing due to court decisions and new state laws addressing the issue. Further complicating the issue are gay activist organizations that present misleading accounts of court rulings and laws reflecting unfavorably on homosexual parenting.

States That Specifically Prohibit Gay Adoption

Three states, Florida, Mississippi, and Utah, have passed statutes specifically prohibiting homosexual adoption. The advocates of gay adoption downplay the Utah statute, asserting that it was not intended to prevent adoption by homosexuals. Liz Winfeld, writing in the *Denver Post*, discusses claims that the Utah law was aimed squarely at homosexuals: "Not true. Utah disallows any unmarried person from adopting regardless of gender or orientation."[1] . . .

In fact, the Utah law was enacted specifically to close loopholes in Utah adoption laws that were being taken advantage of by homosexual couples seeking to adopt children. . . .

The ensuing fight led to the legislature passing a statute barring homosexual adoptions. . . .

States That Specifically Permit Gay Adoption

USA Today reports that seven states, including California, Connecticut, Illinois, Massachusetts, New Jersey, New York, Vermont, and the District of Columbia permit homosexuals to adopt.[2] However, at present the inclusion of California on this list is inaccurate.

States That Permit Second-Parent Adoption

Homosexual couples have adopted children through "second-parent" adoption policies in at least twenty states. There is no evidence that homosexuals in the remaining states are permitted to adopt children, a fact admitted by the gay activist Human Rights Campaign (HRC): "In the remaining 24 states, our research has not revealed any second-parent adoptions."[3]

At least one state has reversed its policy of permitting second-parent adoptions. In November 2000, the Superior Court of Pennsylvania ruled that same-sex couples cannot adopt children.[4] In addition, a court decision in California has reversed that state's policy of permitting homosexuals to adopt children. On October 25, 2001, the 4th District Court of Appeal (San Diego) ruled that there was no legal authority under California law permitting second-parent adoptions.[5] . . .

Homosexual Households in the United States

There are widely varying and unsubstantiated claims about the numbers of children being raised in gay and lesbian households. . . .

- The U.S. Census Bureau reports that there are 601,209 (304,148 male homosexual and 297,061 lesbian) same-sex unmarried partner households, for a total of 1,202,418 individuals, in the United States.[6] If one million children were living in households headed by homosexual couples, this would mean that, on average, *every* homosexual household has at least one child.
- However, a survey in *Demography* indicates that 95 percent of partnered male homosexual and 78 percent of partnered lesbian households do *not* have children.[7] This would mean that the one million children presumed to be living in homosexual households would be divided among the 15,000 (five percent of 304,148) male homosexual and 65,000 (22 percent of 297,061) lesbian households that actually have children. This would result in an astounding 12.5 children per gay and lesbian family.

The cases highlighted by the media to generate sympathy for homosexual adoption typically feature "two-parent" homosexual households. Of course, some children are also being raised by a natural parent who identifies himself or herself as homosexual and lives alone. Nevertheless, the hypothetical calculations above give some indication of how absurdly inflated most of the estimates are concerning the number of children being raised by homosexuals. Far from being the proven success that some claim, homosexual parenting remains a relatively rare phenomenon.

Implications for Homosexual Parenting

Demands that homosexuals be accorded the right to . . . adopt children fit into the gay agenda by minimizing the differences between homosexual and heterosexual behavior in order to make homosexuality look as normal as possible. However, as already shown, only a small minority of gay and lesbian households have children. Beyond that, the evidence also indicates that comparatively few homosexuals choose to establish households together—the type of setting that is a prerequisite for the rearing of children. Consider the following:

- HRC claims that the U.S. population of gays and lesbians is 10,456,405, or 5 percent of the total U.S. population over 18 years of age.[8] The best available data supports a much lower estimate for those who engage in same-sex sexual relations.[9] However, assuming the higher estimate for the purposes of argument, this would indicate that *only 8.6 percent* of homosexuals (1,202,418 out of 10,456,405) choose to live in a household with a person of the same sex.

- HRC asserts that "30 percent of gay and lesbian people are living in a committed relationship in the same residence."[10] Assuming HRC's own figures, that would mean over three million gays and lesbians are living in such households, which, as shown above, is a wildly inflated estimate over the census figures. It is worth noting that the HRC claim amounts to a tacit admission that 70 percent of gays and lesbians choose not to live in committed relationships and establish households together.
- HRC claims that the numbers of gay and lesbian households were "undercounted" by the census. However, if true, it would represent an unprecedented, massive undercount of 260 percent on the part of the U.S. Census Bureau.

The census figures indicate that only a small minority of gays and lesbians have made the lifestyle choice that is considered a fundamental requisite in any consideration regarding adoption, and only a small percentage of those households actually have children. The evidence thus does not support the claim that significant numbers of homosexuals desire to provide a stable family setting for children.

The Nature of Homosexual "Committed Relationships"

Gay activists admit that the ultimate goal of the drive to legitimize homosexual marriage and adoption is to change the essential character of marriage, removing precisely the aspects of fidelity and chastity that promote stability in the home. They pursue their goal heedless of the fact that such households are unsuitable for the raising of children:

- Paula Ettelbrick, former legal director of the Lambda Legal Defense and Education Fund, has stated, "Being queer is more than setting up house, sleeping with a person of the same gender, and seeking state approval for doing so. . . . Being queer means pushing the parameters of sex, sexuality, and family, and in the process transforming the very fabric of society."[11]
- According to homosexual writer and activist Michelangelo Signorile, the goal of homosexuals is to redefine the term *monogamy*.

For these men the term 'monogamy' simply doesn't necessarily mean sexual exclusivity. . . . The term 'open relationship' has for a great many gay men come to have one specific definition: A relationship in which the partners have sex on the outside often, put away their resentment and jealousy, and discuss their outside sex with each other, or share sex partners.[12]

- The views of Signorile and Ettelbrick regarding marriage are widespread in the homosexual community. According to the *Mendola Report,* a mere 26 percent of homosexuals believe that commitment is most important in a marriage relationship.[13] . . .

Even those who support the concept of homosexual "families" admit to their unsuitability for children:

- In their study in *Family Relations,* L. Koepke et al. observed, "Even individuals who believe that same-sex relationships are a legitimate choice for adults may feel that children will suffer from being reared in such families."[14]
- Pro-homosexual researchers, J. J. Bigner and R. B. Jacobson describe the homosexual father as "socioculturally unique," trying to take on "two apparently opposing roles: that of a father (with all its usual connotations) and that of a homosexual man." They describe the homosexual father as "both structurally and psychologically at social odds with his interest in keeping one foot in both worlds: parenting and homosexuality."[15]

In truth, the two roles are fundamentally incompatible. The instability, susceptibility to disease, and domestic violence that is disproportionate in homosexual relationships would normally render such households unfit to be granted custody of children. However, in the current social imperative to grant legitimacy to the practice of homosexuality in every conceivable area of life, such considerations are often ignored.

But children are not guinea pigs to be used in social experiments in redefining the institutions of marriage and family. They are vulnerable individuals with vital emotional and developmental needs. The great harm done by denying them both a mother and a father in a committed marriage will not easily be reversed, and society will pay a grievous price for its ill-advised adventurism.

Notes

1. Liz Winfeld, "In a Family Way," *Denver Post,* November 28, 2001.
2. Marilyn Elias, "Doctors Back Gay 'Co-Parents,'" *USA Today,* February 3, 2002.
3. "Chapter 4: Second-Parent Adoption," in *The Family* (Human Rights Campaign, 2002). . . . .
4. Ibid.
5. Bob Egelko, "Court Clarifies Decision on Adoptions," *San Francisco Chronicle,* November 22, 2001. The decision is under review by the California Supreme Court.
6. "PCT 14: Unmarried-Partner Households by Sex of Partners" (U.S. Census Bureau: Census 2000 Summary File 1).
7. Dan Black et al., "Demographics of the Gay and Lesbian Population in the United States: Evidence from Available Systematic Data Sources," *Demography* 37 (May 2000): 150.

8. David M. Smith and Gary J. Gates, "Gay and Lesbian Families in the United States: Same-Sex Unmarried Partner Households," *Human Rights Campaign* (August 22, 2001): 2.

9. Dan Black et al., "Demographics of the Gay and Lesbian Population," "4.7 percent of men in the combined samples have had at least one same-sex experience since age 18, but only 2.5 percent of men have engaged in exclusively same-sex sex over the year preceding the survey. Similarly, 3.5 percent of women have had at least one same-sex sexual experience, but only 1.4 percent have had exclusively same-sex sex over the year preceding the survey" (p. 141).

10. Ibid.

11. Paula Ettelbrick, quoted in William B. Rubenstein, "Since When Is Marriage a Path to Liberation?" *Lesbians, Gay Men, and the Law* (New York: The New Press, 1993), pp. 398, 400.

12. Michelangelo Signorile, *Life Outside* (New York: HarperCollins, 1997), p. 213.

13. Mary Mendola, *The Mendola Report* (New York: Crown, 1980), p. 53.

14. L. Koepke et al., "Relationship Quality in a Sample of Lesbian Couples with Children and Child-free Lesbian Couples," *Family Relations* 41 (1992): 228.

15. Bigner and Jacobson, "Adult Responses to Child Behavior and Attitudes Toward Fathering," Frederick W. Bozett, ed., *Homosexuality and the Family* (New York: Harrington Park Press, 1989), pp. 174, 175.

POSTSCRIPT

Can Lesbian and Gay Couples Be Appropriate Parents for Children?

Parenting is an area that has so many unknown factors, influences, and outcomes. Two-parent, high-income families sometimes have children who grow up with emotional and/or behavioral problems. Single parents can raise healthy, well-adjusted children. Some heterosexual couples raise children effectively and some do not; some lesbian or gay couples raise children effectively, and some do not. Some parents abuse their children; most do not.

While there is much research exploring correlations between economic health, number of parents, and other factors, literature reviewing the connections between a parent's sexual orientation and the ability to parent remains inconclusive. There are studies maintaining that children need to be raised by a married, heterosexual couple, and there are studies asserting that a same-sex couple can do just as effective a job.

There is also insufficient information about sexual orientation itself, and the effects that having a lesbian, gay, or bisexual parent may or may not have on a child. The lack of information and plethora of misinformation breed fear. When people are afraid, they want to protect—in this case, people who do not understand the basis of sexual orientation feel they need to protect children. In doing so, they sometimes make decisions that are not always in the best interest of the child. For example, in 1996, a divorced heterosexual couple living in Florida was battling over custody of their 11-year-old daughter. The male partner had recently completed an eight-year prison sentence for the murder of his first wife, and had married his third. His ex-wife, however, had since met and partnered with a woman. A judge determined that the man and his new wife would provide a more appropriate home for the child than the child's mother because she was in a relationship with another woman. In the end, the judge believed that the child would do best in a home with a mother and a father, even though the father was convicted of second-degree murder and accused of sexually molesting his daughter from his first marriage.

How do you feel about this? If you feel that heterosexual couples are more appropriate parents than same-sex couples, how would the fact that one of the heterosexual partners had committed a capital crime affect your opinion?

Sometimes, we argue for what we think "should be" in a given situation. A challenge arises when comparing the "should be" to the "is"—what we think is best as opposed to the reality. If you feel that heterosexual married couples make the best parents, what should be done with those same-sex couples who are providing a loving, stable home for their children? Would it be best to leave the child where she or he is, or do you think the child would be better off removed from the existing family structure and placed with a heterosexual couple? Clearly, this is a discussion and debate that will continue as more and more same-sex couples not only adopt, but also have biological children of their own.

Suggested Readings

Jane Drucker (2001). *Lesbian and Gay Families Speak Out: Understanding the Joys and Challenges of Diverse Family Life*. HarperCollins: New York.

Noelle Howey, Ellen Samuels, Margarethe Cammermeyer, & Dan Savage (2000). *Out of the Ordinary: Essays on Growing Up with Gay, Lesbian, and Transgender Parents*. St. Martin's Press: New York.

Patricia Morgan (2002). *Children as Trophies? Examining the Evidence on Same-Sex Parenting*. The Christian Institute: Newcastle upon Tyne, NE, UK.

ISSUE 12

Are Fathers Necessary for Children's Well-Being?

YES: Natasha J. Cabrera, Jacqueline D. Shannon, and Catherine Tamis-LeMonda, from "Fathers' Influence on Their Children's Cognitive and Emotional Development from Toddlers to Pre-K," *Applied Developmental Science* (2007)

NO: Peggy Drexler, from *Raising Boys Without Men* (Rodale Books, 2005)

ISSUE SUMMARY

YES: Professor of human development Natasha J. Cabrera reports that father engagement has positive effects on children's cognition and language, as well as their social and emotional development.

NO: In contrast, Peggy Drexler studied what she terms "maverick" moms to show how boys can succeed in homes without fathers.

O n Father's Day, June 21, 2009, President Obama gave a speech in which he said, "We need fathers to step up." He used his own experiences as a child growing up without a father, as well as his observations as a community organizer and legislator as a basis for his plea. His concerns reflect long-standing assumptions that fathers are necessary for children's well-being. But are they?

For decades there has been active debate about parenting roles and responsibilities. What does it mean to be a responsible parent? Is one sex naturally better at parenting than the other? Are there essential characteristics of fathering versus mothering? Is having parents of two sexes necessary for the well-being of children? Should mothers work or engage in other activities outside the family? Should fathers move beyond the provider or breadwinner role and become more involved in the physical and emotional care of their children? Should fathers emulate mothers' traditional nurturing activities? Or should fathers uphold their role as masculine role models for their children? Are fathers essential?

The twentieth century saw significant changes in the American family. Well over half of mothers are currently in the paid workforce. More than half of all new marriages end in divorce. One-third of all births are to single women.

The traditional family ideal in which fathers work and mothers care for children and the household characterizes less than 10 percent of American families with children under the age of 18.

Mothers' increased labor force participation has been a central catalyst of change in the culture of fatherhood. Mothers began to spend less time with children, and fathers began to spend more time. Thus, the cultural interest in fatherhood increased, and it was assumed that fathers were becoming more nurturant and more essential. The history of the ideals of fatherhood reveals that fathers have progressed from distant breadwinner to masculine sex-role model to equal coparent.

Despite changes in the *ideals* of fatherhood, some family scholars observe that fathers' behavior has not changed. Rather, it appears that mothers' behavioral change may be responsible for the change in the culture of fatherhood. A recent review of comparisons of fathers' and mothers' involvement with their children (in "intact" two-parent families) reveals a gap: fathers' engagement with their children is about 40 percent that of mothers'; fathers' accessibility is about two-thirds that of mothers. Fathers' lesser involvement is even more characteristic of divorced and never-married families. Nearly 90 percent of all children of divorce live with their mothers. Most single-parent fathers are "occasional" fathers. More than one-third of children in divorced families will not see their fathers at all after the first year of separation. Only 10 percent of children will have contact with fathers 10 years after divorce. Yet at the same time, research has documented the important ways in which fathers influence their children. But does this mean that fathers are essential?

Some contend that fathers are not mothers; fathers are essential and unique. Many reject a gender-neutral model of parenting, arguing that mothers and fathers have specific roles that are complementary; both parents are essential to meet children's needs. Proponents of this model assert that fatherhood is an essential role for men and pivotal to society. They maintain that fathers offer unique contributions to their children as male role models, thereby privileging their children. Moreover, fathers' unique abilities are necessary for children's successful development.

The following selections advance two models. Natasha Cabrera and her colleagues' paper suggests that a father's presence has positive effects on children's cognition and language, as well as their social and emotional development, and that the timing of these effects are important. They believe programs that increase fathers' education in particular can contribute to fathers developing positive parenting skills. In contrast, Peggy Drexel's study of boys raised without fathers challenges traditional views of fathering. Her results suggest that boys can thrive without fathers. Responsible parenting can occur in a variety of family structures, including single parents and same-sex parents. Drexel challenges four myths about traditional families and shows that single mothers can be successful, and does so without bashing fathers.

Natasha J. Cabrera,
Jacqueline D. Shannon, and
Catherine Tamis-LeMonda

Fathers' Influence on Their Children's Cognitive and Emotional Development: From Toddlers to Pre-K

In recent years, scholarship on *resident low-income fathers* has made important contributions to our understanding of how fathers affect children's development. It has shown that men are involved with their young children in multiple ways through their accessibility, responsibility, and engagement; the quality of father engagement, or father–child interactions, can be positive and supportive; positive father–child interactions matter for children's development, with different effects emerging at different points in development; and, that father–child interactions are embedded in a larger ecology that includes mother–father relationship and the family human and financial resources. This article presents an integration of findings across several of our recent studies that have contributed to each of these areas.

First, we present findings that address the question of how resident fathers are engaged with their young children at 2 years, 3 years, and pre-kindergarten (pre-K). These findings are important because they are based on observed rather than survey data and show that the quality of father–child interactions is consistent across time and that fathers, like mothers, can be sensitive and supportive to their children.

Second, we highlight central fathers' personal and contextual characteristics that affect fathers' engagement. In particular, we focus on fathers' human and financial resources and mother–child interactions. These findings shed light onto particular personal and contextual factors that are central to positive parenting over time, which programs and policies can target for effective interventions.

Third, we focus on how fathers' engagements affect their young children's cognitive, language and social, and emotional outcomes over and above mothers' contribution. The extant literature on low-income fathers has focused on the effects of absent fathers and men's lack of resources on children's development. In contrast, our findings show that fathers who engage with their children in positive ways have significant effects on their cognition and language at 2 and 3 years and their social and emotional development at 2 and 3 years

From *Applied Developmental Science*, vol. 11, no. 4, 2007, pp. 208–213. Copyright © 2007 by Taylor & Francis Journals. Reprinted by permission.

and at pre-kindergarten. These findings are important because they show that fathers uniquely contribute to children's cognitive and social and emotional development above the effects on mothers' engagement on children.

These studies are guided by the Dynamics of Paternal Influences on Children over the Life Course Model that stipulates the important contribution of parent characteristics, child, and context to parenting and children's outcomes. These findings add to the literature in several ways: First, they focus on an ethnically/racially diverse, low-income sample of fathers who reside with their young children. Second, they show that low-income fathers can make significant contributions to their children's development. Third, these findings are based on observations of fathers and their children and hence move us beyond methodologies that rely on mothers as proxy respondents for fathers.

Methods

Participants

Participants were drawn from research sites that participated in both the National Early Head Start Research and Evaluation Project (EHS study) and the EHS Father Study's Project. Ten of 17 EHS sites participated in the father component of the main study at 2 and 3 years, and 12 participated at pre-K time point. Families ($N = 1,685$ at 2/3 years, $N = 2,115$ at pre-K) were enrolled into the study when they initially applied to have their children receive childcare and parenting services at the local Early Head Start program that is partners in the EHS study. Written consent to participate in the EHS study and family baseline data (e.g., maternal age, race/ethnicity) were obtained from mothers at the start of the research and from fathers at their initial visit.

Because the majority of fathers who participated in the video portion of the study were biological and resident (i.e., 85% at 2 and 3 years, 75% at pre-K), we only include families with a resident biological father at each age point. For the 2 and 3 year time points, we report on a sample of 290, and at pre-K we report on a sample of 313. These samples include families for whom we had father video data on at least one assessment.

Given the design of the study (mothers identified fathers, but not all identified fathers agreed to participate in the study), the fathers who ultimately participated in study 1 (2 and 3 year time point) and study 2 (pre-K time point) of the EHS father study are a select group of men. Compared with those who did not participate in the father study, participating fathers and their children's mothers were more likely to be married and/or cohabiting, White or Latino, completed more years of education, and were more likely to be employed. Additionally, their children had higher scores on cognitive and social and emotional tests than children from nonparticipating families.

The majority of fathers in these reported studies were White (60%, 60%, and 51%, respectively); the remaining fathers were largely African American followed by Latino. Across the three ages, approximately 1/3 to 1/2 of fathers had less than high school degree; remaining fathers had high school degrees or more. Almost all fathers reported working full-time or part-time at the various ages, ranging from 84% to 96%. However, the annual income for families at pre-K was larger ($59,459) than it was at 2 and 3 years ($18,820 and $25,440, respectively). Children averaged 25 months at the time of the 2-year visit, 37 months at the 3-year visit, and 64 months at the time of the pre-kindergarten visit; about half at all three ages were boys.

Procedures

Once fathers had been identified by the child's mother, they were contacted to participate in the study. Participating fathers were administered a father questionnaire and mother–child and father–child dyads were videotaped in separate home visits when children were 2 and 3 years, and about to enter kindergarten. Children's cognitive, language, and social and emotional development were assessed by a trained tester at the mother visit. Fathers were given $20 at the 2- and 3-year visits and $30 at the pre-K visit, and children were given a gift.

Father–child interactions were videotaped during three activities, including 10 or 15 min of semi-structured free play, which was the focus of the investigation. During free play, toys were presented to fathers in three separate bags. Toys were selected to be age appropriate and to offer dyads the opportunity to engage in both concrete and symbolic forms of play (e.g., at 2 years, the father toys included: bag #1—a book, bag #2—a pizza set and telephone, and bag #3—a farm with farm animals). Fathers were asked to sit on a mat with his child, try to ignore the camera, and to do whatever felt most natural. They were instructed to only play with the toys from the three bags and to start with bag #1, move on to bag #2, and finish with bag #3. They were told that they could divide up the 10 min or 15 min as they liked.

Measures

Parent Characteristics

The majority of demographic characteristics were collected from the father interview. Family income was gathered from standards measure of employment. Measures to assess children's development included mental and behavior ratings scales (i.e., emotional regulation and orientation/engagement factors) . . . and children's sociability and emotional regulation.

Parent–Child Interactions

The quality of father–child interactions as well as mother–child interactions were assessed. . . . We assessed three dimensions of positive parenting (i.e., sensitivity, positive regard, and cognitive stimulation) as indicators of fathers' and mothers' *Supportiveness,* which represents parenting that is characterized by emotional support and enthusiasm for the child's autonomous work, responsiveness, and active attempts to expand the child's knowledge and abilities. We included one negative aspect of parenting: *Intrusiveness,* which indicates that the parent is over-controlling and over-involved. All coders were unaware of children's scores on child assessments and father interviews.

Results

Findings from these studies are organized around the three research questions: (1) How do resident fathers engage with their young children? (2) How do human and financial resources and mothers' engagements predict the quality of fathers' engagements with their young children? (3) How do resources and father engagements affect their young children's development, over and above mother engagement?

Fathers' Engagements with Their Young Children

Building on past research that fathers and mothers engage with their children in distinct but also similar ways, our work offers further evidence of the similarities between some parents. Fathers were as sensitive as mothers, and both parents showed low levels of intrusiveness, countering common stereotypes of fathers as aloof. At all child ages studied, fathers and mothers received comparably high scores on their supportiveness . . . and equivalently low scores on their intrusiveness. . . . As observed in the videotaped father–child interaction episodes, children experienced supportive and positive parenting from both their parents.

Financial Resources and Mother–Child Interactions to Father Engagement

Although the samples in our studies represented all resident fathers who were generally higher functioning than nonparticipating fathers, for example, the majority were employed and obtained at least a high school degree, there was variation in the sample that accounted for differences in father engagements.

In terms of human and financial resources, fathers were more supportive at all three ages and less intrusive at 2 years when they had at least a high school education. . . . Income was positively related to fathers' supportiveness at 2 years and pre-K, but not at 3 years . . . , whereas income negatively related to fathers' intrusiveness at these same two ages. . . . At all three ages, mother supportiveness to her child related to father supportiveness. . . . Mother intrusiveness with her child related to father intrusiveness at 2 and 3 years . . . , but not at pre-K. . . .

In summary, fathers' resources and mother supportiveness are significantly related to supportive father engagement at most ages. Also, the finding of covariation between father and mother engagement quality, underscores the need to covary mothers' engagement when considering the unique influence of fathering on children's outcomes.

Human and Financial Resources and Parent Engagement in Relation to Children's Development

Children's scores on the mental scale . . . , language scores . . . and word-recognition and applied problems . . . averaged .5 to 1.0 SD below the national norms. However, children were highly regulated and interactive during the administration of child assessments as indicated by their high scores on the orientation/engagement and emotional regulation factors . . . and on the cognitive-social and emotional regulation composite scales. . . .

Predictors to Children's Cognition and Language

Fathers' education (*more* than high school) was significantly related to children's scores. . . . Family income was significantly related to all child outcomes at pre-K. . . .

After accounting for financial and human resources (and mother engagement), the association between father engagement and child outcomes varied slightly over time depending on type of father engagement. In general, mothers' supportiveness related to children's cognitive outcomes at 2 and 3 years, and at pre-K. . . . Fathers' supportiveness related to children's outcomes at 2 and 3 years, but not at pre-K. . . . Intrusiveness varied in its relation to child outcomes by child age. Neither mother nor father intrusiveness were related to child outcomes at 2 and 3 years. . . .

Predictors to Children's Social and Emotional Behaviors

. . . As with cognitive outcomes, fathers' education (more than high school) consistently predicted children's emotional regulation at 2 and 3 years. . . . Family income, on the other hand, mattered only for children's orientation-engagement at 3 years and emotional regulation at pre-K . . . and approached significance to their cognitive-social behaviors at pre-K. . . .

In terms of parent engagement, surprisingly, maternal supportiveness was unrelated to children's outcomes at all ages . . . , however, father supportiveness, was positively associated with children's emotional regulation at 2 years . . . and marginally related to their orientation-engagement at both 2 and 3 years. . . . Expectedly, maternal intrusiveness was negatively related to children's emotional regulation at 2 years and pre-K as well as their cognitive-social scores at pre-K. At 2 years, father intrusiveness was positively related to orientation-engagement but inversely related to emotional regulation. . . . Father intrusiveness was unrelated to children's social and emotional outcomes at 3 years and pre-K. . . .

Discussion

To date, studies of how fathers matter to their children have produced inconsistent findings. Some studies have reported that father engagement has no direct effect on children's outcomes. First, it is less likely to find an association between father *report* of engagement and child outcomes than when the quality of father engagement is observed. Second, it is possible that fathers have different effects on children's development across time. Findings from this study support both explanations. We also find that fathers' education and income are key predictors of positive father engagement.

It is noteworthy that the quality of fathers' and mothers' parenting is very similar to each other. Insofar as the brief videotape of parent–child interaction provides a window to how children are parented, we find that both parents are more sensitive than intrusive. In line with prior research, we also find that the most consistent predictors of supportive fathering across children's ages are fathers' education and income. It might be that fathers who have more than high school education are more motivated to parent and are more aware of the developmental needs of children than those with less education.

The next question we were interested in was whether parenting has an effect on children's outcomes. Although children in our study scored .5 to 1.0 SD below national norms of cognitive tests, they were highly regulated across ages. As with predictors to father engagement, in general, fathers who have more than high school education have children performing better in all developmental domains—cognition, language, and social and emotional development. Family income, however, matters more at later ages than earlier; presumably as children get older they need more stimulating materials and opportunities to promote learning. This is consistent with resource theories that posit that parents who have more resources are more likely to invest on their children by providing a stimulating environment that promotes growth and learning than fathers with fewer resources.

Once we accounted for the effect of resources on children's development, we examined the unique contribution that parenting had on children's outcomes. For cognitive development, mothers' and fathers' supportiveness were positively related to children's language and cognitive outcomes across ages, although fathers' supportiveness did not matter at pre-K. For social and emotional development, fathers' supportiveness mattered only at earlier ages, while mother supportiveness was not related at any age. It might be that supportive mothering alone might not be enough to teach children to regulate and pay attention. Perhaps supportive parenting coupled with other dimensions of parenting, not measured here, such as discipline, might be more effective, especially with older children. It is also possible parents in our study were not intrusive enough to have a negative effect on children. Our findings are consistent with past research that supportive parenting is important for children's cognitive development across time and it adds to the literature by showing that *supportive fathering* has similar effects on children's cognitive functioning and emotional development especially with younger children, whereas *supportive mothering* only affects cognitive development across ages.

Our results also shed light on the effects of one dimension of negative parenting. We found parent intrusiveness less consistently related to children's development across domains and ages. In contrast to our findings for supportive parenting, intrusive parenting has an expected negative effect on children's cognition and language, but only for older children. Perhaps over controlling parents tend to inhibit older children's autonomy to verbalize and ask questions hence diminishing opportunities for learning. However, parent intrusiveness related to children's emotional regulation differently depending on child's age and gender of parent. At 2 years, both parents' intrusiveness mattered. Parents who are over controlling and over-involved have young children who are less regulated (i.e., less attentive, less able to stay on task) than non-intrusive mothers and fathers. At 3 and pre-K, maternal intrusiveness was almost consistently related to less emotional regulation whereas paternal intrusiveness was not related at all. It is possible that children, especially older children, interpret paternal intrusiveness in a more positive way than they do maternal intrusiveness.

In summary, fathers who have at least a high school education were more supportive and less intrusive than parents with fewer resources. Over and above mother engagements, fathers' supportiveness matters for children's cognitive and language development across ages as well as children's social and emotional behaviors, but less consistently. In contrast, father intrusiveness is not related to older children's social and emotional behaviors; it matters only at 2 years. These findings have important implications for policy and programs. Programs that aim at increasing fathers' education and that promote and encourage father's positive parenting will yield large benefits for children.

Peggy Drexler  **NO**

Raising Boys Without Men

For as long as any of us can remember, parenting theory and popular culture have promoted the notion that Mommy and Daddy—the traditional family unit—produce the best sons. That message has become louder in recent years. In 1992, President George H. Bush announced that children "should have the benefit of being born into families with a mother and father," citing the number and the gender of parents and their biological bond as central to optimal family life. And his son has supported a constitutional amendment to ban gay marriage and thus produce the hallowed nuclear family. Whether conservative politicians and religious leaders like it or not, the family structure has changed—dramatically—and the Bush definition of family seems, well, less than definitive.

Across the country, a lightning bolt has split the trunk of the family tree, and it is growing in new and challenging directions.

Some have labeled this a family crisis, though as Laura Benkov, Ph.D., points out in her book *Reinventing the Family*, "A careful look at other places and other times reveals [the nuclear family] to be but one of many possible human arrangements." Further, according to historian Stephanie Coontz, "Families have always been in flux and often in crisis; they have never lived up to the nostalgic notions about 'the way things used to be.'" We cannot roll back history, nor—once we tear away prevailing misconceptions about the American family—would we want to. So get ready for a little myth-bashing reality check.

Myth #1: Families of the past didn't have problems like families do today. The reality is that desertion, child abuse, spousal battering, and alcohol or drug addiction have always troubled a significant number of families. Many of those perky housewives from 50 years ago depended on mother's little helper (tranquilizers, mood enhancers, and alcohol) to see them through their mind-numbing days. In other words, the good old days weren't what they are cracked up to be.

Myth #2: The 1950s male-breadwinner family is and always has been the only traditional family structure in America. Families have regularly been torn apart and reassembled throughout human history. Not until the 1920s did the majority of children in this country live in a home where the husband was the breadwinner, the wife was a full-time homemaker, and the kids could go to school instead of working for their wages.

Myth #3: The sexual revolution of the 1960s caused the rise in unwed motherhood. The reality is that the sharpest increase in unwed motherhood occurred when it tripled between 1940 and 1958. During the Great Depression, abandonment rates rose, with husbands leaving their wives (and children if they had them). Out-of-wedlock sex shot up during World War II. And below the surface, the underpinnings of traditional marital stability continued to erode. After this shift, nontraditional families (including divorced families, stepfamilies, single parents, gay and lesbian families, lone householders, and unmarried cohabiting couples) would never again be such a minor part of the family terrain that we could count on marriage alone as our main institution for caring for dependents.

While women's out-of-wedlock sex and the breakdown of the nuclear family are issues for politicians who see it as the root to society's ills, women—whether in lesbian relationships, widowed, divorced, or as single mothers by choice—are transforming the way we think about unwed mothers. In my neighborhood and neighborhoods all across this country, single mothers and mothers in pairs are at the forefront of what it means to re-create the new American family. They are a galvanizing force in American society as our nation struggles to accommodate a broader and more useful—yet no less loving—definition of family.

Myth #4: Children of divorced or unwed mothers are sure to fail. The reality is that it's how a family acts, not the way it's made up, that determines whether the children succeed or fail. The number of times you eat dinner with your kids is a better guide to how well they'll turn out than the number or gender of the parents at the dinner table. Marriage is no longer the gold standard when it comes to being a good parent. Though residual condemnation still hits here and there, Dr. Benkov points out that raising children without being married has "emerged as a potentially positive decision, not an unwanted circumstance." We all can understand the appeal of a perfect mom-and-dad family. But we have to wonder, how many children and parents in this country actually live there?

Diversity is taking over America. The U.S. Census Bureau reported that in 2000 only 23.5 percent of households in the United States contained families with a married mom and dad and their children. The percentage of all households that were unmarried in 1950 was 22 percent; in 2000 that number had reached 48 percent. Figures released from the 2000 census show that mothers raising sons (and daughters) alone or in pairs in this new world are just as prevalent as the 1950s Donna Reed mom-and-dad version. The number of families headed by single mothers increased 25 percent between 1990 and 2000, to more than 7.5 million households.

This new breed of mothers without fathers is likely to be financially secure, straight or gay, and of any age and any race. The median age for unmarried mothers is late twenties, and the fastest-growing category is White women. Whether these women are divorced or never married, mothering singly and in pairs has not only entered the popular culture and become acceptable; it also is now considered chic. High-profile moms like Angelina Jolie, Isabella Rossellini, Wendy Wasserstein, Camryn Manheim, and Diane Keaton are parenting sons and daughters without husbands, and lesbian moms such as comedian Rosie O'Donnell and singer Melissa Etheridge are coming out with their partners and are mothering together. Few of these women have men as full-time parenting partners. Yet despite their deviation from what's been deemed a "normal" family pattern, the media routinely refer to their motherhood in a positive light. . . .

The Tarnished Gold Standard

Conservative critics tell us that family life is on the verge of being atomized, that our children are corrupted, that our moral codes are crushed. As we all know, there's a serious movement to define legal marriage as the union of one man and one woman, the conservative ideal for marriage—and for family making. Many in the so-called marriage movement (and, I would argue, in the clinical research field as well) take a pessimistic view of children raised by parents who are not a traditionally married couple. The mom-and-dad family may have its problems, conservative advocates of family values agree, but they pronounce the presence of a strong male family figure to be vital to a child's development.

Marriage proponents, however, ignore the dark side of matrimony. While overall both adults and children get a host of benefits from good marriages, the situation for kids in bad marriages is quite the opposite. Married couples in conflict don't always provide what's best for their children. Further, according to Philip Cowan, Ph.D., professor of psychology at the University of California at Berkeley, the way husbands and wives treat each other has as much impact on their children's academic confidence, social adjustment, and behavior problems in school as the way the parents treat the children. A high-conflict marriage or a marriage that isn't working can negatively affect children in a way that might never happen in a single-mom family.

In addition, social scientists have confused family structure with economic factors that can influence behavior and performance. Researchers who analyze the data of boys having problems, for example, see that a large percentage of these kids come from single-mother homes and assume that mothers' single status has caused their boys to fail. Think back to the days when mothers were blamed for their children's having illnesses they didn't cause. I believe the same thing is happening with single moms and two-mom households: They're blaming the mom instead of the economic situation of the family. A study by researchers at Cornell University found that single mothering did not automatically spell trouble in school for elementary-age sons. How much schooling the mother received and her abilities had the biggest influence on her children's school performance—not the fact that the boys were without fathers.

Similarly, it had been assumed that boys from divorced families had more problems than children of two-parent, mom-and-dad families, until a 2000 study reported by the New York University Child Study Center discovered that the same boys had been demonstrating behavioral problems even prior to the divorce. When the researchers controlled for earlier behavior problems, the differences between boys from intact families and from divorced families were significantly reduced. The researchers concluded that to blame the boys' difficulties after the divorce on the actual divorce or separation limited the scope of understanding. The likely turmoil that preceded the split had to be considered a contributing factor to any problems observed in the boys after the divorce.

So now we have seen a series of bad raps against mothers. I would say that ever since Eve, women have been blamed for the evils of the world (and she gave Adam the apple even before the children were born!). The mother is labeled overprotective when she worries about her children, negligent if she doesn't worry; smothering or bossy if she engages in her children's lives, selfish or icy if she doesn't; overly self-involved if she pursues a career or holds down a job, overly involved with her kids if she doesn't. She can't seem to get it right, and if anything goes wrong with the children, it's her fault.

Snap Judgments

If you think that's a problem, consider how much more severe the judgment is on single or lesbian mothers. Because the economics have not been factored into the difficulties single mothers face, many people assume that single mothers are bound to have trouble raising their sons. And the prejudice against lesbians carries over into the expectation that they can't raise healthy sons. These are the biggest myths of all.

In my research . . . I have found there is absolutely no reason to expect that single or gay moms cannot raise sons on their own. These maverick moms and their families are living their lives with an everyday consciousness of the problems they and their sons face. They are not ideologues working out a theory about different ways to parent in our culture. They are real mothers raising real boys, boys who should not be marginalized in the least. These boys may not live with biological fathers, but they are in no way illegitimate. The families their moms have created are as real and as legitimate as any other, and have much to teach everybody who cares about children. . . .

Throughout my research and the writing of this book, I have come to take a stand against the recent tide of opinion and the rash of books asserting that boys must have a father in the home in order to grow to full manhood. Instead, I have found that loving, growth-encouraging parenting is what boys (and girls, for that matter) need. A good parent, whether mother or father, will enable a boy to develop to his full potential as a young man, as long as his individuality, his manliness, his courage, and his developing conscience are respectfully and fully supported.

The families I studied were all in some way on the fringes of the societal mainstream, and the sons all suffered in one way or another from the ignorance or prejudice of others. Teachers didn't accept drawings of their families; other children teased them about their families; there was a presumption that boys raised by lesbians would be sissies and that sons raised by single mothers would be automatically vulnerable to the worst elements in our society. Then there was a terrible libel against these mothers, that they have no standards or morals.

I found that this very marginalization was a source of tears and concern. But it was also a source of strength for the mothers and their sons.

The boys and mothers I studied had all the ups and downs of every family. Just like the rest of the boys on the planet, they fought, they cried, they got into trouble, they had school problems, they got furious with their parents, they didn't do what they were told. But there was something different in the quality of their relationships, both at home and in the world.

They had a wider range of interests and friendships than the boys I studied from heterosexual parents, and they appeared more at ease in situations of conflict. They developed their "boyishness" at a normal rate, but their sense of justice and fairness and their ability to express their feelings were off the charts. They admired many kinds of men, from scientists to sports heroes, and they accepted their own quirks and interests (and those around them) more readily than did boys from traditional families.

My research showed that it's the quality of parenting, not the gender of the parents, that counts. And yes, two-parent families—including both the mom-and-dad variety and the two-mom variety—work well when they work well.

Does this mean that fathers are not important? Of course not. Do I mean to bash fathers? Under no circumstances. This book describes the strengths of these maverick mothers and how their sons used emotional skillfulness as an antidote to the stigma of being raised by lesbian or single moms. The truth as I see it is that the love, the respect, and the understanding their parents offered was what made for strong and resilient young men. . . .

[There is a] music of love and communication that surrounded the sons of maverick mothers. It is also the secret of sound children: You listen carefully, you respond the best way you can, you foster the children's interests, and you give them loving correction. You know what your own behavior says to them and what good Observers they are.

E. M. Forster said it best 80 years ago on *Two Cheers for Democracy*: "Only connect!" This is the message of the maverick mothers. It's a lesson for us all. Mothers and fathers alike need to connect with their sons, not as clones of themselves, but as free-standing personalities. And they need to understand what their sons are going through, supporting their best instincts and teaching them how to be better men.

What kind of men will the boys I studied become? Only a fortune-teller can answer that question with certainty. But I see that the qualities they exhibited at a young age will serve them well.

From Howard Gardner's path-breaking work on the varieties of intelligence to Daniel Goleman's book on emotional intelligence, the world of social science is emphasizing the importance in interpersonal savvy in life and work. The boys I came to know already exhibited high emotional IQs. They might be a step ahead of many others when they enter the world of work.

And then there's the mountain of medical research about the importance to physical health of having intimate relationships throughout life. These boys already had an extraordinary capacity for closeness. Of course, they could shut down as teenagers (many boys do). But the chances are good that when they emerge as young men, they will once again be at home with intimacy.

These boys will bear close watching over the years to come. And like Judith Wallerstein and others, I will continue to listen to them and spend time with them as they mature. My bet is that living through all the vicissitudes of adolescence, dealing with the prejudices against their families, filling out forms that have no blanks for their family types, and surviving the torments of first love and disappointment will be very hard for these boys. But they already have a set of competencies to meet these difficulties.

We know that many successful women give credit for their courage and energy to the loving support of their fathers. I am beginning to suspect that the same dynamic between mother and son may have a similar effect.

"I've always loved and respected my mother. I thought she was a super-hero," Bruce Addison, then 34, said to me, remembering those economically and emotionally challenging years when his mother raised him and his siblings on her own and worked long hours running different mortgage brokering businesses. "I've never met or read about a woman who is as powerful as she is. She'll tell you that she muddled through it and what have you, but I certainly didn't get that sense. She really lived with purpose. She instilled in me a great deal of that sense of purpose."

What a different view this is from the traditional mother bashing we know so well. Perhaps mothers have been blamed for communicating the cultural norms of the day. Those "smothering mothers" of the past were messengers of the family values of the time: Do what I tell you; go into your father's business; you have to be a doctor/lawyer/banker; no, theater isn't manly enough for you; don't cry—be a man!

By redefining manhood, mothers have the chance to redefine not only the American family but also the face of our society. "My hope is that my sons are going to be the kind of people who will understand that others haven't necessarily had the advantages they have, and not exploit or be blind to the fact that they have had a leg up, but instead use their privileges for good things," one such mother told me. "That is the kind of man who can change the world."

POSTSCRIPT

Are Fathers Necessary for Children's Well-Being?

Researchers have explored under what conditions optimal father involvement is possible. Some state that the three necessary conditions are: (1) when a father is highly motivated to parent, (2) when a father has adequate parenting skills and receives social support for parenting, and (3) when a father is not undermined by work and other institutional settings. The reconstruction of fathering, whatever the redefinition, has proven to be very difficult and contested by many cultural forces.

At issue is the assumption that there is something natural and thus rooted in the basic nature of women and men that makes a two-parent family, with a mother and father, essential and ideal for children's well-being. The fundamental assumption of different parenting styles and roles of men and women has led to debates about whether "fathers can mother." That is, can men and should they begin to fill the role of nurturer? The result is that men's "job description" as fathers is less clear than expectations of women as mothers. Therefore, fathering is very sensitive to context (including the marital or coparental relationship, children, extended family, and cultural institutions). The role of mother is especially delimiting. Mothers often serve as gatekeepers in the father-child relationship. Father involvement is often contingent on mothers' attitudes toward, expectations of, and support for the father.

Many mothers are ambivalent about active father involvement with their children. The mothering role has been a central feature of adult women's identity, so it is no wonder that some women feel threatened by paternal involvement in their domain, which affects their identity and sense of control. In the absence of social consensus on fathering and counterarguments about the deficits of many fathers, many mothers are restrictive of father involvement. However, some maintain that responsible mothering will have to evolve to include support of the father-child bond.

In addition, with increasing latitude for commitment to and identification with their parental role, men are increasingly confused about how to exercise their roles as fathers. This also makes them sensitive to contextual factors such as others' attitudes and expectations. Worse yet, they frequently encounter disagreement among different individuals and institutions in their surrounding context, further complicating their role choices and enactment.

Four other contextual forces challenge a redefinition of fathering. (1) Legal notions of fatherhood disregard nurturing. Adequate fathering is primarily equated with financial responsibility. (2) Concepts of masculinity conflict with nurturant parenting. Nurturant fathers risk condemnation as being "unmanly."

How can nurturant fatherhood fit into notions of maleness and masculinity? (3) Homophobic attitudes further obstruct nurturant fatherhood. Ironically, active legal debate about sexual orientation and parenting might be influential in reconstructing fatherhood. Is there a model of shared parenting within the gay community? (4) Nurturing by fathers and mothers has typically functioned in a single-parent model, whether with a two-parent marriage or with parents living in separate households. One parent usually does most, if not all, of the nurturing. Interestingly, it is the case that nurturance is a better predictor of effective parenting than is sex. Gender neutrality and equality in parenting is undefined. How would you conceptualize a model of shared parenting (taking care not to discriminate against single-parent families)? What would parental equality look like in practice? Is it essential that children be exposed to both female and male role models? If so, why? If women and men were not expected to conform to a specific set of expectations associated with their sex would the sex of the people raising children matter? Which benefits the child more, a heterosexual set of parents who are bound by strict gender-related conventions which results in an overbearing, abusive father, or a loving single father or loving, nurturing gay parents?

Suggested Readings

Andrea Engber and Leah Klungness, *The Complete Single Mother: Reassuring Answers to Your Most Challenging Concerns* (3rd edition) (Avon, MA: Adams, 2006).

Gary Greenberg and Jeannie Hayden, *Be Prepared: A Practical Handbook for New Dads* (New York: Simon & Schuster, 2004).

Meg Meeker M.D., *Strong Fathers, Strong Daughters: 10 Secrets Every Father Should Know* (Washington, DC: Regnery Publishing, 2007).

W. D. Allen and M. Connor, "An African American Perspective on Generative Fathering," in A. J. Hawkins and D. C. Dollahite, eds., *Generative-Fathering: Beyond Deficit Perspectives* (Sage Publications, 1997).

D. Blankenhorn, *Fatherless America: Confronting Our Most Urgent Social Problem* (Basic Books, 1995).

S. Coltrane, *Family Man: Fatherhood, Housework, and Gender Equity* (Oxford University Press, 1996).

Cynthia R. Daniels, *The Unexpected Legacy of Divorce: The 25 Year Landmark Study* (New York: Hyperion, 1998).

Lucia Albino Gilbert and Jill Rader, "Current Perspectives on Women's Adult Roles: Work, Family, and Life," in Rhoda K. Unger, ed., *Handbook of the Psychology of Women and Gender* (Hoboken, NJ: John Wiley & Sons, Inc., 2001), pp. 156–169.

F. Daniel McClure and Jerry B. Saffer, *Wednesday Evenings and Every Other Weekend: From Divorced Dad to Competent Co-Parent. A Guide for the Noncustodial Father* (Charlottesville, VA: The Van Doren Company, 2001).

Ross Parke and Armin Brott, *Throwaway Dads: The Myths and Barriers That Keep Men from Being the Fathers They Want to Be* (New York: Houghton Mifflin, 1999).

Janice M. Steil, "Family Forms and Member Well-Being: A Research Agenda for the Decade of Behavior," *Psychology of Women Quarterly, 25* (2001): 344–363.

ISSUE 13

Should Parents Be Allowed to Choose the Sex of Their Children?

YES: Z. O. Merhi and L. Pal, from "Gender 'Tailored' Conceptions: Should the Option of Embryo Gender Selection Be Available to Infertile Couples Undergoing Assisted Reproductive Technology?" *Journal of Medical Ethics* (2008)

NO: American College of Obstetricians and Gynecologists, from "Sex Selection" Opinion No. 360, *Obstetrics and Gynecology* (2007)

ISSUE SUMMARY

YES: Physicians Z. O. Merhi and L. Pal discuss the conditions under which selection of the sex of a child does not breach any ethical considerations in family planning among infertile couples.

NO: American College of Obstetricians and Gynecologists' Committee on Ethics supports the practice of offering patients procedures for the purpose of preventing serious sex-linked genetic diseases, but opposes sex selection for personal and family reasons.

Gender is influenced before conception, in making decisions to carry a fetus to term. The potency of sex and gender as explanations for differences between males and females escalates early in life. By early childhood, a host of differences are observed between boys and girls as children internalize a sense of themselves and others as gendered. Concern has been raised about inequities and deficits resulting from the effects of sex and gender.

Research has consistently documented the preference and desire for sons in twentieth-century America and in other cultures. In many cultures, such as India and China, maleness means social, political, and economic entitlement. Men are expected to support their parents in their old age. Moreover, men remain with their family throughout life; women, upon marriage, become part of the husband's family. Thus, women are traditionally seen as a continuing economic burden on the family—particularly in the custom of large dowry payments at weddings. In some cultures if a bride's family cannot pay the demanded dowry, the brides are often killed (usually by burning). Although dowries and dowry deaths are illegal, the laws are rarely enforced.

In such cultures, there is an expressed desire for male children and an urgency to select fetal sex. Recently, sex-determination technology is most commonly used to assay the sex of fetuses, although in many cultures the use of such technology has been banned. When the fetus is determined to be female, abortion often follows because of cultural pressures to have sons. Such sex-determination practices have led to many more male than female infants being born. The gap grows even wider because of a high childhood death rate of girls, often from neglect or killing by strangulation, suffocation, or poisoning. Furthermore, women are blamed for the birth of a female child and are often punished for it (even though, biologically, it is the male's sperm, carrying either X or Y chromosomes, that determines sex).

Research shows that in contemporary America, 78 percent of adults prefer their firstborn to be a boy. Moreover, parents are more likely to continue having children if they have all girls versus if they have all boys. Faced with having only one child, many Americans prefer a boy. The availability of sex-selection technology in the last quarter of the twentieth century was met with growing interest and widespread willingness to make use of the technology.

Available technologies for sex selection include preconception, preimplantation, and postconception techniques. Preconception selection techniques include folkloric approaches like intercourse timing, administering an acid or alkaline douche, and enriching maternal diets with potassium or calcium/magnesium, all thought to create a uterine environment conducive to producing male or female fetuses. There are also sperm-separating technologies whereby X- and Y-bearing sperm are separated, and the desired sperm are artificially inseminated into the woman, increasing the chance of having a child of the chosen sex.

Preimplantation technologies identify the sex of embryos as early as three days after fertilization. For sex-selection purposes, the choice of an embryo for implantation is based on sex. Postconception approaches use prenatal diagnostic technologies to determine the sex of the fetus. The three most common technologies are amniocentesis (available after the 20th week of pregnancy), chorionic villi sampling (available earlier but riskier), and ultrasound (which can determine sex as early as 12 weeks but is not 100 percent accurate).

The American demand for social acceptance of sex-selection technologies has increased in the past decade. Preconception selection techniques are becoming quite popular in the United States, and preimplantation technologies (though more expensive) are also more frequently used. It has become more and more socially accepted to use prenatal diagnostic technologies to determine fetal sex. But incidence rates for sex-selective abortions are difficult to obtain. There is mixed opinion about the frequency of sex-selective abortions, tinged by political controversy.

In the following selections The American College of Obstetricians and Gynecologists' Committee on Ethics assert that fetal sex selection is always unethical, except in the case of preventing sex-linked genetic diseases. They suggest that parents are really not interested in the genitalia that their infants are born with. What they are really choosing is an "ideal," defined by gender role expectations: a boy dad can play ball with or a girl who can wear mom's wedding gown when she marries. In contrast, Physicians Merhi and Pal argue that a desire for gender balance in the family is ethical.

YES ⤶

Z. O. Merhi and L. Pal

Gender "Tailored" Conceptions: Should the Option of Embryo Gender Selection Be Available to Infertile Couples Undergoing Assisted Reproductive Technology?

Preimplantation genetic diagnosis (PGD) was introduced at the beginning of the 1990s as an adjunct to the prenatal diagnostic armamentarium, allowing for genetic diagnoses earlier in the gestational period. This diagnostic option allows couples the opportunity of reaching decisions regarding terminating a genetically compromised fetus earlier in the course of the pregnancy, thus minimising the psychological stress as well as medical risks associated with terminations performed at more advanced gestations. Since its inception, PGD testing has been utilised for evaluation of a spectrum of inherited diseases (e.g., cystic fibrosis, sickle cell disease, hemophilia A and B, Lesch-Nyhan syndrome, thalassemia, Duchenne muscular dystrophy, and recently, Marfan's syndrome) allowing parents to avoid the lengthy, fearful wait for results of traditional testing (e.g., amniocentesis, chorionic villous sampling) while their pregnancy continues to progress. However, the application of PGD has raised multiple ethical issues, many of which were addressed by the President's Council on Bioethics in a recent paper in which the council sought to improve the application of PGD. One of the thorniest issues currently being confronted is the use of PGD for gender selection.

The methods used for preconception gender selection have evolved over time. An influence of coital timing on the gender of the conceptus was proposed by Shettles, who described an exaggerated motility by the smaller Y-bearing sperm in the mid cycle cervical mucus, and hypothesised that there would be male offspring dominance if the timing of coitus was proximate to ovulation. The length of the follicular phase of the menstrual cycle (i.e., period of maturation of the ovarian follicle and the contained egg therein), risk modifications by changing vaginal PH, possible effects of ionic concentrations in the woman's body, susceptible to dietary modifications and pre-fertilisation separation of X-bearing from Y-bearing spermatozoa, have all been stated to

From *Journal of Medical Ethics*, vol. 34, 2008, pp. 590–593. Copyright © 2008 by Institute of Medical Ethics. Reprinted by permission of BMJ Publishing Group via Rightslink.

demonstrate varying degrees of success in gender determination. However, while some of these methodologies offer successes greater than predicted by the "toss of a coin," the results remain far from "guaranteed."

Among the prominent motivations driving a demand for preconception gender selection is the desire for children of the culturally preferred gender, and to achieve gender balance within a given family. Recently, an interest in PGD testing for the purpose of "gender selection" for social reasons seems to be escalating, although no concrete data are available. This use of PGD for "family tailoring" has engendered debate and controversy. While the acceptability of PGD for traditional medical indications is generally condoned, utilisation of this modality for non-medical purpose has generated ethical concerns. The American College of Obstetricians and Gynecologists has taken a clear stance on this issue as reflected in the following committee opinion, "The committee rejects the position that gender selection should be performed on demand. . . ." Additionally, the American Society of Reproductive Medicine states that "in patients undergoing IVF, PGD used for gender selection for non medical reasons holds some risk of gender bias, harm to individuals and society, and inappropriateness in the use and allocation of limited medical resources." An introspective assessment of the published literature on clinical practices suggests that, while the stance of the principal governing bodies on the issue of PGD for gender selection is unambiguous, the actual practice of the technology of "gender tailoring on demand" is not uncommon. In fact, a recent survey of IVF clinics in the United States, an access to and provision of PDG services for sex selection was acknowledged by as many as 42% of the providers of assisted reproductive technique (ART) services; furthermore, beyond these geographical boundaries, the literature is replete with documentation of couples undergoing ART specifically wishing for family completion and/or balancing requesting that embryo(s) of a preferred gender be utilised for transfer.

Acknowledging the contrasting stance of the licensing and governing bodies on ethical concerns related to a wider availability and access to gender selection option versus the prevalent practices (as mentioned above), the authors herein attempt to explore whether the explicit utilisation of PGD for the purpose of gender selection by the infertile couple already undergoing a medically indicated ART procedure encroaches on breach of basic dictates of medical ethics.

It is currently not the "standard of care" (an individualised paradigm of diagnostic and treatment plan that an appropriately trained clinician is expected to pursue in the care of an individual patient) to perform PGD in the absence of a medical indication. However, "standards of care" should remain receptive to evolving scientific data, both that which supports and that which stands in opposition to changes in the standard. Accordingly, the opportunity to explore ethical arguments for and against the utilisation of PGD for gender selection by infertile couples undergoing ART is undertaken in this paper. This process might enable the patient and the provider to make informed and rational decisions when considering PGD utilisation for such a non-medical indication.

Beneficence and Non-Maleficence

Within the context of beneficence-based clinical judgment, a physician's inherent obligation towards his/her patient (i.e., the potential benefits of PGD) *must* be balanced against the risks of the proposed technique. For the infertile patients undergoing ART, and therefore already anticipating a procedure with some treatment related inherent risks, that is, minimal and yet real risks of anaesthesia, infection, bleeding, and ovarian hyperstimulation syndrome (a potentially lethal complication of attempts at inducing multiple ovulation), PGD for targeted genetic anomalies has been shown to improve ART outcomes (i.e., successful pregnancy following treatment), and to significantly reduce the risk of aneuploidy and miscarriage rates in a high-risk population. We believe, that in this patient population, use of additional gene probes per request, that is, for sex chromosomes, would not in any way jeopardise the principle of beneficence.

The limiting factor within this prototype of allowing PGD for gender selection "on request" will be the availability of an adequate number of cleaving embryos. A small yet real possibility does exist for a failure to achieve an embryo transfer either because of evidence of aneuploidy in the entire cohort of the tested embryos, a scenario that can be easily conjured for an older woman, or because of a procedure-related embryo loss due to the mechanisms used to create an opening in the zona pellucida (a membrane surrounding the egg) for the explicit purpose of removing a cell from the dividing embryo for PGD. The proposed benefits of PGD for the sole intention of gender selection in a patient undergoing ART must be thus balanced against the small yet real risks of embryo loss, and even failure to achieve an embryo transfer, as well as the incremental costs incurred (approximately $2500 per cycle above the costs of approximately $7500–$10000 for the IVF cycle and related procedures). To date, there are no reports of increased identifiable problems (fetal malformations or others) attributable to the embryo biopsy itself. On the contrary, data suggest that PGD for aneuploidy screening may significantly reduce the risk of spontaneous abortions and of aneuploidies in the offspring of women undergoing IVF, particularly so in the reproductively aging patient population.

The principle of beneficence is maintained in offering PGD to couples undergoing ART (the analysis of risks and benefits being based on the physician's assessment, and the risks being primarily confined to the embryo, and not to the patient). However, the same may not hold for otherwise fertile couples. In that case, the female partner would be subjected to medically unindicated risks as well as substantial financial costs ($10000–$15000), driven solely by a desire for a child of the preferred gender. Such couples may represent a "vulnerable population" whose vulnerability lies within a potential, enticed by a promise of a child of the preferred gender, for making impetuous decisions regarding an expensive and medically non-indicated intervention that has an uncommon, yet real potential for health hazard. For the fertile population, this desire may lead them to "medicalise" the spontaneous procreative process, transforming it into a controlled and expensive process.

While the authors believe that the principles of beneficence and non-maleficence are upheld within the context of allowing couples anticipating undergoing ART for the management of infertility, we believe that the medical community needs to pause and ponder on any potential for generation of *unwanted surplus embryos* of the undesired sex prior to declaring this as an "acceptable practice." Aspects for further "beneficence" may be appreciated within the folds of this latter concern as couples may consider donation of discard embryos of the non-desired gender to the less fortunate infertile patients. These plausible scenarios must be discussed at length with any couple wishing to discuss the possibility of embryo gender selection while undergoing a medically indicated IVF.

In contrast to an infertile patient anticipating undergoing medically indicated IVF and requesting embryo gender selection, a similar request from an otherwise fertile couple merits additional consideration. A decision to discard embryos of an undesired gender may be less onerous to a reproductively competent individual, although data in support of such a conjecture are lacking. Whether or not this concern regarding abandonment of the "unwanted" embryos is legitimate depends on the perception of the status accorded to the embryos. Although debatable, some would agree that since embryos are too rudimentary in the developmental paradigm to have "interests," there is simply no basis upon which to grant the embryos "rights." Additionally, the ethical principle of non-maleficence is not violated since this principle is directed to "people" rather than "tissues." Future debates on this particular concern might be needed to settle this issue.

To summarise, the performance of PGD per request specifically for gender selection in an infertile couple already planning to undergo ART for medical indications may not breach the principle of beneficence nor hold undue harm for the patient. However, the principles of justice and autonomy must also be considered.

Justice

The principle of justice requires an equitable distribution of the benefits as well as the burdens associated with an intervention. While at one end of the spectrum, this concept addresses the concern of societal gender imbalance resulting from utilisation of PGD for gender selection, at the other extreme, there may be concerns of gender imbalance in relation to socioeconomic strata, as an economic differential in the utilisation of ART services is well recognised.

Concerns are voiced regarding a potential of PGD, if deemed acceptable for the explicit purpose of sex selection, for disrupting the societal gender balance. Indeed, examples of gender preferences abound in existing communities and societies. For example, in certain regions of China, termination of pregnancies, infanticide, and inferior medical care for baby girls have created a shift in the population to a ratio of approximately 1.5 to 1 favouring males. Gender preference for the firstborn can thus overwhelmingly favour male gender, particularly if "one child per family" population policies continue to be implemented. Similarly, a preference for male offspring is recognised in other regions across the globe including India and the Middle East. In contrast, in Nigeria, anecdotal tradition suggests that although a son is beneficial for propagating the family's name, a female infant is preferentially hoped for, as a daughter holds promise for eventual financial gains at the time of marriage. Similarly, in Haiti, a female firstborn is welcomed as a potential caregiver to the future siblings (personal communication).

It is important to appreciate that concerns voiced by the community regarding a potential for creating a gender differential across global regions if PGD for sex selection while undergoing a medically indicated IVF indeed achieves wider acceptability, while not unreasonable, appear based on "snap shot" views of cultural preferences. One is reassured by results of a recent cross-sectional web-based survey of 1197 men and women aged 18–45 years in the United States which revealed that the majority of those surveyed were unlikely to utilise "sperm sorting," an already existing, cheaper and less invasive technology, as a means for preferential preconception gender selection (sperm sorting employs flow cytometric separation of the 2.8% heavier "X chromosome" from the relatively lighter "Y chromosome" bearing sperm, thus providing an "X" [destined to contribute to a female fetus] or "Y" [destined to create a male fetus] enriched sperm sample for subsequent utilisation for artificial insemination or ART). Given the lack of enthusiasm for this simpler modality for preconception gender selection (an intervention that involves no risks to the patient or the embryos), at the population level, individuals are even less likely to opt for a more aggressive approach, that is, proceeding with ART and PGD, just for gender selection reasons. Similarly, a study from England on 809 couples revealed that gender selection is unlikely to lead to a serious distortion of the sex ratio in Britain and other Western societies. Yet another survey performed on a sample of German population (1094 men and women aged 18–45 years were asked about their gender preferences and about selecting the sex of their children through flow cytometric separation of X- and Y-bearing sperm followed by intrauterine insemination), revealed that the majority did not seem to care about the sex of their offspring and only a minority expressed a desire for gender selection. These authors concluded that preconception gender selection is unlikely to cause a severe gender imbalance in Germany. Similar conclusions, that is, the lack of an overwhelming interest in preconception gender selection were deduced in a survey of infertile Hungarian couples with regard to utilisation of sperm sorting for gender selection. These data are thus reassuring and suggest that, at least in the developed world, even if given access to technology facilitating preferential gender selection, and subsequently while undergoing a medically indicated IVF, use of such methods is not likely to significantly impact on the natural sex ratio within the communities. It needs to be appreciated however, that surveys generated within the industrialised nations are not representative of global perceptions regarding access to and utilisation of similar technology for ensuring conception of progeny of a preferred gender.

Another concern regarding the possibility of breaching the principle of justice is the ART-related cost as well as the additional expenditure related to the use of PGD. The financial burden is likely to preclude a section of the infertile population from using this service, hence holding the potential for a breach in the principle of justice. However, given that utilisation of PGD for gender selection may be limited secondary to financial constraints, such a differential would render significant shifts in population gender distribution very unlikely (like in ART, the issue of social and economic differences pose a distributive bias here that is beyond the scope of our paper).

Given the lack of information regarding the magnitude of utilisation of technologies for gender selection (PGD or sperm sorting) within societies, it may not be unreasonable to suppose that PGD would not be accessible to large enough numbers of people to make a real difference in the population gender balance. A potential donation of the undesired embryos by couples who opt to utilise PGD for gender selection is likely to negate any concerns regarding eventual disturbance of the sex ratio, enhance the balance towards "beneficence" by offering a possibility of parenthood to those who would otherwise not be able to afford the cost associated with ART and thus address some concerns regarding the principle of "justice" voiced earlier.

To summarise, although the existing literature touches upon aspects of preferential and differential biases in terms of gender preferences in the various communities around the world, data specifically addressing this aspect in infertile couples undergoing medically indicated ART are nonexistent, and voice a need to more formally assess the use of preconception gender selection technologies globally, so as to fully evaluate the impact of these practices on the principle of justice. It follows that performing PGD for gender selection might be consistent with substantive justice–based considerations until more thorough analysis for societal disruptive imbalance of the sexes has been performed.

Patient Autonomy

The freedom to make reproductive decisions is recognised as a fundamental moral and legal right that should not be denied to any couple, unless an exercise of that right would cause harm to them or to others. Access to and use of contraceptive choices, recognition of a woman's right to request for a termination of an unplanned and/or undesired pregnancy, and an emerging acceptance of an individual's right to determine his or her sexual orientation reflect evolving social and societal perceptions as relates to "reproductive autonomy, the authors believe that utilisation of PGD for the purpose of gender selection by infertile couples already undergoing ART may be incorporated within this paradigm of "reproductive autonomy." Across the societies, while parental autonomy in shaping the social identity of their progeny (behaviour, education, attire . . . etc.) is an acceptable norm, this debate proposes that, in defined clinical situations, allowing parents to shape the genetic identity of a much-desired child will be within the purview of patient autonomy.

It is of interest that most of the ethical debates around use of PGD for gender selection stem from concerns regarding termination of pregnancies. Opponents to use of PGD for gender selection project that acceptability of such a practice will add yet another indication to justifying pregnancy termination, namely termination of a conceptus of an undesired gender. This latter concern however pales against the escalating requests for "selective reduction" of fetuses (a procedure in which one or more fetuses in a multiple pregnancy is/are destroyed in an attempt to allow the remaining embryo/s a better chance to achieve viability as well as minimise health risks to the mother) resulting from ART, driven by patients' "demands" for transfer of surplus embryos so as to ensure "success," albeit at escalating health risks for the mother and the fetus(es). If indeed a request for "selective reduction" of fetuses by an infertile couple is an acceptable exercise of parental autonomy, the authors put forth that compliance with a request for "gender selection" by an infertile couple undergoing ART be viewed in a similar vein.

By the same token of parental autonomy, the couple has to assume all responsibility of consequences resulting from such a decision, including a possibility of not achieving an embryo transfer secondary to failure of embryos to demonstrate ongoing development following the biopsy, a possibility of all embryos being of the less desired gender, as well as of the child of the desired gender failing to conform to their expectations! Extensive counselling of the couple must therefore be an integral part of the consenting process, if couples and practitioners are considering utilisation of such procedure.

Conclusion

While concerns regarding a potential for breach of ethical principals related to a generalised acceptance of such a practice are real, this paper attempts to evaluate the integrity of principles of ethics within the context of acceptability and use of PGD for the purpose of gender selection, exclusively in patients undergoing ART for the management of infertility. The authors believe that given the current prevalence of such practices despite a stance to the contrary taken by the licensing bodies, the needs and desires of an individual seeking care within the context of the overall society's perspective be considered; this extrapolation seems not to breach the basic four principles of ethics, nor does it hold harm for the patient/embryos. Accessibility of PGD for gender selection to couples undergoing ART for management of infertility is unlikely to influence the gender balance within this society and is very distant from being in the "bright-line" areas described by the President's Council on Bioethics.

American College of Obstetricians and Gynecologists

 **NO**

Sex Selection

Sex selection is the practice of using medical techniques to choose the sex of offspring. Patients may request sex selection for a number of reasons. Medical indications include the prevention of sex-linked genetic disorders. In addition, there are a variety of social, economic, cultural, and personal reasons for selecting the sex of children. In cultures in which males are more highly valued than females, sex selection has been practiced to ensure that offspring will be male. A couple who has one or more children of one sex may request sex selection for "family balancing," that is, to have a child of the other sex.

Currently, reliable techniques for selecting sex are limited to postfertilization methods. Postfertilization methods include techniques used during pregnancy as well as techniques used in assisted reproduction before the transfer of embryos created in vitro. Attention also has focused on preconception techniques, particularly flow cytometry separation of X-bearing and Y-bearing spermatozoa before intrauterine insemination or in vitro fertilization (IVF).

In this Committee Opinion, the American College of Obstetricians and Gynecologists' Committee on Ethics presents various ethical considerations and arguments relevant to both prefertilization and postfertilization techniques for sex selection. It also provides recommendations for health care professionals who may be asked to participate in sex selection.

Indications

The principal medical indication for sex selection is known or suspected risk of sex-linked genetic disorders. For example, 50% of males born to women who carry the gene for hemophilia will have this condition. By identifying the sex of the preimplantation embryo or fetus, a woman can learn whether or not the 50% risk of hemophilia applies, and she can receive appropriate prenatal counseling. To ensure that surviving offspring will not have this condition, some women at risk for transmitting hemophilia choose to abort male fetuses or choose not to transfer male embryos. Where the marker or gene for a sex-linked genetic disorder is known, selection on the basis of direct identification of affected embryos or fetuses, rather than on the basis of sex, is possible. Direct identification has the advantage of avoiding the possibility of aborting an unaffected fetus or deciding not to transfer unaffected embryos. Despite the increased ability to identify genes and markers, in certain situations, sex determination is the only current method of identifying embryos or fetuses potentially affected with sex-linked disorders.

Inevitably, identification of sex occurs whenever karyotyping is performed. When medical indications for genetic karyotyping do not require information about sex chromosomes, the prospective parent(s) may elect not to be told the sex of the fetus.

Other reasons sex selection is requested are personal, social, or cultural in nature. For example, the prospective parent(s) may prefer that an only or first-born child be of a certain sex or may desire a balance of sexes in the completed family.

Methods

A variety of techniques are available for sex identification and selection. These include techniques used before fertilization, after fertilization but before embryo transfer, and, most frequently, after implantation.

Prefertilization

Techniques for sex selection before fertilization include timing sexual intercourse and using various methods for separating X-bearing and Y-bearing sperm. No current technique for prefertilization sex selection has been shown to be reliable. Recent attention, however, has focused on flow cytometry separation of X-bearing and Y-bearing spermatozoa as a method of enriching sperm populations for insemination. This technique allows heavier X-bearing sperm to be separated; therefore, selection of females alone may be achieved with increased probability. More research is needed to determine whether any of these techniques can be endorsed in terms of reliability or safety.

Postfertilization and Pretransfer

Assisted reproductive technologies, such as IVF, make possible biopsy of one or more cells from a developing embryo at the cleavage or blastocyst stage. Fluorescence in situ hybridization can be used for analysis of chromosomes and sex selection. Embryos of the undesired sex can be discarded or frozen.

Postimplantation

After implantation of a fertilized egg, karyotyping of fetal cells will provide information about fetal sex. This presents patients with the option of terminating pregnancies for the purpose of sex selection.

Ethical Positions of Other Organizations

Many organizations have issued statements concerning the ethics of health care provider participation in sex selection. The ethics committee of the American Society for Reproductive Medicine maintains that the use of preconception sex selection by preimplantation genetic diagnosis for nonmedical reasons is ethically problematic and "should be discouraged." However, it issued a statement in 2001 that if prefertilization techniques, particularly flow cytometry for sperm sorting, were demonstrated to be safe and efficacious, these techniques would be ethically permissible for family balancing. Because a preimplantation genetic diagnosis is physically more burdensome and necessarily involves the destruction and discarding of embryos, it was not considered similarly permissible for family balancing.

The Programme of Action adopted by the United Nations International Conference on Population and Development opposed the use of sex selection techniques for any nonmedical reason. The United Nations urges governments of all nations "to take necessary measures to prevent . . . prenatal sex selection."

The International Federation of Gynecology and Obstetrics rejects sex selection when it is used as a tool for sex discrimination. It supports preconception sex selection when it is used to avoid sex-linked genetic disorders.

The United Kingdom's Human Fertilisation and Embryology Authority Code of Practice on preimplantation genetic diagnosis states that "centres may not use any information derived from tests on an embryo, or any material removed from it or from the gametes that produced it, to select embryos of a particular sex for non-medical reasons."

Discussion

Medical Testing Not Expressly for the Purpose of Sex Selection

Health care providers may participate unknowingly in sex selection when information about the sex of a fetus results from a medical procedure performed for some other purpose. For example, when a procedure is done to rule out medical disorders in the fetus, the sex of a fetus may become known and may be used for sex selection without the health care provider's knowledge.

The American College of Obstetricians and Gynecologists' Committee on Ethics maintains that when a medical procedure is done for a purpose other than obtaining information about the sex of a fetus but will reveal the fetus's sex, this information should not be withheld from the pregnant woman who requests it. This is because this information legally and ethically belongs to the patient. As a consequence, it might be difficult for health care providers to avoid the possibility of unwittingly participating in sex selection. To minimize the possibility that they will unknowingly participate in sex selection, physicians should foster open communication with patients aimed at clarifying patients' goals. Although health care providers may not ethically withhold medical information from patients who request it, they are not obligated to perform an abortion, or other medical procedure, to select fetal sex.

Medical Testing Expressly for the Purpose of Sex Selection

With regard to medical procedures performed for the express purpose of selecting the sex of a fetus, the following four potential ethical positions are outlined to facilitate discussion:

Position 1: Never participate in sex selection. Health care providers may never choose to perform medical procedures with the intended purpose of sex selection.

Position 2: Participate in sex selection when medically indicated. Health care providers may choose to perform medical procedures with the intended purpose of preventing sex-linked genetic disorders.

Position 3: Participate in sex selection for medical indications and for the purpose of family balancing. Health care providers may choose to perform medical procedures for sex selection when the patient has at least one child and desires a child of the other sex.

Position 4: Participate in sex selection whenever requested. Health care providers may choose to perform medical procedures for the purpose of sex selection whenever the patient requests such procedures.

The committee shares the concern expressed by the United Nations and the International Federation of Gynecology and Obstetrics that sex selection can be motivated by and reinforce the devaluation of women. The committee supports the ethical principle of equality between the sexes.

The committee rejects, as too restrictive, the position that sex selection techniques are always unethical (position 1). The committee supports, as ethically permissible, the practice of sex selection to prevent serious sex-linked genetic disorders (position 2). However, the increasing availability of testing for specific gene mutations is likely to make selection based on sex alone unnecessary in many of these cases. For example, it supports offering patients using assisted reproductive techniques the option of preimplantation genetic diagnosis for identification of male sex chromosomes if patients are at risk for transmitting Duchenne's muscular dystrophy. This position is consistent with the stance of equality between the sexes because it does not imply that the sex of a child itself makes that child more or less valuable.

Some argue that sex selection techniques can be ethically justified when used to achieve a "balance" in a family in which all current children are the same sex and a child of the opposite sex is desired (position 3). To achieve this goal, couples may request 1) sperm sorting by flow cytometry to enhance the probability of achieving a pregnancy of a particular sex, although these techniques are considered experimental; 2) transferring only embryos of one sex in assisted reproduction after embryo biopsy and preimplantation genetic diagnosis; 3) reducing, on the basis of sex, the number of fetuses in a multifetal pregnancy; or 4) aborting fetuses that are not of the desired sex. In these situations, individual parents may consistently judge sex selection to be an important personal or family goal and, at the same time, reject the idea that children of one sex are inherently more valuable than children of another sex.

Although this stance is, in principle, consistent with the principle of equality between the sexes, it nonetheless raises ethical concerns. First, it often is impossible to ascertain patients' true motives for requesting sex selection procedures. For example, patients who want to abort female fetuses because they value male offspring more than female offspring would be unlikely to espouse such beliefs openly if they thought this would lead physicians to deny their requests. Second, even when sex selection is requested for nonsexist reasons, the very idea of preferring a child of a particular sex may be interpreted as condoning sexist values and, hence, create a climate in which sex discrimination can more easily flourish. Even preconception techniques of sex selection may encourage such a climate. The use of flow cytometry is experimental, and preliminary reports indicate that achievement of a female fetus is not guaranteed. Misconception about the accuracy of this evolving technology coupled with a strong preference for a child of a particular sex may lead couples to terminate a pregnancy of the "undesired" sex.

The committee concludes that use of sex selection techniques for family balancing violates the norm of equality between the sexes; moreover, this ethical objection arises regardless of the timing of selection (i.e., preconception or postconception) or the stage of development of the embryo or fetus.

The committee rejects the position that sex selection should be performed on demand (position 4) because this position may reflect and encourage sex discrimination. In most societies where sex selection is widely practiced, families prefer male offspring. Although this preference sometimes has an economic rationale, such as the financial support or physical labor male offspring traditionally provide or the financial liability associated with female offspring, it also reflects the belief that males are inherently more valuable than females. Where systematic preferences for a particular sex dominate, there is a need to address underlying inequalities between the sexes.

Summary

The committee has sought to assist physicians and other health care providers facing requests from patients for sex selection by calling attention to relevant ethical considerations, affirming the value of equality between the sexes, and emphasizing that individual health care providers are never ethically required to participate in sex selection. The committee accepts, as ethically permissible, the practice of sex selection to prevent sex-linked genetic disorders. The committee opposes meeting other requests for sex selection, such as the belief that offspring of a certain sex are inherently more valuable. The committee opposes meeting requests for sex selection for personal and family reasons, including family balancing, because of the concern that such requests may ultimately support sexist practices.

Medical techniques intended for other purposes have the potential for being used by patients for sex selection without the health care provider's knowledge or consent. Because a patient is entitled to obtain personal medical information, including information about the sex of her fetus, it will sometimes be impossible for health care professionals to avoid unwitting participation in sex selection.

POSTSCRIPT

Should Parents Be Allowed to Choose the Sex of Their Children?

A primary focus of critics' concern about sex-selection technologies (and cultural biases toward males) is their impact on population sex ratios. A skewed sex ratio, they fear, will cause dire consequences for a society, particularly for heterosexual mating (although it is ironic that the same class of reproductive technological advances not only facilitate sex selection but also make reproduction less reliant on conventional heterosexual mating). But what about social concerns about sex selection? How will the increasing frequency of the use of sex-selection technologies impact families? How will it affect gender assumptions and sex discrimination?

Is the acceptability of sex-selection conditional? If Americans were not as biased toward having just boys or just girls, and therefore the population sex ratio would not be threatened, would sex selection be acceptable to control the birth order of the sexes, to ensure a mixture of boys and girls, or to have an only child of a certain desired sex? Sex-selection technology might reduce overpopulation by helping families who already have a child of one sex "balance" their family with a second child of the other sex, rather than continue to have children "naturally" until they get the sex they want. Is using sex selection as a "small family planning tool" an acceptable use of sex-selection technologies? Many feel that using sex selection to balance a family is not sexist. But others argue that it is sexist because it promotes gender stereotyping, which undermines equality between the sexes.

Some feminists argue that sex selection for any reason, even family-balancing, perpetuates gender roles and thus the devaluation of women. Some people in the disabilities right movement have joined with this perspective, suggesting that if it is permissible to select against female embryos (is sex per se a genetic "abnormality?"), then so it is permissible to select against embryos with genetic abnormalities of all types; and who is to define what is "abnormal"—height, IQ? Then the door is open to increasing discrimination against people with disabilities.

Should abortions solely for the purpose of sex selection be allowed? This is a profound dilemma for many pro-choice feminists for whom a woman's right to choose an abortion for any reason is opposed to gross sex discrimination in the form of sex-selective abortions (usually of female fetuses). It is interesting to note that when parents choose to abort based on fetal sex in an effort to "balance" their family, sex selection is regarded as more acceptable than when only female fetuses are aborted because of a preference for males. What assumptions about sex and gender underlie this judgment? In these selections, the effects of sex and gender on fetuses, children, and adolescents are examined. Is fetal sex selection ethical? Are sex differences located in biology and/or culture? Can children's gender roles be redefined?

Suggested Readings

K. M. Boyd, "Medical Ethics: Principles, Persons, and Perspectives: From Controversy to Conversation," *Journal of Medical Ethics, 31* (2005): 481–486.

John Harris, "Sex Selection and Regulated Hatred," *Journal of Medical Ethics, 31* (2005): 291–294.

S. Matthew Liao, "The Ethics of Using Genetic Engineering for Sex Selection," *Journal of Medical Ethics, 31* (2005): 116–118.

Rosamond Rhodes, "Acceptable Sex Selection," *American Journal of Bioethics, 1* (2001): 31–32.

Susan M. Wolf, *Feminism and Bioethics: Beyond Reproduction* (New York: Oxford University Press, 1996).

See also the following organizations' statements on sex selection:

1. FIGO [International Federation of Gynecology and Obstetrics], "Ethical Issues in Obstetrics and Gynecology" by the FIGO Committee for the Study of Ethical Aspects of Human Reproduction and Women's Health, November 2006.
2. The Ethics Committee of the ASRM, "Preconception Gender Selection for Nonmedical Reasons," *Fertility and Sterility, 75*(5) (May 2001).

Internet References . . .

About Women's Issues

This Web site addresses a number of issues related to gender and the world of work.

**http://womensissues.about.com/od/
genderdiscrimination/i/isgendergap.htm**

International Labour Organization (ILO)

The ILO is dedicated to reducing poverty and promoting opportunities for women and men to obtain decent and productive work. This Web site provides a comprehensive bibliography of materials related to gender issues and women at work.

http://www.ilo.org

World Alliance for Citizen Participation—Gender Toolkits

CIVICUS: World Alliance for Citizen Participation is an international alliance of more than 1,000 members from 105 countries that has worked for over a decade to strengthen citizen action and civil society throughout the world, especially in areas where participatory democracy and citizens' freedom of association are threatened.

http://www.civicus.org/toolkits/gender-toolkits

Gender at Work

The Web site for Gender at Work was created in June 2001 by AWID (Association for Women's Rights in Development), WLP (Women's Learning Partnership), CIVICUS (World Alliance for Citizen Participation), and UNIFEM (United Nations Fund for Women). They state, "We aim to develop new theory and practice on how organizations can change gender-biased institutional rules (the distribution of power, privileges and rights), values (norms and attitudes), and practices. We also aim to change the political, accountability, cultural and knowledge systems of organizations to challenge social norms and gender inequity."

http://www.genderatwork.org

Advancing Women

This Web site offers advice on career and business strategies; provides tools and resources to support one's career, business, and leadership goals; and features a targeted, diversity job board.

http://www.advancingwomen.com/

UNIT 5

From 9 to 5: Gender in the World of Work

*T*here are few places other than the workplace where gendered patterns are more apparent. There are sex-segregated jobs: "pink" collar jobs for women and "blue" collar jobs for men. Within occupational categories, there is sex-stratification, with men more often holding the higher, more prestigious and better-paying positions, such as anesthesiologist versus pediatrician, or corporate lawyer versus family lawyer. Women on average make $.75 for each man's dollar; this holds across race, ethnicity, social class, educational level, and work status (full-time or part-time). Such disparities provoke heated discussion. Are they the result of discrimination against women in the workplace, or are they justifiable differences based on natural talents? In what ways does gender influence women's and men's efforts to balance work and family interests and responsibilities? Why do we ask the question about the impact on children of mothers working outside the home but never the question of the impact of fathers working? What are the ramifications of this question for poor people, especially women? Are these women to be blamed for their status as single mothers on welfare? As you explore the issues raised in this section consider the competing, or perhaps complementary, explanations for gender differences in the workplace: biologically based differences that lead to differences in interests, motivations, and achievement level and/or culturally based differences, such as discrimination in hiring and promotion practices, the devaluing of women's work, the social rejection of competent women, and the lack of role models and mentors.

Are biologically based explanations justified in the face of differential experiences in the workplace based on race, ethnicity, class, culture, and other status-defining attributes, such as disability status or sexual orientation? How do media images of the workplace affect our understanding of the workplace?

- Does the "Mommy Track" (Part-Time Work) Improve Women's Lives?
- Can Social Policies Improve Gender Inequalities in the Workplace?
- Is the Gender Wage Gap Justified?
- Are Barriers to Women's Success as Leaders Due to Societal Obstacles?

ISSUE 14

Does the "Mommy Track" (Part-Time Work) Improve Women's Lives?

YES: E. Jeffrey Hill, Vjollca K. Märtinson, Maria Ferris, and Robin Zenger Baker, from "Beyond the Mommy Track: The Influence of New-Concept Part-Time Work for Professional Women on Work and Family," *Journal of Family and Economic Issues* (2004)

NO: Mary C. Noonan and Mary E. Corcoran, from "The Mommy Track and Partnership: Temporary Delay or Dead End?" *The Annals of the American Academy of Political and Social Science* (2004)

ISSUE SUMMARY

YES: Brigham Young University colleagues E. Jeffrey Hill and Vjollca Märtinson, along with Maria Ferris of IBM and Robin Zenger Baker at Boston University, suggest that women in professional careers can successfully integrate family and career by following a new-concept part-time work model.

NO: In contrast, Mary Noonan, an assistant professor in the department of sociology at the University of Iowa, and Mary Corcoran, a professor of political science at the University of Michigan, document the various costs of the mommy track for female attorneys, including lower salaries and decreased likelihood of promotion to partner.

Women account for about 47 percent of the workforce in the United States and work approximately the same number of hours as men (35–50 hours/week); 60 percent of all women over age 16 are in the workforce. However, women earn less than men on average; this is true across full-time and part-time work, as well as across race, class, and educational levels. One explanation for the earning discrepancy is that women experience more job discontinuity due to family obligations, such as taking time off for childbirth, as well as dual-career conflicts, such as following a spouse who relocates to improve his job status. That is, women are expected to choose family over career in any work-family conflicts. Job interruptions and lower wages can result in women experiencing lower self-esteem and a reduced sense of accomplishment. Often these patterns are attributed to women's own choices and that they "deserve" less. However, others have suggested that society would benefit from recognizing that the childbearing years are also the years during which one is most likely to make the greatest career advancements. Thus, if women get off the career track to have children, they begin to lag and struggle to ever get back on the track. As a solution to this problem, the "mommy track" was proposed in 1989, a phrase coined in the *New York Times* to describe a "career and family" path that would serve as a viable alternative to the traditional "career primary" path typically followed by men. The "career and family" path was intended to offer women—only temporarily—flexible schedules, with reduced salaries and less responsibilities, while they tended to family matters, with the opportunity to return later to the fast track. The debate is whether the mommy track adequately allows for a temporary delay in women's career trajectory or if it really is a dead end. Skeptics question whether it is ever possible to truly get back on the fast track following a timeout for family. Although the concept of the mommy track was to prevent women from being unfairly treated, many argue that all it has done is perpetuate the stereotype that women, who chose, even temporarily, family over career, are not really committed to the workplace. As recently as July 2007, a *U.S. News & World Report* article was focused on how the mommy track can derail a career. In the selections that follow, Hill and colleagues use data from a study of IBM workers to argue that women in professional careers can successfully integrate family and career by following a new-concept part-time work model. The selection by Noonan and Corcoran counters with data from University of Michigan law school graduates to show the costs of the mommy track for female attorneys, including lower salaries and decreased likelihood of promotion to partner.

YES ⬅ E. Jeffrey Hill, Vjollca K. Märtinson, Maria Ferris, and Robin Zenger Baker

Beyond the Mommy Track: The Influence of New-Concept Part-Time Work for Professional Women on Work and Family

The demographic composition of the United States workforce now includes more dual-earner couples who have responsibility to care for children, as well as more dual-professional couples who both have careers, not just jobs. In addition, the trend is toward longer work hours for many segments of American workers, especially for highly educated managers and professionals. The United States is one of the countries with the highest percentage of employees working 50 hours per week or more. This creates what has been termed a time famine for today's families. The time deficit is especially severe for women who choose to have children while pursuing a full-time career in a professional occupation.

Becoming a mother can make having a balanced life very difficult for a professional woman. Some new mothers try to do it all, continuing to work long hours in their professional careers while at the same time investing heavily in their family career. This option often takes a toll in stress and health. Others opt for, or are channeled into the so-called mommy track, moderating their ultimate career aspirations in order to raise their children. Some of these women choose to drop out of the workforce completely or for some period of time. Others take less demanding jobs in order to have more time and energy for their children. Still others choose part-time work.

Voluntary part-time employment after childbirth or adoption is consistently cited as a desirable option to facilitate work and family balance, especially for women. Studies show that part-time work options, especially for women, are increasing, and that this work is associated with lower work-to-family interference, better time-management ability, and improved life satisfaction. However, most professional women do not opt for reduced-hours options because, like other work-life programs, the economic costs in the form of forgone wages and career advancement are perceived to be too great. Generally these part-time jobs are of lower status with less pay and fewer career opportunities.

Because job prestige, income, and career opportunity are important to many professional women, some companies have begun to offer new-concept

From *Journal of Family and Economic Issues*, March, 2004, pp. 121–126, 129–133. Copyright © 2004 by Springer Journals (Kluwer Academic). Reprinted by permission.

part-time employment options, call[ing] it customized work; it [is] a growing trend. In contrast to most part-time jobs, these are high-status, career-oriented reduced-hours options that conserve pro-rated professional salaries and benefits. The hope is that this option might ameliorate the tendency toward mommy track career outcomes and convince women to continue to make professional career contributions as they embark on their family career. [O]ffering reduced work schedules that fit well with employee needs is an important weapon in "winning the war for talent" by retaining "professional employees and managers with critical skills."

Work and Family Balance

Research offers support for the notion that flexible work arrangements allowing individuals to integrate and overlap work and family responsibilities in time and space are instrumental in achieving a healthy work and family balance. Examples of outcomes associated with negative work-to-family spillover include withdrawal from family interaction, increased conflict in marriage less knowledge of children's experiences, less involvement in housework, shorter period of breast-feeding for mothers with full-time employment, depression, greater likelihood to misuse alcohol, and overall decrease in the quality of life.

Less research has focused on family-to-work spillover, the "neglected side of the work-family interface." Examples of outcomes associated with negative family-to-work spillover include more pronounced psychological distress at work due to poor marital and parental role quality, decreased job satisfaction, greater likelihood of leaving the company, and increased absenteeism. $6.8 billion worth of annual work loss in the United States as a result of the absenteeism that is associated with marital distress [has been documented].

Part-Time Employment

The most persistent work characteristic that predicts work-family imbalance is long work hours, especially for women. For those financially able to do so, part-time work seems an obvious option for dealing with the problems associated with long work hours. In fact, many professionals desire to work fewer hours. More than half of the companies in America have a part-time option for parents to transition back to the workforce after childbirth or adoption. A recent study shows that 8% of men and 21% of women employees in the United States work part time. However, due to work responsibilities, perceived diminished career opportunities, and reduction in salary and benefits, relatively few professionals choose to work less than full time. The emergence of new-concept, part-time work, attempts to address these concerns. "These jobs are viewed as permanent, have career potential, include fringe benefits, and their rate of pay is prorated relative to that of comparable full-time jobs." Though many studies examine part-time work in general, relatively few have specifically examined professional women who work reduced hours while their children are young in these new-concept, part-time professional positions. This study attempts to fill that gap.

Research Questions

This study will expand the extensive literature on part-time employment by exploring the influence of new-concept part-time options, used by professional women who are mothers of preschoolers, on work-family balance and perceived career opportunity. In essence, we speculate that these new-concept part-time jobs will enable female professionals to go beyond the mommy track and successfully start their family careers while they simultaneously move forward in their occupational careers. We will attempt to answer the following specific research questions for a sample of new mothers in professional positions:

1. What is the relationship between new-concept part-time work and work-family balance?
2. What is the relationship between new-concept part-time work and perceived career opportunity?
3. How do part-time professional women and full-time professional women differ in how they allocate time to work, child care, and household chores?
4. How do part-time professional women and full-time professional women differ in total income and pay rates?
5. What do those participating in new-concept part-time positions perceive they would have done, had that option not been available?

Method

The data for this paper came from a work and life issues survey administered on-line by IBM in the United States in 1996. The focus of this study was female professionals with preschool children (birth to age 4) who utilized the new-concept part-time option. Originally the study was to look at part-time work for men as well, but there were insufficient male responses for reliable statistical analyses.

Internal surveys revealed that IBM employees perceived the flexibility to choose when, where, and how many hours are worked to be the most beneficial IBM offering to enhance work-family balance. In 1991, as part of an overall flexibility initiative, IBM implemented the Flexible Work Leave of Absence Program, which enabled employees to reduce their scheduled work hours from 40 to 20–32 hours per week. This qualified as a new-concept, part-time program because those participating continued in their same professional position, received pro-rated pay and benefits equivalent to what they had received when working full time, and were eligible for promotion and recognition. This research was conducted when the maximum length of part-time employment allowed by IBM was five years.

Data Collection and Sample

A 9% representative sample of all IBM employees in the United States was invited to take this online survey; 58% ($N = 6,451$) responded. Sample respondents were similar to the broader U.S. population of workers, except that this IBM sample was more highly educated and more highly paid than national norms. The option of part-time employment was probably more feasible in this population than in the overall population.

The survey was administered electronically. IBM has conducted on-line surveys since 1986, and survey data indicate a high degree of confidence in confidentiality and anonymity. For confidentiality reasons, the electronic mail addresses were deleted from the data before data were sent to the survey administrator. . . .

Results

Results related to the research questions are summarized below.

Relationship Between New-Concept Part-Time Work and Work-Family Balance

Being in a new-concept part-time position vis-à-vis a full-time position was strongly and positively correlated to work-family balance. This relationship was maintained in multivariate analyses after controlling for occupational level, family income, age, and job flexibility.

Relationship Between New-Concept Part-Time Work and Perceived Career Opportunity

Being in a new-concept part-time professional position vis-à-vis a full-time position was not significantly correlated to perceived career opportunity. No significant relationship was found in multivariate analyses after controlling for occupational level, family income, age, and job flexibility.

Allocation of Time to Work, Child Care and Household Chores

Those in new-concept part-time professional positions reported that they worked an average of 23 fewer hours per week than those in full-time professional positions (26.3 hours per week vs. 49.3 hours per week). They reported slightly more hours per week in child care (27.3 vs. 25.5) and in household chores (16.1 vs. 13.5).

Differences in Total Income and Pay Rates

Those in the new-concept part-time professional positions reported $20,022 less annual family income than those in full-time professional positions ($100,568 per year vs. $120,590 per year). They also reported $26,624 less annual individual income ($37,954 per year vs. $64,578 per year). When converted to an hourly pay equivalent, those in new-concept part-time professional positions earned slightly more per hour than those in full-time professional positions ($27.94 per hour worked vs. $25.36 per hour worked).

What Professional Women Report They Would Have Done Had the Program Not Been Offered

Most of those participating in new-concept part-time professional positions (74%) reported they would have left IBM if this program had not been available. Almost three-fifths (59%) reported they would have left IBM to find a job with more flexibility. Almost one-fourth (23%) reported they would have left the workforce altogether. Only about one-fifth (19%) reported they would have stayed with IBM and continued to work full time.

Discussion

In this study we consider the possibility that new-concept part-time professional positions might be an alternative to the mommy track. We consider whether this option may better enable professional women to embark on their family career with less stress and fewer negative consequences to long-term career prospects.

Personal/Family Implications

It was not surprising that mothers in new-concept part-time professional positions reported much better work-family balance than those working full time. Considering they work 23 fewer hours per week, it would have been surprising if the part-time group did not report better balance. However, it was surprising that they did not report less perceived career opportunity. This is counter to what would be expected had they been working in traditional part-time jobs based on previous research. Why is this so? It may be the higher status, greater responsibility, and pro-rated pay of new-concept part-time professional positions creates an environment where the employee feels in the loop of future career opportunities.

The personal decision for a professional woman to work a part-time schedule is a matter of trade-offs. This study quantifies some of the advantages and disadvantages for this population. The most obvious advantage of new-concept part-time work for professional women is that more than four and one-half hours per work day are freed up for personal and family needs. This extra time was certainly a major factor in why work-family balance was less problematic for the professional women working part time.

An interesting finding is that women in the full-time group reported an average of almost as many hours in child care as the part-time group (26 vs. 27 hours per week) and almost as much time doing household chores (14 vs. 16 hours per week). Apparently both full- and part-time professional women take the time needed to care for home and family responsibilities. The real benefit for the part-time women, therefore, appears to be the extra 19 more hours per week available to use in individual activities that might reduce stress, such as additional sleep, recreation, and other renewal activities. The literature cited earlier indicates that possible benefits for these new mothers include less marital conflict, increased period of breast-feeding after the birth of an infant, less depression, and better monitoring of children.

The most obvious disadvantage for a new mother considering a new-concept part-time professional position is reduced income. This study documents that the salaries of the part-time professionals averaged about 41% less (about $27,000 less per year) than the full-time professionals. However, because they reported working 47% fewer hours (26 vs. 49 hours per week), their pay equivalent was actually higher than the full-time group ($27.94 vs. $25.50 per hour). The family income of the part-time group was only about 17% less than the full-time group (about $20,000 less per year).

Organizational Implications

Companies today are engaged in what is known as a talent war to "recruit and retain professional employees and managers with critical skills." Data from this study support the notion that offering new-concept part-time professional positions may be a useful weapon in that war. Difficulty managing the demands of work and personal/family life is very problematic, especially for professional women who have chosen to have children. It is considered to be the most important reason why professional women with preschool children would choose to leave their job. Of the reduced-hours group in this study, 23% reported they would have left their job to stay home full time had the part-time work option not been available. Another 58% said they would have left their job to work for another company that offered greater flexibility. Only 19% indicated they would have continued working full time for the company. It appears that new-concept part-time employment is a strategy that may have enabled 81% of these women to stay employed with IBM, rather than going to work for someone else or leaving the workforce altogether.

In summary, the results of this study indicate that new-concept part-time employment offers the promise of enabling professional women opportunities to better balance work and family life while maintaining career opportunity. This option appears to be a true win-win solution to help mitigate the personal toll of increased work demands, with relatively few costs. If visionary business leaders and empowered individuals adopt greater flexibility, we may see the end to the zero-sum game and set up a virtuous cycle in which work-family balance programs leverage on each other to promote individual well-being, family solidarity, and organizational success.

Limitations

One limitation of this study is that respondents all worked for IBM in the United States. IBM employees, in general, are highly educated, have higher salaries, and have more experience with computer technology than the general population. For these reasons, the degree to which these results may be generalized to other companies and in other parts of the world is uncertain. Even if the IBM sample is representative of employees working for large corporations, it may not be representative of the majority of professional women who work for smaller firms or are self-employed. In addition, most IBMers work in or near urban centers, so the applicability of this research to those who work in rural settings is uncertain.

Conclusion

Just as flexibility in family processes diminishes potential family stress, so flexibility in work processes may be key in helping employees effectively manage contemporary stress associated with work and family demands. In fact, this study documents that new-concept, part-time positions may provide the time professional women need at the beginning of their family career when children require the greatest parental investment. Given that these women represent key talent required for meeting business objectives, data like these can reinforce management's efforts to provide greater flexibility in the workforce, especially when the results are so clear and the costs of such efforts are relatively small. Just as important, these data may help encourage professional women to take advantage of the flexibility offered so they can more effectively care for their young children. As more companies offer viable new-concept part-time options and more employees use these options, perhaps we can move beyond the mommy track to enable women to contribute their best to both work and home, at the same time.

Mary C. Noonan and
Mary E. Corcoran

→ **NO**

The Mommy Track and Partnership: Temporary Delay or Dead End?

More than 40 percent of recent law school graduates are women, and almost 40 percent of associates in large firms are women. In 2003, women made up 63 percent of Berkeley Law School's graduating class, 51 percent of Columbia Law School's graduating class, and 47 percent of Harvard Law School's graduating class. Despite the rapid feminization of law since the 1970s, women associates are far less likely than male associates to become partners. According to a recent American Bar Association Commission report, the most pervasive underrepresentation of women lawyers is among partners in law firms. Only 16 percent of partners in law firms are women. . . .

Women now graduate from top law schools and enter prestigious law firms at roughly the same rates as do men. [W]omen "start strong out of the gate." But after leaving law school and entering firms, women increasingly fall behind men. Why is this? [It has been] asserted that women associates make partner at lower rates than do male associates because women face "multiple glass ceilings" that men do not at many stages of the career hierarchy. One such stage is the decision to remain in a firm long enough to be considered for partnership. Partnership typically occurs after six to eight years at a firm, but many women associates drop out of large law practices by their fourth year. Donovan claimed that "the single most important element of women's inability to make partner is the high attrition rate of women from firms . . . women cannot make partner if they have left the firm." Foster . . . stated that "attrition perpetuates the glass ceiling as fewer women are available for promotion and more men remain in decision-making positions as a result."

High attrition in the first years after joining firms is not the only reason offered for women's underrepresentation in partnership ranks. [G]lass ceilings operate at other career stages as well—resulting in lower promotion chances for women associates who remain in firms and in lower earnings and equity shares for women who become partners.

[T]he following institutional factors may marginalize women associates: "rainmaking" demands (i.e., generating new clients for the firm), lack of mentors, sexual harassment and discrimination, high work hours, and part-time work tracks that permanently derail lawyers from partnership tracks. [F]emale associates have fewer opportunities than male associates to develop "social

From *The Annals of the American Academy of Political and Social Science,* vol. 596, no. 1, 2004, pp. 130–135, 137, 139–142, 146–149. Copyright © 2004 by Sage Publications. Reprinted by permission.

capital" within law firms. Researchers who interview women lawyers find that many report experiencing sex discrimination within the firm. [B]oth men and women lawyers identify sex discrimination as one of the main reasons for women's early attrition from private firms and lower rates of promotion to partnership. [W]omen lawyers report lower levels of discrimination at the "front door" (hiring) than on the job (salary, promotion, and assignments).

The primary personal factor identified as constraining women's partnership chances is that some cut back labor supply (e.g., work part-time for a period, take a family leave, work fewer hours per year) to balance the demands of motherhood with the demands of practicing law. As Donovan put it, "The most notorious reason for women to leave [a firm] is motherhood." [C]hild care responsibilities and family leave policies play a significant role in career decisions—jobs, specialties, cases, and work hours—for women but not for men. Common reasons women report for leaving the field of law are the lack of flexibility offered by law firms, long hours, child care commitments, and the stressful nature of the work. Men are less likely to cite "work-family conflict" as a reason for leaving law and are more likely to state the desire to use different skills.

As these authors noted, the distinction between institutional and personal constraints is fuzzy. For instance, a woman associate may "choose" to work part-time for several years, and this choice may reduce her chances of making partner. But this choice may be a response to discrimination within a firm, or this choice may be all that is available in a firm. Furthermore, the "choice" itself may be strongly conditioned by the expectations of others—family, colleagues, the larger culture—expectations that do not constrain men's labor supply choices. . . .

[Many] authors hypothesized that work-family conflicts lead women to reduce their labor supply in ways that increase their chances of exiting law firms and reduce their chances of becoming partners. Two studies of attrition from law firms and several studies of partnership have used relatively recent data on lawyers' outcomes to test this hypothesis.

What do these researchers find? First, sex strongly predicted exits from law firms and promotion to partnership even when controlling for law school quality, academic distinction in law school, *potential* work experience (i.e., years since called to the bar, years since law school graduation), legal specialization, having taken a leave for child care, marital status, children, current work hours, and measures of social capital. Second, labor supply matters. Having taken a family leave was more common among women and reduced chances of partnership in [a] sample of Toronto lawyers. A work-family constraint lowered women's but not men's chances of partnership in [a] sample of Chicago lawyers. Current work hours positively predicted partnership.

The usefulness of this research in assessing for the extent to which women's labor supply choices reduce their chances of becoming partners is limited given the relatively weak measures of labor supply used. No study had a measure of years worked part-time to care for children. Yet [it has been] argued that choosing to work part-time on a "mommy track" can stigmatize women as "not serious" and permanently damage chances of becoming partners. . . . No study had a measure of years practicing law. Instead, all of these prior studies included a measure of potential experience (years since called to the bar or years since law school graduation), but actual years practiced is likely lower for women than for men. . . . Those who do not make partner might well cut back work hours.

Given the limitations of the labor supply measures used in past research, it may be surprising to learn that even with these weak controls for labor supply, mothers are no less likely than childless women to become partners. This does not mean that *sex* does not matter for partnership; mothers and childless women are equally *less* likely than men to become partners.

We use detailed information on the fifteen-year careers of graduates of the University of Michigan Law School to investigate sex differences in promotion to partnership. Because women may be disadvantaged relative to men at multiple career stages, we examine three steps in the partnership process: (1) the decision to attrite early from private practice, (2) the attainment of partnership among those who do not attrite, and (3) determinants of partners' earnings. Because we have direct measures of the labor supply choices made to handle child care responsibilities (e.g., months time out for kids, months worked part-time for kids, and years worked in law), we can more precisely estimate the extent to which cutbacks in labor supply are associated with reduced chances of becoming partner for women who start out in private practice than have past researchers. If, after controlling for sex differences in these precise measures of labor supply, women still have higher early attrition rates from private practice than men, women who stay in private practice are still less likely to be promoted than men, and women who become partners still have lower earnings than men, then this is strong indirect evidence that glass ceilings constrain women's opportunities at multiple points in their legal careers. In addition, if after controlling for labor supply, motherhood has no further effects on early attrition, partnership among stayers, and wages of partners, then it seems unlikely that parenting concerns account for the remaining sex differences in early attrition, partnership, and earnings.

Examining women's experiences at multiple stages of their careers after they first enter firms is important because the experiences of women long-termers in a firm likely inform the career decisions made by new women entrants. If cutting back on labor supply has derailed the partnership of older women, then new entrants who are concerned about balancing work and family may quit private practice for another legal setting. If older women who have not cut back labor supply are less likely than men with similar work histories to become partners, and if women partners earn less than men partners with similar work histories, then even new women entrants who are not concerned about balancing family demands may decide their opportunities are restricted and leave. . . .

We use a sample of University of Michigan Law School graduates to examine these questions. The law school surveys all graduates fifteen years after graduation about their earnings, work hours, work histories (including interruptions and years worked part-time), work settings, and families. These survey data are matched with law school records, giving additional information on graduates' performance while in law school.

The sample includes the graduating classes of 1972 to 1985. Outcomes are observed from 1987 to 2000. The average response rate across all years was 60 percent for women and 64 percent for men. We exclude women and men with missing data on the variables used in the analyses (about 18 percent of the total sample). We use three samples in our analyses: those who spent at least one year in private practice (433 women and 1,876 men), those who spent at least four years in private practice (354 women and 1,694 men), and those who were partners in their fifteenth year (144 women and 1,116 men). . . .

Women were less likely than men to have tried out private practice for at least one year (82 vs. 87 percent), to have stayed in practice for four or more years (67 vs. 79 percent), and to have made partner (27 vs. 52 percent). Among graduates who did not attrite early (those with four or more years' of private practice), 40 percent of women and 65 percent of men were partners.

. . . At three years of experience, the gap between the percentage of men and women still in private practice is minor—94 versus 89 percent, respectively. The gap widens to approximately 10 percentage points after four and five years of work experience. We suspect that this is the period when women become discouraged about their chances of making partner. Between five and eight years, the years in which partnership decisions are typically made, the gap widens another 10 percentage points, reaching nearly 20 percent at year eight. It seems likely that women leave private practice at higher rates after five to eight years of practice either because they expect not to make partner or they do not make partner. The gender gap in attrition is constant over the period from eight to fifteen years.

. . . Sex differences in family characteristics were large: women were more likely to be childless, less likely to be married, and more likely to be married to a lawyer. Women, on average, also worked significantly fewer hours than men—1,966 hours versus 2,493 hours. Women and men were equally likely to have had a mentor and were equally satisfied with the balance of family and work in their lives.

Sex differences in the labor supply of parents are striking. Only 19 of the 1,574 fathers in our sample had worked part-time, and only 17 had taken a leave from work to care for children. In contrast, 47 percent of mothers had worked part-time and 42 percent had taken a leave from work. Mothers who had worked part-time averaged forty-two months of part-time work over the fifteen years since law school graduation, and those who took a leave from work averaged twenty-four months not working. Fathers worked more hours in year fifteen than did mothers—2,519 versus 2,005 hours. . . .

Although women lawyers were more likely than men lawyers to cut back labor supply, 56 percent of women lawyers *never* worked part-time or took a leave. This 56 percent consists of childless women (29 percent of the sample) and mothers who never worked part-time or took time out to care for children (27 percent of the sample). Women who had not worked part-time or dropped out worked high hours—roughly twenty-four hundred at year fifteen. . . .

Women are more likely than men to exit, even after controlling for GPA, marriage, children, labor supply, mentoring, and satisfaction. GPA and years practiced law are significantly associated with lower rates of leaving for both men and women. Marriage, children, time out, and part-time work are not significantly associated with rates of leaving for women or men. . . . Men who left are more likely than men who stayed to be satisfied with their work-family balance at the fifteenth year; this is not true for women. Further analyses show that, for women, having children, taking time out of work, and working part-time are all positively associated with work-family satisfaction. Women who leave private practice are more likely to take time out of work, women who stay in private practice are more likely to work part-time, and both groups are equally likely to have children. Therefore, it appears that both women "leavers" and "stayers" have balanced their work and family lives in different ways, but both approaches are equally satisfying. Since very few men who remain in private practice actually work part-time, it may be that—for men—work-family satisfaction only comes through leaving the stressful world of private practice for other less demanding lines of work.

Sex also affects promotion rates for lawyers who remain in firms for at least four years. Women are less likely than men to be promoted to partner, even when GPA, race, years practiced law, months part-time, months nonwork, marital status, number of kids, mentorship, and satisfaction are controlled. . . . [M]arriage and children are *positively* associated with the probability of becoming partner when experience measures are included. . . . GPA, years practiced law, and having a mentor are positively associated with partnership, and months not worked is negatively associated with partnership. The effects of time out on partnership are significantly larger for men, and the effects of GPA on partnership are significantly larger for women. Part-time work significantly decreases the likelihood of becoming a partner for women but not for men; however, the difference in the effect is not large enough to be statistically different by sex. Having a lawyer as a spouse increases women's but not men's chances of becoming a partner. . . .

The "base" lawyer is a white man who is married with children, has an average GPA, 13.5 years of private practice experience, no leave, no part-time experience, a mentor, is satisfied with his work-family balance, and has a spouse who is not a lawyer. This "base" lawyer has a 9 percent chance of leaving private practice before his fourth year and a 57 percent chance of making partner if he remains in private practice for at least four years. A woman with these same characteristics has a 15 percent chance of leaving practice within four years and a 40 percent chance of making partner if she remains in private practice for at least four years. Thus, "being female" increased the predicted chances of attrition by 6 percentage points and reduced the chances of becoming partner by 17 percentage points.

Conclusion and Discussion

In this article, we use data on graduates of the University of Michigan Law School, a highly ranked law school that provides specialized training and access to well-paid jobs, to examine sex differences in the path to partnership. These men and women started off on an equal footing in the legal marketplace. Despite this, men were almost twice as likely as women to become partners.

How did this happen? The pattern is one of cumulating disadvantages. Women fell behind men in each stage in the progression to partnership. . . . Some argue that women are more likely than men to select themselves out at each stage of the partnership process because men and women handle family responsibilities differently. Certainly, a large minority of women in our sample cut back labor supply to deal with family responsibilities, and virtually no men did so. These cutbacks in labor supply were negatively associated with partnership chances and with partners' earnings. But we found large gaps between the early attrition rates, chances of partnership, and annual earnings of men and women partners with the *same* work histories. . . . At most, one-quarter to one-third of the male/female differences in early attrition and promotion and one-half of the earnings gap between men and women partners are due to labor supply differences. These estimates of reductions may be on the high side since women's labor supply choices are likely influenced by the options firms offer and by women's perceptions of sex differences in promotion opportunities.

A family leave of one year reduced women's chances of making partner by one-third and reduced women partners' earnings by 28 percent. But law school performance and connections had equally strong effects on women lawyers' careers. A woman with a B+ average GPA in law school was 1.5 times as likely to attrite early as was one with an A average (14 vs. 9 percent) and was less likely to make partner (35 vs. 49 percent). Women with mentors were almost 1.5 times as likely to become partners as were those without mentors (35 vs. 24 percent), and women married to lawyers were 1.8 times as likely to make partner as women who were not married to lawyers (54 vs. 35 percent).

The few male lawyers who reduced their labor supply to care for children fared badly economically. A year of leave reduced men's predicted chances of making partner from 58 to 0 percent, and a year of part-time work reduced male partners' predicted earnings by 41 percent. The meaning of these drops is unclear. These could be very unusual men, or it could be that male lawyers who behave in nontraditional ways face high penalties. If the latter were true, it is not surprising that so few male lawyers reduce labor supply. . . .

One could argue that parenting responsibilities reduce women's productivity at work in ways not captured by these analyses. But controlling for labor supply, mothers had the same early attrition rates, promotion rates, and earnings as did childless women; and ever-married women were more likely to be promoted than never-married women. It seems implausible that women's commitment to home and hearth accounts for the remaining sex-based gaps in early attrition, partnership, and partners' earnings.

This brings us to sex-based differences in the ways women are treated in law firms. Posited that direct discrimination and sexual harassment, as well as a wide array of embedded institutional practices, marginalize women within law firms. We could not directly test this proposition, . . . [b]ut our finding of large sex differences at each stage of the progression to partnership, controlling for labor supply differences, suggests that women are disproportionately selected out and discouraged at each of these stages. This is strong indirect evidence that women face multiple glass ceilings.

Researchers who have conducted in-depth, in-person interviews with associates and partners in law firms describe two sets of mechanisms that could systematically disadvantage women. One set constrains associates' labor supply choices and determines the effects these choices have on partnership. For instance, although firms offer part-time tracks, official policies differ on whether part-time work counts for partnership and on whether part-timers can return to partnership tracks. Even when the official policy is that family leaves and part-time work do not disqualify women from partnership, several studies find that some women reported being assigned less important cases and being labeled as less motivated after having worked part-time. . . . This social stigma and fear of not being taken seriously likely keeps many lawyers from pursuing part-time options. . . . A second set of mechanisms can systematically disadvantage women in ways that are unrelated to their actual labor supply choices. [H]igh rainmaking demands, a lack of mentoring, sex discrimination, disproportionate shares of pro bono work, and mixed messages about personal style all may reduce women's chances of making partner.

It is easy to describe institutional arrangements that might make law firms more family-friendly. A report in the *Harvard Law Review* . . . suggested reducing "billable hours" requirements, billing approaches that move away from reliance on billable hours to other indicators of performance, officially counting part-time work toward partnership, developing a work climate in which individuals who work part-time and take family leaves are not stigmatized, part-time partnership, employer-assisted emergency day care, and mixed compensation (compensation consisting partly of time and partly of money).

It is equally easy to list approaches that can change institutional barriers to women's mobility. To the extent that sex discrimination and sexual harassment limit women's chances, there may be legal avenues to pursue. Of course, the individual costs of pursuing such strategies may be high. Other strategies include programs that improve the mentoring women associates receive, broaden the criteria for partnership, and reduce the extent to which women's personal styles are viewed as less effective in a legal setting. We find mentoring has a big impact on women's partnership chances.

Implementing family-friendly policies and changing embedded institutional policies that disadvantage women may require shifts in law firm culture. This is the rub. The *Harvard Law Review* study . . . warned that such changes can "conflict with (firms') institutional norms" and that "law firms and their clients are understandably reluctant to challenge deeply ingrained business practices." [T]hree social processes—traditionalism, stereotyping, and ambivalence—contribute to this institutional inertia.

The *Harvard Law Review* study . . . succinctly summed up the dilemma facing women associates: "Women cannot reach true equality within firms as large numbers of women are considered atypical because they fail to conform to the male-based definition of the ideal worker." Despite this gloomy assessment, the *Harvard Law Review* study contended that the benefits to changing firm culture may be powerful enough to overcome inertia. The *Harvard Law Review* report argues that high hour demands have led to a "time famine" among lawyers and that this "lack of time" can adversely affect health by increasing stress and can inhibit professional development by reducing available time for community service, pro bono work, scholarship, and education.

POSTSCRIPT

Does the "Mommy Track" (Part-Time Work) Improve Women's Lives?

The irony of the mommy track–fast track debate is that it is based on the assumption that women have a choice regarding work. In fact, most women have no choice. Either they are single parents or part of a family that needs two pay-checks to meet the family's financial needs. Thus, for large numbers of working women, this is a meaningless debate. Choice is reserved for the educational elite, according to Mary Blair-Loy in *Competing Devotions*. Rather, the debate serves to perpetuate stereotypes regarding women's commitment to family over work. The reality is that most working women have little control over the hours they work. Indeed, for the lowest income jobs, working hours are not family-friendly hours. Consider the schedules of waitresses and housekeeping staff, for example.

It is worth noting that the family–career conflict that is receiving so much attention currently is in fact a rather current phenomenon. Claudia Goldin (2004) has suggested that this "conflict" has changed over time. For women graduating from college in the early 1900s the choice was clear: family or career. From 1920 to 1945, many women opted for a "job then family" model. From about 1946 to the 1960s, the pattern was reversed to "family then job." In the late 1960s, the language shifted from "job" to "career," with a pattern of "career then family" dominating through the 1980s. Since then the trend has been toward "career and family." Goldin contends that these shifts have been possible due largely to increased career opportunities for women, especially white collar jobs, with improved contraceptive methods also making it easier for women to control their fertility.

Some scholars have suggested that it is the issue of care-giving that needs to be rethought in our society. If society as a whole were committed to the well-being of children, then conceptualizations of child care might well rest on a foundation of shared community support, freeing up all parents to provide qual-ity care to their children. No longer would the parent who wants/needs to stay home with a sick child or attend preschool graduation be looked upon as less than the ideal worker. Only when there is a shift in perceptions of who is respon-sible for child care will even the subtle, but nevertheless powerful, effects of the assumption of women holding the primary responsibility for children subside.

Suggested Readings

Claudia Goldin, "The Power of the Pill: Oral Contraceptives and Women's Career and Marriage Decisions," *Journal of Political Economy* (August, 2002).

Janet C. Gornick and M. K. Meyers, *Families That Work: Policies for Reconciling Parenthood and Employment* (Russell Sage Foundation, 2003).

Kjell Erik Lommerud and S. Vagstad, *Mommy Tracks and Public Policy: On Self-Fulfilling Prophecies and Gender Gaps in Promotion* (Center for Economic Policy Research, 2000).

Mary Blair-Loy, *Competing Devotions: Career and Family among Women Executives* (Harvard University Press, 2003).

Jeanne Marecek, "Mad Housewives, Double Shifts, Mommy Tracks and Other Invented Realities," *Feminism and Psychology, 13* (2003).

Phyllis Moen (ed.), *It's about Time: Couples and Careers* (Cornell University Press, 2003).

ISSUE 15

Can Social Policies Improve Gender Inequalities in the Workplace?

YES: Hilda Kahne, from "Low-Wage Single-Mother Families in This Jobless Recovery: Can Improved Social Policies Help?" *Journal of Social Issues and Public Policy* (2004)

NO: Hadas Mandel and Moshe Semyonov, from "A Welfare State Paradox: State Interventions and Women's Employment Opportunities in 22 Countries," *American Journal of Sociology* (2006)

ISSUE SUMMARY

YES: Hilda Kahne, professor emerita at Wheaton College in Massachusetts, makes the argument that incomplete education and few training programs, rather than gender discrimination, makes it more difficult for low-wage single mothers to raise their earnings.

NO: In contrast, Hadas Mandel of the department of sociology and anthropology and Moshe Semyonov of the department of sociology and labor studies anthropology at Tel Aviv University review extensive data from 22 countries and conclude that social policies have the counterintuitive impact of decreasing women's opportunities for access to more desirable and powerful positions.

According to the U.S. Census Bureau, there are an estimated 9.8 million single mothers in the United States, a number that had tripled in the past 25 years and, as of 1998, there were an estimated 948,000 teen mothers age 15 to 19. About five-sixths of all single parents are women. Approximately 42 percent of single mothers have never married. From 1960 to 1980, the rate of divorce doubled, and although the rate has leveled off since, an increasing number of women find themselves in the role of single mother. Children, because they usually live with their mothers, are affected. Approximately two-thirds of divorces involve children and over one-half of children in the United States will experience parents' divorce. For these children, their standard of living declines 30 to 40 percent, and 25 percent of divorced mothers will fall into poverty within five years. Contributing to this poverty is the likelihood of not receiving child support even when entitled to it. Factors contributing to divorce, as well as single parenthood, for women include younger age of marriage, social attitudes more accepting of divorce, cohabitation and single-parenthood, as well as women's greater independence because of more opportunities in the workforce. At the same time, and perhaps ironically, the employment rates for single mothers has decreased from 73 percent in 2000 to 69.8 percent in 2003, and the steepest loss has been for black mothers.

Numerous debates surround these numbers. Issues being discussed include teen sexuality and unintended pregnancy as well as marriage initiatives. There is a strong belief among religious conservatives as well as economists that there is a relationship between marital stability, job stability, and earnings. One dimension of these debates relates to gender and whether welfare and work policies should be gender sensitive. There are stereotypes of welfare recipients, typically women, as lazy and irresponsible. However, stories of individual welfare recipients call welfare recipient stereotypes into question. In fact, it is common for poor women to combine welfare with work or to get welfare benefits between jobs. Many women use welfare to help them get more education—a critical factor in moving out of poverty. Many factors conspire against poor women: they can't find employment; they can't secure high enough pay, particularly if they have children in their care; they are financially penalized if married; and they have to endure public condemnation and discrimination.

Nevertheless, stereotypes of welfare mothers remain rigid and condemning. These stereotypes reflect three dominant perspectives or beliefs about the causes of poverty and wealth: (1) individualism contends that individuals are responsible for their own lot in life. Those who are motivated and work hard will make it. Those who do not make it (i.e., welfare recipients) have only themselves to blame; (2) social-structuralism asserts that due to economic or social imbalances (e.g., in education, marriage and family life, and even welfare programs themselves), opportunities are restricted for some people, overriding individual agency and affecting the likelihood of success; and (3) "culture of poverty," most often associated with African Americans who are thought to have developed a culture—some would say counterculture—of poverty with values, traits, and expectations that have developed from the structural constraints of living in poverty and that may be intergenerationally transmitted. Such logic demonstrates what social psychologists call the "fundamental attribution error," that is, the tendency to blame individuals for their outcomes while ignoring the situational context. A focus on social structural factors leads to a discussion of the effectiveness of social policies. Can social policies help lift womens from poverty? This is apparent in the selections that follow.

Kahne suggests that wage-related social policies should be developed to improve educational and training opportunities for low-wage single mothers, thereby increasing their earning potential. In contrast, Mandel and Semyonov argues that although policies have indeed increased women's entry into the job market, they have failed to give women increased access to higher paying, more attractive jobs. This would suggest that current policies may actually contribute to gender-related inequalities in the world of work.

YES ↩

Hilda Kahne

Low-Wage Single-Mother Families in This Jobless Recovery: Can Improved Social Policies Help?

This article focuses on the experience of low-wage single-mother families and how they are affected by the current soft economy and jobless recovery that continues to display many of the earmarks of a recession. It suggests that these effects, bringing uncertainty and stress and often temporary loss of income and asset value for many people, are worse for low-wage earners, including single-mother families. They face a difficult labor market and must compete with more-skilled unemployed workers for available jobs, while carrying considerable family responsibilities, often with limited education and no income reserves for coping with emergencies. In the short run they need financial support through an updating of existing social policies that take account of changing economic realities and life style requirements. But their more permanent need is to increase earning ability that can only be assured if training and education programs make possible an increase in their skills and job versatility. . . .

Changing Economic Context

Long Run

The long-run changing economic context provides a valuable backdrop for understanding the linkage between production and well-being of societal groups. In a recent study of productive and related institutions over time, Michael Piore describes the changing nature of four key institutions between the 1950s and today—the family, corporate enterprises, trade unions, and the government. During the earlier period the family was structurally stable and defined as including a male earner and female homemaker. Corporate enterprises were organized for mass production with a labor force having defined skills and tasks. A strong trade union movement negotiated terms of employment. And a federal government provided regulatory legislation and oversight as well as a safety net for persons needing social support. . . .

From *Analyses of Social Issues and Public Policy,* vol. 4, issue 1, 2004, pp. 47–48, 52–56, 58–65. Copyright © 2004 by Blackwell Publishing, Ltd. Reprinted by permission.

More Recent Trends

Given Piore's insightful observations about long-run changing societal trends, what can be said about the shorter-run influences on the well-being of poor single-mother families and the possibility of their achieving an adequate standard of living as a participant in the creation of society's goods and services? How will they be affected by current changing trends? At present, 50% of persons in poverty live in female-headed families and of all female-headed families, over 25% have incomes below the poverty level. Can their existence be made more economically secure through policies that move them further toward economic independence? . . .

Female family heads experienced unemployment rates higher than the overall average. By February 2003, their unemployment rate was 9% compared with a rate of 5.8% for all workers. The higher rate was partly due to the lesser stability of frequently held low-skill jobs that were often temporary or contingent or part time. It was also probably higher than for other groups because some skilled laid-off workers, at least until they found other work, took low-skill jobs, replacing traditional low-skill workers who were then shuffled to the back of the queue and lacked needed abilities to compete for other openings. It was especially high for single mothers who lacked a high school degree—18% in 2002. In addition to high rates, unemployment has shown a continuing increase in its length. Women's long-term unemployment rates now match those of men. . . .

The causes of the growth in income disparity are multiple and economists do not agree on the relative importance among them. Growing earnings inequality undoubtedly explains much of it with rewards given for high skills and educational levels. Bonuses and stock option benefits have also increased income, especially at the high managerial levels, as have relatively greater tax reductions for high-income groups. Some of the disparity has also been due to the effects of technological changes and of globalization. At the other end of the income stream, changes in family structures, erosion of the value of the minimum wage, and a decline in union bargaining strength have undoubtedly had negative effects on income distribution. Continued gender wage discrimination can intensify these effects. But, whatever the causes of growing inequality, the fact remains that in recent years the inequality in income distribution has increased despite the economic growth that has taken place in society as a whole. Although in the past all groups benefited from rising productivity in reduced unemployment and rising wages, this has not happened in recent years. The distribution of income has become more, rather than less, unequal.

Changing Family Structures and Economic Status

. . . The family, as we know, has been a true anchor of social life. But its form and the roles of its members have varied across cultures and nations and through historical time. . . . [I]n the United States, at least, it is "structure" that statistically defines a family unit. Government data on families reflect particular structural forms and have yet to take account of the features that highlight the cohesion that family units represent.

Family data for the United States is reported by the U.S. Census as part of household data. The Census defines a family as two or more people related by birth, marriage, or adoption who reside together. Female householders were 12% of all households and almost one-fifth of all families in 2001. About 60% of all single householders are single parents. The U.S. Bureau of Labor Statistics also reports on several categories of female singlehood such as single women (with or without children), single mothers with one or more children (own and/or step and/or adopted), and female householders (who may or may not have children). If a single mother with children is living in her mother's residence, she may be excluded from a single-family head accounting. Thus, discussions about categories of female family heads must be carefully defined and interpreted.

. . . No regular account is taken of blended families as a category, not infrequently composed of two or more clusters of stepchildren. Nonfamily households that have grown at twice the rate of family households, although not considered to be "families," often fulfill the role of a family unit. Sometimes single mothers and children live in a grandparent household; increasingly, the grandparents alone are the parent figures. But they are not included as a distinct family form in statistics. Widows are often subsumed under other categories such as "single mothers" or "elders." In fact, there are characteristics and issues that are unique to them.

Whereas in the 1950s, about 90% of all families were married couples, with a large majority of wives being homemakers, by 2001, only 76.3% of all families were married couples and over one-half of wives were in the paid labor force. By way of contrast, 10% of all families were female householders with no husband present in 1959; in 2001, they numbered 13.1 million or 17.7% of all families. . . .

For middle-class traditionally married parents, it is often difficult to understand the complexities required of a single parent who must meet not only work demands of inflexible work hours and required production schedules, but also the many immediate family demands that involve time and money and issues of child safety. . . .

But more than this, a high proportion of single-mother families experience low income and high rates of poverty because of limited education and/or job skills. Their treatment as low-paid workers is often further marked not only by wage disadvantage relative to men in comparable jobs, but also by more frequent lay-offs, involuntary part-time work, job severance, and lack of health and pension benefits and severance pay. Their situation can be further compromised by the absence of child support and accompanying stress and always the complexities involved in having to combine paid work with home responsibilities. Income reserves with which to meet emergencies are often absent. Single-mother parenting and poverty reflect a connection that is only somewhat mitigated in recent years by the rising labor force participation of single mothers. . . .

The rapid growth of single-mother families, and their association with high rates of poverty, has led to a number of research studies seeking to identify the causes for the strong growth trend in this family structure. . . .

One factor influencing the rapid growth of the group has been the weakening of the time linkage between marriage and having a child. This extension of time between the two events, found to be true for both white and black women who marry, is perhaps encouraged by the wish to participate in the labor market. But among less-educated black women who do not marry and who have fewer skills, marriage may be postponed but child bearing prior to marriage is not and is more likely than for white women, though both groups more commonly than in the past have children before or without marriage. Other factors may also play a role in the growth of single-mother families, though with varying intensity and direction at any one time. For example, a poor labor market experience of low-skill men (in wages or employment) as well as a low production of marriageable men relative to women can lead to marriage avoidance and an increase in the pool of single mothers. Divorce, greater sexual freedom, the availability of cohabitation as a prelude or alternative to marriage, and a lack of effective birth control availability and usage can also influence the result. Not all factors have the same intensity and direction at any one time—but the fact of their multiplicity and differing strength for specific population groups has made for complexity in explaining growth trends of low-wage single-mother families. What is clear is that single parenting, for low-skill women especially, has grown in size and results for them, as for other single-mother heads, in a complexity of life's functioning and often financial difficulty and poverty in achieving and retaining economic self-sufficiency for the family reliant on the earnings of one low-wage earner who must fulfill and reconcile both work and home demands.

Poverty: Consequences for Single-Mother Families

Changes in family structures, reinforced by the fact that economic growth in itself does not ensure a dispersal of its benefits to all members of society, have resulted in increasingly wide differences in family incomes. Poverty is often the consequence for single-mother families. . . .

[W]e can expect that with increasing income inequality, reduced job creation and prolonged unemployment for those who lose jobs, that family poverty will be a concern for some time to come, even if economic improvement begins for more skilled groups. The interaction of the growth of economically challenged family structures, combined with an uncertain economy with high unemployment, and the lack of adequate social supports including skill training, will continue to frustrate the efforts of poor families to regain an economic foothold in society.

Social Policy Directions

Existing Social Policies to Improve Incomes

A broad range of wage-related social policy measures need consideration and improvement in order to address effectively the downward sliding position and earnings inadequacy of many single-mother families. Each in some way compensates for inadequate wages and has merit. But none provides a means for permanently increasing the skill and productivity, and hence earnings, of the single-mother providers. This concluding section evaluates existing wage-related income-supportive measures and points the way to policies that can help to establish what is most important—an earned income economic independence for the family unit.

1. *Unemployment Insurance.* Unemployment insurance fulfills a distinctive need of helping to stabilize an economy in troubled times and to providing partial earnings replacement to maintain consumer spending for regular workers who experience involuntary temporary job loss. . . .

    Problems in coverage and eligibility for unemployment benefits arise not only because of changes in the law, but because of the changing nature of work and of labor force work patterns since the law's original enactment. Originally, unemployment was viewed as a temporary employment rupture due to cyclical and seasonal variation in employment patterns. But with changing technological and globalization effects causing major and long-term need for structural adjustments, unemployment can require permanent change in job location and work skills. At the same time, regular full-time uninterrupted work affiliation with an employer, by choice or necessity, is no loner the norm for many workers, especially women, who are more likely to work in service and retail industries where nonstandard work is more common.

    Indeed, women and increasing numbers of men, may need to choose such jobs (part-time, part-year, temporary, or other contingent work offering limited benefits, as best) in an effort to balance work and family responsibility. . . . [Thus, t]he unemployment insurance program is in need of review and revision to adapt to the realities of today's work structures and work patterns and to the needs of all groups in the labor force.

2. *Minimum Wage.* Low wage earners need more than the national economic growth and full employment to assure a satisfactory standard of living. Their well-being also requires that they receive adequate earnings to enable them to support their families. Historically, minimum wage legislation has provided an earnings floor. . . .

    Two criticisms, in addition to the low level of the national minimum wage, are directed at the effectiveness of minimum wage policy in fulfilling its purpose. One criticism points to the low-wage teen-age individuals in the group, not all of whom live in poor families. But teenagers constitute only about one-fourth of the minimum wage workers. Their earnings, like those of other family members, help to meet a variety of expenditures, including family needs and education. They are entitled to equal pay for the equal work they perform.

    The second criticism concerns the claim that, consistent with traditional economic theory, an increase in labor costs resulting from an increase in the minimum wage will negatively impact employment levels. Some studies have supported this result. But other recent scholarly research does not show this and, in fact, indicates that employment levels sometimes even increase as a consequence of worker increased motivation and satisfaction when the minimum wage is raised. . . .

3. *Earned Income Tax Credit (EITC).* Complementing the income support provided by the minimum wage is the Earned Income Tax Credit, a form of negative income tax credit applied to wages paid to low-income earners. Non-wage earners are not eligible for these benefits. . . . Single-mother families have especially benefited from the law's provisions. These benefits are viewed as being responsible for the large increase in their labor force participation in recent years.

Under the provisions of the federal law, a small credit is available to low-income single persons with no children and to childless couples. Substantially more, computed on a graduated scale, is payable to one-child families, and higher amounts to families with two or more children. . . .

The tax credit receives high praise from all political sectors. It is seen as providing a major stimulus for low-income single-mother heads of families and others to engage in paid work in order to qualify for an earned income benefit. And it provides a major boost to incomes of the 18.6 million low-wage family recipients. . . .

4. *Training and Education: A Missing Policy Link.* Each of these existing social supports has worthy goals and provides a measure of income support for the low earnings received by a worker or the absence of wages of a regular labor force participant temporarily and involuntarily unemployed. At present, the EITC is the strongest nation-wide measure in this category, giving tax credit and income rebate support specifically for low-earning family units. It provides a stimulus to potential earners in poor families to engage in paid work, with the result that poverty and the degree of family income inequality nationally can be somewhat lessened. It has been a major cause of the reduction of poverty for children and families.

Still, none of the national social policies, though supportive, has as a goal an increase in wages to a level adequate for family self-sufficiency. It is this that should be the long-run goal of social policy. This is what is needed to complement the income policies that buttress and supplement existing low wages.

Low wages and the increasing disparity in wages between low and high earners are thought by many economists to be linked in a major way to the relatively greater demand for more highly skilled and technically proficient workers. This demand is expected to continue to grow in the future as globalization and the use of technology intensify. Although wage supportive policies can buttress income for low earners, it is education and training that raise worker productivity and enable a move to more skilled jobs at higher wages. An added benefit of such a policy would be reducing the inequality in the distribution of income that now exists. . . .

Training and education programs are neither inexpensive nor easy to implement. Well-conceived programs must not only respond to employer and community skill needs but must take place for a period of time long enough to develop well-honed workplace talents. But all of society would benefit from the increased productivity that results from such programs. And the ameliorative social support that now buttresses low earnings would have as its complement a social policy that would both reduce national disparities in family incomes and, at the same time, make possible a permanent rise in the family standard of living for previously low-income families. That would be a welcome achievement for low-wage single mothers who have shown in earlier training programs an ability to respond well relative to other groups to training opportunities that have been offered them. It is time to develop constructive legislation to provide this meaningful steppingstone for single mother earners and other low-income groups to higher skills and more adequate family income.

Hadas Mandel and
Moshe Semyonov

➡ **NO**

A Welfare State Paradox: State Interventions and Women's Employment Opportunities in 22 Countries

In recent decades, an increasing number of researchers have begun studying the role played by the state in affecting women's economic activities and labor market positions. The growing research on this topic points to the role of the state as legislator and implementer of social and family services, as well as to the role of the welfare state as an employer. These two bodies of literature operate under the premise that the welfare state, whether as a legislator or as an employer, strongly affects women's participation rates and economic opportunities. More specifically, researchers have suggested that progressive social policies and a large public service sector are likely to provide women with better opportunities to join the economically active labor force, and, indeed, to increase women's economic activities.

Whereas the impact of the welfare state on women's labor force participation is widely studied, little research has further investigated the ways that state interventions affect women's occupational opportunities. To address this lacuna, we seek in this article to examine systematically the impact of the welfare state on women's integration into the labor market, their working time, and their opportunities to attain powerful and elite occupational positions. We argue that the state, in its roles as a legislator and implementer of family policies, and in its role as an employer, creates sheltered labor markets for women—labor markets in which women's rights are protected and secured. By so doing the welfare state contributes to increased women's labor force participation, enhances the economic independence of women and mothers, and strengthens their power within the household and in society at large. However, these state actions do not enhance women's occupational and economic achievements, since none of them seriously challenge the traditional distribution of market-family responsibilities between men and women. On the contrary, adjusting the demands of employment to women's home duties or allowing working mothers reduced working hours and long leaves from work are likely to preserve women's dominant roles as mothers and wives. As such, these interventions impede women's abilities to compete successfully with men for powerful and lucrative occupational positions.

In what follows we first develop the theoretical rationale in which our arguments are embodied. Next, we test our theoretical expectations with data for 22 industrialized countries, and, finally, we discuss the findings in light of sociological theories on welfare-state policies and gender inequality. By doing so, we will be in a position to better understand the ways through which the welfare state affects the economic participation and occupational attainment of women.

Theoretical Considerations

The Welfare State and Women's Labor Force Participation

The massive entrance of women into the labor markets of Western societies in recent decades has been affected not only by market forces but also by state interventions. The impact of the state on women's employment opportunities is multidimensional and can be attributed to a series of factors, especially to the roles of the state as a legislator, as a provider of social services, and as an employer. The extensive literature on the topic is generally divided into two separate bodies of research, one that focuses on the role of the state as an implementer of family services, and one that focuses on the role of the welfare state as an employer.

In this study we combine the two bodies of research in order to better capture the effects of state interventions on women's employment opportunities. Specifically, we focus on the role of the state as a legislator and as an activator of programs aimed to decrease the conflict between family responsibilities and work, in addition to its role as an employer. For the sake of simplicity we will use the term "welfare state" to refer to all three roles.

In its role as a legislator and family service provider, the state implements and activates a variety of support systems and provides services and benefits targeted mostly at families with children. These programs and benefits, often referred to in the literature as "family policies," reflect both the state's responsibility for the care of young children and its effort to facilitate employment for mothers, by providing women with the necessary conditions to combine work with family responsibilities.

Comparative studies that focus on the relations between family policies and women's labor force participation find a positive correlation between the two. For example, in the Scandinavian countries, which represent the social democratic welfare regime, women's high levels of employment are supported by generous family policies in the form of universal benefits to working mothers. These characteristics stand in contrast to the other welfare regimes (i.e., liberal or market economies and the conservative welfare regime), in which family policies are less developed and women's labor force participation rates are usually lower. The reduced role of the state as a family service provider in the latter regimes leaves a greater role either to the family itself or to the private market.

Variation in the scope of family policies is evident across countries, as well as across welfare regimes. While ranking countries on continuous scales of family policies, Gornick and her associates found a positive and strong association between family policy indices and mothers' rates of labor force participation, reaffirming the argument that such state interventions are likely to facilitate women's, especially mothers', economic activity.

A different body of research links women's economic activities to the role of the welfare state as an employer. Specifically, the rise of the welfare state has led to a substantial expansion of public employment, especially in health, education, and social services. As a provider of public services—a sector overwhelmingly dominated by women—the state has become a major employer of women. By offering a large supply of care and service jobs (which are traditionally designed for women and which partly replace their care duties at home) along with convenient working conditions, the public service sector facilitates women's entry into the labor force by reducing their domestic responsibilities on the one hand, and by supplying them with new job opportunities on the other hand.

The Welfare State and Gender Occupational Inequality

Whereas researchers agree that both the development of family policies and the extension of public services enhance women's opportunities to become economically active, we know very little about the implications of the welfare state for women's occupational opportunities. In what follows we argue that state activities, while facilitating women's entrance into the labor market, do not facilitate their entry into high-authority and elite positions. Rather, the very same characteristics—generous family policies and a large public service sector—seem to reproduce the gendered division of labor and, in effect, decrease women's chances of joining desirable occupational positions. Put differently, state efforts to facilitate and protect women's work may result in lowering and hardening what is usually referred to in the sociological literature as "the glass ceiling."

State-provided benefits can affect women's occupational opportunities and influence their working patterns in a variety of ways. Paid maternity leaves, for example, although often viewed as paving the way for mothers back to the labor market, and thus strengthening women's ties to the labor market, actually remove mothers from paid employment for several months. In countries where family policies are particularly generous (e.g., Finland and Sweden) paid maternity leave can last for an entire year, and in many other places (e.g., Austria, Belgium, France, Germany, Hungary, Italy, Denmark, and Norway) paid maternity leave can be extended with reduced compensation for up to two years and even longer. Although paid maternity leave serves as a device through which women's employment rights are protected and secured, a long absence from paid employment may discourage employers from hiring women to positions of authority and power and thus handicap their ability to compete successfully with men for elite positions.

Likewise, institutional work arrangements, such as regulations mandating reduced working hours, can further depreciate women's economic outcomes.

Part-time employment, for example, is a common arrangement that enables women to combine paid employment with unpaid work. Consequently, part-time work has become one of the major forms of employment for women in most industrial societies, where about one-third of all employed women work on a part-time basis.

Although part-time employment is not a direct product of states' policies, it is reinforced by regulation and protected by the welfare state. This is, indeed, the case in many Scandinavian states. In these countries (with Finland as a notable exception), part-time employment has become a common practice for many mothers. Yet, unlike other countries where part-time employment serves as an institutional mechanism through which mothers are incorporated into paid work (e.g., the Netherlands, the United Kingdom, Germany, Belgium, and Australia), in Scandinavia part-time employees are entitled to full social benefits, paid vacation, and job security. The allocation of full benefits to part-time workers reflects the state's efforts to encourage and support women's economic activities, whether on a full-time or a part-time basis.

Part-time employment is not the only mechanism through which women's working hours are curtailed. In several European countries (e.g., Sweden, Denmark, France) working hours have been reduced through regulations that set the standard below the conventional 40 weekly hours. Although reduced working hours can contribute to decreasing the conflict between work and family responsibilities for both parents, women are more likely than men to utilize this option.

Occupational discrimination.—The tendency of women to adopt reduced working hour arrangements and their tendency to take parental leave are likely to restrict their opportunities for occupational mobility, as they foster employers' reluctance to hire women and to promote them to positions that require costly investment in firm-specific knowledge, as required in most powerful and elite positions. [Research] highlight[s] the importance of "on-the-job training" for occupational mobility, and its consequences for gender occupational and wage inequality. [This work] suggests that the limited access of women to firm-specific training is one of the most significant causes of their low occupational achievements compared to men.

One major explanation for the limited access of women to positions that require costly qualification and training periods can be cast within the framework of the "statistical discrimination model." According to this theoretical model employers have limited access to information on their candidates' characteristics and future productivity. Therefore when searching for workers to fill jobs that require high training costs, employers are likely to discriminate against employees belonging to groups with statistically lower average levels of expected productivity.

In this article we contend that in well-developed welfare states where women's eligibility for social rights supports their absence from work, the exclusion of women from jobs which require costly firm-specific investment will be more acute. In labor markets where women as a group are more protected by regulations and legislation, and where they enjoy social rights that interfere with their work continuity, employers are expected to prefer male workers for positions that require investment in firm-specific human capital. "If women have social rights that do not apply to men, or are seldom used by men, and the practice of these rights is unprofitable for employers, employers may choose to discriminate against female job applicants," as indeed has been demonstrated in many studies of gender inequalities in the Scandinavian labor markets.

The restricted ability of qualified women to enter high-paying jobs, and their limited promotion opportunities in positions of power and authority, can be viewed as part of the glass ceiling phenomenon—"the unseen, yet unbeatable barrier that keeps minorities and women from rising to the upper rungs of the corporate ladder, regardless of their qualifications or achievements." Following other studies that have dealt with the glass ceiling in this study we empirically define "powerful" or "high-level" positions as management positions. We argue that the invisible barriers of the "glass ceiling"—the barriers that prevent women from moving into positions of high authority and high earnings in organizations—are expected to be greater in well-developed welfare states where women are more protected by legislation that supports their absenteeism from the labor force and allows them reduced working hours.

The state as an employer.—The role of the welfare state as an employer completes our argument. With the expansion of public social services, many services have been transferred from the private sphere to the state domain. This process has a twofold effect on employment opportunities for women; first, it enables mothers to allocate more time to paid work, and second, it provides women with new job opportunities. Moreover, the public-welfare sector offers white-collar and service jobs, many of which are "female-typed" service and semiprofessional occupations. It also offers flexible employment hours and programs that tolerate paid absenteeism. As such, the public service sector has become one of the most preferred segments of employment for women. The nature of jobs in the public service sector, coupled with favorable and convenient work conditions, appears to channel women in disproportionate numbers into feminine occupational niches and away from lucrative and powerful positions. Hence, the expansion of the public service sector is likely to increase gender occupational segregation.

Several studies have demonstrated that the overrepresentation of women in the exceptionally large Swedish and Danish public sectors contributes to the lessening of their economic gains. Feminist scholars have also pointed out that the rise of the welfare state, accompanied by a massive entrance of women into the labor force, did not alter the traditional division of labor between men and women. Rather, it actually transferred the gendered division of labor from the private sphere into the public domain. In this process traditional gender roles are perpetuated; women are disproportionately channeled to public services and care roles, while men get hold of more desirable jobs. Hernes referred to this process in terms of "the family 'going public'" where "women have become clients and employees of a highly developed welfare state with a large public service sector."

In fact, a high concentration of women in the protected public sector and the practice of statistical discrimination by employers are not mutually exclusive but rather interdependent. Women's job preferences are influenced by both employers' behavior and labor market opportunities. In labor markets where employers are reluctant to hire women to powerful and high positions, it is less likely that women would be motivated to compete with men for such positions. On the other hand, a large public service sector, which offers job protection and convenient working conditions, is likely to attract women. Although we cannot distinguish between employees' and employers' preferences, these two mechanisms are interrelated; their negative impact on women's occupational attainments are expected to be more pronounced in countries with a highly developed welfare state.

To sum up our arguments: we contend that the massive entrance of women into the labor force of well-developed welfare states has not been accompanied by their equivalent entrance into powerful and desirable positions. On the contrary, in highly developed welfare states the "glass ceiling" has become lower and wider. Social rights attached to women's employment in advanced welfare states are likely to increase employers' tendency to discriminate against women in recruitment to powerful and elite positions in the private sector. Likewise, in a large "protected" public sector women are likely to be relegated mostly to female-typed service jobs. Although under these conditions the concentration of women in feminine niches can be seen as a rational choice, we tend not to view it as a purely free choice, mainly because job preferences are shaped by labor market opportunities, which cannot be separated from employers' discrimination.

Although some of these arguments have been advanced in the feminist literature for quite some time, they have not been systematically tested with cross-national comparative data. Thus, in the analysis that follows we provide a cross-national empirical examination of the hypotheses that developed welfare states—measured quantitatively by their family policies and size of the public service sector—are characterized by high rates of labor force participation among women, while at the same time they also exhibit a high concentration of women in female-typed occupations and low access for women to positions of power, authority, and high economic rewards.

Data Sources, Variables, and Measures

Our data set has information on both individual-level and country-level characteristics. The individual-level variables were obtained from the Luxembourg Income Study (LIS), which serves as an archive for comparable microdata sets for a large number of industrialized countries. The analysis reported here was restricted to the 22 countries that provided detailed information on demographic and labor market attributes of men and women, ages 25–60, during the middle to the end of the 1990s. Information on welfare state characteristics was obtained from a variety of secondary sources. . . .

The individual-level variables included in the analysis are those traditionally employed in models predicting economic activity: gender, marital status, education, age, number of children, and the presence of preschool children. . . .

The dependent variables used in the analysis include two indicators of women's rate of labor force participation, an indicator for the amount of participation (i.e., part-time work vs. full-time employment), and three indicators of gender occupational inequality. The two indicators of participation are rate of labor force participation among women ages 25–60 and rate of participation among mothers of preschool children, respectively. [A] distinction between four categories of employment: full-time employment (more than 39 weekly hours), reduced-hours employment (30–39 weekly hours), half-time employment (15–29 weekly hours), and marginal employment (under 15 weekly hours). Gender occupational inequality was measured by the net odds (women relative to men) to be employed in an occupational category, according to three variables. The first variable captures women's access to powerful and elite positions by the net odds of women (relative to men) to attaining "managerial occupations." Since definitions of managers can vary across countries, and in order to capture confidently elite and top positions, an alternative is to estimate women's access to "lucrative-managerial occupations." While managerial occupations were defined according to the standard classification of occupations for each country, lucrative-managerial occupations were restricted to those that ranked in the top three deciles of the occupational earnings distribution. The third variable captures women's occupational segregation. We measured the net odds of women (relative to men) of being employed in "female-typed occupations." Female-typed occupations were defined according to two combined criteria: the relative proportion of women in an occupational category at the two-digit occupational classification level and a statistical significance test.

The key independent variable utilized in the analysis is an index that reflects the overall protection that the welfare state provides to working mothers. It is designed to capture state interventions that affect the employment of women via both family policies and state employment. . . .

The three indicators were combined to construct the index: the number of fully paid weeks of maternity leave (number of paid weeks multiplied by the percentage of wage replacement during the leave), the percentage of preschool children in publicly funded day-care facilities, and the percentage of the workforce employed in the public welfare sector (public health, education, and welfare). Each of the three components captures somewhat different aspects of the state's activities. Maternity leave policy indicates the benefits that the state offers to working mothers, while publicly funded child-care facilities and the size of the public service sector capture the prevalence of social services provided by the state and the demand for female labor. We believe that when combined into an index the three components represent a broad phenomenon that transcends the unique effect of each component. . . .

Integrative Analysis

An important limitation of previous comparative research in this area is that the multiple dimensions of women's labor market integration are usually studied in isolation from one another. Our comprehensive approach reveals that no country or group of countries approximates unambiguous gender equality.

As anticipated, the social-democratic model of women's integration into the labor market is accompanied by their crowding in female-dominated occupations and their relative exclusion from managerial occupations. On the other hand, the liberal model is less effective in mobilizing women into employment but is more open to their entry into elite positions. Finally, the conservative model typically disadvantages women in both respects.

To underline the cross-national diversity of the opportunity structures that women face, we conducted a factor analysis procedure using all dependent variables utilized in the analysis (labor force participation, working hours, managerial occupations, lucrative-managerial occupations, and female-typed occupations). Two significant factors, representing two unrelated configurations of gendered employment patterns, emerged from the analysis. The first factor, which we dub "participation/segregation," loads strongly on female participation rates, concentration of women in female-typed occupations, and on reduced working hours rather than full-time employment. In our data set Sweden and Finland have the highest scores on this factor while the former socialist countries, Switzerland, and Luxembourg generate the lowest scores. The second factor captures "equality of opportunity"; it singles out gender equality in access to managerial jobs and also a tendency toward full-time employment among working women. In this respect, the North American countries stand at the top of the scale while the Netherlands and Norway are placed at the bottom.

The thesis advanced in this paper suggests that the two labor market profiles (captured by the two factors) should be closely related to the scope and character of the welfare state. In line with our expectations, the correlation between the [Welfare State Intervention Index] (WSII) and the "participation/ segregation" factor is positive ($r = .555$) while the correlation between the WSII and the "equality of opportunity" factor is negative ($r = -.524$). Furthermore, when clustering the countries using the two sets of factor scores, we find that most of them fall into one of three distinctive configurations whose membership [reflects] welfare regimes. Of the 16 countries available for the factor analysis, three with the lowest WSII scores (United States, Canada, and Switzerland) form a liberal cluster characterized by exceptionally high rates of entrance into managerial positions ("equality of opportunity" factor). The Scandinavian countries, representing the social-democratic regime, with the highest scores on the WSII, also have exceptionally high scores on the "participation/segregation" factor and below-average scores for "equality of opportunity." Finally, most of the Continental states and Ireland (representing the conservative welfare state regime) cluster with intermediate levels of WSII and below-average scores on both factors.

Conclusions

The objective of the present research has been to provide a systematic examination of the impact of welfare state activities on the labor force participation of women and on gender occupational inequality. Utilizing data from 22 industrialized countries we found the impact of welfare states on women's employment opportunities to be complex and to vary from one aspect of economic activity to another (i.e., labor force participation and occupational inequality). This impact, therefore, can be properly understood and delineated only when the interrelations among the multiple aspects of women's economic activity are simultaneously considered.

Consistent with theoretical expectations and with previous studies, the data show that women's rate of labor force participation tends to be higher in countries with progressive welfare states. Apparently, expansion of family-oriented services, availability of public child-care facilities, and a large public service sector provide women with better opportunities to become economically active. By increasing the incorporation of women into the paid economy, the welfare state has significantly contributed to increasing women's economic independence, and, by implication, to strengthening their power within the household and the society at large.

However, once women have become economically active, benefits to working mothers and high demand for female labor in the public services serve to restrict their occupational achievements. Our data show that in countries characterized by a progressive welfare system women are disproportionately underrepresented in managerial positions and overrepresented in female-typed jobs. We contend that family-friendly policies and employment practices assume the primacy of women's familial responsibilities. As such they are designed to allow women time off for the care of young children through extended maternity leaves and support of part-time employment. These policies, in turn, discourage employers from hiring women for managerial and powerful positions and foster women's attachment to female-typed occupations and jobs with convenient work conditions. Although we cannot empirically separate employer discrimination from women's employment preferences, we have suggested that the two are interrelated and jointly have detrimental consequences for women's occupational achievements.

Paradoxically, therefore, the same welfare state activities that promote one dimension of gender equality appear to inhibit another dimension. This trade-off can best be understood in relation to specific welfare regimes. The social-democratic regime promotes women's integration into the labor market by providing them with convenient and flexible working conditions. However, this goal is achieved at the cost of greater occupational segregation and restricted opportunities for women to enter the most desirable positions. By contrast, the market-oriented liberal regime neither restricts nor supports women's economic activities, and no special work arrangements are mandated for mothers. In the liberal market economies women, like men, are expected to work continuously and on a full-time basis. These conditions may not meet the justified desire of many women for family-supportive working arrangements, and may discourage mothers from joining the labor force. At the same time, women who become economically active are in a better position to compete for high-status managerial jobs than are their counterparts in social-democratic countries.

POSTSCRIPT

Can Social Policies Improve Gender Inequalities in the Workplace?

A related controversy surrounds the incidence of conception and child-birth while the mother is a welfare recipient (i.e., "subsequent births"). Traditionally, welfare policies grant monetary benefits to families based on the number of children. Thus, the birth of another child would earn the family increased financial support. Critics charge these women with intentionally having additional children to increase their financial benefit and view them as irresponsible and promiscuous (though, on average, welfare recipients have fewer children than individuals not on welfare). Critics fear that subsequent births will promote long-term dependency on federal aid. The 1996 federal welfare reform law allows states discretion to adopt strategies for inhibiting subsequent births.

States have adopted a variety of programs that operationalize supposed solutions to the subsequent birth problem. Efforts include family caps on welfare benefits, enhanced family-planning services, directive counseling (telling mothers they should not have another baby and instructing them in how to prevent pregnancy), and financial incentives for young mothers who do not become pregnant. Additional incentives and programs aimed at keeping women from having additional children and keeping young women from having sex include the "Illegitimacy Bonus," which rewards states that reduce their out-of-wedlock birthrate while also reducing abortion rates for all women, not just those on welfare; the "Abstinence-Only Standard," which offers financial incentives to states that teach abstinence as the expected or only standard; requiring unmarried mothers under the age of 18 to live with their parents; and enforcing child support by performing paternity tests to identify biological fathers and forcing women to turn in fathers of their children or lose benefits, regardless of the risk of physical or emotional harm to the woman or her children.

Most controversial are family cap provisions, which preclude a welfare recipient from receiving additional case benefits for a child conceived while the recipient parent was on welfare (albeit the child would be eligible for Medicaid coverage and other benefits). The desired outcome of family cap provisions would be fewer out-of-wedlock births.

Supporters of family caps believe that the traditional rule that welfare benefits are determined on the basis of the number of children in a family actually provides a financial incentive to have children while on welfare. Therefore, family caps are implemented to send a message to these women that they should not have more children until they can support them.

Opponents of family caps consider them to be in violation of a mother's right to determine whether or when to have children. Others fear that family caps will increase welfare families' hardship and increase abortion rates. Interestingly, some evaluation studies of such programs also look for higher abortion rates as an outcome signifying program success. In fact, program evaluation research to date has been underwhelming, resulting frequently in inconclusive or disappointing results.

Another criticism is that efforts at the "rational econometric control" of reproduction are ignorant of the complexities involved in becoming pregnant. Typically, two individuals are involved in a social interaction that is not always volitional and often includes an array of pressures. To what degree can reproduction be controlled by incentive pressures? It is also noteworthy that males' role in fertility is largely ignored in programs aimed at reducing subsequent births.

Welfare legislation and statistics raise serious questions about gender dynamics and differentials. Why are most welfare recipients women? How is the societal construction of "mother" and "father" related to welfare statistics and policies? How is socioeconomic class associated with women's reproductive rights and freedoms? How do existing gender inequalities contribute to single mothers' low-income status? How does racism amplify the problems for women of color?

Selected Readings

Children's Defense Fund, "Families Struggling to Make It in the Workforce: A Post Welfare Report" (December 2000).

Diane F. Halpern and S. E. Murphy, eds., *From Work-Family Balance to Work-Family Interaction: Changing the Metaphor* (Mahwah, NJ: Lawrence Erlbaum Associates, Inc. Publishers, 2005).

Diane F. Halpern, "How Time-Flexible Work Policies Can Reduce Stress, Improve Health, and Save Money," *Stress and Health, 21* (2005).

K. Edin, L. Lein, T. Nelson, and S. Clampet-Lundquist, "Talking with Low-Income Fathers," *Poverty Research News, 4* (2000).

M. C. Lennon, J. Blome, and K. English, "Depression and Low-Income Women: Challenges for TANF and Welfare-to-Work Policies and Programs," *Research Forum on Children, Families and the New Federalism, National Center for Children in Poverty* (Columbia University, 2001).

Martha Fetherolf Loutfi, ed., *Women, Gender and Work: What Is Equality and How Do We Get There?* (New Delhi: Rawat Publications, 2002).

Gary N. Powell, ed., *Handbook of Gender and Work* (Thousand Oaks, CA: Sage, 1999).

ISSUE 16

Is the Gender Wage Gap Justified?

YES: John Shackleton, from "Explaining the Overall Pay Gap" in *Should We Mind the Gap? Gender Pay Differentials and Public Policy*, London, England: The Institute of Economic Affairs (2008)

NO: Hilary M. Lips, from "The Gender Wage Gap: Debunking the Rationalizations AND Blaming Women's Choices for the Gender Pay Gap." From *Expert Advice for Working Women.* www.womensmedia.com.

ISSUE SUMMARY

YES: John Shackleton, a professor of economics and Dean of the Business School, University of East London, suggests that the gender gap is largely due to nondiscriminatory factors; most notable are those associated with compensation for the differential value of associated with women's choices due to lifestyle, preferences, attitudes, and expectations.

NO: Hilary Lips, a professor of psychology and the director of the Center for Gender Studies at Radford University, documents the continuing gender gap in wages and argues that a continuing undervaluing of women's work, whatever it happens to be, due to stereotypes and prejudice maintains the wage gap. She argues that the language of "choice" is deceptive.

"**E**qual pay for equal work," "Equal pay for comparable work": These two phrases have been hallmarks of the women's movement's list of rights to which women are entitled. And there are several federal laws, enforced by the U.S. Equal Employment Opportunity Commission (EEOC), that are supposed to protect women from discrimination in their compensation. The Equal Pay Act states, "Employers may not pay unequal wages to men and women who perform jobs that require substantially equal skill, effort and responsibility, and that are performed under similar working conditions within the same establishment," but the act does allow for differences in pay under certain conditions: "Pay differentials are permitted when they are based on seniority, merit, quantity or quality of production, or a factor other than sex." These are known as "affirmative defenses" and it is the employer's burden to prove that they apply. Questions arise from these declarations. What constitutes "substantially equal"? By what criteria are judgments of "merit, quantity and quality of pro-duction or a factor other than sex" made? Classic studies in social psychology have shown repeatedly that the same work, whether it is an essay, a painting, or a resume, when attributed to a man receives a more favorable evaluation than when attributed to a woman. Decisions are made on a daily basis regarding who gets hired, who gets a pay raise, and who gets a promotion. To what extent do women's personality, interests, and choices affect these decisions and to what extent do sexism and discrimination affect these decisions? Is the world of work so constructed that its practices and policies result in discrimination against women? These practices might include policies that require out-of-town travel to get a promotion and for the single mother in particular to have adequate child care. Or these practices might include tolerance for sexual harassment that forces a woman to quit her job or suffer in silence because she cannot afford to lose her job. Or perhaps there are policies that are intolerant of a single mother missing work because she has a sick child. So, under such institutional barriers to success women may be forced to forego certain careers and occupations, "choosing" those more compatible with the gender roles society expects them to fulfill. Or, alternatively, perhaps it is the way women are constituted that makes the difference. Are women by nature less ambitious, less competitive, less assertive, and as a consequence less effective leaders? If so, they may freely choose careers, and occupations that are more suited to their nature, careers, and occupations that just happen to pay less.

In the following selections John Shackleton argues that women make employment choices that ultimately determine their wages. He suggests that the division of labor in the home plays a large role in the choices women make and that discriminatory factors are negligible. Hilary Lips could not disagree more. Lips argues that the continued undervaluing of women's work and prejudice against women in the workplace result in a continuing unjustifiable gender wage gap.

YES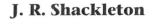

J. R. Shackleton

Should We Mind the Gap?
Gender Pay Differentials and
Public Policy

In this chapter various possible explanations for the differences in male and female earnings are examined.

We should begin by asking what determines pay, in general terms, in a competitive market. In such a market we would not expect everybody to earn the same. In the short run, wages are determined simply by supply and demand. If there is a sudden increase in the demand for construction workers because a new underground line is being built, and a limited supply of those with the necessary skills, wages will rise. But in the longer term, more workers will be attracted into construction, perhaps from abroad, or workers in other occupations will retrain. Longer term, it is possible that big pay differentials can persist if people possess unique skills or talents in high demand. . . .

Compensating Differentials

Even where people are free to enter a well-paid field of employment, however, they may not choose to do so. Long ago Adam Smith, in his *Wealth of Nations*, spelled out several reasons why some workers consistently earn more than others. His reasoning forms the basis for the modern idea of "compensating differentials"—where jobs that are unattractive may have to be rewarded with higher pay if they are to attract sufficient workers.

One factor is what Smith called "the difficulty and expense" of learning a job. Some forms of employment require years of training, education, and work experience—generically classed as human capital. The acquisition of human capital typically involves some cost to the trainee in terms of time and forgone earnings, even if the direct costs are paid by the state or the employer, and the worker will expect to be compensated by higher pay. This is clearly relevant to discussion of the gender pay gap, because women are likely to differ from men in relation to their human capital.

Note, however, that the amount of extra pay required will vary, Smith argues, with the "agreeableness or disagreeableness" of the job. Apparently an academic job in a high-ranking research department at Oxford carries sufficient kudos to offset the higher salary obtainable in other universities. By contrast, a cook on a North Sea oil rig, for example, will normally be paid more than a similarly skilled cook working in a city. But whether a premium is paid, and its size, will depend on the tastes and preferences of individuals. If, over time, Oxford becomes overcrowded and less attractive as a city, the university will have to pay more to attract the best academics. If lots of cooks develop a taste for working at sea, their premium will diminish or disappear. This is pertinent to discussion of the pay gap, for women's preferences in relation to jobs may differ systematically from those of men, as we shall see.

It is rarely discussed in the debate over the pay gap, but part of the explanation for men's higher average pay could well be that there is a compensating differential for less attractive working conditions. Men are more likely to work outside in all weathers. They are more likely to work unsocial hours. Thirty-six percent of male managers work more than 48 hours a week; the figure for women managers is only 18 percent. Men suffer much higher rates of industrial injury.

Looking at the economy as a whole, we see that women's jobs are less at risk: in the three months from November 2007 to January 2008, there were 3.4 redundancies per thousand female employees; the figure for men was 5.3. Women are more likely to get employer-provided training: 13.6 percent of females had received job-related training in the last four weeks in the third quarter of 2007, as against 11.3 percent of males. They have a shorter commuting time to work and take more time off work. No wonder, perhaps, that they report greater job satisfaction than men.

The implication of this is that the "true" gender pay gap may be less than the measured one, as male pay may include an element of compensation for less attractive working conditions. This is ignored in many empirical studies, and it is a serious omission.

Discrimination

Discrimination is often seen as an important explanation of the gender pay gap. The concept needs some clarification before we assess this belief.

Discrimination is a word that has changed its common meaning. Whereas once it was seen as something worthy of praise—as in somebody displaying "a fine discrimination" between paintings or pieces of music—it now usually means something unfair, unacceptable, and, in an increasing number of cases, illegal.

Economic analysis of the subject effectively began with the work of Gary Becker in the 1950s. In Becker's analysis, employers, fellow employees, and governments may engage in discrimination, which he interprets as an economically unjustified preference for one group over another, such that members of the favoured group would be more likely to be given a job, to be paid more, or otherwise treated better than another group or groups. Becker's particular insight was that this preference, this "taste for discrimination," could be seen as an end in itself, something that therefore entailed a "cost" to the discriminator. For example, employers might prefer to hire male rather than female workers even if this were more expensive. In this respect Becker differed fundamentally from Marxists and other critics of capitalism who saw discrimination as a means of exploiting subordinate groups to the benefit of the discriminator.

If this taste for discrimination exists, it *may* be manifested in the existence of a pay gap. This is not necessarily the case, however. If rigorous laws prevent women being paid less than men, discriminating firms may simply hire fewer women, but they will be paid the same as men. So Becker's analysis supports the point made earlier in relation to Italy and Spain: the size of the pay gap in itself does not say very much about the extent of discrimination.

From Becker's analysis, originally applied to racial differences, it followed that discriminating firms would hire white workers, or pay them a higher wage, rather than black workers of identical or superior productivity characteristics. But, he reasoned, this behaviour would raise costs. If other employers who were "colour-blind" entered the market, they would be able to undercut the discriminators and gain a competitive edge.

From this, Becker argued that, in a competitive market where non-discriminators were free to enter, discrimination would be unlikely to persist for long. It could be found where firms had monopsony power;[1] it could also be found where trade unions exercised power to protect white workers against blacks, or, in our context, men against women. But Becker, as a Chicago economist, argued that market power to sustain discrimination is unlikely to persist for any extended period if free entry of firms is allowed and union power is limited. Therefore any sustained discriminatory power is to be attributed to government interference in the free market. Apartheid South Africa is an obvious example. And in the USA, the so-called "Jim Crow" laws in the South sustained labour market discrimination for many years: when they were abolished there was a big increase in the relative pay of black workers—the reduction in the white/black pay gap since then has been relatively modest.

In our current context, it should be remembered that government discrimination against women was often quite explicit in the UK until the mid-twentieth century, with different pay rates for men and women civil servants and teachers, requirements to resign on marriage, and prohibitions on working at all in certain jobs.

A quite different approach to the economics of discrimination was taken by Arrow and Phelps. In their view, employer discrimination was not the result of "tastes" or simple prejudice. Rather, it was a rational response to imperfect knowledge about the characteristics of individual job applicants. This led risk-averse employers to operate with stereotypes, which might be accurate or inaccurate, of common group characteristics. Suppose—and this is true, whatever its cause—that women on average take more time off work than men for sickness, employers might hold this against a female job applicant even if, unknown to the employer, she as an individual had a low sickness risk. Such "statistical discrimination" would be economically rational even if unfair to individuals in particular cases.

As in Becker's reasoning, however, free competition ought to reduce discrimination. Some firms might find it easier than others to acquire more information about individuals, or would be prepared to take a chance on them, because they faced different cost and demand conditions. Not all firms, therefore, will behave in the same way. Furthermore, individuals are not passive. They can signal more information about themselves and market themselves more effectively to potential employers. One way they could in principle do this is to offer to work for less pay during a trial period. In most developed countries, however, such trial arrangements are difficult if not impossible because of legislation on equal pay, minimum wages, and employment protection. Again, governments may be part of the problem.

Some support is given to the common Becker and Arrow/Phelps thesis that free competition tends to eliminate discrimination, while some forms of government intervention assist it, countries with greater economic competition, as measured by the Economic Freedom Index, display lower gender pay gaps. The OECD has recently reached similar conclusions, with the added insight that product market regulation may be an important factor, by protecting disproportionately male "insiders" from new entrants. It finds that "regulatory barriers to competition explain between 20% and 40% of the cross country/time series variation in the gender wage gap."

As overt discrimination is now illegal, direct evidence of its existence is hard to come by. Some studies have used "correspondence tests," where there is some limited evidence that matched job applications from females and males elicit more interview offers for males. Another example is that of "blind" musical auditions which suggest women do better if only their playing is heard. And careful documentation of practices in, for instance, construction indicates prejudice against female employees. But this sort of evidence is sparse.

Those seeking evidence of discrimination might also point to the large number of employment tribunal cases over sex discrimination and equal pay issues as evidence of the problem. It is certainly true that the number of such cases has risen recently: between 2004/05 and 2006/07, the number of sex discrimination cases accepted by tribunals rose from 11,726 to 28,153, while equal pay cases rose from 8,229 to a massive 44,013. There has been little detailed analysis of the growth of these cases, but it is known that there were special factors associated with changes in the law, and with the advent of "no-win, no-fee" lawyers. It is interesting, incidentally, that a disproportionate number of these cases are against public sector employers, although as we have seen, the gender pay gap is much smaller in the public sector. The majority of these claims were multiple claims brought against local authorities and the NHS, paradoxically as a result of the introduction of Job Evaluation Schemes aimed at closing the pay gap.

Looking at the private sector, though, it is clear that only a small proportion of equal pay and sex discrimination claims succeed. The Women and Work Commission examined all private sector equal pay claims from 2000 to 2004 and found that only 25 reached the decision stage, with applicants winning in only five cases.

Despite their growing numbers, tribunal cases are brought by only a tiny proportion of the workforce and cannot really do much to explain the aggregate phenomenon of the overall gender pay gap. They often concern procedural issues rather than more fundamental matters: in the case of sex discrimination tribunal claims, they are often about issues such as sexual harassment, bullying, and other offences rather than issues directly related to pay.

Econometric Analysis of the Pay Gap

Given the limited evidence of direct discrimination, in trying to analyse pay inequality researchers have increasingly concentrated on econometric work.[2] A substantial literature is concerned with separating out that part of the overall gender pay gap that can be accounted for by relevant economic characteristics and that residual part which could possibly be attributable to discrimination—defined as paying different amounts to men and women for identical skills and abilities, and usually seen as conscious or unconscious behaviour by misguided employers.

The large number of studies that have been made of pay gaps in many different countries vary considerably in methodology and conclusions, but there are some common threads. Most studies use a statistical technique first developed more or less simultaneously by Oaxaca and Blinder. This decomposes the gender pay gap into two parts. The first component is the difference in pay associated with differences in observable characteristics such as experience and education. The second is the "residual," which may partly result from discrimination.

The procedure involves first estimating a wage equation, which relates the logarithm of wages to years of education, work experience, and a range of other productivity-related characteristics that are available in the particular dataset the researcher is using. In effect the coefficients of the estimated equation indicate how much the labour market pays for these characteristics. One equation may be estimated for males, and then the regression coefficients are used to calculate what women would have earned had their characteristics been rewarded at the same pay rate as men. This typically reduces the pay gap between men and women quite significantly, leaving the "unexplained" element as the differences in returns to productivity-related characteristics for males and females.

Another wage equation may be estimated from data on women's earnings; the coefficients in this regression can then be applied to see what men would have earned if their characteristics had been paid at the same rate as those of women. This can then be used to give another possible estimate of the proportion of pay explained by worker characteristics, together with the residual potentially attributable to discrimination. Alternatively a pooled regression may be used.

Since the early studies, more sophisticated modelling has developed. One problem with the Oaxaca–Blinder approach is sample selection bias. When calculating the gender pay gap, researchers are using data on men and women who are in employment. Many women, however, especially those with lower levels of skills and qualifications or with less interest in careers, may drop out of the workforce and live on benefits and/or intra-household transfers from partners. So women who work may be untypical of all women—they are the more skilled and committed females, while employed men will cover a far wider spectrum of ability and commitment. The size of the underlying wage gap—between what men and women could earn—may therefore be underestimated, and the statistical explanation of the gap erroneous. The "Heckman correction" gets round this problem by using other variables to estimate the probability of employment of men and women and uses this as a further explanatory variable in the wage equation.

Other refinements have involved the development of international comparisons through the Juhn, Murphy and Pierce methodology. This approach assumes an "institutionalist" view that the structures of pay (including collective bargaining systems) affect gender differentials. It involves decomposing down cross-country differences in the gender pay gap by taking one country as a benchmark, and analysing pay gaps in other countries with reference to the pay structure of that country. So the decomposition involves explaining differences in pay gaps by reference to gender differences in observed characteristics, to a component associated with cross-country differences in wage structures, and to an unexplained element. Some interesting work has been done with this approach.

It is worth emphasising again that analysts are not unanimous in their choice of modelling strategy. And the quality and coverage of the data used in different studies often leave much to be desired. While most studies suggest that there is a sizeable unexplained residual pay gap, this varies considerably in size, as does the proportion of the explained gap associated with relevant individual and job characteristics.

A rather different approach to decomposition is used in work done by Wendy Olsen and Sylvia Walby for the Equal Opportunities Commission. As this has been widely quoted in UK debates, it is worth describing in some detail. Olsen and Walby adopt a novel approach which avoids some of the problems they perceive with the Oaxaca–Blinder technique. They prefer to estimate a single equation for men and women which produces estimates of coefficients on a range of explanatory variables. They then bring out the sizes of the main components of the pay gap by "simulating the hypothetical changes which would be needed to bring women's levels of these components into line with those of men." They use data from the British Household Panel Survey.

How does their approach work? Their wage equation shows a significant relationship between hourly earnings and, for example, the proportion of men in an occupation. This proportion is an indicator of "gender segregation" at work, which is believed by many to be an element in perpetuating pay inequality. The coefficient on this variable is 0.13, which means that, other things being equal, pay rises by 1.3 percent for every 10 percent more males in an occupation. So Olsen and Walby simulate the effect of increasing the proportion of men in every female-dominated occupational category to 50 percent. This is what they mean by an "unsegregated" workforce. If this were to be done, they find, earnings in these categories would rise by an average of 2.5 percent, or about 10 percent of the measured pay gap in their study.

This careful study still shows a largish "unexplained" pay gap, although it's a good deal smaller than some earlier studies, where only tiny proportions of the gap were explained. The large size of the unexplained gap in some of these studies is often the result of poor or proxy data. For example, work experience is used in estimating wage equations, but information on work history is often missing or incomplete, and some studies use the difference between current age and age at (assumed) completion of schooling as a proxy for this. For many women, and some men, with periods outside the workforce, this will exaggerate the true extent of their work experience. This in turn will lead to the role of experience in explaining the pay gap being underestimated because the differential in experience between men and women is inaccurately measured. Moreover, another key explanatory variable in wage equations, education, is often just measured by years of schooling, when it is known that the type and especially the subject of qualification are important, particularly in higher education. Women tend not to study the same subjects as men at university. Overall, in 2006, women accounted for 58.9 percent of the UK student population, but the proportion of women in the major subject areas shown varies considerably. Women are startlingly under-represented in some subjects and over-represented in others.

This in itself might not matter if different subjects were rewarded equally in the labour market, but this is not the case. For example, a study for the Royal Society of Chemistry showed that individuals' rates of return on more narrowly defined degrees varied widely. Engineering, chemistry, and physics, where women are seriously under-represented in the student population, offer rates of return significantly above average. By contrast, psychology degrees (where almost 80 percent of the 66,000 students in 2006 were female) and linguistics, English literature, and Celtic studies (where 72 percent of over 70,000 students were female) give returns that are markedly less than the average.

Variations in rates of return might reflect discrimination or the systematic undervaluing of the jobs of graduates in areas where women dominate. But there are some obvious structural factors at work. One is the sector in which different types of graduates are likely to work. Over a quarter of all women in higher education are studying nursing or education. The vast majority of graduates in these areas will work in the public sector: there are relatively few highly paid jobs in government employment.

Lifestyles, Preferences, Attitudes, Expectations

After allowing for these factors, is that part of the pay gap left unexplained attributable to discrimination, as many claim? Well, possibly, but in addition to [various] factors [such as amount of full-time experience; interruption in employment; education; years of part-time experience, etc.] there is also what econometricians call "unobservable heterogeneity." Here this means differences in attitudes, preferences, and expectations which can cause apparently similarly qualified and experienced individuals to behave very differently.

Catherine Hakim, a sociologist whose work on "preference theory" has created some controversy, claims that, in countries such as the UK, women now have a wide range of lifestyle options and that they can be classified into three relatively distinct groups by their preferences—those who are home-centred, those who are work-centred, and those who are "adaptive."

The first group, which she estimates to be approximately 20 percent of UK women, prioritise family life and children, and prefer not to work in the labour market (though they do so, they are not career-driven). Work-centred women, again about 20 percent, are likely to be childless, committed to their careers, and with a high level of investment in qualifications and training. The largest group, the "adaptives," around 60 percent of UK women, want to work, but they also want families. Their careers tend to be more erratic.

Hakim carried out a national survey which indicated that women's expressed preferences were good predictors of their employment status, whereas, perhaps surprisingly, their educational qualifications were not: some well-qualified women were in the "home-centred" camp. She argues that her preference theory "explains continuing sex differentials in labour market behaviour (workrates, labour turnover, the choice of job etc) and hence also in the pay gap."

Hakim's assertion receives some support from the work of Arnaud Chevalier, who uses data on attitudes and expectations to demonstrate how standard econometric analysis of the gender pay gap often misleads by leaving a large unexplained pay gap which is then too easily attributed to discrimination.

His work is based on a survey that covers more than 10,000 UK graduates who left university in 1995 and provides data on the 42 months following graduation. Unusually, in addition to information on wages, educational attainment, and job history, it provides data on family background, subject of degree, and, most importantly, attitudes and expectations. The survey asked twenty questions, coded on a five-point scale, about character traits, motivation and expectations.

The data indicated a mean raw gender pay gap of 12.6 percent for this group of young graduates. Chevalier's meticulous multistage process illustrates very clearly that the large residual pay gap found in many studies is likely to be the result of model misspecification because of the omission of explanatory variables.

What Chevalier does is fascinating. In essence he recapitulates the development of work on pay gaps in various stages, to show how adding information about individuals can explain more and more of the difference in earnings. His first step is to use a very basic specification using labour market experience, age at graduation, ethnicity, and region of residence as explanatory variables. Many widely cited studies of gender pay gaps tend to be confined to a few variables such as these. As might be expected, given that the group is fairly homogeneous in view of them having a degree and being relatively young, the simple model explains very little, only about 20 percent, of the observed pay gap between men and women.

He then goes on to include further explanatory variables such as A-level score, degree results, type of higher education institution and postgraduate qualifications. These indicators add a little, but not very much, to the explanatory power of the model. Adding in controls for the subject in which these young people graduated, however, increases the explanatory power of the model very significantly, with over 50 percent of the pay gap now accounted for.

A further iteration extends the model to include other objective data such as the characteristics (size and sector) of the workplace, the type of contract, and the "feminisation" of the occupation. This raises the proportion of the wage gap which is explained to 65 percent. The addition of data on the number of jobs held since graduation—a measure of mobility—adds another minor increment to the specification's explanatory power.

The final specification includes information on the values that graduates attach to jobs and their career expectations. Men and women differ significantly with regard to these characteristics: men are more likely to state that career development and financial rewards are very important, and are much more likely to define themselves as very ambitious, while women emphasise job satisfaction, being valued by employers and doing a socially useful job. Two-thirds of women in this sample expect to take career breaks for family reasons; 40 percent of men expect their partners to do this, but only 12 percent expect to do it themselves.

When these attitudinal variables are added to the specification, the result is that 84 percent of the wage gap can now be explained. This suggests that many of the models that generate large "unexplained" wage gaps, and from which non-specialists frequently infer a significant element of employer discrimination, are simply misspecified. They just don't incorporate sufficient explanatory variables for a satisfactory analysis of the causes of the gender pay differential.

How exactly do these attitudes and values lead to women being paid less than men? One way is through different individuals' choices of potential employers. A recent survey of young graduates shows that women's choices of preferred employers are very different from those of men. Of the top 25 ideal employers for women, twelve were in the public or voluntary sectors, as against only four out of 25 for men. The top three ideal employers for women graduates were all in the public sector.

Such preferences mean that many bright women are deliberately choosing jobs where really high earnings are impossible or unlikely. They clearly regard other aspects of the job—a greater sense of moral purpose, perhaps? Or maybe greater job security, less stress, and relatively generous pension provision—as offsetting the reduced chance of very high earnings. This is the compensating differential principle touched on earlier.

Another way in which employee attitudes influence earnings outcomes may be through different approaches to pay negotiations and promotion applications. Particularly at more senior levels, the pay offer an employer makes may be negotiable—if, that is, the employee chooses to negotiate. In their book *Women Don't Ask: Negotiation and the Gender Divide*, American academics Linda Balcock and Sara Laschever claim that women are very reluctant to negotiate over salaries. In one US study eight times as many men as women graduating with master's degrees negotiated their salaries, adding an average of 7.4 percent to their starting pay. This initial gap is likely to persist and grow over time. This is partly because women may have lower expectations: women's salary expectations for their first job are significantly lower than those of men going for similar jobs.

In the UK, an analysis of the pay gap among academic economists indicates that men receive more promotions and higher placings on pay scales, and one of the factors associated with this is the receipt of outside offers. Men receive more outside offers than women and are thus able to negotiate their pay upwards. They also make more pay-oriented moves between jobs than women.

So the conclusion we can draw from empirical analysis of the full-time pay gap is that a high proportion of this gap can be accounted for, given sufficient information on individual and job characteristics and the attitudes and expectations of employees. Males and females make different choices in the labour market, in terms of the trade-off between pay and other job characteristics, choice of education, choice of occupation, and attitudes to work. These strongly influence earnings. Employer attitudes and discrimination seem not to be nearly as important as politicians and lobbyists have suggested.

Summary

There is a sizeable gap between the average hourly earnings of UK men and women working full time: this is the gender pay gap. The gap has, however, declined over time and is expected to decline further given demographic trends and changes in women's qualifications. It could even go into reverse.

The view that the UK has a particularly large gender pay gap by international standards is misleading. The gap is anyway only one indicator of women's economic status. Its size is not necessarily related to other indicators of sex discrimination and it can increase or decrease for reasons that have nothing to do with employers' behaviour.

The pay gap may partly reflect compensating differentials: men's jobs may typically have disadvantages that are reflected in higher pay. Women report greater job satisfaction than men.

There is little evidence of direct discrimination by employers against women. Discrimination is often inferred from the unexplained residual in econometric analyses of the causes of the gender pay gap.

When attitudes and preferences, as well as objective characteristics such as work experience and qualifications, are brought into the picture, however, most of the pay gap can be explained without reference to discrimination.

Notes

1. Where a firm is the dominant employer in an area, it may be able to segment the job market and pay different rates to different groups of workers without being undercut by other firms. Such a situation could also arise if gender segregation occurred as a result of employee job choice.

2. Econometrics uses statistical methods to analyse and test relationships between economic variables.

Hilary M. Lips   **NO**

The Gender Wage Gap: Debunking the Rationalizations

Last year, a labor economist from the Economic Policy Institute made the widely-quoted estimate that the gender pay gap would be closed within 30 years. Other commentators state confidently that the gap does not reflect discrimination, but other factors, such as the high wages of a few white men, and gendered patterns of occupational and educational choice and work experience. The effect of such assertions is to make women feel complacent about the wage gap—and perhaps to feel that they can avoid its impact by making the right educational, occupational, and negotiation-related choices. Such complacency is unwarranted.

The Wage Gap Exists within Racial/Ethnic Groups

White men are not the only group that out-earns women, although the wage gap is largest between white men and white women. Within other groups, such as African Americans, Latinos, and Asian/Pacific Islanders, men earn more than women (Source: U.S. Census Bureau).

What Difference Does Education Make?

Higher levels of education increase women's earnings, just as they do for men. However, there is no evidence that the gender gap in wages closes at higher levels of education. If anything, the reverse is true: at the very highest levels of education, the gap is at its largest.

The Wage Gap Exists within Occupations

Some people think that if women move into male-dominated occupations in larger numbers, the wage gap will close. However, there appears to be a gender-related wage gap in virtually every occupational category. In researching this issue at the Center for Gender Studies, we found only four occupational categories for which comparison data were available in which women earned even a little more than men: special education teachers, order clerks, electrical and

From *Expert Advice for Working Women,* 2009. Copyright © 2009 by WomensMedia.Com. Reprinted by permission.

electronic engineers, and miscellaneous food preparation occupations (Source: Bureau of Labor Statistics).

The movement of women into higher paid occupations, whether male-dominated or not, may not have the impact of narrowing the earnings gap. Social psychologists have demonstrated repeatedly that occupations associated with women or requiring stereotypically feminine skills are rated as less prestigious and deserving of less pay than occupations associated with men and masculine skills. Thus, as more and more women enter an occupation, there may be a tendency to value (and reward) that occupation less and less.

Do Women Earn Less Because They Work Less?

Women are more likely than men to work part-time. However, most gender wage comparisons leave out part-time workers and focus only on full-time, year-round workers. A close look at the earnings of women and men who work 40 hours or more per week reveals that the wage gap may actually widen as the number of hours worked increases. Women working 41 to 44 hours per week earn 84.6% of what men working similar hours earn; women working more than 60 hours per week earn only 78.3% of what men in the same time category earn (Source: Bureau of Labor Statistics). Furthermore, women may work longer to receive the promotions that provide access to higher pay. For example, among school principals, women have an average of 3 years longer as teachers than men do (Source: National Center for Education Statistics). So it is hard to argue that women's lower earnings are simply a result of women putting in fewer hours per week, or even fewer years than men.

Is the Wage Gap Closing?

The U.S. Census Bureau has made available statistics on women's and men's earnings for several decades. By examining this time series of data, it is possible to get a feel for the changes and trends in earnings. One thing revealed by a simple visual examination of the series since 1960 is how closely the shapes of the two lines parallel each other. The dips and bumps in women's and men's earnings seem to move in tandem. Clearly, similar economic and social forces are at work in influencing the rise and fall of earnings for both sexes. Men's earnings do not stand still and wait for women's to catch up.

Another thing that is apparent is that there is some minor fluctuation in the size of the wage gap. For example, the gap widened in the 1960s, closed a little in the 1980s, and widened slightly in the late 1990s. Thus, depending on which chunk of years one examines, it may be possible to conclude that the gap is either widening or narrowing. The only way to get a clear picture of what is happening is to examine the whole series rather than a few years at a time.

The series of data points from 1960 onward provides a basis for a forecast of the future, although such forecasts are always estimates rather than hard certainties. When we used forecasting analyses to project the earnings of women and men into the future, to the year 2010, we found no evidence on which we could base a prediction for a closing (or widening) wage gap. The forecast was, in essence, for the two lines to remain parallel, although the 90% confidence intervals (the range within which we are 90% certain the actual future earnings will fall) do overlap a little.

A Question of Value

As women and men left their jobs this spring because they were called up for military duty, employers scrambled to make sure that these workers did not suffer losses of salary and benefits. In a number of cases, organizations made up the difference between their employees' military pay and their normal pay, held jobs open, and made sure that benefits continued during workers' absence. At the same time, the media made a hero out of a father who chose to ship out with his military unit rather than stay home with his infant son who was awaiting a heart transplant. The message about what we as a society consider important is clear:

- When something perceived as very important needs to be done outside of the workplace, employers feel obligated to provide support for their employees to go and do it.
- In the eyes of society, or at least many employers, family concerns and the care of children do not fall into the category of "very important"—certainly not as important as military duty.

Are these the values we want to live by? If women and men continue to accept the notion that the domestic and caretaking work traditionally classified as "women's work" is not important enough for employers to accommodate, the gender gap in wages will never close. A few individual women may be able to evade the gap by choosing to be childfree, being fortunate enough to have a supportive spouse, and carefully following a model of career advancement that was developed to fit men's needs. However, to make the wage gap disappear will require that we stop buying into the idea that the rules are gender-neutral and that men just follow them better than women do. One by one, employers must be convinced to re-examine assumptions that unwittingly place higher value on the type of work men do than on the type of work women do. The most important step in closing the wage gap is for all of us to give up the notion that, to be paid fairly, a woman must "make it in a man's world."

Blaming Women's Choices for the Gender Pay Gap

A 2006 article in the *New York Times* cited Labor Department statistics that, for college-educated women in middle adulthood, the gender pay gap had widened during the previous decade. The phenomenon was attributed partly to discrimination, but also to "women's own choices. The number of women staying home with young children has risen . . . especially among highly educated mothers, who might otherwise be earning high salaries."

A 2007 report from the American Association of University Women sounded the alarm about a continuing wage gap that is evident even in the first year after college graduation. The authors noted, however, that individual choices with respect to college major, occupation, and parenthood have a strong impact on the gap. Accepting the idea that much of the pay gap can be accounted for by such neutral factors as experience and training, they concluded that, in the first year after college graduation, about 5 percent of the pay gap is unexplained by such factors—and it is that 5 percent that represents the impact of discrimination.

The language attributing women's lower pay to their own lifestyle choices is seductive—in an era when women are widely believed to have overcome the most serious forms of discrimination and in a society in which we are fond of emphasizing individual responsibility for life outcomes. Indeed, it is possible to point to a variety of ways in which women's work lives differ from men's in ways that might justify gender differences in earnings. Women work in lower-paid occupations; on average they work fewer paid hours per week and fewer paid weeks per year than men do; their employment is more likely than men's to be discontinuous. As many economists with a predilection for the "human capital model" would argue, women as a group make lower investments in their working lives, so they logically reap fewer rewards.

At first blush, this argument sounds reasonable. However, a closer look reveals that the language of "choice" obscures larger social forces that maintain the wage gap and the very real constraints under which women labor. The impact of discrimination, far from being limited to the portion of the wage gap that cannot be accounted for by women's choices, is actually deeply embedded in and constrains these choices.

Do Women Choose Lower-Paid Occupations?

Women continue to be clustered in low-paid occupational categories: office and administrative support and various service jobs. While they now make up a majority of university students, they are concentrated in academic specialties that lead to lower paid occupations: education rather than engineering, for example. If women persist in choosing work that is poorly paid, shouldn't the responsibility for the wage gap be laid squarely at their own doorstep?

Actually, within groups graduating with particular academic majors, women earn less than men, as illustrated in the AAUW report cited above. And within occupational categories, women earn less than their male counterparts, as revealed in this chart.

Furthermore, there is a catch-22 embedded in women's occupational choices: the migration of women into an occupation is associated with a lowering of its status and salary, and defining an occupation as requiring stereotypically masculine skills is associated with higher prestige, salary, and discrimination in favor of male job applicants. So convincing women in large numbers to shift their occupational choices is unlikely to obliterate the earnings gap.

As well, using the language of choice to refer to women's career outcomes tacitly ignores the many subtle constraints on such decisions. From childhood

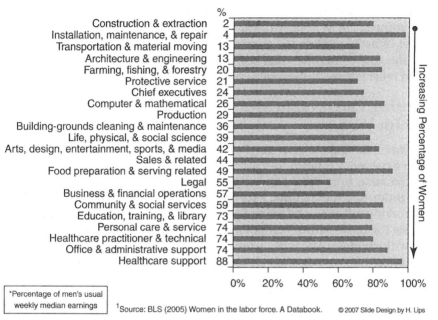

U.S. Women's Earnings as a Percent of Men's*
within Occupational Categories: 2005[1]

Category	%
Construction & extraction	2
Installation, maintenance, & repair	4
Transportation & material moving	13
Architecture & engineering	13
Farming, fishing, & forestry	20
Protective service	21
Chief executives	24
Computer & mathematical	26
Production	29
Building-grounds cleaning & maintenance	36
Life, physical, & social science	39
Arts, design, entertainment, sports, & media	42
Sales & related	44
Food preparation & serving related	49
Legal	55
Business & financial operations	57
Community & social services	59
Education, training, & library	73
Personal care & service	74
Healthcare practitioner & technical	74
Office & administrative support	74
Healthcare support	88

*Percentage of men's usual weekly median earnings

[1]Source: BLS (2005) Women in the labor force. A Databook.   © 2007 Slide Design by H. Lips

onward, we view media that consistently portray men more often than women in professional occupations and in masculine-stereotyped jobs. Not surprisingly, researchers find that the more TV children watch, the more accepting they are of occupational gender stereotypes. Why does the acceptance of gender stereotypes matter? Gender-stereotyped messages about particular skills (e.g., "males are generally better at this than females") lower women's beliefs in their competence—even when they perform at exactly the same level as their male counterparts. In such situations, women's lower confidence in their abilities translates into a reluctance to pursue career paths that require such abilities.

So, there are many problems with treating women's occupational choices as based purely on individual temperament and as occurring within a static occupational system that is unaffected by such choices. Women's employment choices are systematically channeled and constrained—and when women elude the constraints and flow into previously male-dominated jobs, the system apparently adapts to keep those jobs low-paid.

If Women Chose to Work More Hours, Would They Close the Gap?

Women work fewer paid hours per week than men do, but among workers who labor more than 40 hours per week, women earn less than men. Indeed, among workers working 60 hours or more per week at their primary job, women earned only 82% of men's median weekly earnings in 2006. Furthermore, women do not necessarily choose to work fewer hours than men do. One researcher found that 58% of workers want to change their work hours in some way—and that 19% of women report they want the opportunity to work more hours. Also, women have recently brought lawsuits against corporations such as Boeing and CBS claiming discrimination in access to overtime. Thus, in the realm of hours worked for pay, it is probably a mistake to use the number of hours worked as a simple indicator of women's (or men's) choices. As in the case of occupational segregation by gender, the number of hours worked reflects some systematic constraints.

Choosing Parenthood Means Lower Wages Only for Women

For women, having children has a negative effect on wages, even when labor market experience is taken into account. This may be due to mothers' temporary separation from the workforce and/or the loss of the benefits of seniority and position-specific training, experience, and contacts. Among married persons working full-time, the ratio of women's to men's median weekly earnings is 76.4% for those with no children under the age of 18, but only 73.6% for those with children. And when women and men of all marital statuses are considered together, women with children under 18 earn 97.1% of what women without children earn, whereas men with children under 18 earn 122% of what men without children earn.

So, the choice to have children is associated with very different earnings-related outcomes for women and men. In terms of children, it is not that women and men are making different choices, but that the same choices have very different consequences for the two groups. Those consequences reflect society's failure to value the work of parenting. Yet, if most women decided to forego motherhood, the declining birthrate already causing concern in some parts of the developed world would soon become catastrophic.

Women's Choices Are Not the Problem

Individual women can sometimes evade the effects of the gender pay gap by making certain kinds of choices, such as selecting male-dominated occupations, working more hours, avoiding parenthood. However, these choices occur in an environment suffused with subtle sexism and discrimination: there are more barriers for women than for men to making certain choices, and the consequences of some choices are starkly different for women and men.

Moreover, these individual solutions are not effective on a societal level; they work only if the women enacting them remain in a minority. For example, if most women moved into jobs that are now male-dominated, signs are that the salaries associated with those jobs would likely drop. But, by making it difficult to go against the tide, the forces of discrimination ensure that most women don't move into such jobs. And as long as a few women get past the barriers, the illusion persists that any woman could do it if she wanted to—it's a matter of free choice. However, women's choices will not be free until their abilities and their work are valued equally with men's, and until women and men reap equivalent consequences for their choices in the realm of work and family.

POSTSCRIPT

Is the Gender Wage Gap Justified?

Historically, poor women have always worked, perhaps as a housekeeper or a nanny or a seamstress in a sweatshop. In recent U.S. history, women were most likely to enter the workforce in masses during times of war. Their presence was needed to compensate for the lack of male laborers. Rosie the Riveter became the patriotic role model. However, after each of the two major world wars, women were encouraged to return to their rightful place in the home with as much enthusiasm as they had been encouraged to leave the home; Suzi homemaker became the new cultural icon for women. Issues of women's equal treatment in the workplace did not really come to the forefront for debate until large numbers of women entered higher education, and participated in the civil rights movement and the antiwar movement of the 1960s. The second wave of the women's movement was the result. Many believed that as more women obtained more education and began to climb the career ladder gender inequities would begin to dissipate. However, although in forty years there has been progress at the entry level for women, women at the top find themselves in a minority.

Ironically, during the 2008–2009 recession, men held 78% of the jobs lost. As a result, women are actually faring better by comparison. Women now hold almost 50% of all jobs today (compared to 36% 40 years ago). But once again, in the words of Lisa Belkin, "The history of women in the workplace (both their leaps forward and then slips back) is a reaction to what was happening to men." Women currently are returning to the workforce because they have to and they are cheaper to hire than are men.

The glass ceiling has not been broken. Some have suggested that women no longer "want it all"—career and family; rather, women are willingly choosing to opt out of the fast-paced, competitive rat race to be stay-at-home moms. There is evidence that some women with advanced degrees from some of the most prestigious institutions in the United States have done this. However, these women are married to highly successful men who generate enough income to maintain an upper-middle-class lifestyle. Other women have opted out of the corporate race to the top because they realized they were not going to break through the glass ceiling. Women are a fast-growing group to start their own businesses. However, such examples ignore the fact that the vast majority of people (women and men) do not have the resources to begin their own businesses nor can they maintain a comfortable lifestyle without two incomes, and for single mothers, it is not a question of lifestyle but a matter of survival. Economists have evaluated the notions of the mommy track and the fast track. The mommy track had originally been proposed as a career path that recognized women's role as child-bearers; the idea was that a woman's career trajectory would be adjusted to allow for this reality without jeopardizing her chances of advancement. It did not work. Such a choice by women has resulted in subtle discrimination. A self-fulfilling prophecy occurred. An employer is more likely to put a male than a female employee on the fast track, believing that he will not be distracted by child-care responsibilities like a female employee. As a result, effort rather than talent is being rewarded. The man is expected to be on the fast track and to put forth more effort than his partner who is on the mommy track. Only permanent changes in public policy will remove the discrimination.

Suggested Readings

Jeanette N. Cleveland, Kevin R. Murphy, and Margaret Stockdale, eds., *Women and Men in Organizations: Sex and Gender Issues at Work* (Mahwah, NJ: Lawrence Erlbaum Associates, 2001).

Jacqueline DeLaat, *Gender in the Workplace: A Case Study Approach* (New York: Sage, 2006).

Barbara A. Gutek and M. S. Stockdale, "Sex Discrimination in Employment," in F. Landy (ed.), *Employment Discrimination Litigation: Behavioral, Quantitative, and Legal Perspectives* (New York: Jossey-Bass, 2005).

Catherine Hein, *Reconciling Work and Family Responsibilities: Practical Ideas from Global Experience* (Washington, DC: Brookings Institution Press, 2005).

International Labor Office, *Gender Equality and Decent Work: Good Practices at the Workplace* (Washington, DC: Brookings Institution Press, 2005).

Kjell Erik Lommerud and Steinar Vagstad, *Mommy Tracks and Public Policy: On Self-Fulfilling Prophecies and Gender Gaps in Promotion* (London: The Centre for Economic Policy Research, 2000).

Linda Wirth, *Breaking through the Glass Ceiling: Women in Management* (International Labor Organization, 2001).

ISSUE 17

Are Barriers to Women's Success as Leaders Due to Societal Obstacles?

YES: **Alice H. Eagly and Linda L. Carli**, from "Women and the Labyrinth of Leadership," *Harvard Business Review* (September 2007)

NO: **Kingsley R. Browne**, from *Biology at Work: Rethinking Sexual Equality* (Rutgers University Press, 2002)

ISSUE SUMMARY

YES: Alice Eagly and Linda Carli contend that barriers exist for women at every stage of their career trajectories, resulting in, not a glass ceiling, but a labyrinth.

NO: Kingsley Browne asserts that the division of labor by sex is rooted in biologically based differences between women and men. Evolutionarily based natural selection has led to inclinations that make women and men better suited for different types of jobs.

Women continue to face career barriers. Although women hold 40 percent of managerial positions in the United States today, only 2 percent of *Fortune* 500 CEOs are women. The question remains as to why. Explanations tend to fall into one of two camps: human capital theory and discrimination theory. Human capital theories focus on obstacles from within the person. These theories focus on explanations such as differences in women's and men's abilities, interests, education, qualifications, personal investment in their careers, and leadership style, as well as choices related to family-work conflicts that are more likely to result in job discontinuity and turnover for women than for men. On the other hand, discrimination theorists focus on sociocultural factors that result in differential treatment of women and men. Three forms of employment discrimination have been identified: within-job wage discrimination (i.e., disparities within the same job, or unequal pay for equal work), valuative discrimination (i.e., lower wages in female- than male-dominated fields), and allocative discrimination (i.e., biases in hiring, promotion, and dismissal). This latter form of discrimination has invoked various descriptors of discrimination, including the "glass ceiling," "concrete wall," and "glass escalator." The image of the glass ceiling suggests that women ascend the career ladder with the top in sight, but at some rung on that ladder they hit the "glass ceiling." This image was transformed to that of a "concrete wall" to describe the even greater challenges faced by ethnic minority women. The "glass elevator" was a term coined to express the rapid career advancement of men who enter non-traditional, historically female-dominated fields, such as nursing. In the selections that follow the excerpt from Browne is an example of an explanation from the human capital perspective in which he argues that by nature women and men have different interests and talents that better suit them for different jobs. In contrast, Eagly and Carli's selection represents a discrimination theory perspective. In addition to describing all the various ways in which women can be targets of discrimination in the workplace, they coin a new term for allocative discrimination, the "labyrinth."

YES ⤶

Alice H. Eagly and
Linda L. Carli

Women and the Labyrinth
of Leadership

If one has misdiagnosed a problem, then one is unlikely to prescribe an effective cure. This is the situation regarding the scarcity of women in top leadership. Because people with the best of intentions have misread the symptoms, the solutions that managers are investing in are not making enough of a difference.

That there is a problem is not in doubt. Despite years of progress by women in the workforce (they now occupy more than 40% of all managerial positions in the United States), within the C-suite they remain as rare as hens' teeth. Consider the most highly paid executives of *Fortune 500* companies—those with titles such as chairman, president, chief executive officer, and chief operating officer. Of this group, only 6% are women. Most notably, only 2% of the CEOs are women, and only 15% of the seats on the boards of directors are held by women. The situation is not much different in other industrialized countries. In the 50 largest publicly traded corporations in each nation of the European Union, women make up, on average, 11% of the top executives and 4% of the CEOs and heads of boards. Just seven companies, or 1%, of *Fortune* magazine's Global 500 have female CEOs. What is to blame for the pronounced lack of women in positions of power and authority?

In 1986 the *Wall Street Journal's* Carol Hymowitz and Timothy Schellhardt gave the world an answer: "Even those few women who rose steadily through the ranks eventually crashed into an invisible barrier. The executive suite seemed within their grasp, but they just couldn't break through the glass ceiling." The metaphor, driven home by the article's accompanying illustration, resonated; it captured the frustration of a goal within sight but somehow unattainable. To be sure, there was a time when the barriers were absolute. Even within the career spans of 1980s-era executives, access to top posts had been explicitly denied. . . .

Times have changed, however, and the glass ceiling metaphor is now more wrong than right. For one thing, it describes an absolute barrier at a specific high level in organizations. The fact that there have been female chief executives, university presidents, state governors, and presidents of nations gives the lie to that charge. At the same time, the metaphor implies that women

From *Harvard Business Review,* September 2007, pp. 63–71. Copyright © 2007 by Harvard Business School Publishing. Reprinted by permission.

and men have equal access to entry- and mid-level positions. They do not. The image of a transparent obstruction also suggests that women are being misled about their opportunities, because the impediment is not easy for them to see from a distance. But some impediments are not subtle. Worst of all, by depicting a single, unvarying obstacle, the glass ceiling fails to incorporate the complexity and variety of challenges that women can face in their leadership journeys. In truth, women are not turned away only as they reach the penultimate stage of a distinguished career. They disappear in various numbers at many points leading up to that stage.

Metaphors matter because they are part of the storytelling that can compel change. Believing in the existence of a glass ceiling, people emphasize certain kinds of interventions: top-to-top networking, mentoring to increase board memberships, requirements for diverse candidates in high-profile succession horse races, litigation aimed at punishing discrimination in the C-suite. None of these is counterproductive; all have a role to play. The danger arises when they draw attention and resources away from other kinds of interventions that might attack the problem more potently. If we want to make better progress, it's time to rename the challenge.

Walls All Around

A better metaphor for what confronts women in their professional endeavors is the labyrinth. It's an image with a long and varied history in ancient Greece, India, Nepal, native North and South America, medieval Europe, and elsewhere. As a contemporary symbol, it conveys the idea of a complex journey toward a goal worth striving for. Passage through a labyrinth is not simple or direct, but requires persistence, awareness of one's progress, and a careful analysis of the puzzles that lie ahead. It is this meaning that we intend to convey. For women who aspire to top leadership, routes exist but are full of twists and turns, both unexpected and expected. Because all labyrinths have a viable route to the center, it is understood that goals are attainable. The metaphor acknowledges obstacles but is not ultimately discouraging.

If we can understand the various barriers that make up this labyrinth, and how some women find their way around them, we can work more effectively to improve the situation. What are the obstructions that women run up against? Let's explore them in turn.

Vestiges of prejudice. It is a well-established fact that men as a group still have the benefit of higher wages and faster promotions. In the United States in 2005, for example, women employed full-time earned 81 cents for every dollar that men earned. . . .

One of the most comprehensive of these studies was conducted by the U.S. Government Accountability Office. The study was based on survey data from 1983 through 2000 from a representative sample of Americans. Because the same people responded to the survey repeatedly over the years, the study provided accurate estimates of past work experience, which is important for explaining later wages.

The GAO researchers tested whether individuals' total wages could be predicted by sex and other characteristics. They included part-time and full-time employees in the surveys and took into account all the factors that they could estimate and that might affect earnings, such as education and work experience. Without controls for these variables, the data showed that women earned about 44% less than men, averaged over the entire period from 1983 to 2000. With these controls in place, the gap was only about half as large, but still substantial. The control factors that reduced the wage gap most were the different employment patterns of men and women: Men undertook more hours of paid labor per year than women and had more years of job experience.

Although most variables affected the wages of men and women similarly, there were exceptions. Marriage and parenthood, for instance, were associated with higher wages for men but not for women. In contrast, other characteristics, especially years of education, had a more positive effect on women's wages than on men's. Even after adjusting wages for all of the ways men and women differ, the GAO study, like similar studies, showed that women's wages remained lower than men's. The unexplained gender gap is consistent with the presence of wage discrimination.

Similar methods have been applied to the question of whether discrimination affects promotions. Evidently it does. Promotions come more slowly for women than for men with equivalent qualifications. . . . Even in culturally feminine settings such as nursing, librarianship, elementary education, and social work, men ascend to supervisory and administrative positions more quickly than women.

The findings of correlational studies are supported by experimental research, in which subjects are asked to evaluate hypothetical individuals as managers or job candidates, and all characteristics of these individuals are held constant except for their sex. Such efforts continue the tradition of the Goldberg paradigm, named for a 1968 experiment by Philip Goldberg. His simple, elegant study had student participants evaluate written essays that were identical except for the attached male or female name. The students were unaware that other students had received identical material ascribed to a writer of the other sex. This initial experiment demonstrated an overall gender bias: Women received lower evaluations unless the essay was on a feminine topic. Some 40 years later, unfortunately, experiments continue to reveal the same kind of bias in work settings. Men are advantaged over equivalent women as candidates for jobs traditionally held by men as well as for more gender-integrated jobs. Similarly, male leaders receive somewhat more favorable evaluations than equivalent female leaders, especially in roles usually occupied by men.

. . . [A] general bias against women appears to operate with approximately equal strength at all levels. The scarcity of female corporate officers is the sum of discrimination that has operated at all ranks, not evidence of a particular obstacle to advancement as women approach the top. The problem, in other words, is not a glass ceiling.

Resistance to women's leadership. What's behind the discrimination we've been describing? Essentially, a set of widely shared conscious and unconscious mental associations about women, men, and leaders. Study after study has affirmed that people associate women and men with different traits and link men with more of the traits that connote leadership. . . .

In the language of psychologists, the clash is between two sets of associations: communal and agentic. Women are associated with communal qualities, which convey a concern for the compassionate treatment of others. They include being especially affectionate, helpful, friendly, kind, and sympathetic, as well as interpersonally sensitive, gentle, and soft-spoken. In contrast, men are associated with agentic qualities, which convey assertion and control. They include being especially aggressive, ambitious, dominant, self-confident, and forceful, as well as self-reliant and individualistic. The agentic traits are also associated in most people's minds with effective leadership—perhaps because a long history of male domination of leadership roles has made it difficult to separate the leader associations from the male associations.

As a result, women leaders find themselves in a double bind. If they are highly communal, they may be criticized for not being agentic enough. But if they are highly agentic, they may be criticized for lacking communion. Either way, they may leave the impression that they don't have "the right stuff" for powerful jobs.

Given this double bind, it is hardly surprising that people are more resistant to women's influence than to men's. . . .

Studies have gauged reactions to men and women engaging in various types of dominant behavior. The findings are quite consistent. Nonverbal dominance, such as staring at others while speaking to them or pointing at people, is a more damaging behavior for women than for men. Verbally intimidating others can undermine a woman's influence, and assertive behavior can reduce her chances of getting a job or advancing in her career. Simply disagreeing can sometimes get women into trouble. Men who disagree or otherwise act dominant get away with it more often than women do.

Self-promotion is similarly risky for women. Although it can convey status and competence, it is not at all communal. So while men can use bluster to get themselves noticed, modesty is expected even of highly accomplished women. . . .

Another way the double bind penalizes women is by denying them the full benefits of being warm and considerate. Because people expect it of women, nice behavior that seems noteworthy in men seems unimpressive in women. For example, in one study, helpful men reaped a lot of approval, but helpful women did not. Likewise, men got away with being unhelpful, but women did not. . . .

While one might suppose that men would have a double bind of their own, they in fact have more freedom. Several experiments and organizational studies have assessed reactions to behavior that is warm and friendly versus dominant and assertive. The findings show that men can communicate in a warm or a dominant manner, with no penalty either way. People like men equally well and are equally influenced by them regardless of their warmth.

It all amounts to a clash of assumptions when the average person confronts a woman in management. . . . In the absence of any evidence to the contrary, people suspect that such highly effective women must not be very likable or nice.

Issues of leadership style. In response to the challenges presented by the double bind, female leaders often struggle to cultivate an appropriate and effective leadership style—one that reconciles the communal qualities people prefer in women with the agentic qualities people think leaders need to succeed. . . .

It's difficult to pull off such a transformation while maintaining a sense of authenticity as a leader. Sometimes the whole effort can backfire. In the words of another female leader, "I think that there is a real penalty for a woman who behaves like a man. The men don't like her and the women don't either." Women leaders worry a lot about these things, complicating the labyrinth that they negotiate. For example, Catalyst's study of *Fortune* 1000 female executives found that 96% of them rated as critical or fairly important that they develop "a style with which male managers are comfortable."

Does a distinct "female" leadership style exist? There seems to be a popular consensus that it does. . . .

More scientifically, a recent meta-analysis integrated the results of 45 studies addressing the question [comparing three leadership styles]. . . . Transformational leaders establish themselves as role models by gaining followers' trust and confidence. They state future goals, develop plans to achieve those goals, and innovate, even when their organizations are generally successful. Such leaders mentor and empower followers, encouraging them to develop their full potential and thus to contribute more effectively to their organizations. By contrast, transactional leaders establish give-and-take relationships that appeal to subordinates' self-interest. Such leaders manage in the conventional manner of clarifying subordinates' responsibilities, rewarding them for meeting objectives, and correcting them for failing to meet objectives. Although transformational and transactional leadership styles are different, most leaders adopt at least some behaviors of both types. The researchers also allowed for a third category, called the laissez-faire style—a sort of non-leadership that concerns itself with none of the above, despite rank authority.

The meta-analysis found that, in general, female leaders were somewhat more transformational than male leaders, especially when it came to giving support and encouragement to subordinates. They also engaged in more of the rewarding behaviors that are one aspect of transactional leadership. Meanwhile, men exceeded women on the aspects of transactional leadership involving corrective and disciplinary actions that are either active (timely) or passive (belated). Men were also more likely than women to be laissez-faire leaders, who take little responsibility for managing. These findings add up to a startling conclusion, given that most leadership research has found the transformational style (along with the rewards and positive incentives associated with the transactional style) to be more suited to leading the modern organization. The research tells us not only that men and women do have somewhat different leadership styles, but also that women's approaches are the more generally effective—while men's often are only somewhat effective or actually hinder effectiveness.

Another part of this picture, based on a separate meta-analysis, is that women adopt a more participative and collaborative style than men typically favor. The reason for this difference is unlikely to be genetic. Rather, it may be that collaboration can get results without seeming particularly masculine. As women navigate their way through the double bind, they seek ways to project authority without relying on the autocratic behaviors that people find so jarring in women. A viable path is to bring others into decision making and to lead as an encouraging teacher and positive role model. . . .

Demands of family life.   For many women, the most fateful turns in the labyrinth are the ones taken under pressure of family responsibilities. Women continue to be the ones who interrupt their careers, take more days off, and work part-time. As a result, they have fewer years of job experience and fewer hours of employment per year, which slows their career progress and reduces their earnings. . . .

There is no question that, while men increasingly share housework and child rearing, the bulk of domestic work still falls on women's shoulders. We know this from time-diary studies, in which people record what they are doing during each hour of a 24-hour day. So, for example, in the United States married women devoted 19 hours per week on average to housework in 2005, while married men contributed 11 hours. That's a huge improvement over 1965 numbers, when women spent a whopping 34 hours per week to men's five, but it is still a major inequity. And the situation looks worse when child care hours are added.

Although it is common knowledge that mothers provide more child care than fathers, few people realize that mothers provide more than they did in earlier generations—despite the fact that fathers are putting in a lot more time than in the past. . . . Thus, though husbands have taken on more domestic work, the work/family conflict has not eased for women; the gain has been offset by escalating pressures for intensive parenting and the increasing time demands of most high-level careers.

Even women who have found a way to relieve pressures from the home front by sharing child care with husbands, other family members, or paid workers may not enjoy the full workplace benefit of having done so. Decision makers often assume that mothers have domestic responsibilities that make it inappropriate to promote them to demanding positions. . . .

Underinvestment in social capital.   Perhaps the most destructive result of the work/family balancing act so many women must perform is that it leaves very little time for socializing with colleagues and building professional networks. The social capital that accrues from such "nonessential" parts of work turns out to be quite essential indeed. One study yielded the following description of managers who advanced rapidly in hierarchies: Fast-track managers "spent relatively more time and effort socializing, politicking, and interacting with outsiders than did their less successful counterparts . . . [and] did not give much time or attention to the traditional management activities of planning, decision making, and controlling or to the human resource management activities of motivating/reinforcing, staffing, training/developing, and managing conflict." . . .

Even given sufficient time, women can find it difficult to engage in and benefit from informal networking if they are a small minority. In such settings, the influential networks are composed entirely or almost entirely of men. Breaking into those male networks can be hard, especially when men center their networks on masculine activities. The recent gender discrimination lawsuit against Wal-Mart provides examples of this. For instance, an executive retreat took the form of a quail-hunting expedition at Sam Walton's ranch in Texas. Middle managers' meetings included visits to strip clubs and Hooters restaurants, and a sales conference attended by thousands of store managers featured a football theme. One executive received feedback that she probably would not advance in the company because she didn't hunt or fish.

Management Interventions That Work

Taking the measure of the labyrinth that confronts women leaders, we see that it begins with prejudices that benefit men and penalize women, continues with particular resistance to women's leadership, includes questions of leadership style and authenticity, and—most dramatically for many women—features the challenge of balancing work and family responsibilities. It becomes clear that a woman's situation as she reaches her peak career years is the result of many turns at many challenging junctures. Only a few individual women have made the right combination of moves to land at the center of power—but as for the rest, there is usually no single turning point where their progress was diverted and the prize was lost.

What's to be done in the face of such a multifaceted problem? A solution that is often proposed is for governments to implement and enforce antidiscrimination legislation and thereby require organizations to eliminate inequitable practices. However, analysis of discrimination cases that have gone to court has shown that legal remedies can be elusive when gender inequality results from norms embedded in organizational structure and culture. The more effective approach is for organizations to appreciate the subtlety and complexity of the problem and to attack its many roots simultaneously. More specifically, if a company wants to see more women arrive in its executive suite, it should do the following:

> **Increase people's awareness of the psychological drivers of prejudice toward female leaders, and work to dispel those perceptions.** . . .
>
> **Change the long-hours norm.** . . . To the extent an organization can shift the focus to objective measures of productivity, women with family demands on their time but highly productive work habits will receive the rewards and encouragement they deserve.
>
> **Reduce the subjectivity of performance evaluation.** . . . To ensure fairness, criteria should be explicit and evaluation processes designed to limit the influence of decision makers' conscious and unconscious biases.

Use open-recruitment tools, such as advertising and employment agencies, rather than relying on informal social networks and referrals to fill positions. . . . Research has shown that such personnel practices increase the numbers of women in managerial roles.

Ensure a critical mass of women in executive positions—not just one or two women—to head off the problems that come with tokenism. Token women tend to be pegged into narrow stereotypical roles such as "seductress," "mother," "pet," or "iron maiden." . . . When women are not a small minority, their identities as women become less salient, and colleagues are more likely to react to them in terms of their individual competencies.

Avoid having a sole female member of any team. Top management tends to divide its small population of women managers among many projects in the interests of introducing diversity to them all. But several studies have found that, so outnumbered, the women tend to be ignored by the men. . . . This is part of the reason that the glass ceiling metaphor resonates with so many. But in fact, the problem can be present at any level.

Help shore up social capital. As we've discussed, the call of family responsibilities is mainly to blame for women's underinvestment in networking. When time is scarce, this social activity is the first thing to go by the wayside. . . . When a well-placed individual who possesses greater legitimacy (often a man) takes an interest in a woman's career, her efforts to build social capital can proceed far more efficiently.

Prepare women for line management with appropriately demanding assignments. Women, like men, must have the benefit of developmental job experiences if they are to qualify for promotions. . . .

Establish family-friendly human resources practices. These may include flextime, job sharing, telecommuting, elder care provisions, adoption benefits, dependent child care options, and employee-sponsored on-site child care. Such support can allow women to stay in their jobs during the most demanding years of child rearing, build social capital, keep up to date in their fields, and eventually compete for higher positions. . . .

Allow employees who have significant parental responsibility more time to prove themselves worthy of promotion. This recommendation is particularly directed to organizations, many of them professional services firms, that have established "up or out" career progressions. People not ready for promotion at the same time as the top performers in their cohort aren't simply left in place—they're asked to leave. But many parents (most often mothers), while fully capable of reaching that level of achievement, need extra time—perhaps a year or two—to get there. . . .

Welcome women back. It makes sense to give high-performing women who step away from the workforce an opportunity to return to responsible positions when their circumstances change. . . .

Encourage male participation in family-friendly benefits. Dangers lurk in family-friendly benefits that are used only by women. Exercising options such as generous parental leave and part-time work slows down women's careers. More profoundly, having many more women than men take such benefits can harm the careers of women in general because of the expectation that they may well exercise those options. Any effort toward greater family friendliness should actively recruit male participation to avoid inadvertently making it harder for women to gain access to essential managerial roles.

Managers can be forgiven if they find the foregoing list a tall order. It's a wide-ranging set of interventions and still far from exhaustive. The point, however, is just that: Organizations will succeed in filling half their top management slots with women— and women who are the true performance equals of their male counterparts—only by attacking all the reasons they are absent today. Glass ceiling-inspired programs and projects can do just so much if the leakage of talented women is happening on every lower floor of the building. Individually, each of these interventions has been shown to make a difference. Collectively, we believe, they can make all the difference.

The View from Above

Imagine visiting a formal garden and finding within it a high hedgerow. At a point along its vertical face, you spot a rectangle—a neatly pruned and inviting doorway. Are you aware as you step through that you are entering a labyrinth? And, three doorways later, as the reality of the puzzle settles in, do you have any idea how to proceed? This is the situation in which many women find themselves in their career endeavors. Ground-level perplexity and frustration make every move uncertain.

Labyrinths become infinitely more tractable when seen from above. When the eye can take in the whole of the puzzle—the starting position, the goal, and the maze of walls—solutions begin to suggest themselves. This has been the goal of our research. Our hope is that women, equipped with a map of the barriers they will confront on their path to professional achievement, will make more informed choices. We hope that managers, too, will understand where their efforts can facilitate the progress of women. If women are to achieve equality, women and men will have to share leadership equally. With a greater understanding of what stands in the way of gender-balanced leadership, we draw nearer to attaining it in our time.

Kingsley R. Browne → NO

Biology at Work: Rethinking Sexual Equality

Modern evolutionary biology and psychology pose an even more direct challenge to the [Standard Social Sciences Model] (SSSM) with their insight that human behavioral predispositions are ultimately attributable to the same cause as the behavioral predispositions of other animals—evolution through natural selection. The centrality of mating and reproduction to evolutionary success, coupled with the differential investment of mammalian males and females in offspring, makes behavioral and temperamental identity of the sexes highly improbable. Just as no farmer expects to see identical patterns of behavior from the mare as from the stallion, from the cow as from the bull, or from the hen as from the rooster, no social scientist should expect to see identical patterns of behavior from men and women.

Claims for the existence of a recognizable "human nature" or for predictable behavioral differences between the sexes should be inherently suspect only to those who believe that the forces that created humans were importantly different from those that created the rest of the animal kingdom. If males and females are at their core psychologically identical, they are unique among mammals. This is not to deny the importance of social influences or the fact that societies have certain emergent characteristics that no amount of atomistic study of individuals could ever predict. But it is critical to understand that some social practices are more likely to arise than others precisely because human *minds* are more likely to settle on some social practices than others and that males and females tend to have different psychologies independent of the influence of cultures that expect them to be different.

The Division of Labor by Sex

A proper understanding of psychological sex differences would go far toward an understanding of the modern workplace, the study of which has heretofore been heavily biased toward the SSSM orientation. One human universal that is apparently a product of human nature is the division of labor by sex. All societies label some work "men's work" and other work "women's work." Although the content of the categories is by no means fixed—what some cultures label "men's work" is "women's work" in others—there are, nonetheless, some consistent patterns. Big-game hunting and metalworking are almost always "men's

work" and cooking and grinding grain are almost always "women's work."
While some divisions are obviously related to physical capacity, this is not
always the case. For example, carrying water is almost always "women's work,"
and manufacture of musical instruments is almost always "men's work."

Modern Western societies are breaking down these age-old divisions,
so that workers increasingly find themselves in what anthropologists call an
"evolutionarily novel environment"—an environment that differs from that
in which our hominid ancestors evolved—in this case a workplace environment in which men and women work side by side and compete for position
in the same status hierarchies. Today, almost all positions in the labor market are formally open to women, the primary exception being certain combat
positions in the military. Nonetheless, a high degree of de facto occupational
segregation continues to exist, so that in practice there are many occupations
that remain "men's work" and "women's work." Thus, most men work mostly
with other men, and most women work mostly with other women. Moreover,
even in largely integrated occupations, men are more likely than women to
achieve the highest organizational positions.

The architects of sexual equality appear to have assumed that lifting formal
barriers to women in the workplace would result in parity with men because
men and women inherently have identical desires and capacities. When prohibitions on formal discrimination have not resulted in sexual parity, hidden
discrimination is often assumed responsible. If hidden discrimination can be
disproved, then informal barriers, such as sexist attitudes of parents or teachers
are identified as the culprit. If direct external forces must finally (and reluc-
tantly) be abandoned because the paths that women's lives have taken must
be attributed to their own choices, then their choice becomes a "choice" that
is attributed to their internalization of "patriarchal" notions about the proper
role of the sexes and to their life constraints. While the causal attribution may
shift over time, what does not change is the persistent invocation of causes
other than women's inherent predispositions. Given the human propensity
for self-deception, it may not be possible to answer the question whether these
shifting arguments reflect actual beliefs or are merely opportunistic arguments
to advance a political agenda.

The social-role view of sex differences is that "men and women have
inherited essentially the same evolved psychological dispositions" and that
behavioral sex differences are simply results of "two organizing principles of
human societies: the division of labor according to sex and gender hierarchy."
How is it that a sexually monomorphic mind came up with the division of
labor by sex and gender hierarchy? Certainly the social explanation is not
the most parsimonious explanation for sex differences in behavior. Humans
evolved from other creatures surely having sexually dimorphic minds. The
notion that humans evolved away from the primate pattern of behavioral sex
differences—presumably because it was advantageous to do so—but simultaneously replaced the preexisting biological pattern with cultural patterns having the same effect is difficult to credit. Moreover, the direction of causation
in this explanation is implausibly unidirectional. Even if behavioral sex differences originated from a sexually monomorphic mind, one would expect that

they would be reinforced through selection over the hundreds of thousands or millions of years that these social phenomena existed.

Stasis and Change

Trends in women's work-force participation are not easily explained in terms of broad themes such as "patriarchy," "subjugation of women," or even the waning power of a monolithic male hierarchy. The progress of women has not been uniformly slow or uniformly fast, as might be expected if it were solely a consequence of such wide-ranging forces; instead, the pattern has been much more complex, and it is that pattern that any theory of workplace sex differences must attempt to explain.

In some respects, the role of women in the work force has been massively transformed in just a few decades. In 1960, women constituted just one-third of the American work force compared to over 46 percent today. During that same period, the percentage of married women who work doubled to 61 percent. Only 4 percent of lawyers in 1970 were women, while today the figure for law school graduates exceeds 42 percent. The percentage of female physicians increased from 10 to 24 percent between 1970 and 1995, and the percentage of female medical students now exceeds 40 percent. In business, the change has been no less impressive. In 1972, women held only 18 percent of managerial and administrative positions, compared to 43 percent of such positions in 1995. These changes represent a genuine revolution in the American workplace.

Despite these striking advances, however, women are far from achieving parity in a number of areas. They constitute only 5 to 7 percent of senior executives in the largest corporations, and the average full-time female employee makes less than 75 cents for every dollar earned by the average full-time male, if factors that influence wages such as hours worked and nature of the occupation are not considered. Many occupations remain highly sex segregated. Among the occupations in the United States that remain 90 percent or more female are bank teller, receptionist, registered nurse, and preschool and kindergarten teacher. Among the occupations that are less than 10 percent female are engineer, firefighter, mechanic, and pest exterminator. Large numbers of women pursue education in some scientific fields—such as biology and medicine—yet far fewer are found in other scientific fields—such as mathematics, physics, and engineering. Despite frequent assertions that women are victims of widespread discrimination, for the past two decades unemployment rates of the two sexes have not diverged by as much as a percentage point. Thus, women's progress has not been uniformly stifled nor has it uniformly advanced; instead it has been quite patchy.

The question is why. Part of the answer lies in the sexually dimorphic human mind. . . . The means by which any animal "makes a living" is intimately related to the animal's physical and psychological makeup. If the physical and psychological makeup of a species varies substantially by sex, we would expect that males and females may make their livings in a somewhat different manner. The culturally universal division of labor by sex appears to be a manifestation of that principle.

Even in today's relatively egalitarian Western societies, men and women tend to seek different jobs, favor different occupational attributes, and sometimes even perform the same jobs in a somewhat different manner. Because workplace choices often influence both tangible and intangible rewards, systematically different preferences tend to result in systematically different rewards. A social environment in which individuals of both sexes are free to pursue their own priorities cannot therefore be expected, a priori, to produce identical rewards to members of the two sexes.

Sex differences in temperament and cognitive abilities, as well as occupational preferences, are at least partially responsible for a number of workplace phenomena that are sometimes labeled "problems"—the "glass ceiling," the "gender gap" in compensation, and occupational segregation. Although sex discrimination can also play a role, complete understanding of workplace patterns requires us to look honestly at other factors. Some individuals, for example, are more likely to seek, and make the requisite sacrifices and investments to achieve, the highest positions in business, government, and academia. Those who achieve positions of high status tend to be those for whom status is a high priority. Those who have high earnings tend to be those for whom high earnings are a sufficiently high priority that the sacrifices and tradeoffs necessary to achieve them are worthwhile. Because men and women vary systematically along these and other dimensions, occupational outcomes for men and women are not identical. Whether this is a problem or merely a fact is to some extent a value judgment. However, one's beliefs about the causes of the outcomes—for example, discrimination by employers or personal choice of the affected individuals—may influence the extent to which the outcomes are deemed acceptable. . . .

Conclusion

The evidence and arguments put forward in this book will be troubling to many. Some may believe that invocation of biology is implicitly (or perhaps even explicitly) a defense of the status quo—a paean to the virtue of existing arrangements or at least a testament to their inevitability. The defense, however, is more limited. It is that many of the workplace patterns that are laid at the foot of nefarious causes such as discrimination by employers or sexist socialization have causes that are less invidious and less attributable to an anti-female ideology than is commonly recognized.

A consensus about the causes of workplace patterns does not foreordain consensus about policy responses. One's values are important, and values are not directly derivable from scientific fact. Proponents of laissez-faire policies will likely draw free-market implications, while those more inclined toward governmental intervention may settle on more activist approaches. Everyone interested in workplace policy, however, whatever his political or social outlook, should desire an accurate understanding of the underlying causes of current patterns.

It would be a mistake to interpret average temperamental or cognitive sex differences as limitations on the potential of individual girls and women. Nothing contained in this book implies that women cannot or should not be corporate presidents or theoretical physicists, only that equal representation of women in these positions is unlikely to occur unless selection processes are modified with the specific purpose of guaranteeing proportional representation.

Sufficient overlap exists on most traits that there are few occupations that should be expected to remain the exclusive domain of one sex, but many occupations will remain overwhelmingly male or overwhelmingly female if people continue to select occupations on the basis of their preferences and abilities. Expansion of the choices available to women (and to men) increases the influence of individual preferences on workplace outcomes. To the extent that individuals' preferences differ, we should expect them to seek different workplace rewards. Because the average endowment of men and women differs—in temperament, cognitive ability, values, and interests—it would be astonishing if their occupational preferences and behaviors were identical.

Modern attitudes about preferences are somewhat conflicted. The value that Western liberals place upon individual liberty rests heavily on the assumption that the preferences of individuals differ. Each individual should be free, within broad limits, to pursue his own ends. There is, therefore, something vaguely illiberal about both the assumption that all individuals *should* have the same preferences and attempts to ensure the outcomes that would result if they did.

Some people believe that even if sex differences exist, there is harm in publicizing them because they can become self-fulfilling prophecies. Even if the "correct" ratio of professional mathematicians is, say, 5 males to 1 female, it is harmful to make that fact widely known, because then mathematics will be labeled a "male field," and girls will assume that it is *only* for males. Although that is a rational concern, it is not well supported empirically. Clark McCauley found, for example, that when asked to estimate the proportion of males or females in a number of sex-stereotyped occupations, subjects showed no evidence of stereotypic exaggeration. The correlation between estimates and actual percentages was high, indicating that people rank-ordered them accurately, but where the subjects erred, it was almost always in the direction of underestimating the difference between men and women in the occupation. Similarly, Mary Ann Cejka and Alice Eagly found that participants systematically underestimated the extent to which male-dominated and female-dominated occupations were segregated.

It may seem odd that this book implies the near-inevitability of disproportionate male representation at the highest levels in corporate and other hierarchies, at least under current incentives, at the same time that other writers are predicting seemingly contrary trends. In 1999, two books appeared on the market, coincidentally both by Rutgers University anthropologists: *The First Sex* by Helen Fisher and *The Decline of Males* by Lionel Tiger. Both chronicled changes in the workplace, in education, and in broader social forces such as increasing female control over reproduction. Fisher's book emphasized the positive—the ascendancy of females—but gave little attention to the social effects of the "displaced males" that ascendancy of females implies. Tiger analyzed many of the same trends, but his view was more pessimistic, as the specter of large numbers of marginalized males does not bode well for any society. Neither Fisher's nor Tiger's analysis is inconsistent with that provided here, however. [T]he gender gap in compensation shrinks with changes in work that favor women. Nonetheless, men will continue to dominate the scarce positions at the top of hierarchies as long as it is necessary to devote decades of intense labor-market activity to obtain them, even if women come to predominate in middle-management positions and even if men also disproportionately occupy the bottom of hierarchies. Men will similarly continue to dominate math-intensive fields, as well as fields that expose workers to substantial physical risks.

The extent of one's willingness to live with the sex differences in outcomes described here depends to some extent on one's definitions of equality. If current workplace outcomes are a cumulative consequence of millions of individual choices made by men and women guided by their sexually dimorphic psyches, are the outcomes of those choices rendered suspect because those sexually dimorphic minds incline men and women to make their choices in systematically different ways? This question resembles, if not entails, the familiar question of whether the equality that ought to be of importance to policy makers is "equality of opportunity" or "equality of result." Those who place primary importance on equality of opportunity may say that as long as both men and women are given the opportunity to pursue the opportunities that the workplace provides, the outcomes are unimportant. Those who look to group outcomes, on the other hand, may say that the critical question is what the different groups end up with. However, we cannot say that the "outcome" for women is deficient without specifying with precision what that outcome is. We cannot, that is, simply look at women's income and occupational attainment without also considering what they get in return for the occupational tradeoffs that they make.

The question of agency is at the core. Are women, like men, active agents in their own lives, making rational decisions based upon their own preferences? Or are they pawns of both men and society—making suboptimal "choices" that are forced on them by others? All indications are that the former is closer to the mark. Women, though somewhat constrained by life circumstances, as are men, make rational and responsible choices that are most compatible with their temperaments, abilities, and desires.

POSTSCRIPT

Are Barriers to Women's Success as Leaders Due to Societal Obstacles?

Women's leadership style has been cited frequently as a barrier to success at the top of the corporate ladder. Leadership can be viewed from either the human capital perspective or the discrimination perspective. The human capital view would suggest that women, due to their natures, simply do not have the dominance-related and assertive dispositions that are presumed to be correlates of leadership. From a discrimination perspective, one can argue that women have not been given opportunities to learn and practice leadership skills. Furthermore, research shows that many people prefer a male to a female boss. The irony is that much of the research suggests that women's leadership styles, when they differ from those of men, can be more effective, although the job description rather than the sex of the person usually better predicts what type of leadership style one will use.

How can the contradictions between women being effective leaders and still have difficulty exercising leadership be resolved? Alice Eagly has suggested that the view of female leadership is complex and is a mixture of advantage and disadvantage. On the one hand, women's styles have been described as transformative, in that they promote innovation, trust, and empowerment in followers. On the other hand, expectations regarding competitiveness and toughness, coupled with old-fashioned prejudice against women, can interfere with effective leadership, especially in male-dominated domains.

Suggested Readings

Jean Lau Chin, B. Lott, J. Rice, and J. Sanchez-Hucles, *Women and Leadership: Transforming Visions and Diverse Voices* (Teachers College Press, 2007).

E. E. Duehr and J. E. Bono, "Men, Women and Managers: Are Stereotypes Finally Changing?" *Personnel Psychology* (Winter 2006).

Robin J. Ely, D. E. Meyerson, and M. N. Davidson, "Rethinking Political Correctness," *Harvard Business Review* (September 2006).

Anna Fels, "Do Women Lack Ambition?" *Harvard Business Review* (March 2005).

B. R. Ragins, J. M. Cornwell, and J. S. Miller, "Heterosexism in the Workplace: Do Race and Gender Matter?" *Group & Organizational Management* (vol. 28, 2003).

Internet References . . .

Advocates for Youth

This Web site, established in 1980 as the Center for Population Options, works to help young people make informed and responsible decisions about their reproductive and sexual health, fostering a positive and realistic approach to adolescent sexual health.

http://www.advocatesforyouth.org/%20%09%20index.php?option=
com_content&task=view&id=46&Itemid=75

WebMD Sexual Health Center

This Web site provides information from a medical perspective on gender identity disorder.

http://www.webmd.com/sex/gender-identity-disorder

Susan's Place for Transgender Resources

This Web site provides access to a wealth of information for transgendered persons, including information on health sex reassignment surgery, links to various support groups, activism, and spirituality.

http://www.susans.org/

American Psychological Association

This section of the APA Web site provides definitions of transgender and related concepts and answers a number of questions about development and mental health.

http://www.apa.org/topics/sexuality/transgender.aspx

Information for Health

The INFO Project (Information and Knowledge for Optimal Health Project), based at the Johns Hopkins University Bloomberg School of Public Health's Center for Communication Programs, is focused on understanding how knowledge and information can improve the quality of reproductive health programs, practice, and policies.

http://www.infoforhealth.org/

Go Ask Alice!

Go Ask Alice! is a health question-and-answer site sponsored by Columbia University's health education program. The mission of this site is to provide in-depth, factual, and nonjudgmental information to assist individuals' decision making about their physical, sexual, emotional, and spiritual health. Questions about sexuality, sexual health, and relationships are frequent. This site includes hundreds of relevant links.

http://www.goaskalice.columbia.edu/

Gender and Sexuality: Double Standards, Triple Standards?

*M*any contemporary scholars view sexuality as a cultural construction. Cultures provide individuals with knowledge and "lenses" that structure institutions, social interactions, beliefs, and behaviors. Through cultural lenses or meaning systems, individuals perceive the "facts" of sex and gender. Conceptualizations of sex and gender and the importance of sex and gender as social categories vary from culture to culture. However, within a particular culture, because individuals are usually limited to their own cultural lens, definitions of sex and gender seem fixed or even natural. In fact, cultural scholars argue, culture so completely defines us that we are usually oblivious to its presence in our own society. We think of culture as something that other societies have.

How do adolescents first experience sexual attractions—developing a "crush," falling in love, making the decision to "go all the way"? How does a child grow into a sexual being? What does it mean to be sexual? How does a child learn to think about his or her own genitals? These are profoundly personal and important questions, the answers to which are shaped by our cultural understanding of sexuality.

In this section, we examine cultural constructions of sex, gender, gender identity, and sexuality, especially messages sent to children and adolescents. Specifically, how are cultural institutions and mores structured by cultural definitions of the importance of sex and gender and by cultural gender proscriptions? What does culture dictate about the significance and characteristics of the social categories "male" and "female"? Where is there space for people who identify as other than male or female? Does one's standpoint or location within the culture prescribe one's sexual experiences? Consider how assumptions about the biological basis of sexuality as a prime force in human behavior influence how cultures attempt to control sexuality through various sex education strategies. Does the assumption that the expression of sexuality is based on biological drives affect messages that are delivered via the media? How can media images of sexual expression operate as both informational and normative sources of influence? Is it possible to resist media images?

- Should "Abstinence-Until-Marriage" Be the Only Message for Teens?
- Is "Gender Identity Disorder" an Appropriate Psychiatric Diagnosis?
- Should Transgendered Women Be Considered "Real" Women?

ISSUE 18

Should "Abstinence-Until-Marriage" Be the Only Message for Teens?

YES: Bridget E. Maher, from "Abstinence Until Marriage: The Best Message for Teens," *Family Research Council* (2004)

NO: Debra Hauser, from *Five Years of Abstinence-Only-Until-Marriage Education: Assessing the Impact* (2008)

ISSUE SUMMARY

YES: Bridget Maher argues that far too much funding has gone into programs that teach young people about sexuality and contraception— programs that she concludes are ineffective.

NO: Debra Hauser, in an evaluation of numerous abstinence-only-until-marriage programs that received funding under the Title V Social Security Act, concludes that they show few short-term benefits and no lasting, positive effects; rather such programs may actually worsen sexual health outcomes.

In 1996, President Clinton signed the welfare reform law. Attached to this law was a federal entitlement program allocating $50 million per year over a five-year period to abstinence-only-until-marriage educational programs. This Act specifies that a program is defined as "abstinence-only" education if it:

- has as its exclusive purpose teaching the social, psychological, and health gains to be realized by abstaining from sexual activity;
- teaches that abstinence from sexual activity outside of marriage is the expected standard for all school-age children;
- teaches that abstinence from sexual activity is the only certain way to avoid out-of-wedlock pregnancy, sexually transmitted diseases, and other associated health problems;
- teaches that a mutually faithful monogamous relationship in the context of marriage is the expected standard of sexual activity;
- teaches that sexual activity outside the context of marriage is likely to have harmful psychological and physical side effects;
- teaches that bearing children out-of-wedlock is likely to have harmful consequences for the child, the child's parents, and society;

- teaches young people how to reject sexual advances and how alcohol and drug use increases vulnerability to sexual advances; and,
- teaches the importance of attaining self-sufficiency before engaging in sexual activity. (*Section 510(b) of Title V of the Social Security Act, P.L. 104-193*)

In order to access these funds, an entity must agree to teach all of these points, not just a few. Failure to do so would result in loss of the funding.

Those who support the teaching of comprehensive sexuality education disagree with the tenets that abstinence-only-until-marriage (AOUM) supports. They present research that demonstrates how comprehensive sexuality education programs help young people to delay the onset of risky sexual behaviors, and to use contraceptives more effectively once they do start engaging in these behaviors. Some argue that AOUM is exclusionary, excluding non-heterosexual youth; is fear- and shame-based; and is wildly out of touch with the reality in which young people are living. They are quick to point out that AOUM supports have yet to provide empirical evidence that their programs "work."

AOUM supporters believe that comprehensive sexuality education programs teach "too much, too soon." They believe strongly that providing information about abstinence, along with safer sex information, confuses teens, and gives them permission to become sexually active when the potential consequences for sexual activity are much more serious.

Take a look at the language of the legislation. The language refers to "sexual activity." We know that for many people "having sex" means only sexual intercourse. It does not include oral or anal sex, for example. We know that many teens are having sexual intercourse outside of marriage, and although this number is going down, the number of youth engaging in oral and anal sex is increasing. What does "sexual activity" mean to you? Would you be able to support the legislation if it included some behaviors, but not others? Are there some messages you agree with and not others? If you were an educator, would you be able to teach all eight points, especially given what you know about adolescent sexual behavior?

As you read these selections, think about any sexuality education classes you may have had—do you think they should have taught you more? Less? Consider, too, young people who are already sexually active. Would abstinence messages work for them? Did a more comprehensive program "fail" them?

In the following selections, Bridget Maher outlines some of the negative consequences of teen sex, and why abstinence is the only 100 percent effective option for avoiding those negative consequences. She argues that more comprehensive sexuality education programs, while purporting to teach about abstinence, actually rarely, if ever, do. Debra Hauser describes what she perceives to be flaws in the assertions made by AOUM proponents, such as the idea that if educators teach only abstinence, teens won't have sex. In reviewing abstinence-only programs, she concludes that although most show changes in attitudes towards abstinence, many actually discourage safe practices in youth who are sexually active and thereby increase the risks of the very problems the programs were designed to prevent.

YES ⤶

Bridget E. Maher

Abstinence Until Marriage: The Best Message for Teens

The federal government has provided some abstinence-until-marriage funding in recent years, but comprehensive sex education and contraception programs are vastly over-funded in comparison. In 2002, abstinence-until-marriage programs received $102 million, while teen-sex education and contraception programs received at least $427.7 million. In his last budget, President Bush proposed an increase of $33 million for abstinence-until-marriage programs, following upon his campaign promise to try to equalize funding between comprehensive sex education and abstinence programs. This is a good first step, but it still doesn't bring true parity between these programs. It's time for our government to get serious about fulfilling the president's promise to at least level the playing field with regard to funding of the positive and healthy message of abstinence-until-marriage versus that of promoting premarital sex and contraception.

Teens are greatly influenced by the messages they receive about sex in school. Unfortunately, the majority of schools teach "safe sex"—"comprehensive" or so-called "abstinence plus" programs—believing that it's best for kids to have all the information they need about sexuality and to make their own decisions about sex. Abstinence is downplayed while sexual activity and condom use are encouraged in these curriculums, because it's assumed that children are eventually going to have sex. A 2002 report by the Physicians Consortium, which investigated comprehensive sex programs promoted by the Centers for Disease Control, reveals that abstinence is barely mentioned and condom use is clearly advocated in these curriculums.

Abstinence-until-marriage programs, on the other hand, teach young people to save sex for marriage, and their message has been very effective in changing teens' behavior. Today, there are over one-thousand abstinence-until-marriage programs around the United States and one-third of public middle and high schools say that abstinence is "the main message in their sex education." Abstinence organizations do more than just tell teens to say no to unwed sex: they teach young people the skills they need to practice abstinence. Classes cover many topics including self-esteem building, self-control, decision-making, goal-setting, character education, and communication skills. Choosing the Best, Teen-Aid, Inc., and Operation Keepsake are just a few of the many effective abstinence programs in the U.S. . . .

Teens want to be taught abstinence. Nearly all (93 percent) of teenagers believe that teens should be given a strong message from society to abstain

From *Family Research Council*, June 12, 2004. Copyright © 2004 by Family Research Council. Reprinted by permission.

340

from sex until at least after high school. A 2000 pool found that 64 percent of teen girls surveyed said sexual activity is not acceptable for high-school age adolescents, even if precautions are taken to prevent pregnancy and sexually transmitted diseases.

Those who do not abstain from sex are likely to experience many negative consequences, both physical and emotional. Aside from the risk of pregnancy, teens have a high risk of contracting a sexually transmitted disease (STD). Each year 3 million teens—25 percent of sexually active teens—are infected with an STD. About 25 percent of all new cases of STDs occur in teenagers; two-thirds of new cases occur in young people age 15–24. Teens who engage in premarital sex are likely to experience fear about pregnancy and STDs, regret, guilt, lowered self-respect, fear of commitment, and depression. . . .

Public opinion polls show that teens value abstinence highly. Nearly all (93 percent) of teenagers believe that teens should be given a strong message from society to abstain from sex until at least after high school.[1] A 2000 poll found that 64 percent of teen girls surveyed said sexual activity is not acceptable for high-school age adolescents, even if precautions are taken to prevent pregnancy and sexually transmitted diseases.[2] Moreover, teens who have not abstained often regret being sexually active. In 2000, 63 percent of sexually active teens said they wish they had waited longer to become sexually active.[3]

Negative Consequences of Unwed Teen Sex

Teens need to be taught to save sex for marriage, because premarital sex has many negative consequences, both physical and emotional. One of the most obvious outcomes of engaging in premarital sex is having a child outside marriage; today, one-third of all births are out-of-wedlock.[4] Teen birthrates have declined since the early 1990s, but the highest unwed birthrates are among those age 20–24, followed by those 25–29.[5] This shows that many young girls abstain from sex while they are in high school, but not afterward.

Teen unwed childbearing has negative consequences for mothers, children, and society. Unwed teen mothers are likely to live in poverty and be dependent on welfare, and only about 50 percent of them are likely to finish high school while they are adolescents or young adults.[6] Children born to teen mothers are more likely than other children to have lower grades, to leave high school without graduating, to be abused or neglected, to have a child as an unmarried teenager, and to be delinquent.[7] Teen childbearing costs U.S. taxpayers an estimated $7 billion per year in social services and lost tax revenue due to government dependency.[8] The gross annual cost to society of unwed childbearing and its consequences is $29 billion, which includes the administration of welfare and foster care programs, building and maintaining additional prisons, as well as lower education and resultant lost productivity among unwed parents.[9]

Aside from the risk of pregnancy, teens have a high risk of contracting a sexually transmitted disease (STD). Each year 3 million teens—25 percent of sexually active teens—are infected with an STD.[10] About 25 percent of all new cases of STDs occur in teenagers; two-thirds of new cases occur in young people age 15–24.[11]

Chlamydia and gonorrhea are two of the most common curable STDs among sexually active teens. According to the Centers for Disease Control, gonorrhea rates are highest among 15- to 19-year-old females and 20- to 24-year-old males, and more than five to 10 percent of teen females are currently infected with chlamydia.[12] If these diseases are untreated, they can lead to pelvic inflammatory disease, infertility, and ectopic pregnancy.[13] Studies have found that up to 15 percent of sexually active teenage women are infected with the human papillomavirus (HPV), an incurable virus that is present in nearly all cervical cancers.[14]

In addition to being at risk for STDs, unwed sexually active teens are likely to experience negative emotional consequences and to become both more promiscuous and less interested in marriage. Teens who engage in premarital sex are likely to experience fear about pregnancy and STDs, regret, guilt, lowered self-respect, fear of commitment, and depression.[15] Also, adolescents who engage in unwed sex at a younger age are much more likely to have multiple sex partners. Among young people between the ages of 15–24 who have had sex before age 18, 75 percent had two or more partners and 45 percent had four or more partners. Among those who first had sex after age 19, just 20 percent had more than one partner and one percent had four or more partners.[16] Premarital sex can also cause teens to view marriage less favorably. A 1994 study of college freshmen found that non-virgins with multiple sex partners were more likely to view marriage as difficult and involving a loss of personal freedom and happiness. Virgins were more likely to view marriage as "enjoyable.". . .[17]

"Safe Sex" or "Comprehensive Sex Education" Programs

In addition to the influence of their parents, teens are also affected by the messages on sex and abstinence that they receive in school. Unfortunately, the majority of schools teach "safe sex," "comprehensive," or so-called "abstinence plus" programs, believing that it is best for children to have all the information they need about sexuality and to make their own decisions about sex.[18] Abstinence is downplayed and sexual activity and condom use are encouraged in these curriculums, because it is assumed that kids are eventually going to have sex. A 2002 report by the Physicians Consortium, which investigated comprehensive sex programs promoted by the Centers for Disease Control, reveals that abstinence is barely mentioned and condom use is clearly advocated in these curriculums. Not only do students learn how to obtain condoms, but they also practice putting them on cucumbers or penile models. Masturbation, body massages, bathing together, and fantasizing are listed as "ways to be close" in one curriculum. . . .[19]

The Effectiveness of Abstinence-Until-Marriage Programs

Abstinence-until-marriage programs, on the other hand, teach young people to save sex for marriage, and their message has been very effective in changing teens' behavior. According to the Physicians Resource Council, the drop in teen birth rates during the 1990s was due not to increased contraceptive use among teens, but to sexual abstinence.[20] This correlates with the decrease in sexual activity among unwed teens. In 1988, 51 percent of unwed girls between the ages of 15 and 19 had engaged in sexual intercourse compared to 49 percent 1995. This decrease also occurred among unwed boys, declining from 60 percent to 55 percent between 1988 and 1995.[21]

Today, there are over one thousand abstinence-until-marriage programs around the United States, and one-third of public middle and high schools say both that abstinence is "the main message in their sex education" and that abstinence is taught as "the only option for young people."[22] Started by nonprofit or faith-based groups, these programs teach young people to save sex for marriage. However, abstinence organizations do more than just tell teens to say no to unwed sex: They teach young people the skills they need to practice abstinence. Classes cover many topics including self-esteem building, self-control, decision making, goal setting, character education, and communication skills. Sexually transmitted diseases, the realities of parenthood and anatomy are also discussed.[23] The effectiveness of birth control may be discussed, but it is neither provided nor promoted in these programs.

Choosing the Best, an abstinence program based in Marietta, Georgia, and started in 1993, has developed curriculum and materials that are used in over two thousand school districts in 48 states. Students in public or private schools are taught abstinence by their teachers, who have been trained by Choosing the Best's staff. Appropriate for 6th through 12th graders, the curriculum teaches students the consequences of premarital sex, the benefits of abstaining until marriage, how to make a virginity pledge, refusal skills, and character education. Choosing the Best involves parents in their children's lessons and teaches them how to teach abstinence to their children. . . .

This abstinence program has contributed to lower teen-pregnancy rates in Georgia. In Columbus, Georgia, Choosing the Best's materials were used in all 8th grades for a period of four years. A study requested by the Georgia State Board of Education to examine the effectiveness of this curriculum found a 38-percent reduction in pregnancies among middle-school students in Muscogee County between 1997 and 1999. Other large school districts that did not implement Choosing the Best's program experienced only a 6-percent reduction in teen pregnancies during those same years.

Teen-Aid, Inc., based in Spokane, Washington, has been promoting abstinence until marriage and character education for over twenty years. This program seeks to teach young people the knowledge and skills they need to make good decisions and to achieve goals. Parent-child communication is a key component of the Teen-Aid curriculum, as parents are involved in every lesson. In 1999–2000, over 41,000 families in public schools, churches, and community organizations used these materials.

A 1999 study conducted by Whitworth College in Spokane, Washington found many positive results among teens in Edinburg, Texas who were taught the Teen-Aid curriculum. On the pretest administered to students after the course, 62 percent said "having sex as a teenager would make it harder for them to get a good job or be successful in a career," compared to 71 percent on the post test. When asked if they were less likely to have sexual intercourse before they got married, 47 percent responded yes on the pretest, compared to 54 percent after taking the course. . . .[24]

Operation Keepsake, a Cleveland, Ohio-based abstinence program started in 1988, has its "For Keeps" curriculum in 90 public and private schools in the greater Cleveland area. It is presently taught to over 25,000 students, including those in middle and high school, as well as college freshmen. Along with a classroom component, this program also includes peer mentoring, guest speakers, opportunities to make an abstinence pledge, and parental involvement.

Case Western Reserve University evaluated Operation Keepsake's program in 2001, finding that it is having a positive impact on adolescents' beliefs and behavior regarding abstinence. Over nine hundred 7th and 8th graders completed the pretests and post tests. According to the study, the program had "a clear and sustainable impact on abstinence beliefs" because students in the program had "higher abstinence-until-marriage values" at the follow-up survey than did those in the control group, who did not attend the abstinence program. . . .[25]

Virginity pledges are also successful in encouraging sexual abstinence among unwed teens. A 2001 study based on the National Longitudinal Study of Adolescent Health . . . found that teens who take a virginity pledge are 34 percent less likely to have sex before marriage compared to those who do not pledge, even after controlling for factors such as family structure, race, self-esteem, and religiosity. . . .[26]

Conclusion

These are only some of the many abstinence-until-marriage programs in the United States. Their success in changing young people's views and behavior regarding abstinence is due to their telling the truth about sex to young people: that it is meant to be saved for marriage and that it is possible to live a chaste life. Along with this message, they give kids the encouragement and skills they need to save themselves for marriage. . . .

Notes

1. "The Cautious Generation? Teens Tell Us About Sex, Virginity, and 'The Talk,' " National Campaign to Prevent Teen Pregnancy, April 27, 2000.
2. Ibid.
3. "Not Just Another Thing to Do: Teens Talk About Sex, Regret and the Influence of Their Parents," National Campaign to Prevent Teen Pregnancy, June 30, 2000.
4. Joyce A. Martin et al., *Births: Final Data for 2001*, National Vital Statistics Reports 51, December 18, 2002, National Center for Health Statistics, Table C.
5. Bridget Maher, *The Family Portrait: A Compilation of Data, Research and Public Opinion on the Family*, Family Research Council, 2002, p. 73, 162.
6. Rebecca Maynard, *Kids Having Kids: Economic and Social Consequences of Teen Pregnancy*, The Urban Institute, 1997, p. 2–5.
7. Ibid, p. 205–229, 257–281, Judith Levine, Harold Pollack and Maureen E. Comfort, "Academic and Behavioral Outcomes Among the Children of

Young Mothers," *Journal of Marriage and Family* 63 (May 2001): 355–369 and Amy Conseur et al., "Maternal and Perinatal Risk Factors for Later Delinquency," *Pediatrics* 99 (June 1997): 785–790.

8. Rebecca A. Maynard, ed., *Kids Having Kids: A Robin Hood Foundation Special Report on the Costs of Adolescent Childbearing,* The Robin Hood Foundation, 1996, p. 19.

9. Ibid, pp. 20, 88–91.

10. The Alan Guttmacher Institute, "Teen Sex and Pregnancy," *Facts in Brief,* 1999.

11. Linda L. Alexander, ed., et al., "Sexually Transmitted Diseases in America: How Many Cases and at What Cost?" The Kaiser Family Foundation, December 1998, 8.

12. Centers for Disease Control, *Tracking the Hidden Epidemics: Trends in the United States 2000,* 4.

13. The Alan Guttmacher Institute, "Teen Sex and Pregnancy."

14. Ibid. See also the Kaiser Family Foundation, "HPV (Human Papillomavirus) and Cervical Cancer," *Fact Sheet,* July 2001.

15. Tom and Judy Lickona, *Sex, Love and You* (Notre Dame: Ave Maria Press, 1994), 62–77.

16. Centers for Disease Control, "Current Trends: Premarital Sexual Experience Among Adolescent Women—United States, 1970–1988," *Morbidity and Mortality Weekly Report* 39 (January 4, 1991): 929–932.

17. Connie J. Salts et al., "Attitudes Toward Marriage and Premarital Sexual Activity of College Freshmen," *Adolescence* 29 (Winter 1994): 775–779.

18. Tina Hoff and Liberty Greene et al., "Sex Education in America: A Series of National Surveys of Students, Parents, Teachers, and Principals," Kaiser Family Foundation, September 2000, 16.

19. The Physicians Consortium, "Sexual Messages in Government-Promoted Programs and Today's Youth Culture," April 2002.

20. Cheryl Wetzstein, "Drop in Teen Birthrates Attributed to Abstinence," *The Washington Times,* February 11, 1999, A6.

21. Joyce C. Abma and Freya L. Sonenstein, *Sexual Activity and Contraceptive Practices Among Teenagers in the United States, 1988 and 1995,* Series 23: Data from the National Survey of Family Growth, National Center for Health Statistics, Washington, D.C., April 2001, Table 1.

22. Tina Hoff and Liberty Greene et al., "Sex Education in America: A Series of National Surveys of Students, Parents, Teachers, and Principals," 14.

23. Barbara Devaney et al., "The Evaluation of Abstinence Education Programs Funded Under Title V Section 510: Interim Report," Mathematica Policy Research, Inc., April 2002, 14.

24. Raja S. Tanas, "Report on the Teen-Aid Abstinence-Education Program Fifth-Year Evaluation 1998–1999," Whitworth College, Spokane, WA, July 1999.

25. Elaine Borawski et al., "Evaluation of the Teen Pregnancy Prevention Programs Funded Through the Wellness Block Grant (1999–2000)," Case Western Reserve University, March 23, 2001.

26. Peter S. Bearman and Hannah Bruckner, "Promising the Future: Virginity Pledges and First Intercourse," *American Journal of Sociology* 106 (January 2001): 859–912.

Debra Hauser

NO

Five Years of Abstinence-Only-Until-Marriage Education: Assessing the Impact

Introduction

Since 1991, rates of teenage pregnancy and birth have declined significantly in the United States. These are welcome trends. Yet, teens in the United States continue to suffer from the highest birth rate and one of the highest rates of sexually transmitted infections (STIs) in the industrialized world. Debate over the best way to help teens avoid, or reduce, their sexual risk-taking behavior has polarized many youth-serving professionals. On one side are those that support comprehensive sex education—education that promotes abstinence but includes information about contraception and condoms to build young people's knowledge, attitudes, and skills for when they do become sexually active. On the other side are those that favor abstinence-only-until-marriage—programs that promote "abstinence from sexual activity outside marriage as the expected standard" of behavior. Proponents of abstinence-only programs believe that providing information about the health benefits of condoms or contraception contradicts their message of abstinence-only and undermines its impact. As such, abstinence-only programs provide no information about contraception beyond failure rates.

In 1996, Congress signed into law the Personal Responsibility & Work Opportunities Reconciliation Act, or "welfare reform." Attached was the provision, later set out in Section 510(b) of Title V of the Social Security Act, appropriating $250 million dollars over five years for state initiatives promoting sexual abstinence outside of marriage as the only acceptable standard of behavior for young people.

For the first five years of the initiative, every state but California participated in the program. (California had experimented with its own abstinence-only initiative in the early 1990s. The program was terminated in February 1996, when evaluation results found the program to be ineffective.) From 1998 to 2003, almost a half a billion dollars in state and federal funds were appropriated to support the Title V initiative. A report, detailing the results from the federally funded evaluation of select Title V programs, was due to be released more than a year ago. Last year, Congress extended "welfare reform" and, with it, the Title V abstinence-only-until-marriage funding without benefit of this, as yet unreleased, report.

As the first five-year funding cycle of Title V came to a close, a few state-funded evaluations became public. Others were completed with little or no fanfare. This document reviews the findings from the 10 evaluations that Advocates for Youth was able to identify. Advocates for Youth also includes evaluation results from California's earlier attempt at a statewide abstinence-only initiative.

Available Evaluations

Ten states made some form of evaluation results available for review. For Arizona, Florida, Iowa, Maryland, Minnesota, Oregon, Pennsylvania, and Washington, Advocates was able to locate evaluation results from state Title V programs. For Missouri and Nebraska, Advocates located evaluation findings from at least one program among those funded through the state's Title V initiative. Finally, the evaluation of California's abstinence-only program was published in a peer-reviewed journal and readily available.

Funding*

During the first five years of abstinence-only-until-marriage Title V programming, the 10 states received about $45.5 million in federal funds. To further support the initiatives and to cover their required funding match, these states appropriated about $34 million in additional funds over the five years. In addition, California spent $15 million in state funds between 1991 and 1994 to support its abstinence-only initiative. In sum, the program efforts discussed in this paper cost an estimated $94.5 million in federal and state dollars.

Program Components

For the most part, Title V funds were administered through states' departments of health and then sub-granted to abstinence-only contractors within each state. Program components varied from state to state and from contractor to contractor within each state. However, all programs discussed in this document included an abstinence-only curriculum, delivered to young people in schools or through community-based agencies. Popular curricula included: *Education Now Babies Later (ENABL)*, *Why Am I Tempted? (WAIT)*, *Family Accountability Communicating Teen Sexuality (FACTS)*, *Choosing the Best Life, Managing Pressures before Marriage,* and AC Green's *Game Plan,* among others. Some programs

---

* In federal fiscal year 2003, the 10 states discussed here with evaluations of Title V programs received $8,810,281 in federal funds. Under the law, states are required to provide matching funds of three state-raised dollars for every four federal dollars received. Thus in 2003, the 10 states supplied $7,268,060 in state dollars, bringing the total of public monies to Title V funded abstinence-only-until-marriage programs to $16,078,341.

included peer education, health fairs, parent outreach, and/or *Baby Think it Over* simulators. Some states supplemented their educational programs with media campaigns, also funded through Title V.

Evaluation Designs

The 11 evaluations summarized in this document represent those Advocates for Youth could uncover through extensive research. The quality of the evaluation designs varied greatly. Most evaluations employed a simple pretest/posttest survey design. Slightly fewer than half (five) assessed the significance of changes from pre- to posttest, using a comparison group. Additionally, seven evaluations included some form of follow-up to assess the program's impact over time, although results are not yet available for two. Three of these seven also included a comparison group. For those programs that included follow-up, surveys were administered at three to 17 months after students completed their abstinence-only-until-marriage program.

Because the quality of the evaluation designs varied from state to state, Advocates relied heavily on the evaluators' own analyses and words to describe each program's impact.

Summary of Results

Evaluation of these 11 programs showed few short-term benefits and no lasting, positive impact. A few programs showed mild success at improving attitudes and intentions to abstain. No program was able to demonstrate a positive impact on sexual behavior over time. A description follows of short- and long-term impacts, by indicator.

Short-Term Impacts of State Abstinence-Only Programs

In 10 programs, evaluation measured the short-term impact of the program on at least one indicator, including attitudes favoring abstinence, intentions to abstain, and/or sexual behavior. Overall, programs were most successful at improving participants' attitudes towards abstinence and were least likely to positively affect participants' sexual behaviors.

Attitudes Endorsing Abstinence—10 evaluations tested for short-term changes in attitudes.

- Three of 10 programs had no significant impact on attitudes (Maryland, Missouri, and Nebraska).
- Four of 10 showed increases in attitudes favorable to abstinence (Arizona, Florida, Oregon, and Washington).
- Three of 10 showed mixed results (California, Iowa, and Pennsylvania).**

** Mixed results indicated that attitudes changed in both desired and undesired directions, either by survey questions within one initiative, or by individual programs within an initiative.

Intentions to Abstain—Nine evaluations measured short-term changes in intentions.

- Four of nine programs showed no significant impact on participants' intentions to abstain (California, Maryland, Nebraska, and Oregon).
- Three of nine programs showed a favorable impact on intentions to abstain (Arizona, Florida, and Washington).
- Two of nine programs showed mixed results (Iowa and Pennsylvania).**

Sexual Behaviors—Six evaluations measured short-term changes in sexual behavior.

- Three of six programs had no impact on sexual behavior (California, Maryland, and Missouri).
- Two of six programs reported increases in sexual behavior from pre- to posttest (Florida and Iowa). It was unclear whether the increases were due to youth's maturation or to a program's effect, as none of these evaluations included a comparison group.
- One of the six programs showed mixed results (Pennsylvania).**

Long-Term Impacts of State Abstinence-Only Programs

Seven evaluations included some form of follow-up survey to assess the impact of the abstinence-only programs over time. Results from two of these are not yet available (Nebraska and Oregon). Of the remaining five, three were of statewide initiatives (Arizona, California, and Minnesota). Two were evaluations of programs within statewide initiatives (Missouri's *Life Walk* Program and Pennsylvania's LaSalle Program). All five evaluations included questions to assess changes in participants' attitudes and behaviors between pretest/posttest and follow-up. Four also measured changes in intentions to abstain. Three evaluations included a comparison group.

- **Attitudes Endorsing Abstinence**—Five evaluations included assessment of changes in attitudes. Four of five evaluations showed no long-term positive impact on participants' attitudes. That is, participants' attitudes towards abstinence either declined at follow-up, or there was no evidence that participating in the abstinence-only program improved teens' attitudes about abstinence relative to the comparison groups, at three to 17 months after taking the abstinence-only program (Arizona, California, Missouri, and Pennsylvania's LaSalle Program). Follow-up surveys in Minnesota showed mixed results.
- **Intentions to Abstain**—Four evaluations measured long-term intentions to abstain. Three of four evaluations showed no long-term positive impact on participants' intentions to abstain from sexual intercourse. That is, participants' intentions either declined significantly at follow-up or there was no statistically significant difference in participants' attitudes relative to controls at follow-up (Arizona, California, and Minnesota). In one of the four (Pennsylvania's LaSalle Program),

evaluation showed a positive impact at follow-up on program participants' intentions to abstain relative to comparison youth.
*   **Sexual Behavior**—Five programs measured long-term impacts on
    sexual behavior. No evaluation demonstrated any impact on reducing
    teens' sexual behavior at follow-up, three to 17 months after the pro-
    gram ended (Arizona, California, Minnesota, Missouri, or Pennsylvania's
    LaSalle Program).

Comparisons of Abstinence-Only-Until-Marriage versus Comprehensive Sex Education

Two evaluations—Iowa's and the Pennsylvania's Fulton County program—
compared the impact of comprehensive sex education with that of abstinence-
only-until-marriage programs.

In Iowa, abstinence-only students were slightly more likely than comprehensive sex education participants to feel strongly about wanting to postpone
sex but less likely to feel that their goals should not include teen pregnancy.
There was little to no difference between the abstinence-only students and
those in the comprehensive sex education program in understanding why
they should wait to have sex. Evaluation did not include comparison of data
on the sexual behavior of participants in the two types of programs.

In Fulton County, Pennsylvania, results found few to no differences
between the abstinence-only and comprehensive approaches in attitudes
towards sexual behavior. Evaluators found that, regardless of which program
was implemented in the seventh and eighth grades, sexual attitudes, intentions, and behaviors were similar by the end of the 10th grade.

Discussion

These evaluation results—from the first five-year cycle of funding for abstinence-
only-until-marriage under Section 510(b) of Title V of the Social Security
Act—reflect the results of other studies. In a 1994 review of sex education
programs, all the studies available at the time of school-based, abstinence-
only programs [were assessed] that had received peer review and that measured attitudes, intentions, *and* behavior. [It was] found that none of the three
abstinence-only programs was effective in producing a statistically significant
impact on sexual behaviors in program participants relative to comparisons.
In a 1997 report for the National Campaign to Prevent Teen Pregnancy, Doug
Kirby reviewed evaluations from six abstinence-only programs, again finding
no program that produced a statistically significant change in sexual behavior. This was again confirmed in 2000, when another review by Kirby found
no abstinence-only program that produced statistically significant changes in
sexual behaviors among program youth relative to comparisons. This failure
of abstinence-only programs to produce behavior change was among the central concerns expressed by some authors of the evaluations included in this
document. . . . It is important to note that a great deal of research contradicts
the belief that changes in knowledge and attitudes alone will necessarily result
in behavior change.

A few evaluators also noted the failure of abstinence-only programs to address the needs of sexually active youth. Survey data from many of the programs indicated that sexually experienced teens were enrolled in most of the abstinence-only programs studied. For example:

In Erie County, Pennsylvania, researchers found that 42 percent of the female participants were sexually active by the second year of the program.

In Clinton County, Pennsylvania, data collected from program participants in the seventh, eighth, and ninth grades showed a dramatic increase in the proportion of program females who experienced first sexual intercourse over time (six, nine, and 30 percent, respectively, by grade).

In Minnesota, 12 percent of the eighth grade program participants were sexually active at posttest.

In Arizona, 19 percent of program participants were sexually active at follow-up. Concurrently, Arizona's evaluators found that youth's intent to pursue abstinence declined significantly at follow-up, regardless of whether the student took another abstinence-only class. Eighty percent of teens reported that they were likely to become sexually active by the time they were 20 years old.

Abstinence-only programs provide these youth with no information, other than abstinence, regarding how to protect themselves from pregnancy, HIV, and other STIs.

A third, related concern of evaluators was abstinence-only programs' failure to provide positive information about contraception and condoms. Evaluators noted more than once that programs' emphasis on the failure rates of contraception, including condoms, left youth ambivalent, at best, about using them.

In Clinton County, Pennsylvania, researchers noted that, of those participants that reported experiencing first sexual intercourse during ninth grade, only about half used any form of contraception.

Arizona's evaluation team found that program participants' attitudes about birth control became less favorable from pre- to posttest. They noted that this was probably a result of the "program's focus on the failure rates of contraceptives as opposed to their availability, use and access." . . .

Conclusion

Abstinence-only programs show little evidence of sustained (long-term) impact on attitudes and intentions. Worse, they show some negative impacts on youth's willingness to use contraception, including condoms, to prevent negative sexual health outcomes related to sexual intercourse. Importantly, only in one state did any program demonstrate short-term success in delaying the initiation of sex; none of these programs demonstrates evidence of long-term success in delaying sexual initiation among youth exposed to the programs or any evidence of success in reducing other sexual risk-taking behaviors among participants.

POSTSCRIPT

Should "Abstinence-Until-Marriage" Be the Only Message for Teens?

The *Healthy People 2010: Understanding and Improving Health* report (U.S. Department of Health and Human Services, 2000) suggests that as many as 50 percent of all adolescents are sexually active. The *National Youth Risk Behavior Survey* (2007) reported similar findings, with rates higher for boys than girls, and with 7.1 percent of youth having sexual intercourse before age 13. Approximately 35 percent of students surveyed had had sexual intercourse in the three months before the survey, and only 61.5 percent used a condom during the most recent sexual intercourse. The *National Survey of American Attitudes on Substance Abuse XIV: Teens and Parents* (2009) found strong relations among teen drunkenness, marijuana use, and harmful sexual behaviors. The high rates of sexual activity among young people are especially troubling, given that a large and disproportionate percentage of sexually transmitted diseases and unintended pregnancies occur among adolescents. In March of 2008, the Centers for Disease Control released results of a survey of teens that indicates that at least 25 percent of teen girls have a sexually transmitted disease (STD), in spite of the fact that many claimed they had not had sexual intercourse. Among those who admitted to sexual intercourse, 40 percent had an STD. The discrepancy is likely due to the fact that some STDs are oral, and many youth do not consider oral sex "real" sex. There is no doubt that STDs have become a serious public health issue among teens.

In reality we know that during the teen years, young people go through many powerful hormonal, emotional, and social changes. They discover sexual feelings without fully understanding their meaning or what to do with them. They often end up engaging in sexual activity that is not pleasant (especially females) and often do not practice safe sex (using condoms or dental dams, for example). There are powerful gender-related dating and sexual scripts that make it more difficult for adolescents to negotiate their sexual experiences. These scripts guide expectations: notions of "real" sex, who is supposed to initiate, and what the experience is supposed to be like (e.g., an ideal), as well as the consequences for engaging (or not) in sexual activity. Males may feel like they have to be sexually active to be seen as a "real" man and run the risk of being called "gay" if they refrain. Females have to deal with the stereotypes of "prude" or "slut." Many adolescent girls report they engage in oral sex to be popular.

Each side of the sexuality debate is working with what it considers to be a logical presumption. For AOUM proponents, the surest way to avoid an unintended pregnancy or STI is to not do anything sexually until in a committed, monogamous relationship—which, to them, is only acceptable within the context of marriage. If people do not engage in the behaviors, they cannot be exposed to the negatives. Since AOUM supporters also believe that marriage is a commitment that is accompanied by a promise of monogamy, or sexual exclusivity, it is, for them, the only appropriate choice for teens.

For comprehensive sexuality education proponents, the logic is that sexual exploration is a normal part of adolescents' development. They believe that the "just say no" approach to sexual behaviors is as unrealistic as it is unhealthy. Rooted in education, social learning, and health belief theories, comprehensive sexuality education programs believe that youth can make wise decisions about their sexual health if given the proper information. Comprehensive programs can address the psychosocial issues, and the role of gender-role expectations in ways that AOUM cannot.

Suggested Readings

Charles Abraham, Mary Rogers Gillmore, Gerjo Kok, and Herman P. Schaalma, "Sex Education as Health Promotion: What Does It Take?" *Archives of Sexual Behavior, 33* (2004): 259–269.

Paul Florsheim, *Adolescent Romantic Relations and Sexual Behavior: Theory, Research, and Practical Implications* (Mahwah, NJ: Lawrence Erlbaum Associates, 2003).

Douglas Kirby, "The Impact of Schools and School Programs upon Adolescent Sexual Behavior," *The Journal of Sex Research, 9* (2002): 27–33.

J. Mark Halstead and Michael J. Reiss, *Values in Sex Education: From Principles to Practice* (London: Routledge Falmer, 2003).

PM Medical Health News, *21st Century Complete Medical Guide to Teen Health Issues, Teenage Nutrition, Teen Violence, Teenage Sexual Health, Authoritative Government Documents, Information for Patients and Physicians* (CD-ROM, 2004).

Deborah A. Stanley, *Sexual Health Information for Teens: Health Tips about Sexual Development, Human Reproduction, and Sexually Transmitted Diseases* (Detroit, MI: Omnigraphics, 2003).

ISSUE 19

Is "Gender Identity Disorder" an Appropriate Psychiatric Diagnosis?

YES: Mercedes Allen, from "Destigmatization versus Coverage and Access: The Medical Model of Transsexuality" at http://dentedbluemercedes.wordpress.com/2008/04/05/destigmatization-versus-coverage-and-access-the-medical-model-of-transsexuality/ (2008)

NO: Kelley Winters, from GID Reform Advocates, "Issues of GID Diagnosis for Transsexual Women and Men" from http://www.gidreform.org/GID30285a.pdf (2007)

ISSUE SUMMARY

YES: Mercedes Allen, educator, trainer, and founder of AlbertaTrans.org, recognizes the bias in the DSM's classification of Gender Identity Disorder as a mental disorder but argues that changes run the risk of leaving the trans community at risk of losing medical care and treatment.

NO: Kelley Winters, Ph.D., writer and founder of GID Reform Advocates, argues the inclusion of Gender Identity Disorder in the DSM adds to the stigma faced by transpersons and that reclassification is necessary to adequately address the population's health care needs.

Gender identity can be a difficult concept to describe. Many people have probably never given much thought to questions of how they feel about themselves in terms of maleness or femaleness. It is assumed that most people have a gender identity that is congruent with their anatomical sex. While some men may feel more (or less) masculine than others, the majority strongly *identify* as male. The same could be said for most women—regardless of how feminine they feel (or don't feel), the majority *identify* as women. If asked, most women would probably say they feel like a woman. Most men simply feel like a man. But what does it mean to "feel" like a woman or a man? What is it to "feel" feminine or masculine? Is there only one type of femininity? One style of masculinity?

And what about those who feel that their gender identity, their feeling of maleness or femaleness, doesn't match their birth sex? For those whose gender does not match societal expectations for a person of their anatomical sex, gender identity can be hard to ignore. Their gender identities do not fit the binary gender system that is firmly in place in American society. Because of this, a diagnosis of Gender Identity Disorder (GID) has been applied to those who identify as transgender or transsexual. This diagnosis can be found in the *Diagnostic and Statistical Manual of Mental Disorders,* commonly referred to as the DSM, published by the American Psychiatric Association.

In 2012, an updated, fifth edition of the DSM will be published (Melby, 2009). Over the years, new editions have been greatly anticipated to see what changes occur. With each edition, new disorders have been identified, adding to the list of mental illnesses. Diagnostic criteria for others have been refined, and some behaviors, once defined as disordered, have been removed because they no longer meet the criteria for diagnosis as a mental illness. An example of this is homosexuality. In the DSM-II, published in 1968, homosexuality was considered a mental illness. The 1973 publication of the DSM-III did not list homosexuality as a disorder. This declassification erased some of the stigma associated with same-sex attraction and provided a boost to the gay rights movement in the United States (Melby, 2009).

As the release of the DSM-V draws closer, experts from various fields, appointed to an array of work groups, are holding meetings to discuss what should be added, revised, or removed. For those interested in the field of human sexuality, much attention is being given to the status of GID. There has even been controversy over those appointed to the Sexual and Gender Identity Disorders Work Group (National Gay and Lesbian Task Force, 2008). The changes made to the upcoming DSM-V concerning GID, or the lack thereof, could have great impact on the lives of transgender individuals.

In an essay entitled "Destigmatization versus Coverage and Access: The Medical Model of Transsexuality," Mercedes Allen argues that the removal of Gender Identity Disorder from the DSM would put access to mental health care, hormonal treatments, and surgeries needed by some transsexual individuals at risk of being denied. Kelly Winters, in an essay called "Issues of GID Diagnosis for Transsexual Women and Men," argues that the inclusion of GID in the DSM only serves to stigmatize the transgender and transsexual community, while failing to promote hormonal or surgical treatments as medical necessities.

References

T. Melby, "Creating the DSM-V," *Contemporary Sexuality* (vol. 43, no. 3) (2009).

National Gay and Lesbian Task Force, "Task Force Questions Critical Appointments to APA's Committee on Sexual and Gender Identity Disorders," accessed at http://www.thetaskforce.org/press/releases/PR_052808 (2008).

YES ↵

Destigmatization versus Coverage and Access: The Medical Model of Transsexuality

In recent years, the GLB community has been more receptive to (and even energized in) assisting the transgender community, but regularly asks what its needs are. One that is often touted is the "complete depathologization of Trans identities" (quoting from a press release for an October 7, 2007, demonstration in Barcelona, Spain) by removing "Gender Identity Disorder" (GID) from medical classification. The reasoning generally flows in a logic chain stating that with homosexuality removed from the Diagnostic and Statistical Manual (DSM, the "bible" of the medical community) in 1974, gay and lesbian rights were able to follow as a consequence—and with similar removal, we should be able to do the same. Living in an area where GRS (genital reassignment surgery) is covered under provincial Health Care, however, provides a unique perspective on this issue. And with Presidential candidates proposing models for national health care in the U.S., it would obviously be easier to establish GRS coverage for transsexuals at the ground floor, rather than fight for it later. So it is important to note, from this "other side of the coin," how delisting GID could do far more harm than good.

Granted, there are concerns about the current classification as a "mental disorder," and certainly as a transgender person myself, it's quite unnerving that my diagnosis of GID puts me in the same range of classification as things such as schizophrenia or even pedophilia. And when the emotional argument of "mental unfitness" can lead to ostracism, discrimination in the workplace or the loss of custody and/or visitation rights of children, there are some very serious things at stake. But when the lobbies are calling for a reclassification—or more dramatically a total declassification—of GID, one would expect that they had a better medical and social model to propose. They don't.

Basic Access to Services

The argument for complete declassification is a great concern, because unlike homosexuals, transgender people—especially transsexuals—do have medical needs and issues related to their journey. Genital reassignment surgery (GRS), mastectomies and hysterectomies for transmen, tracheal shave, facial hair removal and breast augmentation for transwomen . . . there are clear medical applications that some require, even to the point of being at risk of suicide from the distress of not having these things available (which is an important point to keep in mind for those in our own communities who assume that GRS is cosmetic surgery and not worthy of health care funding). And we need to use caution about taking psychiatry out of the equation: GID really does affect us psychologically, and we do benefit from having a central source of guidance through the process that keeps this in mind, however flawed and gated the process otherwise might be.

Declassification of GID would essentially relegate transsexuality to a strictly cosmetic issue. Without being able to demonstrate that GID is a real medical condition via a listing in the Diagnostic and Statistical Manual (DSM), convincing a doctor that it is necessary to treat us, provide referrals or even provide a carry letter that will enable us to use a washroom appropriate to our gender presentation could prove to be very difficult, if not impossible. Access to care is difficult enough *even with* the DSM-IV recommending the transition process—imagine the barriers that would be there without it weighing in on that! And with cases regarding the refusal of medical services already before review or recently faced in California, Ontario and elsewhere, the availability of services could grow overwhelmingly scarce.

A Model of Medical Coverage

And then there is health care coverage, which often causes a lot of issues of itself, usually of the "not with my tax money" variety. But no one just wakes up out of the blue and decides that alienating themselves from the rest of the world by having a "sex change" is a good idea. Science is developing a greater understanding that physical sex and psychological gender can, in fact, be made misaligned, causing a person to be like a stranger in their own body. In extreme cases (transsexuals), this often makes it impossible to function emotionally, socially, sexually, or to develop any kind of career—and often makes one constantly borderline suicidal. The medical community currently recognizes this with the existing medical classification, which is why GRS surgery is the recognized treatment, and why it (GRS, that is, and usually not things like breast augmentation) is funded by some existing health plans.

Canada provides an interesting model on this, as the nation has universal health care, and several provinces fund GRS with some limitations (British Columbia, Newfoundland, Saskatchewan and Quebec fund vaginaplasty, hysterectomy and breast reduction for FTMs, Alberta funds those plus phalloplasty, and Manitoba funds 60% of GRS-related costs). Funding may be restored in Ontario and gained in Nova Scotia, pending some ongoing activism.

This exists specifically because it is classified as a medical issue, and is treated according to the recommendations of WPATH. There are some idiosyncracies, of course—a diagnosis of Intersex, for example, overrides a diagnosis of GID, and if someone is diagnosed as IS, the treatment is different (namely, GRS is not covered). Phalloplasty and metoidioplasty (FTM surgeries) are not covered in several areas because they are considered "experimental." Some provinces insist on treatment only in publically-funded hospitals, resulting in the rather unusual situation of Quebec sending patients to the U.S. or overseas, even though one of the top-rated (but privately-owned) GRS clinics in the world is located in Montreal. And many provinces direct transsexuals to the notoriously restrictive and obstacle-laden Clarke Institute (CAMH in Toronto) for treatment. Waiting lists can be long, and only a select few GID-certified psychiatrists are able to be a primary signature on letters authorizing surgery and funding. Still, the funding provides opportunity that many non-Canadian transsexuals would leap at within a moment, if they could.

Future Considerations

This possibility, remote as it may seem, is also out there for future American transsexuals. Both Democratic Presidential nominees have discussed developing a national health care program. The time is now for the trans, gay/lesbian/ bisexual and allied communities to lobby insurance companies to develop policies that cover GRS. The time is now to lobby companies to seek out group policies for their employees with such coverage, and with more emphasis than the HRC's impossibly easy Corporate Equality Index (CEI), in which providing mastectomies for breast cancer patients qualifies as "transgender-related surgeries." The more prevalent health care coverage is for transgender persons when a national program is developed, the more effective the argument is that a national program should include it. Certainly, it will be much harder to lobby to have it specifically added later.

This possibility, remote as it may seem, exists because of the current classification. Even some existing coverage of and access to hormone treatment is called into question in a declassification scenario. And certainly, where coverage is not available, it is the impoverished, disenfranchised and marginalized of our community—who quite often have more to worry about than the stigma of mental illness—who lose the most.

So a total declassification is actually not what's best for the transgender community. Too, if anyone had been thinking that proclaiming that "transsexuality is not a mental disorder" would magically change the way that society thinks about transfolk, then they are spectacularly and embarrassingly wrong.

The Question of Reclassification

At some point in the future, I expect that we will find more biological bases for GID, and that transgender people will perhaps become a smaller part of the larger intersex community (rather than the other way around). Recent studies in genetics have demonstrated some difference in chromosomal structure in male brains versus female brains, and the UCLA scientists who conducted the study have also proposed that their findings demonstrate gender dysphoria as a biological characteristic. Other studies into endocrine disrupting chemicals (EDCs) could open new discoveries related to variance in gender correlation. A reassessment of GID is almost certainly something that will be on the medical community's table at some point in the future, but it definitely needs to be in the DSM somewhere. But for now, GID is not something that can be determined by a blood test or an ultrasound, and is not easy to verifiably place with biological conditions. The science is not there; the evidence and solutions are not yet at hand.

This is why reclassification is not yet feasible. It's difficult to convince scientific and medical professionals to move a diagnosis when the current model is workable in their eyes (even if not perfect), while the alternatives are not yet proven, cannot be demonstrated as more valid than the current listing, and no modified treatment system has been devised or proposed. Any move of the diagnosis is not likely to be very far from the current listing, and from the literature I've seen, I doubt that those in the community who advocate to changing or dropping the current classification would be happy with that. For some, even listing it as a "physical disability" could constitute an "unwanted stigma." I have heard one WPATH doctor suggest the term "Body Morphology Disorder"—for many, I suspect, this would still be too "negative."

"Unnecessary Mutilation"

That's not to say that complacency is an answer. In the face of conservative reluctance and new activism on the left by the likes of Julie Bindel, claiming that GRS is "unnecessary mutilation," we need to demonstrate the necessity of treatments, in order to ensure that any change would be an improvement on the existing model, rather than a scrapping of it. This is, of course, something that affects a small portion of the transgender community in the full umbrella stretch of the term, but the need for those at the extreme on the spectrum is profound—not simply a question of quality of life, but often one of living at all—or at least a question of being able to function. If and when a reclassification occurs, it will need to be this sense of necessity that will determine the shape of what will be written into any revision.

The solution isn't to destroy the existing medical model by changing or eliminating the current classification of "Gender Dysphoria." Collecting data, demonstrating needs, fighting for inclusion in existing health plans, examining verifiable and repeatable statistics on transgender suicide and success rates and other information relevant to the medical front is where medical-related activism should be focused, for the moment.

NO

GID Reform Advocates

Issues of GID Diagnosis for Transsexual Women and Men

Gender Identity Disorder in Adolescents or Adults, 302.85

Section: Sexual and Gender Identity Disorders
Subsection: Gender Identity Disorders

"Gender Identity Disorder" (GID) is a diagnostic category in the *Diagnostic and Statistical Manual of Mental Disorders* (DSM), published by the American Psychiatric Association (APA, 1994). The DSM is regarded as the medical and social definition of mental disorder throughout North America and strongly influences the *International Statistical Classification of Diseases and Related Health Problems* (ICD) published by the World Health Organization. GID currently includes a broad array of gender variant adults and children who may or may not be transsexual and may or may not be distressed or impaired. GID literally implies a *"disordered"* gender identity.

Thirty-four years after the American Psychiatric Association (APA) voted to delete homosexuality as a mental disorder, the diagnostic categories of "gender identity disorder" and "transvestic fetishism" in the *Diagnostic and Statistical Manual of Mental Disorders* continue to raise questions of consistency, validity, and fairness. Recent revisions of the DSM have made these diagnostic categories increasingly ambiguous, conflicted and overinclusive. They reinforce false, negative stereotypes of gender variant people and at the same time fail to legitimize the medical necessity of sex reassignment surgeries (SRS) and procedures for transsexual women and men who urgently need them. The result is that a widening segment of gender non-conforming youth and adults are potentially subject to diagnosis of psychosexual disorder, stigma and loss of civil liberty.

A Question of Legitimacy

The very name, Gender Identity Disorder, suggests that cross-gender identity is itself disordered or deficient. It implies that gender identities held by diagnosable people are not legitimate, in the sense that more ordinary gender identities are, but represent perversion, delusion or immature development. This message

From http://www.gidreform.org/GID30285a.pdf, 2007, pp. 1–5. Copyright © 2007 by Kelley Winters. Reprinted by permission.

is reinforced in the diagnostic criteria and supporting text that emphasize difference from cultural norms over distress for those born in incongruent bodies or forced to live in wrong gender roles.

Under the premise of "disordered" gender identity, self-identified trans-women and trans-men lose any rightful claim to acceptance as women and men, but are reduced to mentally ill men and women respectively.

DIAGNOSTIC CRITERIA

A. A strong and persistent cross-gender identification (not merely a desire for any perceived cultural advantages of being the other sex). In adolescents and adults, the disturbance is manifested by symptoms such as a stated desire to be the other sex, frequent passing as the other sex, desire to live or be treated as the other sex, or the conviction that he or she has the typical feelings and reactions of the other sex.
B. Persistent discomfort with his or her sex or sense of inappropriateness in the gender role of that sex. In adolescents and adults, the disturbance is manifested by symptoms such as preoccupation with getting rid of primary and secondary sex characteristics (e.g., request for hormones, surgery, or other procedures to physically alter sexual characteristics to simulate the other sex) or belief that he or she was born the wrong sex.
C. The disturbance is not concurrent with a physical intersex condition.
D. The disturbance causes clinically significant distress or impairment in social, occupational, or other important areas of functioning.

Specify if (for sexually mature individuals) Sexually Attracted to Males, . . . Females, . . . Both, . . . Neither.

Maligning Terminology

Of the disrespectful language faced by gender variant people in North America, none is more damaging or hurtful than that which disregards their experienced gender identities, denies the affirmed gender roles of those who have transitioned full time and relegates them to their assigned birth sex. Throughout the diagnostic criteria and supporting text, the affirmed gender identities and social role for transsexual individuals is termed "other sex." In the supporting text, subjects are offensively labeled by birth sex and not their experienced affirmed gender. Transsexual women are repeatedly termed "males," and "he." For example,

> For some <u>males</u> . . . , the individual's sexual activity with a woman is accompanied by the fantasy of being lesbian lovers or that <u>his</u> partner is a man and <u>he</u> is a woman.

Perhaps most disturbing, the term "autogynephilia" was introduced in the supporting text of the DSM-IV-TR to demean lesbian transsexual women:

> Adult <u>males</u> who are sexually attracted to females, . . . usually report a history of erotic arousal associated with the thought or image of oneself as a woman (termed *autogynephilia*).

The implication is that all lesbian transsexual women are incapable of genuine affection for other female partners but are instead obsessed with narcissistic paraphilia. The fact that most ordinary natal women possess images of themselves as women within their erotic relationships and fantasies is conspicuously overlooked in the supporting text.

Medically Necessary Treatment of Gender Dysphoria

Gender Dysphoria is defined in the DSM-IV-TR as:

> A persistent aversion toward some or all of those physical characteristics or social roles that connote one's own biological sex.

The focus of medical treatment described by the current World Professional Association for Transgender Health Standards of Care is on relieving the distress of gender dysphoria and not on attempting to change one's gender identity. Yet, the DSM-IV-TR emphasizes cross-gender identity and expression rather than the distress of gender dysphoria as the basis for mental disorder. While criterion B of Gender Identity Disorder may imply gender dysphoria, it is not limited to ego-dystonic subjects suffering distress with their born sex or its associated role. Ego-syntonic subjects who do not need medical treatment may also be ambiguously implicated. In failing to distinguish gender diversity from gender distress, the APA has undermined the medical necessity of sex reassignment procedures for transsexuals who need them. It is little wonder that the province of Ontario and virtually all insurers and HMOs in the U.S. and have denied or dropped coverage for sex reassignment surgery (SRS) procedures. Since gender dysphoria is not explicitly classified as a treatable medical condition, surgeries that relieve its distress are easily dismissed as "cosmetic" by insurers, governments and employers.

The transgender community and civil rights advocates have long been polarized by fear that access to SRS procedures would be lost if the GID classification were revised. In truth, however, transsexuals are poorly served by a diagnosis that stigmatizes them unconditionally as mentally deficient and at the same time fails to establish the medical necessity of procedures proven to relieve their distress.

Overinclusive Diagnosis

Distress and impairment became central to the definition of mental disorder in the DSM-IV (1994, p. xxi), where a generic clinical significance criterion was added to most diagnostic categories, including criterion D of Gender Identity Disorder. Ironically, while the scope of mental disorder was narrowed in the DSM-IV, Gender Identity Disorder was broadened from the classification of Transsexualism in prior DSM revisions and combined with Gender Identity Disorder of Adolescence or Adulthood, Nontranssexual Type (GIDAANT) from the DSM-III-R (1987, pp. 74–77).

Unfortunately, no specific definition of distress and impairment is given in the GID diagnosis. The supporting text in the DSM-IV-TR lists relationship difficulties and impaired function at work or school as examples of distress and disability (2000, p. 577) with no reference to the role of societal prejudice as the cause. Prostitution, HIV risk, suicide attempts and substance abuse are described as associated features of GID, when they are in truth consequences of discrimination and undeserved shame. The DSM does not acknowledge the existence of many healthy, well-adjusted transsexual or gender variant people or differentiate them from those who could benefit from medical treatment. These are left to the interpretation of the reader. Tolerant clinicians may infer that transgender identity or expression is not inherently impairing, but that societal intolerance and prejudice are to blame for the distress and internalized shame that transpeople often suffer. Intolerant clinicians are free to infer the opposite: that cross-gender identity or expression by definition constitutes impairment, regardless of the individual's happiness or well-being. Therefore, the GID diagnosis is not limited to ego-dystonic subjects; it makes no distinction between the distress of gender dysphoria and that caused by prejudice and discrimination. Moreover, the current DSM has no clear exit clause for transitioned or post-operative transsexuals, however well adjusted. It lists postsurgical complications as "associated physical examination findings" of GID (2000, p. 579).

Pathologization of Ordinary Behaviors

Conflicting and ambiguous language in the DSM serves to confuse cultural nonconformity with mental illness and pathologize ordinary behaviors as symptomatic. The Introduction to the DSM-IV-TR (2000, p. xxxi) states:

> Neither deviant behavior . . . nor conflicts that are primarily between the individual and society are mental disorders unless the deviance or conflict is a symptom of dysfunction. . . .

However, it is contradicted in the Gender Identity Disorder section (p. 580):

> Gender Identity Disorder can be distinguished from simple nonconformity to stereotypical sex role behavior by the extent and pervasiveness of the cross-gender wishes, interests, and activities.

The second statement implies that one may deviate from social expectation without a diagnostic label, but not too much. Conflicting language in the DSM serves the agendas of intolerant relatives and employers and their medical expert witnesses who seek to deny transgender individuals their civil liberties, children and jobs.

In the supporting text of the Gender Identity Disorder diagnosis, behaviors that would be ordinary or even exemplary for ordinary women and men are presented as symptomatic of mental disorder on a presumption of incongruence with born genitalia. These include passing, living and a desire to be treated as ordinary members of the preferred gender. For example, shaving legs for adolescent biological males is described as symptomatic, even though it is common among males involved in certain athletics. Adopting ordinary behaviors, dress and mannerisms of the preferred gender is described as a manifestation of preoccupation for adults. It is not clear how these behaviors can be pathological for one group of people and not for another.

POSTSCRIPT

Is "Gender Identity Disorder" an Appropriate Psychiatric Diagnosis?

It is important to realize that, while Allen and Winters take opposing sides to the question presented, both oppose the labeling of transgender or transsexual individuals as mentally ill. To a certain extent, the debate over the inclusion, reclassification, or exclusion of GID in the upcoming edition of the DSM exemplifies the phrase "You're damned if you do, you're damned if you don't." To remove GID from the DSM would in all likelihood help to reduce some of the stigma attached to transsexuality. However, many transsexual individuals need a diagnosable condition in order to receive adequate coverage for medical care. Could there possibly be a "correct" answer in this situation?

Allen's essay, which acknowledges the stigma attached to the label of mental disorder and notes the possible benefits of re- or declassification of GID, focuses on the issue of access to medical care. The point is made that declassification would impact transgender and transsexual individuals in much different ways than the declassification of homosexuality affected gay men and lesbians. Unlike other sexual minorities, "transgender people—especially transsexuals—do have medical needs and issues related to their journey," Allen states. What would be the risks of removing GID from the upcoming DSM? Why would some transgender advocates argue for its continued inclusion? Allen also mentions the impact of nationalized health care on the GID debate. How would the discussion be different if the United States implemented health care coverage for all citizens?

Winters focuses on deconstructing the current diagnosis of GID. Despite recent revisions, she states, the diagnostic criteria are "increasingly ambiguous, conflicted and overinclusive." After reading the most recent DSM criteria for GID, included in her essay, would you agree? Fears that a revised classification would endanger medical care for the transgender community are essentially moot, states Winters, given the fact that the current diagnosis "fails to establish the medical necessity of procedures proven to relieve their distress." With the criteria put in place by the DSM, Winters argues, many insurers are already refusing to cover treatments, dismissing surgeries as "cosmetic" in nature, rather than necessary for treatment.

Do you feel that total declassification is the correct step to take? Or would a revision of the current classification be more appropriate? What if these changes resulted in the denial of access to medical care for transgender or transsexual individuals? Is there a middle ground that reduces stigma while maintaining access to medical treatment?

Suggested Readings

P. T. Cohen-Kettenis, "The Treatment of Adolescent Transsexuals," *Journal of Sexual Medicine* (vol. 5, no. 8, 2008).

R. Ehrbar, "Clinical Judgment in the Diagnosis of Gender Identity Disorder in Children," *Journal of Sex and Marital Therapy* (vol. 34, no. 5, 2008).

K. Hausman, "Controversy Continues to Grow over DSM's GID Diagnosis," *Psychiatric News* (vol. 38, no. 14, 2003). Accessed at http://pn.psychiatryonline .org/cgi/content/38/14/25.full.

ISSUE 20

Should Transgendered Women Be Considered "Real" Women?

YES: Lisa Mottet and Justin Tanis, from *Opening the Door to the Inclusion of Transgender People: The Nine Keys to Making Lesbian, Gay, Bisexual and Transgender Organizations Fully Transgender-Inclusive* (The National Gay and Lesbian Task Force Policy Institute, 2008)

NO: Jaimie F. Veale, Dave E. Clarke, and Terri C. Lomax, from "Sexuality of Male-to-Female Transsexuals" *Archives of Sexual Behavior* (2008)

ISSUE SUMMARY

YES: Attorney and activist Lisa Mottet and program manager of the National Center for Transgender Equality Justin Tanis argue for recognizing diversity in all aspects of people's lives and reject efforts to categorize on the basis of rigid definitions.

NO: Jaimie Veale, a graduate student, along with university faculty compared the sexuality of male-to-female transsexuals to biological females and found a number of differences that distinguish the groups in terms of patterns of sexual attraction to males.

In 1999, a controversy erupted between the organizers of the Michigan's Womyn's Music Festival (MWMF) and Camp Trans over MWMF's policy towards permitting transgendered women to attend the festival. To understand this conflict, some background is necessary. According to the MWMF founder Lisa Vogel, "Since 1976, the Michigan Womyn's Music Festival has been created by and for womyn-born womyn, that is, womyn who were born as and have lived their entire life experience as womyn." Camp Trans, an alternative music festival founded in 1994 to protest MWMF, is held on Forest Service land across from the MWMF. They believe that anyone who is a woman, regardless of the sex they were born as, should be permitted to attend. Vogel sent a letter to a member of Camp Trans that stated, "I deeply desire healing in our communities, and I can see and feel that you want that too. I would love for you and the other organizers of Camp Trans to find the place in your hearts and politics to support and honor space for womyn who have had the experience of being born and living their life as womyn. I ask that you respect that womyn born womyn is a valid and honorable gender identity. I also ask that you respect that womyn born womyn deeply need our space—as do all communities who create space to gather. . . . As feminists, we call upon the transwomen's community to help us maintain womyn only space, including spaces created by and for womyn-born womyn. As sisters in struggle, we call upon the transwomen's community to meditate upon, recognize and respect the differences in our shared experiences and our group identities even as we stand shoulder to shoulder as women, and as members of the greater queer community. . . . the need for a separate womyn-born womyn space does not stand at odds with recognizing the larger and beautiful diversity of our shared community."

This controversy raises the question of what is a "real" woman. It is clear that according to the MWMF credo, the lived experiences of womyn born womyn is different from that of those women who were born biologically male and then chose to live their lives as female. This is the case in spite of the fact that the MWMF founders embrace all forms of gender variant women as long as they were born biologically female. This would include lesbians, bisexual, and polyamorous women who present their gender in a variety of ways (butch, bearded, androgynous, femme, etc.). One question to ponder as you read these selections is how "common" do people's experiences have to be in order for them to have a common bond.

Furthermore, what is the role of the patterns of sexual attraction in defining what it means to be a "woman"? The assumption is that heterosexual women have a clearly defined pattern of attraction to men. Gender variant women, on the other hand, may be lesbian or bisexual or polyamorous (i.e., having more than one intimate partner of the same or different sex at the same time); thus, for the womyn born womyn movement, it would appear that a variety of patterns of sexual attraction are acknowledged. Research has shown that among male to female transgendered persons as well, a variety of sexual attraction patterns are possible, and some of these patterns would qualify as gender variant, that is, something other than females attracted to males.

In the selections, Veale and colleagues take a close look at the variety of ways male to female transsexuals experience sexual attraction. They rely heavily on Ray Blanchard's theory that there are 15 aspects of sexuality that can be used to categorize people. Male to female transsexuals can be classified as gynephilic (or lesbian, exclusively sexually attracted to adult females), bisexual, androphilic (or heterosexual, exclusively sexually attracted to adult males), asexual, and narcissistic or automonosexual gender-variant persons (sexually aroused by the idea or impression of themselves as females). Veale's research indicates that male to female transsexuals differed from biological females in a variety of ways, suggesting, at least when it comes to sexual attraction, this group really is different from women born as women. However, Mottet and Tanis argue against categorizing people based on gender identity or patterns of sexual attraction and then using those categories as a basis for discrimination. They suggest that some members of gender variant communities may in fact be transphobic. As you read these selections, consider this possibility. How exclusionary must an organization be before it is considered to be transphobic?

YES

Lisa Mottet and
Justin Tanis

Opening the Door to the Inclusion of Transgender People: The Nine Keys to Making Lesbian, Gay, Bisexual and Transgender Organizations Fully Transgender-Inclusive

Introduction

Thank you for picking up this guide and for your desire to discover new ways to help your lesbian, gay, bisexual and transgender (LGBT) organization become a more inclusive place for transgender people. It is exciting to see the ways in which our movement continues to grow and challenge ourselves to be more inclusive and more effective as we serve our communities.

In this guide, you will find practical ideas for how LGBT organizations can take concrete steps to provide a more welcoming environment for transgender people. We'll address directly the challenges and opportunities that present themselves in this process.

This resource is specifically written for LGBT groups and organizations that want to be more inclusive of transgender people. This will mean various things to different kinds of groups—from welcoming more transgender people on your soccer team to passing transgender-inclusive legislation to running transgender-specific programs at your community center. We encourage you to take the ideas in this guide and think of ways in which you can apply them to your unique organization and mission.

LGBT organizations are made up of a wide range of people, including family, friends, and allies. Our volunteers, staffs, and constituencies identify as lesbian, bisexual, straight, gay, transgender, non-transgender, queer, and more. When we refer to LGBT organizations in this guide, it is our intention to speak to this diverse group of people with the goal of helping our community become increasingly inclusive.

Other organizations that are not LGBT-specific in their focus may also find this guide helpful. Please feel free to translate the information from the LGBT experience to your own in ways that are useful to you.

Transgender Inclusion

Transgender people have been a part of the LGBT movement from its beginnings. As people began to see their sexual orientation as a healthy part of their identity and found the prejudice they faced oppressive, they found common cause with those who expressed their gender differently than the majority of society. Together, they began the work that we continue—striving to create a world where we are free to be ourselves and where our identities are never a justification for discrimination and violence.

Those who oppose our rights see LGBT people as a common community. We are targeted for stigmatization and violence together as a group because we break stereotypes. Our common vulnerabilities may have brought us together, but the LGBT community works together because we are working towards a common purpose, for the freedom to be who we are and the right to live with dignity and justice.

When we talk about transgender-inclusion in this guide, it is with the understanding that transgender people are inherently a part of the LGBT community and have been from the beginning. In some ways, the term "transgender-inclusion" is not perfect; it could be taken to mean that transgender people aren't inherently a part of something called the LGB(T) movement and that instead, transgender people have been added to the LGB movement. We use this term, despite this perceived limitation, because we believe it is the best term to describe the process of integration of transgender people throughout one's LGBT organization, and it is the term that our movement has been using for over a decade.

We also realize that the term "LGBT" sometimes glosses over the gap that exists between the realities of our community organizations (that they are not always inclusive) and the diverse and vast world of LGBT people. We know that our organizations want to accurately reflect and meaningfully serve LGBT people. Working together can be challenging, and we need to be intentional in order to create a truly diverse and vibrant community.

As Suzanne Pharr has noted in her ground-breaking book, *Homophobia: A Weapon of Sexism*, homophobia is driven by a rigid gender code. A long-time feminist, Pharr observed that women who break out of constricting gender roles and take leadership in their communities are often branded as "lesbian" to make them stop pushing for change—whether that change means better schools for their children, clean-up of a toxic waste dump, or marriage equality. Similarly, men who visibly challenge gender conformity—by confronting male violence, expressing emotion, or embracing their artistic or "feminine" sides— are punished both socially and in the world of work. Simply, gender bias and homophobia are inextricably entwined.

Gay, lesbian, and bisexual people have often constituted a significant share of our society's gender outlaws, standing side by side on the gender non-conforming continuum with our transgender peers and bearing the consequences of not matching the gender stereotypes of straight society. Accordingly, bias against gender non-conformity threatens access to employment and other key societal institutions for all of us and exposes us to violence and prejudice. While we may not all be in the exact same boat, we are certainly all in the same water.

The divisive and disappointing federal legislative battle around the removal of gender identity/expression protections from the Employment Non-Discrimination Act in 2007 should not confuse any of us. There is no secure equality for LGB people without protections for gender bias. On a parallel course, there is no true community and no authentic expression of queer life or culture without transgender people. Often the most stigmatized people in our ranks, gender non-conforming people have consistently led the charge for change in our movement and the society at large. We marginalize them/us at our own peril.

In different times and in different places, the LGBT community has varied between close-knit cohesion and an uneasy alliance between lesbian, gay, bisexual, and transgender activists. We have been divided along lines of gender, gender identity/expression, race, class, abilities, and more. But we believe that at the heart of the LGBT movement is a passion for inclusion and that at our best, and most effective, the LGBT community strives to open our doors to all who want to work together with people of all sexual orientations and gender identities and expressions.

We hope this book provides you with the concrete tools you need to fully realize your vision for a fully transgender-inclusive organization. There is so much work to do and so many challenges facing our movement. We must draw on the vast talents and strengths that our brilliant, diverse communities have to offer to achieve our goal of full equality.

Our Perspectives

The authors of this manual bring a variety of view points to our writing. One of us is transgender, and the other is a long-time ally. We have both had significant others who are transgender people. Both of us have spent our careers working within the LGBT movement, which significantly informs our perspective. We have also been active in a number of LGBT community organizations as participants, taking part in book clubs, political advocacy organizations, sports teams, and other groups.

We have been both leaders and members of the very kinds of organizations that we hope will benefit from this manual. In some cases, we've been very successful in bringing about the changes that we outline here. At other times, we've been met with resistance and have had the opportunity to learn how difficult this work can be.

Ultimately, we believe in LGBT communities—we believe in our drive for inclusiveness and in the strength of our vision. We have been proud to be a part of this movement and hope that this guide lends some ideas and experience that will help us move forward together into an even better future.

Opening the Door to a Transgender-Inclusive Movement

The question before us now is not whether transgender people are part of our movement, but rather how to build organizations in which the participation of transgender people is affirming for both them and for the groups to which they belong. The purpose of this guide is to consider how we can strengthen that partnership so that the political and social organizations that we have worked so hard to build can truly be as diverse, effective, and inclusive as we want them to be.

The Challenges We Face

One of the most significant challenges LGBT organizations face is that transgender (and bisexual) labels have often been added in name (the addition of the "B" and "T" to LGBT) without any authentic effort to integrate transgender and bisexual people and experiences into the organization. While often well-intentioned, changes in name only render the impact of adding those letters almost meaningless, as transgender people have learned the hard way. Because the addition of the "T" only sometimes translates into concrete programs or even a genuine welcome, trans people may view the "T" with suspicion or simply ignore it altogether.

Transgender people have also encountered overt hostility in some LGBT organizations. Some people—regardless of their sexual orientation—are uncomfortable with transgender people because of the transphobia that they have learned from the larger society. Sometimes lesbian and gay people recycle the homophobia they have heard and use it against transgender people, saying things like, "that's not natural," or "it's just a phase." Not intending to be hostile, some LGB people have pointed out the real differences between being LGB and T, and the different ways in which people experience discrimination, and have said that their organization should treat these issues differently. Whatever the reasoning, the result is that transgender people have learned, through painful experience, that lesbian, gay, and bisexual spaces are not always welcoming, safe environments for them. Using prejudice to exclude others based on their identity weakens our movement, and, as leaders, we must take whatever steps we can to counteract it.

Sometimes, gay, lesbian, and bisexual people genuinely want to welcome transgender people but don't know how. We may inadvertently include people in a way that demonstrates ignorance of the issues of gender identity/expression. For example, we might write a newsletter article on "LGBT marriage issues," failing to recognize that marriage rights for transgender people pose a different set of questions than same-sex marriage rights for non-transgender people. Or we might ask people if they are gay, lesbian, bisexual, *or* transgender, rather than seeing that a person can be lesbian, gay, or bisexual, *and* transgender. . . .

Looking at Our Missions

It is important that our organizations look carefully at our mission statements and make a decision about the inclusion of transgender people. While we would advocate that LGBT organizations are strongest when they are fully inclusive, you will have to make your own choices.

It is not acceptable, however, to just add the "T" to the mission or name of an organization out of perceived pressure to conform to a movement standard and then proceed to ignore transgender people. It is more honest to decide that transgender people are not part of your organization's mission and to say so than it is to try to *appear* inclusive but not *be* inclusive. If you feel your organization might fall into that category, you cannot change the past, but you certainly can change the future of your organization to fully live up to your name and desire for inclusion.

Mission statements of organizations that are fully inclusive of LGBT people should include gender identity/expression as well as sexual orientation. If transgender people are part of our mission, then we should do everything we can to fulfill the mission of our organization, including providing an equal place at the table for transgender people.

Transgender people can bring incredible gifts to our organizations to help us achieve the goals that we have as a community. Transgender people are often resilient, creative, and strong. They have survived the prejudices thrown at them by family, friends, and an all-too-often hostile world. They also seek what all of us seek in our LGBT organizations—safe and affirming places in which to be ourselves. By opening our programs—and our hearts and minds—to transgender people, we help to achieve the purpose that brought all of us together in the first place. . . .

Conclusion

By now you have a very good idea of what it is going to take to move your LGBT organization along in its journey to become fully transgender-inclusive. If you have a long way to go, you may feel overwhelmed. Rest assured, by slowly taking steps one by one, you will get where you need to go, and bring along the others in your organization with you. Many hands make light work. You will likely find the process enlightening and empowering. It certainly has been for us in our work in building transgender-inclusive LGBT organizations.

The work of trans-inclusion is critically important. Have no doubt that each of us doing our part will create a new world where it is safe and acceptable to identify as any gender and express our gender in any form we choose. As LGBT organizations demonstrate trans-inclusion, our example will be noted by other organizations and institutions we work with; indeed, we should be actively encouraging them to adopt these practices. Ultimately, our hope is that through each of us making our part of the world trans-inclusive, we will help spread trans-friendly attitudes and behaviors everywhere.

As Mahatma Gandhi said, "You must be the change you wish to see in the world." The power to change the world is yours and ours; we must recognize that power and use it to create a dynamic, inclusive LGBT movement. Hopefully, this guide will support that process. We look forward to working with you and your organization as we build an ever stronger, more powerful, and fully integrated movement for justice.

Transgender Inclusion: The Nine Keys for Success

#1 Work Toward Full Integration at Every Organizational Level

- Transgender people should be more than just clients; trans people should be in key leadership positions, serve on the board, act as volunteers, and be on the staff of an inclusive organization.
- Avoid the pitfall of tokenization or having one transgender person that the organization consults with on all trans issues.
- Unless trans people are fully integrated, transgender people will not be fully represented in and by your organization, which hurts not only the organization, but robs the movement of the chance to develop more experienced community members.

#2 Recruit a Broad Range of Trans People

- The work is never done; so one can never put this issue aside as complete.
- Not knowing trans people isn't an adequate excuse; there are transgender people interested and excited to work on LGBT issues. They can be found.
- The differences between transgender people must be recognized, both in gender identity and expression, but also in class, race, ability, age, and religious affiliation.

#3 Create a Welcoming Environment

- Physical space is important. Trans people need trans-friendly bathrooms. Some need a place to change into their gender presentation before a meeting or event.
- What you say really matters. Watch language on forms asking about gender and sexual orientation and think about whether the names of your organization and events are inclusive.

#4 Deal with Prejudice

- There is serious transphobia within LGB communities which must be addressed, not swept under the rug. Racism, classism, ableism, sexism, and other oppressions are also problems in nearly every environment and must also be addressed.

#5 Acknowledge Past Mistakes Regarding Trans Inclusion

- If your organization has previously done something that was not transgender-friendly, it is important to put aside defensiveness in the process of healing and repairing any rift that exists between LGB and T people in the organization.
- This is not always a fast process; typically, it will take time to rebuild trust.

#6 Have Trans-Inclusive Programming, Services, and Advocacy Positions

- There should be trans-specific programming/services; but they shouldn't be the only places trans people are expected to show up.
- Remember that not all trans people are gay/lesbian/bisexual, so include heterosexual transgender people and their families.
- For legislative- and policy-related organizations, the organization must take a non-negotiable stance on transgender-inclusion.

#7 Understand Transgender Experiences

- Be conscious of social and cultural differences that transgender people may have. Being trans is different than being gay.
- Do one's own education about trans issues; read a book, look on the internet, or do research so you better understand all of the different ways to be transgender and how that affects one's life.

#8 Understand One's Role as an Ally

- Being an ally means that one should help facilitate the trans community's goals and agenda, without undue influence on setting the agenda.
- However, you can (and should) still use your own critical thinking skills and contribute to agenda-setting and strategy when invited to do so by transgender leaders and colleagues.

#9 Have Fair Employment Practices

- Implement strong nondiscrimination policies, include nondiscrimination statements in job listings, establish transgender-friendly hiring practices, and provide trainings for employees on sensitivity.
- Provide transgender-related health care, integrate transgender-sensitivity into staff evaluations, ensure employees can update their name and gender in files, ensure that transgender status is confidential, and ensure that transgender employees are safe from harassment on the job.

Jaimie F. Veale, Dave E. Clarke
and Terri C. Lomax

➡ **NO**

Sexuality of Male-to-Female Transsexuals

Since its beginnings in the early 20th century, research investigating the sexuality of male-to-female transsexuals has classified them into groups based on their sexual orientation. However, this approach has been disputed by a number of transsexuals. The present study attempted to shed some light on this issue by assessing aspects of male-to-female transsexuals' sexuality, including sexual orientation, autogynephilia, sexual attraction to transgender fiction, and factors relevant to evolutionary theory, among a non-clinical population. These variables were also compared to a group of biological females to ascertain similarities and differences in the sexuality of male-to-female transsexuals. Before outlining these aspects of sexuality, a brief review of some previous studies of male-to-female transsexual sexuality is given. In this article, the term transsexual refers to male-to-female transsexuals unless otherwise stated.

Research has shown that gynephilic (exclusively sexually attracted to adult females), bisexual, androphilic (exclusively sexually attracted to adult males), asexual, and narcissistic or automonosexual gender-variant persons can be distinguished. Automonosexuals are sexually aroused by the idea or impression of themselves as females.

Gynephilic transsexuals reported cross-gender fetishism that was not seen among androphilic transsexuals. Androphilic transsexuals also reported a greater level of childhood feminine gender identity than gynephilic transsexuals. . . . One relatively strong factor included erotic attraction to women and fetishism . . . , and low childhood feminine gender identity and less erotic attraction to males. . . . Thus, there were two distinct "types" of transsexuals: gynephilic and androphilic.

Using standardized self-report questionnaires, Blanchard provided evidence for the two-type model of transsexuality. . . .

He introduced the concept of *autogynephilia* . . . to refer to "a male's propensity to be sexually aroused by the thought of himself as a female." This concept formed the basis of Blanchard's hypothesis that there are two distinct manifestations of male-to-female transsexualism: "homosexual" and "autogynephilic." . . . Nonhomosexual gender dysphoria is the result of autogynephilia. Autogynephilic transsexuals are sexually aroused by stimuli

From *Archives of Sexual Behavior*, vol. 37, 2008, pp. 586–597. Copyright © 2008 by Springer Journals (Kluwer Academic). Reprinted with kind permission of Springer Science+Business Media via Rightslink.

that result in them to perceiving themselves in a more feminine way. Cross-dressing is the most striking example here—Blanchard believed that there was much commonality between autogynephilic transsexuals and transvestites. However, he believed autogynephilia can also encompass erotic ideas of feminine situations in which women's clothing plays little or no role at all, such as going to the hair salon or even doing knitting.

Blanchard believed that the sexual interest in males that arises in bisexual transsexuals was fundamentally different from the androphilic group. According to Blanchard, in bisexual transsexuals, autogynephilia produces a secondary interest in males to go along with the transsexuals' basic erotic interest in females. The interest was not in the male body or physique as it is for the androphilic group, but rather in the perception of themselves as a woman that males are attracted to. The inclusion of a male can add to the fantasy of being regarded as a woman for the bisexual group, and the attraction to a male would diminish if the bisexual transsexual was not being regarded as a woman. . . . Bisexual transsexuals were significantly more likely to report autogynephilic interpersonal fantasy—erotic fantasies of being admired by another person—than all of the other transsexual groups.

Autogynephilic sexual arousal may diminish or even disappear due to age, hormone treatment, and sex reassignment surgery (SRS), and yet the desire to live as a woman does not diminish, and often grows stronger, . . . like a heterosexual pair bonding: after years of marriage, sexual excitement with a partner tends to decrease; however, one continues to be just as attached to that person. Similarly, the desire to have a female body continues in a "permanent love-bond."

A number of subsequent findings have relevance to Blanchard's theory. Among transsexuals, gynephilia was significantly positively correlated with sexual arousal to cross-gender fantasy, and significantly negatively correlated with feminine gender identity in childhood. More recent studies have also reported the existence of cross-gender sexual arousal among transsexuals. Two further studies have found that transsexuals who were sexually attracted to males were significantly more feminine as a child and significantly less likely to report sexual arousal when cross-dressing.

Another interesting observation that has relevance to Blanchard's theory is the existence of erotic narratives that are found in transvestite publications and on the Internet that appear to be created for individuals with transvestic and autogynephilic fantasies. Nearly half of the stories ended with the indication that the main character will go on to live as a woman—an indication of transsexual fantasy among consumers of such fiction. The experiences in the transvestite fiction differed sharply from what the transvestite experienced in real life. These stories illustrate wish fulfillment of desires that are deprived of expression in reality. The themes of these stories merely provide insight into what transvestites find most pleasurable, but they are of little use in distinguishing individual's motives or reasons for cross-dressing. Many of these narratives can be interpreted as autogynephilic fantasies because the male is transformed into a female, not just through a change of clothes, but also through changes via a surgical, magical, or science fiction means.

One question this research is addressing is whether transsexuals are sexually attracted to this fiction.

Many transsexuals oppose Blanchard's theory of autogynephilia. It is clear that many transsexuals do not accept the underlying assumption of Blanchard's theory that persons with autogynephilia are males with a sexual fetish. Another phenomenon that added fuel to the argument was the release of Bailey's book [*The Man Who Would Be Queen: The Science of Gender Bending and Transsexualism*]. In this book, Bailey supported Blanchard's theory, and explained it in layperson terms in an attempt to popularize it among the general public. However, this has been very unpopular among transsexuals because among other things Bailey asserted that all transsexuals who do not believe in Blanchard's model are lying, either to themselves or to others.

Some further aspects of sexuality were of interest for the present study: sexual attraction to feminine males, sadomasochism, and aspects of sexuality relevant to evolutionary theory. . . .

Little previous research has examined attraction to femininity in males among gender-variant persons. Transvestites tend to avoid sexual encounters with males, with the exception of other transvestites; 26% of personal advertisements looking for transsexuals and transvestites were placed by self-described cross-dressers.

Several researchers have noted sadistic and masochistic tendencies in transsexuals and transvestites. If autogynephilia is a type of paraphilia as Blanchard contends, then we would expect to see a positive relationship between autogynephilia and sadomasochism and other fetishistic fantasies.

In accordance with sexual selection theory, males are more likely than females to report interest in uncommitted sex, interest in visual sexual stimuli, preference for younger partners, to value partner physical attractiveness, and experience of sexual jealousy more strongly than emotional jealousy. On the other hand, women were more likely than men to report concern with partner status, and to report experiencing emotional jealousy more strongly than sexual jealousy.

The aim of this research was to measure these aspects of sexuality among male-to-female transsexuals and compare them to those of a group of biological females, to ascertain similarities and differences in the sexuality of transsexuals.

Method

Participants

Transsexual participants were recruited from transgender social/support groups in New Zealand, and biological female participants were recruited through an undergraduate psychology class at Massey University in Auckland, New Zealand. These participants were given the option of either completing the questionnaire on the Internet or completing a paper version. Transsexual and biological female participants were also recruited via the Internet. The link to the survey was posted on a number of transgender, women's, and psychology online interest groups and email lists. Participants recruited via the Internet were given only the option of completing the survey over the Internet.

The questionnaire received a total of 361 completed responses; 327 of these were via the Internet questionnaire. Paper surveys were given to 71 people; 34 of these were returned completed, giving a response rate of 48%. Of the total, 127 responses came from biological females and 234 came from transsexuals.

Transsexuals ($M = 39.21$ years, $SD = 14.03$) were on average significantly older than biological females ($M = 30.63$ years, $SD = 11.90$), $t(359) = 5.83$, ($p < .001$). The majority (90%) of participants identified as European. Ethnic minorities were represented in 14% of participants. Participants in highly skilled occupations were well represented in this sample, with 46% of participants classified in the three most highly skilled categories on the New Zealand Standard Classification of Occupations. A large proportion (23%) of participants were students. The current sample appeared to be well-educated: 27% reported having a bachelor's degree, 16% reported having a master's or doctoral degree, and only 6% reported achieving 3 years of high school or less. Transsexual and biological female groups did not differ significantly in ethnicity, occupation classification, or level of education. Most of the transsexual participants (83%) had not undertaken SRS, and 61% of transsexuals reported that they were currently taking female hormones.

Differences between participants who completed and did not complete the entire survey were examined. Participants who did not complete the entire questionnaire were significantly less likely to be European, and significantly more likely to be Asian. . . . Completers and non-completers did not differ significantly in terms of gender identity, occupation classification, marital status, age, level of education, number of biological children, sexual orientation, or on any of the remaining variables.

Measures

Sex-Linked Behaviours Questionnaire
Sexual orientation was determined by responses to eight questionnaire items on sexual fantasy, sexual arousal, and sexual attraction, for example, "Rate the degree to which in your current sexual fantasies you are aroused by males." . . .

Attraction to Male Physique
This scale contains six items measuring sexual attraction to the male physique. . . .

Attraction to Feminine Males Scale
This scale contains six items measuring sexual attraction to femininity in males. . . .

Recalled Gender Identity/Gender Role Questionnaire
This scale measures recalled childhood gender identity and gender role; for example, "As a child, I put on or used cosmetics (make-up) and girls' or women's jewellery." This scale uses 5-point responses, with one or two extra

response items to allow participants to indicate that they did not remember or that the behavior did not apply. . . .

Core Autogynephilia Scale

This 8-item scale was developed by Blanchard to measure sexual attraction to the fantasy of being a woman, for example, "Have you ever been sexually aroused at the thought of being a woman?" Changes were made to six of the questions so that participants were asked if they have ever been sexually aroused when picturing themselves with attractive or more attractive female physical features. The "attractive or more attractive" part was added to Blanchard's original version of the scale to make the questions more applicable to biological females. . . .

Autogynephilic Interpersonal Fantasy Scale

This 4-item scale measures the sexual arousal of being admired by another person as a female, for example, "Have you ever been sexually aroused while picturing yourself as a woman in the nude being admired by another person?" . . .

Fetishism Scale

This scale measures sexual attraction to inanimate objects, for example, "Were you ever more strongly sexually attracted by inanimate things than by females or males?" . . .

Masochism Scale

This scale measures masochistic tendencies, for example, "Has imagining that you were being humiliated or poorly treated by someone ever excited you sexually?" . . .

Sexual and Emotional Jealousy

This 4-item scale was designed to assess sexual and emotional jealousy, for example, "Rate how distressing imagining your partner falling in love with that other person would be." . . .

Preference for Younger Partners

This 11-item scale measures age preference for sexual partners, for example, "If someone showed definite signs of aging it would be difficult for me to be very sexually attracted to them." Nine of the items were scored on a 7-point Likert-scale format from *strongly agree* to *strongly disagree*. Two of the items ask participants to specify an age of desired partner. This was then subtracted from the participant's age to give a difference score. . . .

Interest in Uncommitted Sex

This scale is a 10-item measure of attraction to casual sexual relationships, for example, "Monogamy is not for me." . . .

Interest in Visual Sexual Stimuli

This scale is a 12-item measure of sexual interest in visual stimuli, for example, "Seeing my sexual partner undress is a real turn-on." . . .

Importance of Partner Status
This scale is a 12-item measure of concern with the amount of resources held by a partner or potential partner, for example, "I would like my partner to be from a higher social class background than I.". . .

Importance of Partner Physical Attractiveness
This scale is a 10-item measure of concern with the physical attractiveness of partners, for example, "I would be happy if my partner were more sexually attractive than I." . . .

Attraction to Transgender Fiction Scale
This scale contains 12 items measuring sexual attraction to erotic narratives containing transgender themes. . . .

Transgender Identity Scale
This 9-item scale measures cross-gender identification, and continuous commitment to cross-gender behavior through the desire to live entirely in the female role, for example, "If it were possible, I'd choose to live my life as a woman (or I now do so)." This scale was only completed by transsexual participants. . . .

Additional information was collected from transsexual participants about the age they first desired to change their sex, how long they had been taking female hormones, and whether they had undertaken SRS.

Results

Comparisons Between Biological Females and Transsexuals

. . . After adjusting for age differences, transsexuals scored significantly higher on Attraction to Feminine Males, Recalled Feminine Gender Identity, Core Autogynephilia, Preference for Younger Partners, Importance of Partner Status, Importance of Partner Physical Attractiveness, and Attraction to Transgender Fiction. Biological females scored significantly higher on Emotional Jealousy.

Comparisons among Autogynephilic Transsexuals, Non-Autogynephilic Transsexuals, and Biological Females

Transsexual participants were categorized as autogynephilic or non-autogynephilic based on their scores on the Core Autogynephilia, Autogynephilic Interpersonal Fantasy, Attraction to Feminine Males, and Attraction to Transgender Fiction scales. These scales were selected because they were found most effective for classifying transsexuals into groups in a taxometric analysis using the same data as the present study. . . .

All of the scales . . . yielded a significant difference between the three groups except for the sexual orientation scales, and Attraction to Male Physique.

. . . Non-autogynephilic transsexuals scored significantly lower on Masochism and Interest in Visual Sexual Stimuli than autogynephilic transsexuals and biological females, who did not differ significantly from each other. Autogynephilic transsexuals scored significantly higher on Attraction to Feminine Males, Autogynephilic Interpersonal Fantasy, Preference for Younger Partners, and Attraction to Transgender Fiction, and lower on Sexual Jealousy than non-autogynephilic transsexuals and biological females, who did not differ significantly from each other. For Fetishism and Interest in Uncommitted Sex, autogynephilic transsexuals scored significantly higher than biological females, who scored significantly higher than non-autogynephilic transsexuals. Biological females scored significantly lower on Recalled Feminine Gender Identity than both transsexual subgroups, which did not differ significantly from each other. Autogynephilic transsexuals scored significantly lower than biological females on Emotional Jealousy and significantly higher on Importance of Partner Status; non-autogynephilic transsexuals did not differ significantly from autogynephilic transsexuals or biological females for these variables. For Core Autogynephilia and Importance of Partner Physical Attractiveness, autogynephilic transsexuals scored significantly higher than non-autogynephilic transsexuals, who scored significantly higher than biological females.

Comparisons were made between autogynephilic and non-autogynephilic transsexuals on the measures that were only completed by transsexuals. Autogynephilic transsexuals had a significantly later age of first desire to change sex . . . , were less likely to be taking female hormones . . . , had fewer months taking hormones . . . , and less likely to have had SRS . . . than non-autogynephilic transsexuals. These groups did not differ significantly in age or scores on the Transgender Identity Scale.

Correlational Analyses

. . . Sexual Attraction to Males correlated positively with Core Autogynephilia among biological females and with Autogynephilic Interpersonal Fantasy among all participants. Sexual Attraction to Females correlated positively with Core Autogynephilia among all participants and with Autogynephilic Interpersonal Fantasy among transsexuals. Attraction to Male Physique correlated positively with Autogynephilic Interpersonal Fantasy among biological female participants. Attraction to Feminine Males correlated positively with Core Autogynephilia and Autogynephilic Interpersonal Fantasy among all participants. Attraction to Transgender Fiction was positively correlated with Core Autogynephilia among all participants and with Autogynephilic Interpersonal Fantasy among transsexuals. Recalled Feminine Gender Identity was not related to Autogynephilia variables for transsexual or biological female participants. However, Recalled Feminine Gender Identity was positively correlated with Sexual Attraction to Males among both transsexuals . . . and biological females . . . , and negatively correlated with Sexual Attraction to Females among both transsexuals . . . and biological females. . . .

Finally, in testing Blanchard's hypothesis that bisexual autogynephilic transsexuals are not attracted to the male physique, we found among transsexual participants classified as autogynephilic . . . , Attraction to Male Physique correlated significantly positively with Sexual Attraction to Males . . . , and this correlation was comparable to non-autogynephilic transsexuals . . . and biologi-cal females. . . .

Discussion

The results showed that male-to-female transsexual sexuality differed from biological females on a number of variables, and the largest differences were found when transsexuals were classified into two groups. Those classified as autogynephilic scored significantly higher on Attraction to Feminine Males, Core Autogynephilia, Autogynephilic Interpersonal Fantasy, Fetishism, Prefer-ence for Younger Partners, Interest in Uncommitted Sex, Importance of Part-ner Physical Attractiveness, and Attraction to Transgender Fiction than those transsexuals not classified as non-autogynephilic and biological females. Sub-ject to further investigation, these erotic preferences—especially Attraction to Feminine Males and Attraction to Transgender Fiction—can be seen as notable components or correlates of autogynephilia.

Both groups of transsexual participants scored significantly higher than biological female participants on Recalled Feminine Gender Identity, and Importance of Partner Physical Attractiveness. It was unexpected that trans-sexuals would score on average higher on childhood feminine gender iden-tity, because transsexuals would be given less opportunity to express their femininity and would be discouraged from doing so in their childhood. One possible explanation for this finding is that a large number biological females reporting sexual attraction to females were included in this study—such per-sons have been shown to recall less femininity in childhood. Transsexual participants, even those categorized as non-autogynephilic, reported placing greater importance of physical attractiveness of potential partners than bio-logical females. The reason for this phenomenon is unclear—it is possible that transsexuals, being biological males, have been shaped by natural selection to view physical attractiveness as a marker of partner fertility; however, non-autogynephilic transsexuals did not score in a significantly more "masculine" direction than biological females on any of the other sexuality parameters relevant to evolution, but autogynephilic transsexuals scored in the more "masculine" direction than other participants on five out of seven of these variables. Overall, biological female and transsexual participants also did not differ on levels of Interest in Visual Sexual Stimuli. This is in spite of [the] claim that male-to-female transsexuals are more responsive to visual erotic stimuli, similar to other biological males.

The finding that transsexuals—even those classified as autogynephilic—did not differ significantly on Masochism from biological females was unex-pected given previous reports of the prevalence of masochism in transsexuals, and reports of co-occurrence of fetishism.

Autogynephilic transsexual participants reported a significantly greater amount of sexual attraction to transgender fiction themes than biological females. Transsexuals most commonly endorsed themes of magical transfor-mation into a female, having to be transformed into a female as part of a deal, bet or dare, and gender body swaps. However, some transsexuals endorsed all of the themes, and no clear pattern appeared among them. We conclude that sexual fantasy to certain transgender fiction themes does not appear to be predictive of transsexualism. This finding . . . [suggests] that these themes are of little use in distinguishing individual's motives.

Contrary to Blanchard's findings, when the transsexual participants were divided into autogynephilic and non-autogynephilic groups, they did not differ significantly on sexual orientation measures. Among transsexual participants, the Core Autogynephilia Scale positively correlated with Sexual Attraction to Females—in line with Blanchard's research. However, further analysis of the transsexual subgroups revealed notable diversity within the groups. The average score of Sexual Attraction to Males was higher for transsexuals classified as autogynephilic than for transsexuals classified as non-autogynephilic, although this difference was not significant, this is at variance with Blanchard's theory. Also, 68% of transsexuals classified as non-autogynephilic scored the highest possible score . . . on the Sexual Attraction to Females scale. Finally, among the transsexuals classified as autogynephilic, none scored low scores . . . on both the Sexual Attraction to Males and Females scales that would be expected if they were asexual—one of the sexuality subgroups of Blanchard's autogynephilic transsexuals. Possible explanations for this lack of asexuality include more liberal attitudes towards sexuality in today's culture, and participants in Blanchard's research reporting a greater asexuality if they believed this would increase their chances of receiving medical intervention. Attraction to Male Physique was positively correlated with Sexual Attraction to Males among autogynephilic transsexuals. If Blanchard's hypothesis that the sexual attraction to males experienced by bisexual transsexuals is to include them as props in the fantasy of being regarded as a woman, as opposed to sexual interest in the male body is true then we would not expect to see this positive correlation, or we would at least expect this correlation to be lower than the corresponding correlations for non-autogynephilic transsexuals and biological females. However, it is still possible that this attraction to the male physique could develop along with the secondary emergence of attraction to males that Blanchard describes. Also, contrary to expectation Recalled Childhood Feminine Gender Identity Scale did not correlate with autogynephilia measures.

We conclude that while Blanchard's two-group classification of male-to-female transsexuals appears to have merit for significant proportion of transsexuals, there is still diversity in the experiences of transsexuals, and a simple categorization may not completely represent this diversity.

Limitations

In the questionnaire, changes were made to the questions in the Core Autogynephilia scale so that participants were asked if they have ever been sexually aroused when picturing themselves with attractive or more attractive female physical features. The responses were also altered from a yes/no format, and the skip instructions were changed. All of these alterations to the scale made these research findings less comparable to Blanchard's research. Also, the Sex

Linked Behaviours Questionnaire, Core Autogynephilia, Autogynephilic Inter-personal Fantasy, Fetishism, and Masochism scales . . . were altered. . . .

A further limitation of this research was that it relied entirely on self-report. Blanchard reported that the group that he would later label auto-gynephilic may over report their femininity and under report the extent of their cross-gender sexual arousal. From clinical and research observations, pre-vious researchers have claimed that non-androphilic transsexuals may con-sciously or unconsciously distort their responses to appear less autogynephilic. It is beyond the scope of this research to assess whether participants were dis-torting their answers. However, we believe participants would be less likely to consciously distort their responses in this study because their answers were anonymous and had no implications for whether they will receive treatment in a clinical setting.

Another limitation was the susceptibility of this research to manipula-tion. Although this is an issue with most Internet surveys, the contentiousness of the subject matter in this survey would make it more susceptible to dishon-esty. Many transsexuals have strong feelings about autogynephilia and could have manipulated the survey by completing it many times with answers that they believe would either discredit or confirm the theory, depending on their beliefs. However, the length of the survey (162 questions) may have discour-aged participants from answering it many times—our system showed us that most participants took longer than 25 min to complete it. In addition, we did not see any suspicious responding in the data, such as a lot of responses in a short period. Furthermore, distinct and often thoughtful comments were made by 71.4% of transsexual participants who completed the questionnaire on the Internet when given the opportunity to comment on Blanchard's theory of autogynephilia and on the survey in general. Although we did not see any signs of suspicious activity, we are aware that this may have been a possibility, and this is a considerable limitation to our findings.

The recruitment methods used in this research also contributed to a biased sample. The biological female participants were either recruited through first-year psychology classes or through Internet mailing lists and message boards for persons with interests in psychology, sex research, or transsexualism (e.g., support groups for family and friends of transsexuals). The significant propor-tion of university students in the biological female sample resulted in a large number of participants in the 18–22 year age group. Among the transsexual sample, those who access online transsexual support groups and mailing lists were also likely to be overrepresented. Europeans were also overrepresented in the overall sample, and the participants appeared to be more educated than the general population. Also, a number of previous studies have shown that females volunteering for sexuality research are less sexually inhibited than the general population. It is likely that the present sample was biased in this way as well.

Finally, our findings bring up an area in need of further research. The con-cept of sexual attraction to oneself as a woman (autogynephilia) has never been assessed among biological female participants previously. Although a number of biological female participants endorsed items on the Core Autogynephilia and Autogynephilic Interpersonal Fantasy scales, no previous studies have reported biological females with such sexual attraction. Because of this, it is unlikely that these biological females actually experience sexual attraction to oneself as a woman in the way that Blanchard conceptualized it. However, the scales used in this research were not sufficient for examining this, so further research is needed to confirm it.

POSTSCRIPT

Should Transgendered Women Be Considered "Real" Women?

In July of 2008, it was announced that four Olympic athletes failed a gender test, the latest in a long series of challenges to the sex of female athletes. In 1968, the International Olympic Committee (IOC) began requiring certain female athletes, those for whom their masculine appearance and superior athletic ability raised questions about whether they were "real" women, to submit to genetic and blood tests. The goal was to determine their sex. The rule is that only women with two X chromosomes can compete as women (contrary to the opinion of most geneticists), with the exception of male to female transsexuals, but they must wait to compete for two years after the sex change surgery. In 1992, compulsory testing was abandoned but can be requested. Other questions arise for female athletes with other sex-related anomalies. The most recent case arose when the 2009 World Championship runner Mokgadi Caster Semenya was accused of being a hermaphrodite. The legitimacy of her gold medal has been called into question. Would this condition give her an advantage over other "normal" women? According to media reports in September of 2009, genetic testing revealed that Semenya is indeed intersexed; she has internal testes but no womb or ovaries and has testosterone levels three times higher than those typical of females. At the time of this writing (October 2009) the International Association of Athletics Federations (IAAF) states that these reports should be viewed with caution; they will not make a final decision for weeks on the status of her medal. Regardless of the final ruling of the Semenya case, it raises intriguing questions regarding what determines one's sex.

Because we now know that sexual development occurs on a continuum, from variation in number of chromosomes to various concentrations of estrogen and androgens (i.e., growth hormones) at different stages of prenatal development, the concept of sex as a simple dimorphic category is now questioned. For example, there are people who are intersexual, a group formerly termed hermaphrodite. These are individuals who are born with a blend of female and male sexual organs (approximately 1.7% of all live births). For many intersexuals, as well as infants with prenatal exposure to atypical levels of sexual hormones, genital size at birth becomes the primary basis for declaration of sex at birth. In these infants, it is the same tissue, but differences in size result in one of three natural configurations of external genitalia: female, male, or ambiguous. Gender identity for these persons is strongly influenced by whichever sex is declared at the time of birth. In contrast, transsexualism is seen as a medical condition in which a person identifies with the sex they were not born, that is, they are sexually dysmorphic (self-concept and biological sex do not match), and varies on a continuum in strength of the desire to become the other sex (ranging from cross-dressers to those seeking surgical alterations). Transgenderism refers to one's "gender identity," that is, identification as woman, man, mixed, or neither, that does not match one's assigned, or genetic, sex. It is estimated that there are from 10,000 to 30,000 trans people worldwide, and that male to female outnumber female to male transgendered people. There are also people who consider themselves gender nonconformists. That is, they are neither transsexuals nor have a biological disorder. Rather, they oppose traditional standards.

What are the implications for what we now know about the varieties of gender identity and possibilities for being born intersexual or with ambiguous genitalia have for the concept of womyn born womyn? Is womyn-born womyn a valid gender identity? What are the criteria for being considered a womyn-born womyn—XX chromosomal composition only? What about females with XO (Turner's syndrome) or XXX chromosomal make-ups? Must external genitalia be unambiguous? As long as women with any of these conditions are gender variant, do they qualify for the label womyn-born womyn? What are the implications of these variations for shared experiences and group identities?

Consider other cultures in which more than two categories of sex are recognized and sometimes even celebrated (see Issues 2 and 19). How does an appreciation of such cultural variation help us discuss transsexuality, transgenderism, and gender variance? Does this knowledge strengthen or weaken the case that there are distinct and different gender identities that should be honored?

Suggested Readings

John Colapinto, *As Nature Made Him: The Boy Who Was Raised as a Girl* (New York: HarperCollins, 2000).

Alice Domurat Dreger, *Hermaphrodites and the Medical Invention of Sex* (Cambridge, MA: Harvard University Press, 2000).

Judith Rich Harris, *The Nurture Assumption: Why Children Turn Out the Way They Do* (New York: Free Press, 1999).

Sharon E. Preves, *Intersex and Identity: The Contested Self* (Piscataway, NJ: Rutgers University Press, 2003).

Sandra L. Samons, *When the Opposite Sex Isn't: Sexual Orientation in Male-to-Female Transgender People* (New York: Routledge, 2009).

Contributors to This Volume

EDITOR

JACQUELYN W. WHITE is professor of psychology and former director of Women's and Gender Studies at the University of North Carolina at Greensboro. She received her Ph.D. in social psychology from Kent State University.

Dr. White has conducted research in the area of aggression and violence for over 30 years, publishing numerous articles and chapters. She has conducted one of the few longitudinal studies of sexual assault and dating violence among adolescents and college students (funded by NIMH, NIJ, and CDC). Recent publications reflect an ecological developmental perspective to aggression and violence. She is a frequent speaker at national and international conferences. She is co-editor with Dr. Cheryl Travis of the University of Tennessee on *Sexuality, Society, and Feminism: Psychological Perspectives on Women,* published by the American Psychological Association. She completed the "Gendered Aggression" chapter for the *Encyclopedia of Gender* (Academic Press) and "A Developmental Examination of Violence Against Girls and Women" for the *Handbook of the Psychology of Women and Gender* (Wiley).

In addition to her research activities, Dr. White served as the editor of the *Psychology of Women Quarterly* (2000–2004) and is a consulting editor for *Aggressive Behavior.* She has been president of the Southeastern Psychological Association, has been the treasurer of the International Society for Research in Aggression, and was the 2007–2008 president of the Society for the Psychology of Women Division 35 of the American Psychological Association. She has been a consultant on a project with the U.S. Navy examining the impact of pre-military experiences with physical and sexual abuse on military experiences. She has been the recipient of a number of awards, including the Women's History Committee Service Award given by the Commission on the Status of Women and the Greensboro YWCA and Kent State University's Honors Alumna of 2000. She was UNCG's 1996 Senior Research Excellence Award recipient, the highest research honor the university can bestow on a faculty member. She is also a fellow of the American Psychological Association.

Dr. White was the 2008 recipient of the Carolyn Wood Sherif Award, given by the Society for the Psychology of Women. She currently co-chairs the National Partnership to End Interpersonal Violence and is co-editor of a two-volume series *Violence Against Women and Children: Consensus, Critical Analysis, and Emergent Priorities.* She is currently working on an NIDA-funded project on trauma and substance use.

AUTHORS

MERCEDES ALLEN is the founder of AlbertaTrans.org, a network designed to help foster and support the transgender community in Edmonton, Calgary, and rural Alberta, Canada.

AMERICAN PSYCHOLOGICAL ASSOCIATION'S COUNCIL OF REPRESEN-TATIVES is the elected governing body of the American Psychological Association. Among various activities it creates task forces charged with drafting resolutions based on research reviews that the Council can then consider for adopting as official APA policy.

SUSAN W. BAKER, M.D., is an assistant professor in the Department of Pediatrics, Adrenal Steroids Disorders Program, at Mount Sinai School of Medicine. As a psychoendocrinologist, she has followed patients with classical and non-classical congenital adrenal hyperplasia (CAH), both clinically and through research. She has investigated cognitive strengths and weaknesses in CAH, as well as the effects of prenatal treatment on the condition.

ROBIN ZENGER BAKER has been a lecturer at the Boston University School of Management and has a Ph.D. in organization studies from UCLA.

KINGSLEY R. BROWNE is a professor at Wayne State University Law School. He specialized in labor and employment law when he was previously a partner in the San Francisco-based law firm of Morrison & Foerster. He has written *Co-ed Combat: The New Evidence That Women Shouldn't Fight the Nation's Wars* (Sentinel, 2007). His work deals primarily with employment discrimination law and the legal implications of evolved differences between the sexes.

MOLLY BUTTERWORTH is a graduate student in the clinical psychology program at the University of Utah.

NATASHA J. CABRERA, Ph.D., is an associate professor of human development at the University of Maryland. She directs the Family Involvement Laboratory at the University of Maryland, which explores ways that mothers and fathers are involved in their young children's lives and the influence that parents have on their children's development. Her research interests include parent-child relationships, children's social and emotional development in different types of families and cultural/ethnic groups, school readiness, fatherhood, predictors of adaptive and maladaptive parenting, and translation of research into practice and policy.

LINDA L. CARLI, Ph.D., is an associate professor in the psychology department at Wellesley College, where she has been since 1991. Her current research focuses on women's leadership, particularly the obstacles that women leaders face and ways to overcome those obstacles. Dr. Carli teaches a variety of courses, including organizational psychology, the psychology of law, and research in applied psychology.

DAVE E. CLARKE is a senior lecturer in the School of Psychology, Massey University, Albany Campus, Auckland, New Zealand, and studies stress, personality, motivation, gambling.

MARY E. CORCORAN is professor of political science, public policy, social work, and women's studies at the University of Michigan. Her research focuses on the effects of gender and race discrimination on economic status and earnings and on welfare and employment policies.

JOHN CORNYN is a United States Senator from Texas, who chairs the Senate Judiciary subcommittee on the Constitution, Civil Rights and Property Rights. He is a former state supreme court justice and state attorney general.

TIMOTHY J. DAILEY, senior research fellow at the Center for Marriage and Family Studies, has a Ph.D. in religion and specializes in issues threatening the institutions of marriage and the family. He has authored three books, including *Dark Obsession: The Tragedy and Threat of the Homosexual Lifestyle* (Broadman and Holman, 2003).

ANTHONY D'AMATO is the Leighton professor of law at Northwestern University School of Law, where he teaches courses in international law, international human rights, analytic jurisprudence, and justice. He was the first American lawyer to argue and win a case before the European Court of Human Rights in Strasbourg, and is the author of over 20 books and over 110 articles.

LISA M. DIAMOND, Ph.D., psychology, University of Utah, focuses on two distinct but related areas—the nature and development of affectional bonds and the nature and development of same-sex sexuality. Her primary research questions are: (1) what are the basic psychological and biobehavioral processes underlying the formation and functioning of affectional bonds; (2) how are these processes related to sexual desire and sexual orientation; (3) what are the implications of affectional bonding for mental and physical well-being at different stages of life? In addressing these questions, she uses a diverse range of research methods, including in-depth qualitative interviews, controlled social-psychophysiological experiments, and assessment of naturalistic interpersonal behavior.

CURTIS DOLEZAL, Ph.D., is a research scientist at the HIV Center for Clinical and Behavioral Studies at New York State Psychiatric Institute and Columbia University. He is a co-investigator and data analyst for several projects at the HIV Center and has documented and manages several data sets covering the entire history of the Center. His research interests have included sensation seeking, drug and alcohol use, couple relationship quality, childhood sexual experiences, psychoendocrinology, and sexual risk behavior.

PEGGY DREXLER, an assistant professor of psychology in psychiatry at the Weill Medical College of Cornell University, has been a clinician and lecturer at the New York Hospital/Cornell Medical School, and a researcher at Stanford University as a Gender Scholar. Her research focuses on the new American family.

ALICE EAGLY, a social psychologist, is the James Padilla Chair of Arts and Sciences, professor of psychology, faculty fellow of the Institute for Policy Research, department chair of psychology, all at Northwestern University. She has received numerous awards including the 2007 Interamerican Psychologist Award from Interamerican Society of Psychology for contributions to psychology as a science and profession in the Americas, as well as the 2005 Carolyn Wood Sherif Award from the Society for the Psychology of Women for contributions to the field of the psychology of women as a scholar, teacher, mentor, and leader.

MARIA FERRIS currently works for IBM managing their Global Workforce Diversity and Work/Life programs. During her 27-year career with IBM, she has held a variety of staff and management positions within the HR organization in staffing, employee relations, management development, benefits, and diversity. She is a current member and former co-chair of the Conference Board's Work-Life Leadership Council and a founding member of the Leadership Forum for Women's Advancement.

ADRIAN FURNHAM, Ph.D., is a professor of psychology in the Research Department of Clinical, Educational and Health Psychology at the University College London. His research interests include complementary medicine; cross-cultural psychology, especially mental health and migration; organizational psychology; psychometrics, especially personality assessment; and economic socialization. He is the author of 46 books including: *Culture Shock, The New Economic Mind, The Psychology of Money, The Incompetent Manager*, and *The Dark Side of Behaviour at Work*.

MAHIN HASSIBI, M.D., is a professor of clinical psychiatry (ret.) at New York Medical College and in private practice in New York City. He is also co-author with Stella Chess of *Principles and Practice of Child Psychiatry*.

DEBRA HAUSER, MPH, is the vice president of Advocates for Youth. Advocates for Youth is a national, nonprofit organization that creates programs and supports policies that help young people make safe, responsible decisions about their sexual and reproductive health.

JEFFREY HILL, Ph.D., has been an associate professor in the School of Family Life at Brigham Young University since 1998. His research interests include home and family living, and he teaches a variety of classes in the School of Family Life and a Work and Family class in the Marriott School of Management.

JANET SHIBLEY HYDE, Ph.D., is currently a professor of psychology and women's studies at the University of Wisconsin at Madison. Dr. Hyde's research spans the fields of the psychology of women, human sexuality, and gender-role development. Her current research project is the Wisconsin Study of Families and Work, which focuses on working mothers and their children. She is also working on the Moms and Math (M&M) Project, funded by the National Science Foundation, which focuses on studying mothers as they interact with their fifth- and seventh-grade children to complete math homework.

PETER K. JONASON, Ph.D., is a visiting assistant professor at the University of West Florida in experimental social psychology. He is interested in adaptive individual differences, conditional mating strategies, sex/dating research, personality research, animal models, dark triad personality traits, personality in nonhumans, religiousness, mate choice, mating strategies, short-term vs. long-term mating, intersexual conflict, and evolutionary psychology.

NORMAN P. LI, Ph.D., is an associate professor of psychology at the Singapore Management University, School of Social Sciences, and adjunct assistant professor at the University of Texas at Austin Department of Psychology. He received his doctorate from Arizona State University and has numerous publications on evolutionary perspectives.

QING LI, Ph.D., is an associate professor of educational technology at the Faculty of Education, University of Calgary Faculty of Education, Canada. Her funded research and development programs mainly focus on the use of technology to enhance student learning of mathematics and science as well as equity and social justice in relation to technology. She has a project entitled "Virtual Visitation and Feminist Pedagogy: Would They Make Any Difference?" The primary goal of this research program is to develop new learning practices with the support of technology that can enhance equity in math and science education.

HILARY M. LIPS, a professor of psychology and the director of the Center for Gender Studies at Radford University, has published numerous books and articles related to the psychology of gender, including *Sex and Gender: An Introduction* (Mayfield, 2000).

TERRI C. LOMAX is located at the School of Computer and Information Sciences, Auckland University of Technology, Auckland, New Zealand.

BRIDGET E. MAHER, policy analyst at the Center for Marriage and Family Studies at Family Research Council. She has authored several Family Research Council publications including two editions of *The Family Portrait,* a comprehensive book of data, research, and polling on the family.

VJOLLCA K. MÄRTINSON received her Ph.D. from the Marriage, Family, and Human Development Department at Brigham Young University in 2005.

ZAHER O. MERHI, M.D., is on the staff of Maimondes Medical Center, Brooklyn, NY, specializing in gynecology and obstetrics.

HEINO F. L. MEYER-BAHLBURG is a professor of clinical psychology (in psychiatry) at the New York State Psychiatric Institute and Department of Psychiatry, Columbia University, and associate director of the HIV Center for Clinical and Behavioral Studies at New York State Psychiatric Institute, as well as director, Interdisciplinary Research Methods Core, HIV Center. He is also a full professional psychologist at New York Presbyterian Hospital. His primary research interests include developmental psychobiology of gender and sexuality; intersexuality/disorders of sex development; gender identity disorder; sexual risk behavior; and assessment of gender and sexuality.

LISA MOTTET, J.D., has staffed the Transgender Civil Rights Project at the National Gay and Lesbian Task Force since helping to establish it in 2001. In this role, she assists transgender activists and allies with all transgender-related legislation and policy. She co-authored *Transitioning Our Shelters: A Guide to Making Homeless Shelters Safe for Transgender People,* a joint publication with the National Coalition for the Homeless. Before joining the Task Force, Lisa was involved in leadership positions with various other LGBT organizations. Lisa currently serves on the Board of Advisors of the National Center for Transgender Equality and is on the board of the local LGBT soccer club in Washington, D.C.

MARIA I. NEW, M.D., Department of Pediatrics, Mount Sinai School of Medicine, New York, is a professor of pediatrics of genetics and genomic sciences. She is the director of the Adrenal Steroid Disorders Program at the Mount Sinai School of Medicine. She conducts research on adrenal disease.

MARY C. NOONAN is currently a professor in the department of sociology at the University of Iowa, where she has taught since 2001. Her research interests include gender, family, work, stratification, and quantitative research methods.

LUBNA PAL, M.D., is an assistant professor in the Department of Obstetrics, Gynecology and Reproductive Sciences at the Yale University School of Medicine, New Haven, CT. She was the recipient of 2006 Prize Paper given by the Society of Reproductive Endocrinology and Infertility.

STEVEN PINKER is now the Johnstone Family Professor of Psychology at Harvard University. Until 2003 he was in the department of brain and cognitive sciences at MIT. His empirical studies focus on linguistic behavior. He also conducts theoretical analyses of the nature of language and its relation to mind and brain. He has authored several books including *The Blank Slate: The Modern Denial of Human Nature* (Penguin Books, 2003).

IGNACIO LUIS RAMIREZ, Ph.D., is a professor in the department of sociology at Texas Tech University. His research interests include violence in intimate relations. His teaching includes social problems as well as law and policing.

JUDITH REISMAN is president of the Institute for Media Education, author of, among other publications, the U.S. Department of Justice, Juvenile Justice study, *Images of Children, Crime and Violence in Playboy, Penthouse and Hustler* (1989), *Kinsey, Sex and Fraud* (Reisman, et al., 1990), *Soft Porn Plays*

Hardball (1991), and *Kinsey, Crimes* and *Consequences* (1998, 2000). She is also a news commentator for *WorldNetDaily.com* and has been a consultant to four U.S. Department of Justice administrations, the U.S. Department of Education, and the U.S. Department of Health and Human Services.

JOHN L. RINN, Ph.D., Department of Molecular Biophysics and Biochemistry, Yale University, is an assistant professor of pathology at Harvard Medical School and Beth Israel Deaconess Medical Center and an associate member of the Broad Institute. His research aims to understand the role of large non-coding RNA in establishing the distinct epigenetic states of adult and embryonic cells and their misregulation in cancer.

DAVID P. SCHMITT, Ph.D., is a professor of psychology at Bradley University and founding director of the International Sexuality Description Project. His research interests include evolutionary and cross-cultural approaches to understanding personal relationships, sexual strategies, romantic attachment styles, and gender differences in human mating. He is also interested in the "Big Five" model of personality traits, risk factors for HIV/AIDS, and predictors of both sexual aggression and domestic violence across cultures.

JOHN SHACKLETON is professor of economics and dean of the Business School, University of East London. He was formerly dean of Westminster Business School and has taught at Queen Mary, University of London, and the University of Buckingham. Educated at King's College, Cambridge, and the School of Oriental and African Studies, he has also worked as an economist in the civil service, published widely in academic journals, and written for several leading think tanks. He has given evidence to parliamentary committees, has appeared frequently on radio and TV, and has lectured in many countries.

JACQUELINE D. SHANNON, Ph.D., is assistant professor of early childhood education at Brooklyn College, CUNY. She is a member of the National Early Head Start Research Consortium. Prior to joining Brooklyn College she was a research scientist at NYU and post-doctoral research fellow with NICHD. She also directed a home-based child development program in East Harlem serving families with children birth to three years. Her research interests include parenting (with a special focus on fathers) and young children's cognitive and social-emotional development within families living in poverty, using mixed methods.

DAVID L. SNOW, Ph.D., is a professor of psychology in the departments of psychiatry, child study center, and epidemiology and public health at Yale University School of Medicine and is director of the Consultation Center and Division of Prevention and Community Research in the Department of Psychiatry. His work has focused extensively on the design and evaluation of preventive interventions and on research aimed at identifying key risk and protective factors predictive of psychological symptoms, substance use, and family violence. He also has special interests in the protective and stress-mediating effects of coping and social support and in methodological and ethical issues in prevention research.

MICHAEL SNYDER, Ph.D., has recently moved to Stanford University. Previously he was the Lewis B. Cullman Professor of Molecular, Cellular and Developmental Biology, professor of molecular biophysics and biochemistry, and director of the Yale Center for Genomics and Proteomics at Yale University. He uses global approaches to explore protein function and dissect regulatory networks.

ELIZABETH SPELKE is the Marshall L. Berkman Professor of Psychology at Harvard University. Her most recent honors include the William James Award, American Psychological Society 2000; Distinguished Scientific Contribution Award, American Psychological Association, 2000; Ipsen Prize in Neuronal Plasticity, 2001; America's Best in Science and Medicine, *Time Magazine*, 2001; Fellow, American Association for the Advancement of Science, 2002. She is currently publishing research on numerical cognition in infants and young children.

MURRAY A. STRAUS, Ph.D., is currently a professor of sociology at the University of New Hampshire where he has taught since 1968. Dr. Straus is also the co-director for the Family Research Laboratory at the University of New Hampshire. He has been collaborating with researchers in 23 nations on a cross-national study of violence between partners in the dating relationships of university students.

SUZANNE C. SWAN is an assistant professor in the department of psychology and the Women's Studies Program at the University of South Carolina. Before coming to the University of South Carolina, she was the director of Family Violence Programs at the Yale School of Medicine's Department of Psychiatry. She received her Ph.D. from the University of Illinois in 1997. Her recent work has focused on research with women who use violence in intimate relationships, with a particular emphasis on the contextual factors underlying women's violence. She teaches courses on the psychology of women, social psychology, and relationship violence.

CATHERINE TAMIS-LeMONDA is a professor of applied psychology at New York University. Her research is focused on the cultural and social contexts of language and cognitive and social development in infants' first years of life. Through longitudinal inquiry she follows infants from birth through preschool, visiting babies and families in their homes, schools, and communities using naturalistic observations, interviews, and direct assessments of development. She is the principal investigator (for NYU as a local site) on the Father Involvement in the Lives of Low Income Children Project.

JUSTIN TANIS, Ph.D., joined the staff of the National Center for Transgender Equality as program manager in August of 2005. He works as a writer, Web manager, and designer for NCTE, creating publications, resources, and newsletters for the organization. Justin is the author of *Transgendered:*

Theology, Ministry and Communities of Faith and contributed to the *Queer Bible Commentary* and *Take Back the Word: A Queer Reading of the Bible.*

JAIMIE R. VEALE is a graduate assistant in the School of Psychology, Massey University, Albany Campus, Auckland, New Zealand, whose doctoral dissertation is testing a model to explain the development of gender-variance, e.g., transsexualism, transvestism, and other forms of gender diversity.

GREGORY D. WEBSTER, Ph.D., is an assistant professor in the department of psychology at the University of Florida. He conducts research on prosocial and aggressive behavior from an evolutionary social psychological perspective. His research examines within-family resource allocation as a function of relatedness and emotional closeness. His aggression research examines relationships between different domains of self-esteem and aggression.

KELLEY WINTERS formerly under pen-name Katherine Wilson, is a writer on issues of transgender medical policy, founder of GID Reform Advocates, and an Advisory Board Member for the Matthew Shepard Foundation and TransYouth Family Advocates.